AF394211

The Texture of Contact

The Iroquoians and Their World

Editors
JOSÉ ANTÓNIO BRANDÃO
WILLIAM A. STARNA

UNIVERSITY OF NEBRASKA PRESS | LINCOLN AND LONDON

The Texture of Contact

European and Indian Settler Communities
on the Frontiers of Iroquoia, 1667–1783

David L. Preston

Portions of chapter 2 originally appeared as "George Klock, the Canajoharie Mohawks, and the Good Ship *Sir William Johnson*: Land, Legitimacy, and Community in the Eighteenth-Century Mohawk Valley," *New York History* 86, no. 4 (2005): 473–99.

Portions of chapter 3 originally appeared as "Squatters, Indians, Proprietary Government, and Land in the Susquehanna Valley," in *Friends and Enemies in Penn's Woods: Indians, Colonists, and the Racial Construction of Pennsylvania*, ed. William Pencak and Daniel K. Richter (University Park: Pennsylvania State University Press, 2004), 180–200.

© 2009 by the Board of Regents of the University of Nebraska

All rights reserved
Manufactured in the United States of America

Library of Congress Cataloging-in-Publication Data

Preston, David L. (David Lee), 1972–
The texture of contact : European and Indian settler communities on the frontiers of Iroquoia, 1667–1783 / David L. Preston.
p. cm. — (The Iroquoians and their world)
Includes bibliographical references and index.
ISBN 978-0-8032-1369-2 (cloth: alk. paper)
ISBN 978-0-8032-4352-1 (paper: alk. paper)
1. Iroquois Indians—Government relations. 2. Iroquois Indians—History—18th century. 3. Iroquois Indians—History—17th century. 4. Europe—Colonies—America. 5. United States—History—Colonial period, ca. 1600–1775. 6. Iroquois Indians—Canada—History—18th century. 7. Iroquois Indians—Canada—History—17th century. 8. Frontier and pioneer life—United States. 9. Frontier and pioneer life—Canada. I. Title.
E99.I7P75 2009
974.7004'9755—dc22
2009012833

Set in Quadraat.

Contents

Illustrations

Figures

Maps

Tables

Acknowledgments

My gratitude and respect for the many teachers, colleagues, and friends who have shaped my work are ineffable. These terse acknowledgments cannot begin to do them all justice. It is impossible for me to imagine a more perfect mentor than James Axtell. His example of a scholar's life has been inspirational. Colleagues at the College of William and Mary and the Citadel have guided me with their wisdom and blessed me with their friendship. I particularly wish to thank Mike McGiffert, Carol Sheriff, and Jim Whittenburg, for their friendship and encouragement. At presentations of my research at various meetings of the Iroquois History Conference, the Omohundro Institute, the Society for Ethnohistory, the Pennsylvania Historical Association, and the Western Frontier Symposium, I have benefited from conversations with James Carson, George Hamell, William Hart, James Merrell, Jane Merritt, Jon Parmenter, Daniel Richter, Tony Wonderley, and the late Mary Druke Becker.

Many institutions have facilitated my research and writing through generous financial support. The Citadel Foundation in Charleston, South Carolina, has been exceedingly generous in awarding me yearly research grants and travel grants. The College of William and Mary also provided research support early in the project. A Price Fellowship from the William L. Clements Library and a Larry Hackman Research Grant from the New York State Archives were also critical in my research. Until I met Dr. James Folts at the New York State Archives, I never fully realized how deeply historians are indebted to archivists. He generously shared his consummate knowledge of colonial sources and has remained a gracious colleague and friend. I also thank the staffs at the New York State Archives and Library, New York State Historical Association, New-York Historical Society, New York Public Library, Albany Institute of History and Art, Hamilton College Archives, Montgomery County Department of Archives and History, Historical Society of Pennsylvania, Pennsylvania State Archives, Beinecke Library, Huntington Library, William L. Clements Library, National Archives of Canada, and Archives Nationales du Quebec (Montreal). Especially deserving of thanks are Steve Bielinski, John Dann, Brian Dunnigan, Bill Evans, Kelly Farquhar, Clayton Lewis, Doug MacGregor, and Jonathan Stayer. I also owe many thanks to the interlibrary loan staffs of Swem Library at William and Mary and Daniel Library at the Citadel.

Many friends either read and commented on various drafts of this work or improved it through conversation and friendship: Jody Allen, Emily Blanck, Bill Carrigan, Dave Corlett, Steve Feeley, Paul Moyer, Sharon Sauder Muhlfeld, Pat O'Neil, Jim Piecuch, and Mike Simoncelli. I wish to thank my beloved parents and brother, whose selfless love, true character, and quiet encouragement have always sustained me. Finally, I wish to dedicate this work to my wife, English: my best friend, my spiritual companion, and my "joint-heir in the grace of life" through Christ (I Peter 3:7).

Introduction

Under the Tree of Peace

In 1734 a unique map came before the eyes of New York's royal governor, Col. William Cosby. Mohawk Iroquois leaders had sent a petition to the governor complaining about people encroaching on their lands southwest of Albany near the headwaters of Schoharie Creek, a tributary of the Mohawk River. The culprits turned out to be the Mohawks' neighbors in the Hudson Valley—Mahican Indians—who claimed the right to sell six thousand acres of Schoharie Valley land to three European colonists who had in turn obtained a formal land title (letters patent) for the vast tract. There were, then, three sets of inhabitants—Mohawks, Mahicans, and Germans—who occupied and claimed the land. How did these peoples who lived in the same valley deal with one another on a routine basis? The petition and the map vividly illustrate the notion that the boundaries between people could be firm in principle but extremely blurry in practice, and they provide unique insight on how people in early America actually experienced the land. The map that the sachems drew to define their particular claims provides a revealing glimpse of the Mohawks' view of the world. In contrast to mechanical European maps, the Mohawk landscape was framed by a network of creeks, rivers, and waterfalls; activities such as travel, trade, hunting, fishing, and warfare all unfolded for them on the water. Prominent hills and ridge lines of the Catskill Mountains were landmarks that held spiritual, territorial, and emotional significance. But one of the most revealing features of the Mohawks' map is its juxtaposition of the "Schohary Wigwams" and the German villages of "Schohary." The Mohawks' actual settlements on the east and west sides of Schoharie Creek are marked by a longhouse with a central fireplace—the symbol of the Haudenosaunee, or Iroquois, who are the People of the Longhouse. The Natives also represented their closest neighbors, the Palatine Germans, as inhabiting four small log houses with smoke billowing from their chimneys. But why did the Mohawks draw the Palatine villages on their map? There is something significant in this juxtaposition. This was a world in which Mohawks were said to have "lived intermixed with the Christians" and "daily resort[ed] to the Christians Houses."[1] Indeed, the map accurately reflects the fact that Mohawk and German villages were located literally across from each other on Schoharie Creek; the Mohawks had given the German immigrants permission to settle there after the Palatines had approached them in a friendly manner, and they continued to trade and socialize in personal, intimate, and often contentious ways. What, then, was everyday life like in this eighteenth-century world where Indians "lived intermixed with the Christians"? And what actually happened when they "daily resorted" to European settlers' houses?

My purpose in writing this book is to help readers understand the texture of human contact among ordinary European and Indian frontier settlers whose everyday lives were profoundly interwoven. I have also tried to evoke the landscape itself—for another important element of this texture of contact is how humans occupied, lived on, and used the land. The details of the tapestry can be gleaned from a host of meetings, scenes, places, and conversations described in eighteenth-century records: three French-Canadian sisters who lived

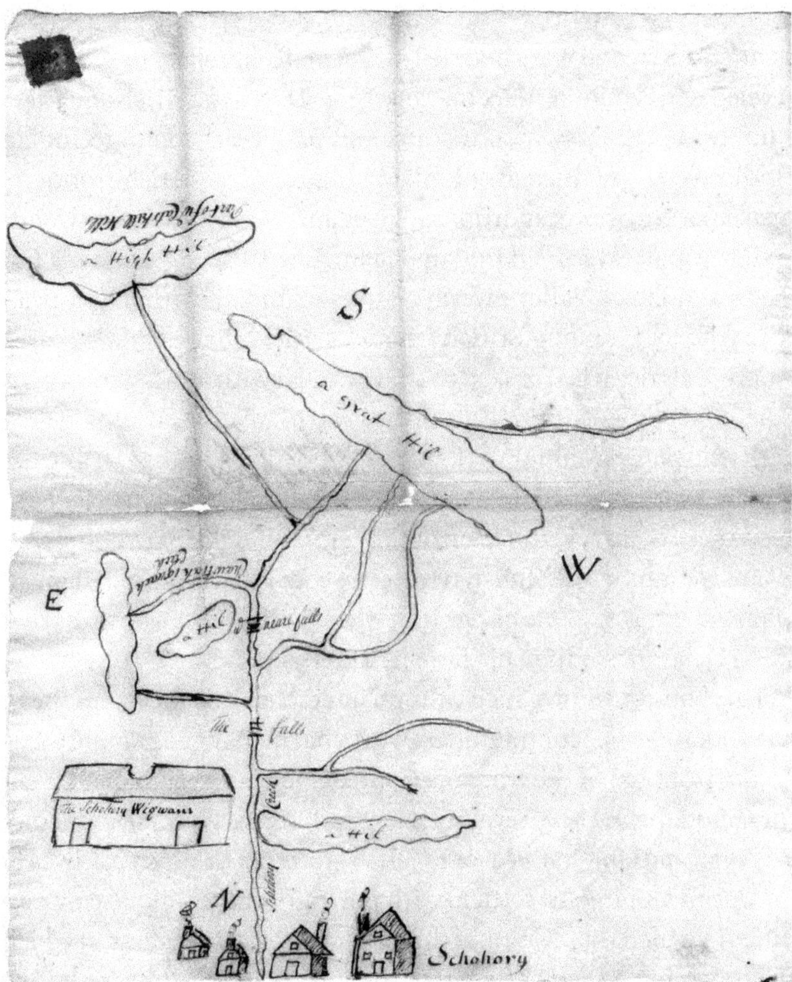

Fig. 1. Schoharie Mohawk map, 1734, from "Petition of the Sachems or Chiefs of the Schoharie Mohawk Indians," Applications for Land Grants, A0272, vol. 11, fol. 106. Courtesy of New York State Archives, Albany NY.

among Catholic Iroquois for over two decades and operated a trading store in their village; Indians wandering the streets of colonial Montreal and drinking beer at Crespeau's tavern; German immigrants who approached Mohawks for permission to settle among them; Christian Mohawks who insisted that they would live out their lives as brothers with German Christians, who baptized and christened their children and were married in German churches; Indians who reveled with white settlers on Christmas Day; Scots-Irish squatters who lived peaceably with Indians and paid yearly rents to Indian landlords, in defiance of colonial landlords; Scots-Irish frontiersmen enjoying a friendly drink with Iroquois warriors at a backwoods Pennsylvania tavern; an Indian playing European tunes on his fiddle in a Mohawk Valley tavern; a Mohawk Indian with a European wife who lived among British frontier settlers in the Ohio Valley; a Palatine settler who refused to share a meal with an Iroquois in his home and pushed him away from the hearth; Palatine farmers in New York who made wampum belts, spoke Iroquoian languages, and negotiated with the French in Canada; a hatchet cleaving the skull of a Swiss settler, attacked at his frontier farm by English-speaking Delaware Indians with English names; a Scots settler murdered on an Ohio Valley farm while harvesting wheat with a man whose mother was a Delaware Indian, his father an Englishman.

This book examines such cultural interactions between European and Indian settler communities, with a particular geographic focus on the frontiers of the Iroquois Confederacy in the eighteenth century (modern Quebec, Vermont, New York, Pennsylvania, Maryland, Virginia, and Ohio). It weaves together stories of the everyday lives of European and Indian settlers with portraits of the unique communities in which they lived and the larger historical contexts in which they operated. When I began this study years ago, I was intrigued by glimpses in the historical record of the everyday interactions of Indians and Europeans who shared and contested places like the Mohawk Valley. This work especially focuses attention on the grassroots dimension of social and economic life that has largely escaped historians' attention.[2] This study thoroughly explores the entire spectrum of intercultural negotiations—from frontier farmers' informal contacts with Natives to colonial officials and Indian leaders' diplomacy. French-Canadian, Palatine, Scots-Irish, Dutch, English, and African settlers and slaves not only lived close to Indian villages but frequently interacted with Iroquois, Delawares, Shawnees, and other Native peoples. Frontier farms, forts, churches, mills, taverns, and towns were scenes of frequent face-to-face meetings. Ordinary people powerfully shaped the larger social, economic, and diplomatic patterns of cultural contact through their routine negotiations. The everyday lives of European and Indian settlers were far more complex and, at times, more harmonious and stable than our histories have allowed. In the absence of clear racial or frontier dividing lines, frontier inhabitants made sense of their worlds primarily through the face-to-face human relationships they formed. Local relationships between European and Indian communities were as important in maintaining peace as the formal alliances orchestrated by British, French, and Iroquois diplomats.

The Iroquois Confederacy—or the Six Nations, as it was referred to after 1722—was supremely important in shaping early American history. Historians have deeply explored the political, diplomatic, military, and imperial contours of the Six Nations' relations with Dutch, French, and English colonizers. Recent scholarship has mainly focused on Iroquois diplomacy, warfare, and political structures.[3] Indeed, the Iroquois policy of neutrality was partly responsible for a sustained period of peaceful relations in the early eighteenth century. The Five Nations pursued peace with New France at the Treaty of Montreal in 1701 and subsequently expanded their "Covenant Chain" alliance with New York to include other British colonies such as Pennsylvania. The late Francis Jennings rightly concluded that the Iroquois alliances with the French and British were examples of "accommodation and cooperation between peoples of different ethnicity, different cultures, and different social and political structures."[4]

But as I read the major works on Indian-European relations in early America, I wanted to know more about the texture of human contact in the eighteenth century—the threads in the tapestry of daily life that are often absent from recent frontier/backcountry and ethnohistorical studies. With a few notable exceptions, histories of the backcountry do not bring the settlers' nearest neighbors and enemies—the Indians—into their stories of settlement, land disputes, economic development, and agrarian rebellions.[5] On the other hand, many studies of Indian peoples only address the common European settlers of the frontier insofar as their "Indian hating" and violence affected larger diplomatic relations. Scholars have frequently typecast European frontier folk as land-hungry, violent, and ethnocentric catalysts of conflict with Indians. But such casual characterizations are often based on loose research or an uncritical acceptance of colonial elites' writings, with their jaundiced views of the "lower sort." Moreover, recent ethnohistorical work remains focused on empires, diplomacy and foreign policy, trade, and the perspectives of "cultural brokers"—the politically important sachems, interpreters, and colonial officials who helped to structure formal alliances. This book explores what was happening on the ground and treats both European and Indian communities with equal ethnographic justice and exhaustive research.[6]

Another imbalance that exists in historical literature is that far more is known about colonial communities than Indian ones; detailed treatments of Native communities are far and few between (the historical focus has always been on the "tribe"). The historian Joshua Piker's recent study of a single Creek town in the colonial southeast suggests the promises of such an approach.[7] Throughout this work I refer to European and Indian *settler* communities to emphasize the similarity of their inhabitants' lives and aspirations. Simply put, Indians were settlers too: many of the Indians whom colonists encountered were themselves new settlers seeking security in the land. As John Mack Faragher observes, "The American conflict with the Indians came not because they were so alien to each other but precisely because they were so much alike."[8] The ordinary colonial and Native peoples who lived in close proximity on the frontiers were a diverse blend of villagers, farmers, squatters, tavernkeepers, rural artisans, hunters, traders, soldiers, and warriors. They often had no official role in diplomacy, yet they profoundly shaped their worlds at a local level; they directly negotiated with one another, and they understood and misunderstood their cultural conversations. Locality was a crucial dynamic in Iroquois society, as anthropologist William N. Fenton has observed, and the same can be argued for European frontier societies.[9] This book specifically investigates the contacts between European and Indian settler communities and how they changed over time in the St. Lawrence, Mohawk, Susquehanna, Juniata, and Ohio river valleys. These five river valleys are notable in that Indian and European settlers coinhabited in them for extended periods of the eighteenth century.[10] They were the main avenues of European settlement expansion in New France, New York, and Pennsylvania. With rich alluvial soil, forest resources, and emotional and spiritual significance, they were hotly contested in numerous land disputes by Native and non-Native settlers, land speculators, provincial elites, and imperial officials. Each of the following chapters thus begins with a descriptive sketch of a particular Indian or European settlement or neighborhood and the rhythms of life on the frontier. Without reference to this "village world," it would be impossible to appreciate the complex character of Indian-European interactions in the eighteenth century.[11]

The emotional relationships between European and Indian communities exerted a powerful bearing on official diplomatic relations. The treaties, conferences, and diplomacy usually emphasized in the histories of early America cannot be understood apart from this very local frontier world. As William Fenton's work plainly reveals, the Iroquois Confederacy did not function according to Western ideals of diplomacy and foreign policy. Rather, the decisions that individuals or localities made were crucial determinants of how the Confederacy as a whole functioned. Ideals of community, kinship, and reciprocity—and the ceremonies preserving them—remained the bedrocks of human relationship to the Indians. Kinship metaphors such as "brothers" or "children" defined how the Iroquois perceived their closest European neighbors. From the Natives' perspective peace and stability were sustained locally by Indian and European communities, not simply by pen, ink, and parchment. In Philip Reid's words, peace was "primarily a matter of the mind": it was not simply a "negotiated agreement backed by the sanctions of international law and mutual self-interest. It was a matter of 'good thoughts' between two nations, a feeling as much as a reality." Indians desired that their alliances with Europeans would join together entire peoples, not mere political entities, and unite the peoples' hearts and minds. When the Delaware sachem Sassoonan spoke before assembled colonists and Indians in the Great Meeting House in Philadelphia in 1728, he expressed his wish that "they may all know that the Christians & Indians ought to have but one Head, one Heart, & one Body; that he looks on them all as one People." Indian peoples scrutinized the behaviors and attitudes of nearby European settlers for tangible signals and evidence of the alliance's vitality. Scholars have long recognized that "words and good thoughts were tremendously important, for only if everyone shared in the climate of good will could peace be preserved." A French officer wrote admiringly that the Iroquois Confederacy had a "constant preoccupation to preserve the good will of its allies," and for that reason "examples of the violation of treaties [among the Iroquois] are rare." Local relations between Indian and European communities had the power to sustain or undermine the goodwill and good feelings that were among the most important foundations of alliances from the Indians' viewpoint.[12]

The diplomatic records of the colonial era contain abundant references to the significance that Indian leaders attached to their local relationships with frontier settlers. Whenever they decried land frauds, murders, assaults, or inhospitable treatment, the Indians placed more emphasis on the sinister *motives* and *feelings* that such actions betrayed. In 1767, for example, an Onondaga sachem expressed his "uneasiness" over British officials' hardhearted responses to Indian complaints. As William Johnson recounts, the sachem cited as evidence the "hostile behaviour of [the British settlers] these 2 years past." Such behavior aroused Iroquois suspicions and apprehensions that the settlers "were not so Sincere as [Johnson] always represented." In 1761, for example, a frontier tavernkeeper, Eve Pickerd, made a few Mohawk Indians drunk and cajoled them into signing a deed to lands. Mohawk sachems "in a violent passion" subsequently protested not merely her unjust actions but "the deceitfulness, and unbrotherlike behaviour of the white people towards them." In the Mohawks' view Pickerd's malicious motives "seemed to aim at their entire extirpation" and betrayed the Mohawks' past faithfulness and goodwill toward her.[13]

In sum, everyday relations between Indian and colonial communities hold a richness, depth, and sophistication that have yet to be fully explored. As noted earlier, past historical studies have often emphasized "cultural brokers," and indeed, as Daniel Richter explains, without cultural brokers' savoir-faire, "peoples with vastly differing political structures, economic systems, and cultural beliefs could hardly talk to each other, much less work together." James Merrell's admirable work on the Pennsylvania frontier, for example, primarily focuses on politically important negotiators; in his interpretation these few go-betweens were responsible for averting conflict between two cultures that seemingly always stood at the precipice of war.[14] My research builds upon these analyses of cultural brokers by showing how ordinary Indians' and colonists' everyday lives were elaborately interwoven, but it differs by showing that cultural negotiations did not in fact depend on a small class of negotiators. Culture did not always overshadow the settlers' common humanity. Ordinary people carried on cross-cultural conversations independent of official mediators, and just as skillfully. They frequently communicated, traded, negotiated over land, and even conducted their own forms of diplomacy separate from colonial governments or Indian councils. As a group of Europeans living near the Mohawk settlement of Canajoharie emphasized, "None of your [New York] Gentlemen knows the way of the Indians yet as we that lives amongst them."[15] Indeed, colonial gentlemen frequently condemned their frontier subjects' unauthorized "intermeddling" or "tampering" with Indians under their assumed jurisdiction. In that respect official mediators and the governments they represented were often peripheral to events taking place on the frontiers.[16]

The familiar historical portrait of overweening colonial empires did not prepare me for the portrait of colonial empires that emerged from eighteenth-century records. I was struck by the outright fear and anxiety that colonial officials expressed about the frontiers and the Indian nations that surrounded them. At times British and French imperial officials operated in a highly theoretical world: they asserted claims to lands that they could not possibly control; they viewed distant frontiers with a great degree of uncertainty and, at times, ignorance of actual conditions; and as a result they often reacted to developments with great trepidation. This is not to say that colonial power was trivial, irrelevant, or unfelt by the Indians. Clearly, the presence of rival colonial governments that tried to breathe life into their imperial claims structured the lives of Indian peoples to a degree. But we often forget how mightily and painfully British and French leaders struggled for dominion, while never fully achieving it.

British colonial correspondence contains voluminous evidence of this sense of weakness and the fear of Iroquois independence and power. The members of the New York colonial council, for example, often remarked on the defenseless, "naked and exposed" condition of Albany and Schenectady and their lack of effective military forces. But their worst nightmare was the possibility of the Six Nations defecting to the French. For most of the colonial era British officials had magnified the military significance and fighting strength of the Five Nations, and in a sense they were now prisoners of their own inflated rhetoric. In 1745, for example, the New York Council feared that Albany itself would soon fall to French and Indian attack, in which case "there would be nothing less to expect than the Revolt of the Six Nations" and a total shift in the balance of power toward the French. Governor George Clinton predicted that the British would then have to completely abandon their frontiers and retreat to the coast.[17] So much for the lofty British claims that the Iroquois were the subjects of the British monarch and that their lands were technically part of the king's dominion, according to Article 15 of the 1713 Treaty of Utrecht. "The Iroquois laugh when you talk to them of obedience to kings," the English trader John Long wrote in 1768, "for they cannot reconcile the idea of submission with the dignity of man." An Onondaga speaker explicitly rejected British claims in a 1748 speech to the governor general of New France: "They had not ceded to any one their lands," he emphasized, "which they hold only of Heaven." Gen. Thomas Gage, the commander in chief of British forces in North America in 1772, agreed, privately remarking to Sir William Johnson that "as for the Six Nations having acknowledged themselves subjects of the English, that I conclude must be a very gross mistake and am well satisfied were they told so, they would not be well pleased."[18]

The French colonial correspondence also provides a powerful argument against the dominance of imperial powers. Although the French had an obvious interest in denying and disproving British claims over the Six Nations, their outside commentary only confirms what British leaders like Gage privately admitted. One French document stated that the British claim of "sovereignty is a chimera. . . . The Iroquois are very far from acknowledging any sovereign." French governors certainly coveted sovereignty over their Native allies, but the Marquis de Beauharnois and Gilles Hocquart plainly admitted in 1731 "the impossibility of subjugating the Indians at present." Another report concluded, "There is not an Indian nation in North America that ought to be considered in any other light than as friends and allies." The correspondence of Philippe de Rigaud de Vaudreuil, the governor general of New France from 1703 to 1725, repeatedly emphasized that the colony's existence depended upon peace with the Iroquois: avoiding renewed warfare was the bedrock of New France's policy toward the Six Nations.[19]

The histories of frontier communities often demonstrate the weak grasp of distant colonial capitals and the hollow nature of imperial claims of sovereignty over frontier lands and Native nations. Modern readers have been conditioned to accept the inevitability of European domination; most maps of colonial America in textbooks privilege British and French imperial claims and show nothing about the territories of Indian nations. For example, when I decided to pursue a broader study encompassing much of northeastern North America, I initially expected to engage a longstanding debate over whether the Middle Colonies constituted a distinct region. But I found that works like William Brewster's *The New York and Pennsylvania Frontier* (1954) obscured the great degree to which the lands northward, southward, and westward of those colonies remained an Indian world and landscape.[20] A term like *Pennsylvania frontier* projects colonial power and boundaries onto places where neither of these categories was absolute. Pennsylvania's evolving boundaries, for example, were contested by the Six Nations, Ohio Indians, Virginia, Maryland, Connecticut, and New York. Native peoples themselves treated colonial charters and land claims as though they were peripheral, if not invisible, and continued to travel, hunt, fight, and settle in areas they had occupied for centuries. The process to be explained was how these distinctively Iroquoian borders and territories of the early eighteenth century were transformed into rigid colonial, state, and national possessions.[21]

The Six Nations possessed enduring prestige during the eighteenth century as the most powerful Indian confederation in eastern North America. The Haudenosaunee, or People of the Longhouse, inhabited a metaphorical longhouse stretching from the Mohawks' eponymous valley to the Great Lakes; their population actually increased over the eighteenth century, so that by the 1770s they numbered over seven thousand, not including nearly two thousand Iroquois settlers living in the St. Lawrence, Susquehanna, and Ohio valleys.[22] The keepers of the longhouse's eastern door were the Mohawks, while the Senecas guarded the western door. The Oneidas, Onondagas, Cayugas, and Tuscaroras (after the 1720s) inhabited the lands between the door keepers. The Six Nations' country sat astride one of the most strategic transportation routes in eastern America—the Mohawk Valley corridor. Moreover, the Iroquois exercised (or at least claimed) a great degree of influence over their Native neighbors such as the Delawares and Shawnees; they invited displaced or oppressed peoples such as the Tuscaroras, Nanticokes, Tutelos, and Mahicans to settle on their southern borders in the eighteenth century (the Tuscaroras became the sixth nation after their adoption in the 1720s). Europeans at the time simply did not perceive the Six Nations as a colonized, dependent, and declining set of peoples.[23] Although the Mohawks and Oneidas faced significant encroachment from European settlements, the Six Nations as a whole retained the vast majority of their ancient homelands until the 1770s and 1780s, when the American Revolution resulted in displacement or dispossession for many Iroquois. The Six Nations, then, deftly avoided becoming dependent. They succeeded in preserving their neutrality, power, and independent course of action for most of the eighteenth century.[24]

The countless French and British admissions of the limits of their authority and the many proofs of Iroquois sovereignty convinced me that historians needed new vocabularies and new vantage points on northeastern North America. Terminology should, as historian Daniel Richter encourages, "shift our perspective to try to view the past in a way that faces east from Indian Country."[25] The term *Iroquoia* has often been used by historians and anthropologists to describe the core lands occupied by each of the Five Nations for hundreds of years.[26] The places where European and Indian communities coexisted, I argue, are more accurately described as *Iroquoian frontiers* or *Iroquoian borderlands*, in contrast to, for instance, the *Pennsylvania frontier*. This shift in emphasis underscores that the Iroquois did not operate in nebulous and boundaryless borderlands but with definite senses of boundaries among themselves and with other nations.[27] Terms like *Iroquoia* and *Iroquoian borderlands* best describe the realities of the contested contact zone between the Six Nations and New France, New York, Pennsylvania, and Virginia.[28] The European farmers and settlers who lived among the Iroquois operated in a distinctly Indian context and landscape. Geographically, I define these Iroquoian frontiers as the areas on the Six Nations' periphery that either fell under Iroquois influence or were settled by Iroquois and other Native emigrants in the 1700s. Like "the extremities of our Confederacy" that an Oneida Indian once spoke of, the Iroquoian borderlands stretched from the St. Lawrence down the Champlain Valley to the Mohawk Valley, across the Catskills to the Delaware and Susquehanna valleys, then westward across the ridge and valley country of the Appalachians to the headwaters of the Potomac and Ohio rivers.[29]

This model points us toward Native understandings of boundaries, human movement, the landscape, and historical change.[30] Iroquois political thought and diplomatic ceremony, ancient and modern, symbolized peaceful relations through a Tree of Peace.[31] The four roots of the Tree of Peace spread beyond Iroquoia itself so that other nations might live under the tree's peaceful shade or as "props" of the longhouse. At the peace of Montreal in 1701, for example, Iroquois speakers spoke of giving the Tree of Peace "roots to reach the Far Nations, in order that it may be strengthened."[32] In the early eighteenth century the Six Nations extended the roots of peace to Delawares, Shawnees, Tutelos, Nanticokes, and Mahicans who settled on Iroquoia's southern frontiers under their auspices—though never their direct control. Christian Frederick Post, a Moravian missionary with a vast knowledge of Indian peoples, described how the arrangement worked: the Iroquois "settle these New Allies on the Frontiers of the White People and give them this as their Instruction. 'Be Watchful that no body of the White People may come to settle near you. . . . We will secure you and defend you against them.'"[33] The Tree of Peace, then, very much structured the mindsets and actions of the Iroquois toward their French, British, and Indian neighbors.

The roots of the Tree of Peace were strengthened and lengthened in the eighteenth century. Many Iroquois settlers—mainly Senecas, Oneidas, Tuscaroras, and Mohawks—also migrated into the Iroquoian borderlands and established new communities in the upper Ohio, Susquehanna, and St. Lawrence valleys from the late seventeenth to the mid-eighteenth centuries.[34] This outward thrust of new communities challenges our conventional portrait of Indians constantly retreating before Europeans. In the St. Lawrence Valley, for example, Kahnawake (1667), Kanasetake (1721), Akwesasne (1755), and Oswegatchie (1750s) were founded by Mohawks, Oneidas, Cayugas, and Onondagas. Seneca Iroquois also established new settlements in the Ohio and Allegheny valleys. And Tuscaroras journeyed all the way from Carolina to live securely among the Five Nations. As Victor Konrad states, these new communities were an "extension of the homeland," not a diminishment of it. In light of the Iroquois population's growth and expansion, the colonial settlements in Pennsylvania and New York appear not as inexorable juggernauts but as weaker entities on the periphery of a powerful Indian confederation.[35]

The extensive movements of Iroquois peoples in the colonial period make it impossible to focus narrowly on one colony's frontier experience. Recent studies of Pennsylvania, for example, suffer from their lack of contextual attention to New France and New York. What is true for Indian-white relations in Pennsylvania is not necessarily true for those in New York or Canada. Studying the entire geographic area that the Six Nations influenced enables us to see in a comparative way the structural similarities and differences of Indian and European settler societies as they merged.[36] Both New York and Pennsylvania, for example, had a common alliance with the Six Nations that sustained a period of peaceful relations in the early eighteenth century. But there were significant differences in the stability of the two colonies' relations with their Indian neighbors. Despite William Penn's vision of peace with Natives at Pennsylvania's founding in 1681, the colony endured grueling conflict at an early date (1755); peaceful relationships there between Native and European communities were more circumscribed and truncated. During the French and Indian War (or the Seven Years' War) (ca. 1754–63), Delawares, Shawnees, Mingos, and their French allies inflicted tremendous destruction on Pennsylvania's defenseless frontiers.[37] The French and Indian War and Pontiac's War in Pennsylvania and Virginia set in motion processes such as unrestrained settlement and racial violence that the American Revolution merely exacerbated. The racial violence of common settlers against Indians, for example, surfaced in Pennsylvania in the 1760s, but not in the Mohawk Valley or the St. Lawrence Valley to the north.

Of all the British North American colonies, New York enjoyed the longest span of peace with the Indian nations on its borders. Relations in the Mohawk Valley defy current interpretations that portray all British colonists as violent Indian killers after 1763. Quite simply, there were no mass murders or massacres of Indians in colonial New York, as there were in Pennsylvania. Strong religious, economic, social, and military ties enabled Iroquois and New York colonial communities to coexist peacefully until the early 1770s. Indeed, cultural relations in the Mohawk Valley reflected those in the St. Lawrence Valley of New France, where "certain *habitants* had a good knowledge of Indian languages, were aware of Native traditions and customs and, not infrequently, entertained close and friendly contacts with their Indian neighbours" near Montreal and Quebec.[38] It was not until the American Revolution that the Iroquois and the New York colonists experienced the same destructive and racially charged warfare that Pennsylvania, Virginia, and other British colonies had experienced much earlier. The Revolution sparked civil wars that pitted loyalists against rebels and Oneidas and Tuscaroras against Mohawks and Senecas. It uprooted the British-Iroquois alliance and

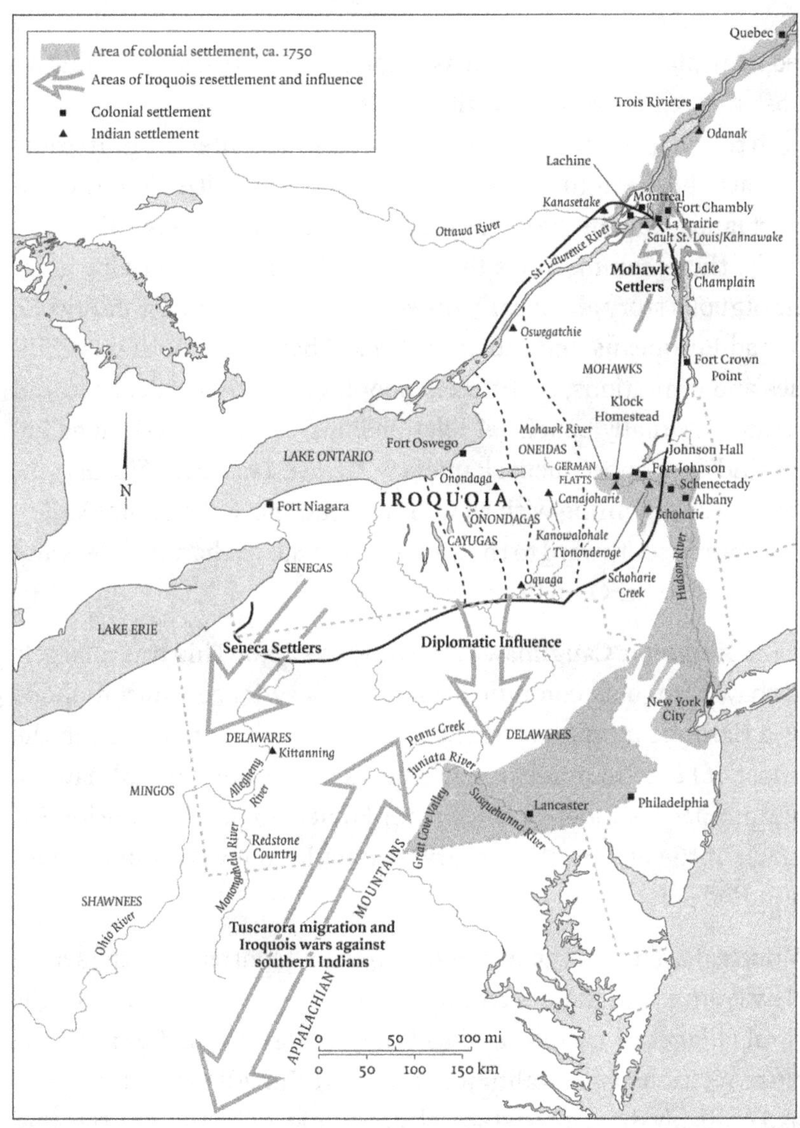

Map 1. European and Iroquoian Communities in the Eighteenth Century

led to displacement and dispossession for many Iroquois in punitive postwar treaties with the United States.

In the chapters that follow readers will encounter the grassroots contacts between Indian and European communities and the distinct landscapes of the river valleys in which they coexisted. Collectively, these communities tell a more complex and perhaps more ambiguous story about early America than the simple morality tale of bad Europeans and Indian victims. They reveal both possibilities and limitations, as different peoples, for a time, coexisted and created mutually beneficial relationships. As the descriptions below indicate, subsequent chapters will trace a vast arc of local communities, beginning with New France and the St. Lawrence Valley, continuing southward to the Mohawk and Susquehanna valleys and westward to the Ohio Country.

Kahnawake (or Caughnawaga), ca. 1700–1750: This was a largely Mohawk Iroquois community in the St. Lawrence Valley founded as a Catholic mission settlement in 1667. Although located in the midst of French-Canadian settlements near Montreal, Kahnawake maintained its independence from French colonial authority. For much of the eighteenth century its population was around twelve hundred persons.

Montreal, ca. 1700–1750: Founded in 1642, Montreal was the seat of New France's fur trade and Indian diplomacy. Along with the nearby rural villages of Lachine and La Prairie, Montreal had particularly close relations with Kahnawake. French-Canadians and Iroquois had probably the strongest social, economic, religious, martial, and marital ties of all the peoples surveyed here.

Schoharie, ca. 1700–1720: In the early 1700s a few Mohawk settlements were founded in the Schoharie Valley southwest of Albany, New York. Distressed and landless Palatine (German) immigrants peacefully approached the Schoharie Mohawks for permission to settle in the valley in 1712. From that point until the American Revolution the history of the Palatines and Mohawks became intertwined in fascinating ways.

Tiononderoge, ca. 1700–1750: The "lower Mohawk castle," numbering about three to four hundred residents in the early 1700s, was one of the principal Mohawk Iroquois settlements. Located at the confluence of the Mohawk River and Schoharie Creek, this community faced significant pressure from nearby Anglo-Dutch colonists at Albany and Schenectady. But the people of Tiononderoge had a particularly strong relationship with the influential Irish trader William Johnson, who intermarried among them and became their chief benefactor.

Canajoharie, ca. 1700–1750: The "upper Mohawk castle," further west of Tiononderoge, was surrounded by Palatine settlements at German Flatts and Stone Arabia and a small white community called Canajoharie. The Mohawk population here, it was said, was more prosperous than the surrounding European farmers, and the Mohawks here often imbibed the architecture, customs, and economy of their European neighbors. The Canajoharie Indians also pursued a unique method of dwelling in peace with British colonists: renting the land to trustworthy families.

Great Cove Valley, ca. 1730–55: This valley's name refers to the geography of the surrounding mountains, which essentially created an isolated cove in the valley below. European squatters inhabiting the Great Cove, Susquehanna, and Juniata valleys lived among Delaware, Shawnee, and other Algonquian communities; they often approached the Indians for permission to share the land, and some even paid annual rents to Native landlords, just as the settlers at Canajoharie had done.

Penn's Creek, ca. 1755: This was a largely Swiss, German, and English settlement on the west side of the Susquehanna River on land that Ohio Indians believed had been fraudulently obtained by the Pennsylvania government in 1754. The Delawares' attack on Penn's Creek in 1755 sheds light on the nature of the violence, warfare, and racial hatred between Indians and colonists that erupted during and after the French and Indian War.

Kittanning, ca. 1756: A Delaware community on the Allegheny River northeast of Fort Duquesne, Kittanning was the object of a devastating attack by colonial Pennsylvanians in 1756. This place symbolizes the erosion of the common world that had once existed between colonists and Natives and the beginning of lasting hostilities in the Ohio Valley.

German Flatts, ca. 1750s–60s: This was the westernmost colonial settlement in the Mohawk Valley, situated between Canajoharie to the east and Oneida villages to the west. Located at an Indian crossroads, the German Flatts community had strong personal, economic, diplomatic, and marital ties with Native communities in the Mohawk Valley. The story of German Flatts reveals the complex diplomacy that took place between the Germans and Iroquois, despite the fact that war was raging between 1756 and 1763.

Redstone Creek, in the Monongahela Valley, ca. 1760s: The Ohio Country was the focal point of an imperial crisis on British North America's frontiers in the 1760s. English settlers came into the valley by the thousands, following in the British army's train as it militarily occupied the west from 1758 until 1772. Despite a vicious cycle of killings and murders, and continued conflict over land and authority, colonists, Iroquois, and Algonquians who lived there still dealt with one another in peaceful ways.

The epilogue demonstrates how the American Revolution affected Indian and European communities on the New York–Pennsylvania–Six Nations borders, dissolving the close social, economic, religious, and personal bonds that had once linked Indian and colonial communities together. The Mohawk Valley in particular suffered tremendous devastation from 1777 through 1781 in a civil war that pitted neighbor against neighbor, loyalists against rebels, and Iroquois against Iroquois. Indians' and Euroamericans' racial hatred, born of the Revolution's warfare, made any postwar accommodation tenuous. Though the process was not inevitable, the Iroquoian borderlands in which Indian and European settlers had coinhabited for most of the eighteenth century were truly revolutionized by greater numbers of American settlers moving westward. The settlers on the ground brought reality and legitimacy to the land claims of individual states and the new American republic, which to this point had been but shadows.

Finding evidence about the daily lives of European and Indian settlers was not as difficult an enterprise as one might imagine. These peoples left behind comparatively few documentary traces as colonial governments, but in general historians, as I discovered, have not yet begun to mine the rich archival materials on colonial New York, Pennsylvania, and New France. I examined some manuscript collections that historians have seldom or never consulted in studies of Indian peoples. Manuscript collections from the National Archives of Canada, the New York State Archives, the New York State Library, the New York Historical Society, the Pennsylvania State Archives, the Pennsylvania Historical Society, the William L. Clements Library, and other institutions provide the principal foundations of this work. I have also buttressed the work with the standard published sources such as government records, accounts of Indian treaties and conferences, missionaries' writings, traders' and merchants' account books, travel narratives, captivity narratives, land records, church records, newspapers, letters, and diaries. In all of these cases I read the primary sources for what they revealed about everyday life on the frontiers, finding many rich pieces of evidence. A historian should also personally visit and study the actual vestiges of the historical landscape that survive today. Accordingly, this work has been enriched by my personal explorations of the many colonial forts, taverns, houses, barns, churches, graveyards, and windmills that have survived for over 250 years. Visits to places like Quebec, Montreal, Kahnawake, the Champlain Valley, Schoharie, Canajoharie, German Flatts, the Great Cove, and Pittsburgh shortened the distance between the eighteenth and the twenty-first centuries. I also realized what a great debt is owed to the keepers of those sites and records and to the historians, editors, and chroniclers who have come before. The nineteenth-century historian Francis Parkman, though much maligned today, was a deeply influential historian who was no less afflicted by cultural blind spots than we are. Accordingly, I have taken great inspiration from his methods:

> The whole of this published and unpublished mass of evidence has been read and collated with extreme care, and more than common pains have been taken to secure accuracy of statement. The study of books and papers, however, could not alone answer the purpose. The plan of the work was formed in early youth; and though various causes have long delayed its execution, it has always been kept in view. Meanwhile, I have visited and examined every spot where events of any importance in connection with the contest took place, and have observed with attention such scenes and persons as might help to illustrate those I meant to describe. In short, the subject has been studied as much from life and in the open air as at the library table.[39]

1. The Tree of Peace Planted
Iroquois and French-Canadian Communities in the St. Lawrence Valley

Montreal: The Great Peace of 1701

A tree was planted in Montreal in 1701, and a peace grew from its roots that altered the history and character of colonial America and its peoples. From July 25 to August 4, 1701, one of the largest and most important treaties between Indians and Europeans was negotiated. By the waters of the St. Lawrence, Indians and French colonists assembled with hope to end the Iroquois wars of the seventeenth century. Approximately thirty-nine different Indian nations had traveled to Montreal that summer, including Hurons, Crees, Mississaugas, Miamis, Illinois, Potawatomis, Ojibwas, and many others. In addition to six hundred delegates from the Iroquois Confederacy, there were over seven hundred Indians in two hundred canoes who converged on Montreal from the Great Lakes region to the west-northwest. Over nine hundred miles inland, the Montreal area marked the westernmost limit of settlement on the St. Lawrence River. Founded in 1642, Montreal very much remained a frontier post and fur-trading entrepôt, and its population in 1701 was a little over two thousand inhabitants; it was also the epicenter of New France's diplomatic relations with its Native allies. During the summer Indians strolled the streets of Montreal, visiting French merchants' shops and exchanging furs for trade goods such as copper pots, blankets, tools, gunpowder, and hats.[1]

As many as three thousand French and Indian men, women, and children gathered together in an elaborate ceremony to sign the peace on the final day of the treaty, August 4, 1701.[2] On a plain near the St. Lawrence River the French had constructed a large gardenlike arena for order and decorum. The governor general of New France, Louis Hector de Callière, was the presiding French official. Seated on an ornate platform covered with tree branches and surmounted by the French royal arms, Callière's entourage faintly reflected the bright grandeur of France's "Sun King," Louis XIV. Surrounding him were the intendant of the colony, Jean Bochart de Champigny, and Philippe de Rigaud de Vaudreuil, a French officer who would later succeed Callière as governor general. The elite of Montreal society also turned out to witness the proceedings. Their long wigs, ruffled shirts, black robes, and silk dresses had a counterpoint in the ceremonial dress of the Indian participants: painted faces, beaver robes, feather and even bison headdresses, and French hats and coats. One by one Native leaders rose to speak and to sign the treaty. The language they used expressed hope for a future of good feelings and peace. French and Indian leaders exchanged calumets, and pungent tobacco smoke certainly filled the air that day. They spoke of burying their hatchets in a deep trench and of giving "the Tree of Peace that [Onontio had] erected such strong, deep roots, that neither winds nor storms, nor other misfortune will be able to uproot it."[3]

The Tree of Peace planted in Montreal in 1701 ended the chronic and devastating warfare between the Iroquois and New France and its western Indian allies and ushered in a new era of Iroquois neutrality. The seventeenth century had been plagued by wars, crippling outbreaks of disease, and increased competition over hunting territories and access to trade. The Five Nations had waged war against

New France in the St. Lawrence Valley and its Indian allies further west. Iroquois warrior losses in the decade of the 1690s may have approached 50 percent. French military retaliation against Onondagas, Senecas, and Mohawks in 1666, 1684, 1687, and 1693 had only weakened, not destroyed, the Five Nations. The exhausted parties occasionally arranged truces, but there were far more years of actual warfare than of peace in the 1600s. The treaty of 1701 eliminated some of the reasons for these wars, for the Iroquois were able to secure French recognition of their hunting rights in the west and the freedom to trade at the French posts of Detroit and Fort Frontenac.[4]

At Montreal new foreign policy goals emerged for both New France and the Iroquois Confederacy. The Five Nations pledged to remain neutral in any future Anglo-French imperial conflicts. But this neutrality was an "armed neutrality," as William Fenton writes, and it enabled the Iroquois Confederacy to become an assertive and independent power as the French and British competed for its favor. In fact, at the very same moment that Iroquois ambassadors journeyed to Montreal, around two hundred Iroquois leaders were meeting with English officials in Albany. An English writer, Peter Wraxall, believed that preserving "the Ballance between us and the French is the great ruling Principle of the Modern Indian Politics." In the eighteenth century the Five Nations would also develop new alliances with the far-western Indian nations and maintain a guardianlike role over Algonquian peoples in the Susquehanna and Delaware valleys to the south. In the language of diplomacy the Great Tree planted at Montreal was to be a beacon of peace to all nations.[5]

In the years following 1701 King Louis XIV orchestrated the French policy of containing the British colonists east of the Appalachians: alliances with Indians, fortified trading posts along interior waterways, and a new colony in Louisiana were all part of this imperial design. To block the English the French desperately wished to preserve the Iroquois Confederacy in its neutral course. The French desired to preserve peace with the Iroquois at all costs, and their tremendous fear of renewed warfare is a healthy reminder that the Iroquois, though they had suffered tremendously, were far from broken. Governor Vaudreuil, who witnessed the 1701 peace, later spoke of preserving the peace as the guiding principle of French diplomacy with the Five Nations. He also wished to avoid the possibility that the Iroquois would commit military forces to the English in New York in any future conflict. Shortly after 1701 Vaudreuil negotiated a secret agreement with New York in which each colony refrained from attacking the other. In this way the Tree of Peace's shade covered New York.[6]

The Tree of Peace was an incredibly resonant symbol and metaphor for coexistence. It structured the ways that Iroquois, French, British, and Algonquians spoke to one another in the colonial era, and it remains to this day the symbol of the Haudenosaunee Confederacy. Given how frequently it is mentioned in colonial diplomacy, it is surprising how little attention it has received from modern historians. The tree demonstrated death and rebirth: from the dark warfare of the seventeenth century to the long peace of the eighteenth century. The parties buried their hatchets and implements of war, then planted and nurtured the tree of peace over their dark past. Iroquois speakers described a process of giving the tree roots, adding leaves to it, and bringing shade. This was a peace process that required frequent pruning. In 1700 an Iroquois speaker told the French governor, "We now give it roots to reach the Far Nations." Iroquois delegates repeatedly emphasized that the function of the four roots was to "reach all the nations round about us," inviting them to dwell in peace. The shade of the tree's branches represented a place of repose and security.[7]

The Tree of Peace was more than a quaint diplomatic metaphor, for it reflected a great degree of historical reality. The tree's branches provided shade in which French Canadians and Indians in the St. Lawrence Valley dwelled together in largely peaceful ways in the eighteenth century. To recognize that relationship as unique and unprecedented is not to romanticize "some mystical affinity between

Frenchmen and Indians," as historian Richard White warns, but simply to observe that this relationship is without parallel in comparison to other places in colonial North America. The Iroquois community of Kahnawake and its neighborhood with the French-Canadian settlements at La Prairie, Montreal, and Lachine allow us to see some of the religious, political, and demographic streams that watered the Tree of Peace, nurturing such vitality.

In the eighteenth century significant numbers of Indian peoples lived among the French settlers, concentrated near the urban centers of Quebec, Trois Rivières, and Montreal.[8] For example, Christian Hurons had settled the town of Lorette, a short distance from the town of Quebec, in the 1670s. Abenakis lived in the towns of Wolinak (Bécancour) and Odanak (St. Francis), which were both located across the St. Lawrence River from Trois Rivières. Finally, Iroquois peoples had founded many new communities in the St. Lawrence Valley in the late 1600s and early 1700s. Kahnawake (1667) and Kanasetake (or Lake of the Two Mountains) (1721) were largely Mohawk settlements located to the south and west of Montreal. La Présentation (Oswegatchie) (1750s), and Akwesasne (St. Regis) (1755) were Iroquois towns located further up the St. Lawrence Valley. All of these places had common religious origins as Catholic mission towns. As a result of their close proximity to the French settlers and missionaries, most of these communities reflected both Native and French cultural influences. The Swedish naturalist Peter Kalm noted that the Lorette Hurons had "built all their houses after the French fashion." Louis Antoine de Bougainville, a French officer who visited the Huron town of Lorette in the 1750s, also described the stone houses and noted that the Hurons "hold their lands with the same rents and rules as do the French inhabitants. They are all Catholics, good or bad." He was moved by the women's choir at Lorette. "One would take them for a choir of our nuns," he mused, "except that almost all of our Indian women have singularly melodious voices." Indian communities in the St. Lawrence Valley were not impoverished reservations, but towns that flourished both spiritually and materially. In the late 1600s, in fact, the settled Indian population briefly exceeded that of the French on the Island of Montreal. The Indian population of the St. Lawrence Valley grew tremendously in the eighteenth century: historian Gilles Havard writes that "in the final two decades of the French regime, the number of Indian 'domiciliés' oscillated between 3,500 and 5,000 persons, which corresponded to a little less than 10% of the population between Quebec and Montreal." Both their numbers and their importance as trading partners and military allies of the French gave the settled Indians the ability to assert their autonomy and independence in the face of French claims.[9]

Of all the mission communities, Kahnawake was the most renowned among the French. Founded in 1667, Kahnawake ranks as one of the oldest towns in eastern America, older than many notable colonial towns such as Charleston (1680), Philadelphia (1682), and Savannah (1732).[10] This was an exceptionally large Indian town, notable for its size: Luc-François Nau, a Jesuit who served at the mission from 1734 to 1744, called it "the most agreeable and flourishing mission" in Canada, with nearly twelve hundred inhabitants in the 1730s. Situated on the southern bank of the St. Lawrence River about ten miles from Montreal, Kahnawake—the name means "at the rapids"—was always generally located near the Lachine Rapids, or as the French called them, Sault St. Louis. The town shifted westward approximately four times from 1667 until its final remove in 1716 to its current location. The name Kahnawake also hearkened back to the Mohawk Valley settlement of Caughnawaga, which had existed in the seventeenth century. This place is variously referred to in colonial records as "Caughnawaga," "Mission du Sault St. Louis," and the "Canada Indian praying Castle." The multiplicity of names is itself evidence that Kahnawake meant many things to many peoples. Its residents were known to the French as "domiciliated Indians," "Sault Iroquois," and "Christian Iroquois." But the English accused these "praying Indians" or "French Indians" of doing the savage work of their civilized masters. This kind of terminology for Kahnawake and other settlements in the St. Lawrence Valley is misleading, however, for it obscures the very real independence that the Indians there enjoyed.[11]

The Kahnawake Iroquois were often accused by English officials of having "deserted the Five Nations," but they always maintained ties with their families and kin who lived in the Mohawk Valley or elsewhere, who "look[ed] on the Caughnawagas as a part of themselves." The St. Lawrence Valley, then, was more a northern frontier of the Iroquois Confederacy than a purely French possession. The area's long history of Iroquois use and occupation was reinforced when Mohawks, Oneidas, and Onondagas resettled there in the 1700s. Iroquois towns now "stand in the very gates of the French," as Canasatego argued in 1744. The Iroquoian name for the island where the village of Hochelaga—and later Montreal—was situated is "Kawennote Tiohtia:ke." The Mohawk historian Gerald Alfred notes that this marked "recognition of a place where Kanienke [Mohawk lands] and other native nations' territories began to divide." The extension of Iroquois settlements to the St. Lawrence River gave greater flexibility to the Iroquois when pressure mounted on them to commit to either the French or the British alliance. For example, during King George's War in the 1740s, an Iroquois delegation told Albany officials that "it was very hard for them to enter into a War [for] the French Indians and the Indians of the Six Nations are sprang of one blood. They have made alliances and Marriages with each other . . . all of them [are of] some Relation or another living at Cachnawage so that they could not go to War against one another." The Kahnawake Iroquois reciprocated this belief that they remained part of the Iroquois world: in 1745 two of their warriors presented a belt of wampum to the Senecas, pledging their intent to "be [neutral]" and their hope that the Senecas "would likewise[,] they said the white people might fight for themselves." Increasingly, the Kahnawake Iroquois played an important role as mediators among the French, the Six Nations, and the English in New York and New England.[12]

Kahnawake was itself a new creation that emerged from the meeting of Indians and Europeans in early America: a new people (Kahnawake Iroquois), a new identity and faith (Christian Iroquois), and a new community living at peace with the French. The story of Kahnawake's founding, however, is a point of contention among historians. Jesuit writers from the 1600s onward celebrated the mission's history and hailed pious Christian Iroquois such as Kateri Tekakwitha. But many recent histories downplay Christianity's significance in Kahnawake's founding as a "legend" or a mythic contrivance of fervent missionaries; some writers explain the mission's founding more as a product of demographic, economic, or political trends. A subsequent line of argument highlights the survival of traditional Iroquois religious practice, as if to disprove any real adherence or attraction to Christianity. But Christianity owes its existence as a world religion to the fact that its message greatly appealed to the polytheistic peoples of the Roman Empire; during its first three hundred years it had no official support from the Roman state. The historian James Axtell has shown that Jesuit missionaries likewise effectively made Catholic teaching understandable to the Natives, attracting willing and well-versed converts. As a result, he concludes, "we are left with an impressive sum of more than 10,000 natives, mostly adults, who chose to become Christians after long and painstaking instruction by the priests."[13]

In the year 1667 a number of events fortuitously (the Jesuits would say providentially) unfolded that enabled Frenchmen and Iroquois to create a unique, if short-lived, settlement at La Prairie. First, Iroquois and French leaders had met in Quebec in 1665, where an Onondaga chief, Garakontié, proposed a peace to end the chronic warfare that had afflicted New France and the Iroquois Confederacy. But in 1666 a French officer, Alexandre de Prouville de Tracy, led a force of French regular troops in a punitive expedition against the Mohawks and burned a number of their villages. The Mohawks nevertheless not only made peace with the French in 1667 but agreed to allow Jesuit missionaries into their villages. Finally, the Jesuits were awarded a seigneurial land grant of their own, called La Prairie de la Magdeleine, on the south shore of the St. Lawrence River near Montreal. To the Jesuit Pierre Raffeix the peace of 1667 offered the possibility of developing those lands that had constantly been subject to Iroquois attack. Father Raffeix invited some French colonists to settle at La Prairie, including some veterans of the Carignan-Salières Regiment who had campaigned against the Mohawks.[14]

Around the same time a small but significant Iroquois family journeyed to Quebec. The life stories of Tonsahoten and Gandeacteua (or Ganneaktena) are marked by incredible transformations in personal and religious identities. Tonsahoten was a Huron by birth, baptized and converted to Christianity through the teaching of the Jesuit missionary Léonard Garreau. During the Huron-Iroquois wars François-Xavier Tonsahoten was adopted by the Oneidas. Around 1656 Tonsahoten met a woman in the village whose origins were similar to his own: Gandeacteua was originally of the Erie Indian peoples, whom the Five Nations had recently attacked and assimilated. Years passed before this Huron-Iroquois and Erie-Iroquois couple encountered the Jesuit missionary Jacques Bruyas, visiting their village in 1667. The only written sources about the couple, the Jesuit *relations*, make Gandeacteua the principal influence on her husband's decision to journey to New France for medical help. During their visit to Quebec Gandeacteua was baptized as Catherine and was married to François-Xavier according to church rites. When the couple afterward visited Montreal, Pierre Raffeix invited them to winter at the new settlement he was building.[15]

Raffeix, Tonsahoten, Gandeacteua, and a handful of French and Indian settlers became the nucleus of the La Prairie community. The Iroquois knew the place as Kentake, an Iroquoian word that means "the prairie," from which Kentucky's name is most likely derived.

By 1670 eighteen to twenty families had settled at La Prairie; in 1673 a Jesuit *relation* stated that Mohawk warriors were "more numerous at Montreal than they are in their own country"—only a slight exaggeration and a reflection of just how many Natives appeared to be flocking to the mission community.[16]

Indians resettled at La Prairie for many of the same reasons that zealous Europeans emigrated to the American colonies. The Indians' devotion to Christianity was initially their most important motive. The emigrants created a "colony of Christian Iroquois" among a different people—the French Canadians. They were also seeking "an asylum among the French where they might make a true profession of Christianity"—asylum from the scourge of alcohol and from the harassment and persecution of the English and of fellow Iroquois. For the many refugees or captives who came in the eighteenth century, other motives were at work—hunting, "freedom of trade," the attractiveness of the community itself. Situated near the junction of the St. Lawrence and Ottawa rivers, and with access to the Lake Champlain–Richelieu River corridor, Kahnawake was fixed in a strategic place. Its location also provided residents with many economic and trading opportunities. In 1766 a Mohawk speaker remembered that "our Forefathers going to hunt mostly in this Neighbourhood was one of the principal Reasons for our Settling upon the River St. Lawrence," along with "being well received and flattered by the french."[17]

But the zealousness of the founding generation is borne out in the Natives' life stories and the testimonies of many visitors who were uniformly moved by the devotion of Onkwehonwe Tehatiisontha: "real men who make the sign of the cross." The Mohawk woman Kateri Tekakwitha, perhaps the most famous resident of the Sault mission, was "utterly single-minded in her pursuit of God's grace" when she came there in 1677. She and a small group of women at the mission pursued an intensely austere life to mortify sin: long prayer sessions, confessions, self-flagellation, fasting, and vows of perpetual chastity.

After her death in 1680 she was venerated by both French and Indian Catholics in New France and was beatified in 1980 by Pope John Paul II. Another Mohawk, Togouiroui, who would become known to the French as "the Great Mohawk," was attracted to Mohawk Christianity after he encountered some devout neophytes from the St. Francis Xavier mission while hunting near Chambly in 1672. Their earnest example moved him deeply, as did the teaching of the missionary Jacques Frémin. The following year Togouiroui, his wife, and forty others moved from the Mohawk Valley to La Prairie. Togouiroui was baptized and became one of the principal Mohawk war leaders of the mission. A New York gentleman visiting Montreal in 1700 quizzed a Mohawk about why he had recently resettled in Kahnawake. "He had a great inclination to be a Christian," he responded, proceeding to attack Protestant teachings. Indeed, Jesuit accounts point to at least four Kahnawake Christians who were willing to lay down their lives for their newfound faith, remembered by both French and Kahnawake settlers in the eighteenth century.[18]

Initially, from 1667 to 1676, the French and Indian inhabitants of La Prairie lived together in a common settlement. An early Jesuit, Claude Chauchtière, described these early years as a time when "the french and savages all acted as one body." The people shared a chapel ("as was seen in the public rejoicings") and together supported the community's needs ("the little services that they rendered one another"). The Jesuits even compared early La Prairie to the early New Testament church. But this "unique experiment in bicultural living," as historian John Demos has written, did not last long. While the Jesuits believed and prayed that the seeds of the Christian Gospel had fallen onto good soil at La Prairie, where they might take root, by the early 1700s Father Louis Davaugour related that the "triple tares" of "drunkenness, superstition, and lewdness" had choked Christian growth. In fact, Iroquois who had "come to settle at Sault St. Louis in the hope of escaping the annoyances of this evil of drunkenness" were disappointed to find liquor "as common and as frequent as in their own country." French Christians—at least those who ran taverns and sold liquor—became "stumbling blocks" to the Iroquois converts.[19]

French colonial officials, however, were more concerned that the Sault Iroquois present another kind of stumbling block: Kahnawake was described as "the chief defense" of Montreal against the English. French officials were thus highly pleased to have Christian Indians settled in their midst, for they functioned as a buffer against possible attacks from enemy Indians and, above all, British military expeditions. The Marquis Duquesne wrote in 1754 that the network of mission towns "will form a barrier which will protect the government of Montreal against all incursions." Any British armies coming from New York up the Champlain-Richelieu Valley would first have to confront Kahnawake and the forts at St. Jean and Chambly before advancing on Montreal.[20]

Kahnawake, then, lay precisely at the intersection of New France and Indian country. Most eighteenth-century visitors and travelers came to the settlement for peaceful ends, as Indians maintained close trading, diplomatic, and religious ties with nearby French communities. The village of Lachine was a little over half a mile across the St. Lawrence River, to the north. Westward of Kahnawake was Lake St. Louis, formed by the junction of the St. Lawrence and Ottawa rivers: it was so broad that one "could hardly see anything but sky and water." Isle Perrot, in Lake St. Louis, along with Lachine, was crucial to the fur trade. French voyageurs typically disembarked and unloaded canoes at Lachine to bypass the nearby rapids of Sault St. Louis, whose rushing waters could be easily heard as they dropped some forty-five feet before Montreal. Kahnawake's orientation toward the important waterways of the area is reflected in an artist's sketch of the village in the mid-eighteenth century. This sketch allows us to imagine what the community and its landscape looked like and to connect it with details available in written sources.[21]

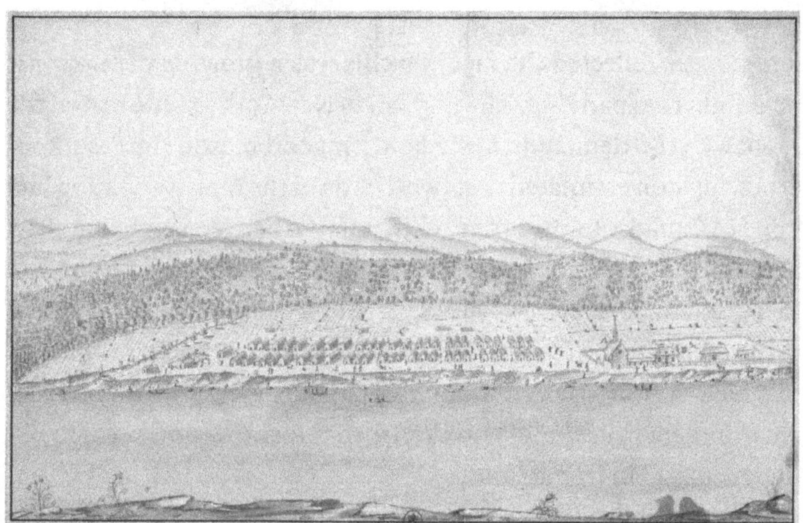

Fig. 2. *View of the Mission of Sault Saint Louis*, contemporary sketch. Courtesy of Bibliothèque nationale de France.

The Iroquois du Sault paradoxically lived in deeply traditional Iroquoian ways and in traditional Catholic ways. At first glance this sketch reveals many features of Kahnawake in the years after 1716 that were Iroquoian in nature. According to a Jesuit account, the soil at the previous location (Kanatakwenke) had become exhausted, and nearby woodlots had been depleted. Yet even this pattern of periodically relocating settlements was rooted in the Iroquois past. The fields around the village perimeter, with corn, beans, squash, and pumpkins, continued to be cultivated by women. Men continued to be responsible for hunting, trapping, and fishing, as the sketch shows in the foreground. We may also envision young men playing lacrosse, as a British trader once witnessed. The rows of longhouses with central fireplaces hearkened back to the seventeenth century. By the mid-1700s, in contrast, many Mohawks living in the Mohawk Valley had ceased to live in longhouses, instead building the small family–unit log houses typical of the British settlers living in their midst. At Kahnawake longhouses were arranged by clan affiliation, and the Iroquois governed themselves through a village council. The outlying longhouses reflected the fact that this was a growing community, its numbers expanding. The English in New York greatly feared the Mohawk resettlement in Canada, with good reason. In 1700 Robert Livingston estimated that two-thirds of the Mohawk nation had gone to Canada. In the year 1716 there were between eight hundred and one thousand souls at Kahnawake; by 1741 the population had increased to nearly twelve hundred people. One of the area's deepest attractions, as historian Daniel Richter has argued, was "the way in which the Christian communities paradoxically provided a social environment in keeping with cherished values that now seemed seldom to exist" in Iroquoia.[22]

But the sketch also abounds with evidence of French cultural influences upon this Iroquois community. This blending of Iroquois and French Catholic ways is not surprising in one sense: a "fundamental fact" about the Kahnawake Iroquois, argues historian Allan Greer, is that "they had come to live on the St. Lawrence in the full knowledge that this entailed close alignment with the French." The Iroquois' traditional combination of agriculture and hunting, for example, was "integrated with the festivals of the Catholicism they had adopted." Departures and returns from hunting trips and maple-sugar gathering were timed to coincide with Christian celebrations. Although the longhouse prevailed for most of the 1700s as the primary Iroquois dwelling place, European writers noted that Kahnawake residents had begun to build in stone, in the style of the French *habitants*, by the 1750s. One French governor thought their homes were "as well built as in the French settlements." And Louis Franquet, a French army engineer who visited in 1752, recorded that the Iroquois were "building houses in the French fashion, with squared frames and even in masonry. To this end, they have brought in French laborers of every kind." The stockaded longhouse at the far left of the sketch undoubtedly contained poultry, cattle, or the horses that most Iroquois kept. Bougainville particularly noted the villagers' fondness for horses, though they were mainly used as beasts of burden, hauling firewood from the ever-receding tree line.[23]

The community's economic life was also interwoven with that of their French neighbors. Bougainville noted that the Indians "sell, buy and trade just like Frenchmen"—activities that took place in the nearby French communities at La Prairie, Lachine, Isle Perrot, and Montreal itself. Furs were only one item frequently exchanged with nearby French settlers or merchants. In 1716 the Jesuit missionary Joseph-François Lafitau discovered that ginseng (*Aureliana Canadensis*) grew in Canada, sparking a feverish search for the plant for export to China, where it was valued as a medicine and an aphrodisiac. A similar ginseng craze began in the Mohawk Valley as well, linking Iroquois, British, French, and Chinese in a worldwide trade network. One European traveler noted that the "Indians in the neighborhood of [Montreal] were likewise so much taken up with the business that the French farmers were not able during that time to hire a single Indian, as they commonly do, to help them in the harvest." Indians apparently found it profitable to work on French settlers' farms in the fall season. But the women of Sault St. Louis had their own harvesting to do: some cultivated wheat and undoubtedly had their grain ground at the Jesuits' nearby gristmill.[24]

The rough-looking wooden palisade that surrounded the chapel and other buildings on the west side of town was itself evidence of how the Iroquois resisted French efforts to militarize the town. Colonial records reveal the Sault Iroquois' long struggle against the presence of French garrisons, accused of brawls, drunkenness, and debauchery of the village women.[25] A small stone chapel stood on the west side of the town, completed by 1722. It was flanked by a house for the missionaries—a stone building with a steep sloping roof in the French colonial style, reminiscent of northwestern France. The chapel itself symbolized that the Kahnawake Iroquois were "strongly attached to us by Religion" and—as the French writer's comments betray—that the French missionaries were also strongly attached to the Iroquois. Both structures were praised by François Lafitau, as "each in their own kind two of the finest edifices in all Canada"; Bougainville described the chapel as "pretty and well decorated." The chapel bell sounded forth the spiritual rhythms of Catholic France. Inside, we may imagine Indians assisting at mass, as the Jesuits encouraged them to do, with a choir singing the *Te Deum* in Huron, which was the preferred liturgical language. Father Nau described a typical day as beginning with morning prayers and mass, with Indian choirs singing prayers and hymns, followed by catechism of unbaptized youths and adults, and finally, evening prayers. Many observers noted that Christian Indians displayed much musical skill and derived great joy from singing hymns and prayers in their own languages. Certainly, not all Iroquois had the same devotion to the Christian faith; the Indians whom early Jesuits publicly shamed for drunkenness are ample evidence of this. But without question, Jesuits and devout Iroquois created a Catholic culture that pervaded the community. This culture was not achieved easily, because of the town's diverse and ever-increasing population.[26]

French colonists and missionaries were also vital to the community's daily life. Indians visited the homes of French settlers at La Prairie and Lachine, trading, drinking, and socializing with them. In the fort itself three French-Canadian women, daughters of a prominent Montreal merchant, operated a trading store for the Natives. The Jesuit priests who resided at the missionaries' house adjoining the chapel often remained for a large portion of their careers. Father Luc-François Nau, who lived at the mission from 1734 to 1744, was adopted into the Bear clan and given the name of Hatériate, hearkening back to an older chief who was a "great-hearted man." In his final days at the mission Father Nau was unable to walk because of his severe gout, but he continued to administer the sacraments to the Sault Iroquois from a stretcher. Nau's determination reflects the advantages the Jesuits brought to Native communities: they fought vociferously to defend their flocks from outside intrusions, even to the point of becoming alienated from their own countrymen for their lax and immoral behavior. Father Nau, for example, came to believe that "our Iroquois are much better christians than the French." His colleague Joseph-François Lafitau authored one of the most articulate and forceful denunciations of the alcohol trade in the entire colonial period.[27]

Kahnawake was one of the most ethnically diverse communities anywhere in eastern North America. Although a small majority of the population was Mohawk, there were also Oneida, Onondaga, Cayuga, and Seneca Iroquois present. As many as twenty different Indian peoples were represented there, including Abenakis, Mahicans, Hurons, Catawbas, and Chickasaws. One of the great challenges that the missionaries encountered was the sheer number of different languages spoken in the mission community. With so many new war captives being brought into Kahnawake, it was often difficult to instruct them in Christian doctrine when they were still learning Iroquoian. Kahnawake warriors also captured English, German, and Dutch colonists in the imperial wars that lasted from the 1690s to the 1750s. Most captives or refugees were subsequently assimilated into a community that few of them wished to leave, even when given the opportunity. A nineteenth-century historian asserted that "because of this mixing, there is not a single purely Iroquois family at Caughnawaga. . . . There are only a few individuals who claim to be Iroquois without a mixture of white blood."[28]

British captives among the Indians and French also pursued intermarriages at Kahnawake. Over the entire colonial era there were well over two hundred New England captives who chose to remain among their French or Indian captors—a figure that does not include those from colonial New York. The best-known English captive was Eunice Williams, daughter of the Puritan minister John Williams, who was taken captive during the French-Indian attack on Deerfield, Massachusetts, in 1704. Young Eunice took on a new identity as a Catholic Iroquois, married a Kahnawake man, and resisted all entreaties to return to her New England home. Such stories have an enduring appeal and fascination because they suggest the power of the frontier. Why did English captives like Eunice Williams and James Delisle embrace both Catholicism and Caughnawaga, preferring, like Delisle, to be "a slave with the Indians [rather] than [to be] in his country [New England] where there is no religion"?

The very openness of the community facilitated people becoming new creations. Ethnicity was an unreliable marker among a people composed of varying European, African, and Indian heritages. One Kahnawake Indian named Atiatoharongwen, or Louis Cook, had a particularly fascinating lineage. His family was most likely taken captive during a 1745 French attack on the New York frontier settlement of Saratoga. His father was a black man, his mother an Abenaki woman from the St. Francis mission (Odanak). Louis Cook, raised at Kahnawake, became a notable warrior during and after the French and Indian War. Captives were not barred from prominence as warriors or chiefs. The brothers Silas and Timothy Rice (ages nine and seven) were captured from Marlborough, Massachusetts, in 1704. Both boys were adopted into the Kahnawake community and took French and Mohawk names: Silas became Jacques Tannhahorens and married Marie Tsiakohawi. Timothy, or Jacques Oserokohton, became a "great chief" at Kahnawake, a position he may have inherited or earned. Little is known of Mary Harris's life in Puritan New England before her capture at age nine in 1704. This Deerfield native eventually married a Kahnawake man with whom she had several children. She and other Kahnawake people enjoyed great freedom of movement, her family resettling in the Ohio Valley by the 1740s. Mary probably would have disappeared from written records were it not for a young British explorer, Christopher Gist, who visited a branch of the Muskingum River called "White Woman's Creek" in 1751 and met its namesake: "Her name is Mary Harris. She still remembers they used to be very religious in [New England]

and wonders how the White men can be so wicked as she has seen them in these woods."[29]

Kahnawake, in sum, was born out of the chronic warfare between New France and Iroquoia in the seventeenth century, the Jesuits' missionary work among the Iroquois, and the desire of many Iroquois to participate in a cultural and religious renaissance on lands that Mohawk peoples had always used and claimed. The people of Kahnawake had the potential to become dominated domiciles of the French government, but this did not occur during the eighteenth century. Unlike their brethren settled near New York, the Kahnawake Iroquois did not face relentless and unyielding encroachment on their lands by neighboring French *habitants*. Kahnawake was a self-governing community that maintained an independent course of action in its relationship with New France. Although many Kahnawake villagers had been baptized as Roman Catholics, they did not see their Christian Iroquois identity as contradictory, but complementary. Even the Natives' clothing appeared to have many European influences: the cloth, the cut, even the style of the French *capot* (overcoat). The Sault Iroquois were also distinguished by the crucifixes and scapulars they wore on their clothing. But as Lafitau knew well, the Indians had "changed only the material of their clothing, keeping their former style of dressing." The community, then, strongly reflected Iroquoian cultural patterns more than it did French influences. But this reality was a point of frustration for many French, as Intendant Antoine-Denis Raudot made despairingly clear: "It is surprising that of so many nations, there is still not one that has taken on our ways and, despite being among us and in daily contact with the French, they still govern themselves in the same manner as they have always governed themselves. It will require labor and an infinite amount of time . . . to compel them to accept our ways and our customs. . . . It is, I assure you, the work of several centuries."[30]

French officials were also anxious about the undue influence of Indians on their own people in the New World. They were right to be concerned: the society and culture of New France was profoundly shaped by contacts with the Natives. Its history and development were so intertwined with the neighboring Indian peoples as to make the two almost indistinguishable. Cooperation was evident in diplomacy, trade, warfare, and everyday interactions. The governor general's fatherly role as "Onontio"—Great Mountain—necessitated a mastery of Indian diplomacy and metaphor. Voyageurs and Indians in the fur trade shared canoes, campfires, and pipes; paddled together; and in some cases intermarried. French-Canadian militiamen fought side-by-side with Indian warriors in their campaigns against the English. Finally, French social and economic interactions with Indian communities in the St. Lawrence Valley were quotidian. Many travelers and writers in the eighteenth century commented on this Franco-Indian world. Pierre de Charlevoix believed that "the example and frequent intercourse with its natural inhabitants [the Indians] are more than sufficient to constitute this character" of the French Canadians. Another writer, Louis Antoine de Bougainville, worried that his French regular troops were in danger of being corrupted by "the example of the Indians and Canadians, breathing an air permeated with independence."[31]

New France's consistently small population made it less likely that the French would dispossess neighboring Indians and more likely that they would have to approach the Natives on their own terms. When the explorer Jacques Cartier made his first forays down the St. Lawrence River in the 1530s and 1540s, he encountered Iroquoian peoples living in the valley and visited the villages of Stadacona and Hochelaga (at the modern sites of Quebec and Montreal, respectively). But by the early 1600s these Iroquoians had mysteriously disappeared from the area, leaving the St. Lawrence Valley largely devoid of inhabitants. Historian Allan Greer rightly observes that "the French moved into this devastated landscape, not as conquering invaders, but as a new tribe negotiating a place for itself in the diplomatic webs of Native North America." When colonization efforts resumed under Samuel de Champlain in 1608, the French were able to settle in the depopulated St. Lawrence Valley, not directly intruding on any Indian nation's lands. This geographic and demographic fact presents a striking contrast to the British colonies' histories: large numbers of immigrants coming to New England, New York, Pennsylvania, Virginia, and the Carolinas all stimulated destructive wars over land with their immediate Indian neighbors. By 1700 New France's population was perhaps 15,000, although it had increased to about 70,000 by the 1760s.[32]

The low rate of immigration to New France also meant that the French did not settle near Native communities in overwhelming numbers. As many as 27,000 immigrants came to Canada from 1608 to 1760, but most did not stay: New France retained about 10,000 of these immigrants as colonists. The British colonies, however, attracted twenty-five times this number from 1700 to 1775 alone. The vast majority of French immigrants came from northwestern France: Bretagne, Normandie, Île-de-France, Poitou, Saintonge, and Aunis, many from an urban and middling sort of background. Not only did the settlers have a similar social and geographic background, but virtually all were Roman Catholic, as required of immigrants by French law. As a result New France was "more culturally homogenous and more thoroughly Roman Catholic than France itself."[33]

Settlement patterns in New France also curtailed the kind of relentless and destructive expansion and land-grabbing that afflicted many British colonies. The landscape of French Canada, past and present, is defined by a distinctive pattern of "long lots": strips of land stretching back from the river upon which French-Canadians established their farms and occasional gristmills and windmills. The lots themselves were part of larger *seigneuries*—land grants given to important French elites, who were responsible for settling and improving the land. Most long lots had river frontage, because the immigrants were very much oriented toward the water for food, trade, and transportation. In addition, the only arable land was located on the riverfronts. In this kind of extended settlement neighborhoods tended to be defined by the *seigneury* to which they belonged; St. Lawrence neighborhoods were also defined by certain *côtes*: distinct coastlines or peninsulas, such as "côte de Beaupré" or "côte de St. Paul," opposite Kahnawake. The *habitants'* whitewashed stone or wood houses were built in a distinctively Canadian architectural style called *pièce-sur-pièce*, using squared timber frames—a method that Kahnawake Indians also learned when they brought Canadian builders to their villages. The *habitants'* homes were usually situated on ground rising up from the St. Lawrence, giving the landscape "the appearance of a continued village." Traveler Peter Kalm best explained this phenomenon. When he came to particularly straight channels of the St. Lawrence, the farmhouses in the distance blended together in a single, unbroken line. Canadian farmers typically cultivated wheat and peas and, as we have seen, hired Indian neighbors to help during harvest time. Agricultural surpluses went to French colonies in the West Indies, but on at least one occasion a Jesuit priest purchased wheat for the Indians of Lorette to supplement a meager corn harvest in 1742. All in all, French-Canadian *habitants* enjoyed a greater degree of prosperity than peasants in France, and many commentators noted that the harsh winter climate actually improved their health, reducing the predominance of disease. Many European travelers discerned at least a surface contentment among the *habitants*, because "everyone here is possessed of the necessaries of life." The traveler Baron de Lahontan disparagingly wrote that the "easiness of their Life, puts 'em upon a level with the Nobility." Further, this degree of contentment and the *habitants'* access to the river alleviated the fierce competition for river frontage that was very common among wealthier and poorer colonists in New York and Pennsylvania.[34]

The French settlements nearest to Kahnawake were located in the *seigneury* of La Prairie, which numbered 550 persons in 1721 and 1,650 persons in 1752. The Iroquois and French not only traded regularly but also celebrated social and religious occasions together. The historian Louis Lavallée documented that Kahnawake Indians and French settlers at La Prairie cooperated in the fur trade between Albany and Montreal—a trade that French authorities deemed illegal. A 1720 government document reveals that Iroquois undoubtedly visited Beauvais's tavern and La Veure's tavern at La Prairie, where they drank and slept overnight after one too many rounds. These two taverns were authorized, but many other French farmers clandestinely sold liquor to the Natives. In one episode that came to the attention of a French court, Marie Jeanne Parent of Lachine gave soup to a party of Sault Iroquois at her home, but when her father, Mathieu, offered them liquor, they refused and promptly went to a local justice. Historian Jan Grabowski has found that ordinary French colonists commonly referred to the Natives as "neighbors"; they gave their Indian friends French names and were given Indian names in return.[35]

Although the early French and Indian communities at La Prairie had separated in the 1670s, in a sense their inhabitants always remained a spiritual community as fellow Catholics. Throughout the rest of New France's history ordinary French settlers held a particular devotion to the remarkable Mohawk Christian Kateri Tekakwitha. Father Nau noted that colonists "flock from all sides to the tomb of the servant of God, Catherine Tegahkouita, to accomplish the vows made in time of sickness." Miraculous cures were attributed to Kateri's intercession by ordinary *habitants*, including Claude Caron of La Prairie (respiratory problems) and Jean Bochart de Champigny, the intendant of New France, who had lost his voice for a long period of time. A French soldier who visited Sault St. Louis in the 1750s was struck by the veneration of Indian martyrs. He noted that "the lame and the paralyzed have been cured by the trip to Sault St. Louis to pray at the new saints' tombs." In his memoirs he recorded the martyrdom accounts of four Sault Iroquois and noted that in the neighborhood of Montreal "four fetes are celebrated in honor of the four savage martyrs of the village St. Louis, and some of the neighboring parishes go in procession once a year, to sing high mass."[36]

The character of the town of Montreal was also deeply shaped by the presence of Indian peoples. By the mid-eighteenth century New France was a highly urban colony with three principal towns: Quebec, Trois Rivières, and Montreal. Quebec was the Atlantic-oriented administrative center of New France, as W. J. Eccles observes, but Montreal retained an unflinching westward gaze by virtue of its role in the fur trade. Founded in 1642, Montreal marked the end of major French settlement in the St. Lawrence Valley. It was at the head of navigation on the St. Lawrence River because of the nearby Lachine rapids, but the nearby Ottawa River stretched another eight hundred miles into the interior, giving Montreal traders access to the vast *pays d'en haut*—the "upper country" of the Great Lakes region. As a trading and commercial center, Montreal grew steadily, but its population was only 1,200 in 1700, increasing to about 4,000 persons by 1750. Most of the residents were French, but there were a few hundred African and Indian domestic slaves. Traveler Peter Kalm described the city as a "rectangular parallelogram" in shape. It was a walled city, but French regular troops scoffed at its rotten ramparts. By the mid-1700s Montreal was an impressive city with a governor's house, lavish churches, a seminary, courts, dockyards, granaries, warehouses, military barracks, convents, and hospitals.[37]

But Montreal "never really emerged very far from the conditions of a frontier town," as historian E. R. Adair has famously noted. Native peoples were an everyday presence in the town's streets, and descriptions of Montreal rank among the more salty in colonial-era writings. In the seventeenth century the settlement hosted annual fur-trading fairs. Hundreds of Indians from the Great Lakes region came to these fairs, and as one Frenchman reported, "every body turns Merchant upon such occasions." Catholic priests and clergy were horrified by reports of brawls, violence, and revelry among the Montrealais and Indians. Father Vachon de Belmont described the place as "a little Babylon which has overwhelmed and intoxicated all the [Indian] nations with the wine of its prostitution." Marie-Andrée

Duplessis, a sister of the Hospitalière order, described her shock at seeing Indians wearing only a breechcloth: "one sees in Montreal, where the Indians abound from all areas, tall and well-made men who stroll in the streets in this garb as impudently as if they were fully clothed; others wear only a shirt, some have a blanket negligently thrown over a shoulder." Montreal's sordid reputation is borne out in legal and court records detailing the gamut of crimes involving Indian and French inhabitants. In fact, city officials established taverns for different Indian nations, to prevent misunderstandings and violence. It takes little effort to imagine a variety of street scenes in Montreal: Kahnawake Indians selling basketry and crafts; white captives such as Eunice Williams seeing her father John Williams; a group of three Indians drinking "some cider at Laverdure, then beer at Crespeau's and afterwards [going] door to door to say our farewells"; Indians poking fun at the French, comparing their language to that of "ducks and geese, which cry out, . . . and which talk all together like the French."[38]

The raison d'être of both New France and Montreal—the fur trade—led to new creations, new customs, and new peoples. Hundreds of young Canadian men undertook at least one stint as a voyageur—mainly to supplement their family incomes and escape the drudgery of agricultural life. Most came from the vicinity of Montreal and Trois Rivières. French officials and missionaries scorned the *coureurs de bois* for their libertine ways and their illicit sales of liquor to the Indians. "I cannot emphasize enough," the Marquis de Denonville wrote, "the attraction that this Indian way of life has for these youths." The incredible journey by canoe from Montreal, up the Ottawa River to the Great Lakes and beyond, provided an initiation into Indian ways, and it was during this long voyage that French-Canadian and Indian beliefs and practices merged. The relentless hours of paddling and portaging, broken by song and story, left a Native imprint on French-Canadian folk tales, voyageur songs, and religious beliefs. In 1686 a French explorer, Chevalier de Troyes, noted that the voyageurs would ritually baptize beginners at a mountain "where the Indians make their sacrifices, shooting their arrows over it, which have small bits of tobacco tied to the ends. Our French have the custom of baptizing at this place those who have yet never before passed."[39] Both French soldiers and fur traders who lived in the *pays d'en haut* inhabited a world that was still very much defined by Indian customs.[40]

The *pays d'en haut* is perhaps best known for the intermarriage and sexual relations reputed to have occurred between French men and Indian women. Traders and voyageurs did indeed live among the western Indians, and some had marriages *à la façon du pays*. It is impossible to quantify the intermarriages among French and Indians, because so many were undocumented. But one study has identified 33 marriages in the seventeenth century and 116 in the eighteenth century that had the blessing of clergy and the benefit of the written record. The degree of intermarriage in New France has no parallel in colonial North America, certainly not among the British colonies. Although the numbers as a percentage of the total population are small, they were disproportionately significant in shaping relations with the Indians. Whether through intermarriage, trade, or captivity, New France had an impressive array of multilingual interpreters with influence among the Natives. For example, Louis-Thomas Chabert de Joncaire and his son Philippe-Thomas lived among the Senecas as influential French agents; Charles-Michel Mouet de Langlade was the son of a French trader and an Ottawa Indian who had an illustrious military career.[41]

One of the great advantages that New France enjoyed in keeping the more populous British colonies at bay for so long was its class of talented military and political leaders whose experience was rooted in cooperation with Indian allies.[42] Some native-born Canadians attained noble status and rose even to the highest positions, of governor general and intendant. By contrast, native-born British Americans in general did not gain noble status. Literally only a handful of British Americans ever received titles of nobility or became governor

Fig. 3. "A Canadian Going to War on Snowshoes," from Bacqueville de la Potherie, *Histoire de l'Amérique septentrionale* (1722). Courtesy of the Library and Archives Canada.

of their colony. In New France military service was a route to promotion and advancement, for the officer commissions in the *troupes de la marine* were typically reserved for Canadian nobles' sons. As a result Canadian nobles brought with them a wealth of experience in trade, negotiation, and warfare with their Native allies. The government of New France organized Canadian settlers into parish militia companies that were usually commanded by respected *habitants*. During wartime Kahnawake warriors often served with French-Canadian militiamen, operating against New England and New York settlements.[43]

Jacques Hertel, for example, came to Canada as a young lieutenant from Normandy, probably in the 1620s; he became a skilled interpreter of Indian languages in the seventeenth century. His son Joseph-François Hertel de la Fresnière, born in 1642 at Trois Rivières, was schooled "in an atmosphere of continual wars" against the Iroquois. His brief captivity among the Onondagas gave him an opportunity to learn the Iroquois language, and he applied Indian war tactics to frontier raids against New England in the 1690s. Joseph-François's son Jean-Baptiste Hertel de Rouville, born in 1668, also began soldiering early in life, as he accompanied his father on different expeditions. Rouville was famous or infamous, depending on one's ancestry, for leading the Canadian, Abenaki, and Kahnawake war party that destroyed Deerfield, Massachusetts, during Queen Anne's War in 1704.[44]

Through diplomacy, the fur trade, military service, religion, and the daily presence of Indians in settled areas, French colonists' life experiences were decisively shaped by contact with Native peoples. The colony's existence was premised on its network of Indian alliances, designed to limit English expansion into the interior. In his travels through New France from 1749 to 1751, the Swedish botanist Peter Kalm observed many ways in which New France's society bore a deep Indian imprint. He concluded: "The French in Canada in many respects follow the customs of the Indians, with whom they have constant relations. They use the tobacco pipes, shoes, garters, and girdles of the Indians. They follow the Indian way of waging war exactly; they mix the same things with tobacco; they make use of the Indian bark boats and row them in the Indian way; they wrap a square piece of cloth round their feet, instead of stockings, and have adopted many other Indian fashions."[45]

Kalm could have accurately included the government of New France in his list of the ways in which the French in Canada followed Indian customs. From the beginnings of colonization in the St. Lawrence in the early 1600s, French alliances with the Natives were characterized by a great degree of mutual dependence and adaptation of Indian diplomatic protocols. Indian peoples referred to the French governor as "Father" and "Onontio," but they ascribed to their French father the attributes of an ideal Indian father: gentle, loving, reconciling, resolute, and exceedingly generous. Although they did not always understand or believe in the spiritual intent of Indian diplomacy, French officials certainly mastered its ceremonial forms: they spoke of their love for their Indian children, lit council fires, buried hatchets, sang songs of war, nourished the tree of peace, and smoked the calumet of peace.[46] New France simply did not have the military capacity to coerce its Native neighbors. Admissions of this weakness in French colonial correspondence are voluminous, and they stand in stark contrast to historical accounts that place Indians in an imperial context, as opposed to Europeans in an Indian world. Governor General Vaudreuil, in a 1711 letter to Gov. Francis Nicholson of New York, acknowledged that New France's allies "are not dependent upon us enough for us to make them change their customs and habits." In 1731, for example, the Marquis de Beauharnois and Gilles Hocquart, respectively the governor general and the intendant of New France, wrote candidly to their superiors in France: "We can easily admit the impossibility of wholly subjugating the Indians at present. It can be eventually effected by inspiring them, by degrees, with more fear and more respect for the government. These are the principles we apply in our negotiations with them." This letter reveals that French officials desperately coveted dominion over the Indian nations but did not have the means to dominate them; they thus resorted to manipulation, intimidation, intrigue, and blunt force, if they could get away with it. French regular army officers who came to Canada during the French and Indian War (1754–60) were shocked by the degree to which Indian diplomacy governed their actions. On one occasion the Marquis de Vaudreuil, the Canadian governor general, cautioned the Marquis de Montcalm that "the colony owes its safety to the Indians, that these tribes require much gentleness and complaisance." But to officers like Montcalm and his aide Bougainville, who wanted the ability to command "savages," it seemed that "one is a slave to the Indians in this country." This was an aspect of New France that many Old World officers never fully accepted or understood.[47]

As historian W. J. Eccles has written, the three principal French goals—planting Christian missions, garnering the fur trade, and blocking British expansion—"depended upon the Indians." The French alone did not have sufficient military force to confine the more numerous British; they depended on the military strength of their Native allies, especially the Iroquois and Abenakis of the mission communities. Even when French regulars were sent against the Iroquois in the seventeenth century, the results were inconclusive; the French military successes against the Fox, Natchez, and Chickasaws were only accomplished with the aid of Native allies. Although the Ministre de la Marine stationed regular companies in New France from 1683 to 1760, there were usually never more than eight hundred troops spread out over half a continent. This basic military dependency was compounded by the fact that the fur trade itself had become a means to a political end. Maintaining the fur trade, garrisoned posts, and alliances, however, was an expensive game. French diplomats had to distribute gifts such as tools, tobacco, cloth, ammunition, and food to their allies; posts and forts had to be maintained; troops had to be paid. "Managing native alliances typically accounted for one-fifth to one-fourth of Canada's colonial expenditures," historian Catherine Desbarats has estimated. "The costs of native alliances," she notes, often "exceeded trade revenues flowing into the colonial coffers: from a mercantilist point of view Canada was thus not paying for itself, let alone yielding profits for the crown." In the end it was the collapse of these alliances that contributed to New France's downfall by 1760.[48]

The community of Kahnawake, in this context of French dependency, was able to assert an independent course of action and avoid outright domination by the French and English. Imperial powers classified the Kahnawake Iroquois as "French Indians," "domiciliès," and "praying Indians" who were "subject to the French." But French officials felt that they could neither dominate nor trust the Kahnawake Iroquois—an ironic conclusion given the British assumption that they were fully in the grip of French Catholics. In 1740 the Marquis de Beauharnois reminded his superiors in France of the "inconstancy" of the domiciled Indians. During their military campaigns with the French the Kahnawake Iroquois assiduously avoided any combat actions with fellow Iroquois to the south. The intendant during Beauharnois's governorship, Gilles Hocquart, also acknowledged "the total freedom of movement that the savages have always enjoyed, and the degree of independence that characterizes their lives." Both Beauharnois and Hocquart lamented their inability to suppress the clandestine fur trade between Kahnawake and Albany. Beauharnois concluded, "Sault St. Louis, My Lord, has become a sort of Republic," and accused its people of having "English hearts."[49]

A republic is self-governing. One of the strongest tests of sovereignty in the colonial era was the ability of European governments to extend their jurisdiction and laws over the Indian republics on their frontiers. The government of New France claimed jurisdiction over the "domiciliated Indians" in its midst, and, as historian Jan

Grabowski states, "this legal fiction was maintained until the end of the French regime." In his superb study of legal relationships between the French and the Indians in Montreal, Grabowski finds that clashing concepts of justice resulted in a "curious blend of French criminal procedure and of Indian tradition." In criminal cases involving Kahnawake, Kanasetake, and other nearby towns, the French were often unable to apply their ideals of law and justice to the Indians. French justices, for example, often accepted the Natives' argument that, because liquor itself was to blame for their actions, liquor distributors should be prosecuted rather than Indians. Cases of Indians being sentenced or executed for crimes were exceedingly rare, though many were brought to court. Justices also allowed Natives to "cover the graves" of murdered French colonists with beaver pelts and other gifts, as was traditionally done among the Iroquois. French colonial officials feared provoking or alienating their allies, as they desperately needed their military services.[50]

Perhaps the most convincing proof of the utter inability of either the French or the English to assert any real dominion over areas that both claimed was the fur trade between Albany and Montreal. From the French government's perspective the Montreal-Albany trade was illegal. The French Compagnie des Indes held the monopoly on the fur trade and was entitled to collect duties on furs, and trading with English colonies was forbidden. But because the trade was conducted on Iroquois territory by Iroquois carriers, it was legal. This commerce was rooted in the Indians' preference for the British-manufactured woolen fabric called stroud and the higher purchasing power of beaver pelts in Albany. Although French trade goods were generally superior to British ones, no substitute for the British strouds was ever produced that could satisfy Indian consumer demands. Named after the English town of Stroud in Gloucestershire, the scarlet-colored strouds were the Indians' most favored woolen broadcloths. Montreal merchants were thus satisfied when they obtained strouds via Albany, but they took an enormous risk in violating French laws forbidding exports to British colonies. The Albany merchants, who were blocked from the western trade, benefited because they received the superior beaver furs of the northern forests. The Iroquois perspective is best summarized in a statement made by an Iroquois leader to the Marquis de La Jonquière in 1751: that he would sooner part with his life than be deprived of the right to obtain merchandise from the English.[51]

The trade existed only because Iroquois men and women of Kahnawake and Kanasetake acted as carriers. Only they were able to transverse Mohawk territories without much interference. The trade had a long history, almost as old as Kahnawake itself. It most likely developed out of the Mohawks' movements back and forth between their old homelands and the St. Lawrence Valley. As early as 1681 the French governor Louis de Buade, Comte de Frontenac, identified Sault St. Louis as the "entrepôt for this traffic." The French traveler Baron de Lahontan mentioned the trade during his 1684 visit to Fort Chambly on the Richelieu River. The practice became even more significant and voluminous between 1713 and 1744—the "long peace" between Britain and France. But even imperial warfare did not stop the clandestine trade, which continued until the British conquest of New France in 1760. The French Compagnie des Indes, which held the fur trade monopoly after 1717, was hurt by the diversion of furs to New York. The volume of trade to Albany was significant: it is estimated that from 10 to 50 percent of Canadian furs were diverted from Montreal to Albany. One New York merchant, Cornelius Cuyler, received three hundred packs of beaver from Canada in a single season. Attempts by the French and British colonial governments to interdict this trade were usually fruitless. Even the presence of French forts at Chambly and Crown Point had no discernible effect on the smuggling. One officer reported that no less than 400,000 livres' worth of beaver were smuggled past Fort Chambly between 1710 and 1712.[52]

What ultimately made the Albany-Montreal trade so threatening to French and British officials was not so much the volume, as the way it unhinged national loyalties and allegiances. The French government, for example, feared that repeated visits to Albany by Canadian Iroquois would result in their eventual defection to the English. The diversion of furs to Albany not only reduced the profits of the Compagnie des Indes but compromised the very profitability of New France to the mother country. The fur trade, in theory, should have covered the expenses of Indian diplomacy, but during many years the French Crown ran a deficit to maintain New France. Imperial-minded New Yorkers such as William Johnson wanted British traders to expand westward directly into French territories. Accordingly, they assailed the Albany-Montreal trade because "it removed any incentive the Albany merchants might have to contest the hold of the French over the western nations." The strouds, wampum, and other trade goods that Montreal merchants obtained via Albany were used to sustain New France's large network of Indian alliances, which in turn weakened the British colonies' strategic position. Finally, New England colonists greatly resented New York merchants because the trade shielded them from Canadian attack, while the French continued to attack the New England frontiers.[53]

The fascinating set of characters involved in the Albany-Montreal trade often operated in an Iroquoian world and context. John Henry Lydius's life illustrates the ways identities changed in a frontier world. Lydius was born in Albany in 1704 to a Dutch Calvinist family; years later he surfaced in Montreal, converted to Roman Catholicism, and married a woman named Geneviève Massé, who had Indian parentage. Lydius engaged in the fur trade with the people of Kahnawake and Kanasetake, "by visiting them or by receiving them in his house." When French authorities finally deemed Lydius a "dangerous man," in 1731, he was banished from the colony. The following year Lydius surfaced again in the Hudson Valley, north of Albany, this time in the British camp, his trading post strategically situated to intercept furs being carried from Canada by his Mohawk contacts.[54]

Lydius's trial and his fur-trading activities intersected with another peculiar case of eighteenth-century French-Indian contact, the Desauniers affair. Three young women, Marguerite, Marie-Anne, and Marie-Madeleine Desauniers, daughters of a prominent Montreal merchant, Pierre Trottier Desauniers, had established themselves in 1727 at Kahnawake, where they operated a trading store and lived among the Iroquois for over two decades.[55] Their store was located directly across from the village chapel, and it is likely that the Jesuits approved the store to prevent the Iroquois from visiting unscrupulous traders at nearby taverns. The sisters spoke Iroquois fluently and even acted as interpreters at times.[56] The Desauniers sisters first came to the attention of French authorities in 1741. When the Marquis de Beauharnois described Kahnawake as a "sort of republic," he offered as evidence the Desauniers sisters' involvement in the illegal fur trade.[57] Subsequent investigations yielded much evidence and a spate of accusations.[58] The French women were engaged in the smuggling among Albany, Kahnawake, and Montreal. In fact, the Desauniers sisters' success was partly due to their connections with Iroquois women who carried beaver pelts out of Montreal in baskets and also carried pelts to Albany. The French commandant at the Sault, Alexandre Dagneau Douville, had been engaged in the fur trade since the age of eighteen; Jean-Baptiste Tournois, a popular and effective missionary, may also have been involved. A Sault Iroquois chief, Tegariogrin, further informed the French governor that the Jesuits were complicit in the Desauniers' smuggling operation.[59] The sisters maintained that they had only developed a ginseng trade and had lived "honorably, without anyone in the colony having been able to reproach them." Other Jesuits testified that the sisters "edified all by their piety and their honesty in the trade. They were charitable to the poor and the sick; they were zealous for the welfare of the Indians."[60] No official action was taken for nine years, until a new governor general, the Marquis de La Jonquière, succeeded in having the Desauniers sisters and Father Tournois expelled from Sault St. Louis in 1751. La Jonquière believed that the sisters had assumed an undue influence over the Sault Iroquois and inspired them with "sentiments of independence, even of rebellion."[61] French officials made examples of the Desauniers sisters, Tournois, and Lydius because they were French subjects and expendable targets. But they never once dared to suppress the trading activities of the Canadian Iroquois, for fear of alienating them. In 1751 La Jonquière personally visited Kahnawake and found that the village was still filled with English merchandise.[62]

In 1751 Iroquois *porteurs*, or carriers, who journeyed over two hundred miles from Kahnawake or Montreal down the Champlain Valley to Albany, went through a region that remained Mohawk country and a largely Indian landscape. They would have followed a crude path, later improved to a military supply road, that ran from La Prairie to Fort St. Jean on the Richelieu River. At first glance the presence of French forts, *seigneuries*, and colonists in the Champlain Valley seemed to herald imperial dominance over this borderland contested with the English. But this so-called empire, as Colin Calloway puts it, "constituted a veneer of French population and culture spread thinly over an Indian world." Forts St. Jean, Chambly, and St. Frédéric did not possess military garrisons formidable enough to control anything beyond musket range of the fort, if that. Bougainville was thoroughly unimpressed by St. Jean's tiny thirty-five-man garrison and remarked that "the fort could very easily be burned by a winter raiding party." Iroquois traveled back and forth from Albany through their ancestral lands as though imperial borders did not exist; they maintained ties with friends and kinfolk settled in the Mohawk Valley as well. Abenaki Indians were also present in large numbers in the Champlain Valley; one of their principal towns, Missisquoi, was located on the lake's eastern shore. As key French allies, the Abenakis and the Kahnawake Iroquois often used Missisquoi as a base of operations for their combined expeditions against the New England frontiers. The Champlain Valley was shared by both groups as well, though the Mohawks claimed its western side as an extended hunting territory. Shared religious sites dotted the landscape as well. Indian travelers left offerings of tobacco to Odzihozo, an Abenaki deity, at a rock outcropping in the middle of the lake. The French Fort St. Frédéric was situated at the rugged, mountainous southern end of the Champlain Valley. St. Frédéric was built in the 1730s near a narrow neck of the lake, and a small French colonial settlement known as Pointe à la Chevelure emerged around the fort. It represented a major threat to English frontiers, but the fort's garrison was ineffective in halting the movements of Iroquois traders.[63]

South of Fort St. Frédéric, Indian travelers began to enter an Anglo-Dutch world as they approached the frontier town of Albany. They followed either Lac St. Sacrament (Lake George) or Wood Creek toward the British settlements. At the end of each route Indians portaged their canoes and cargoes over to the Hudson River. John Henry Lydius had relocated his trading activities to this portage area after his expulsion from New France. From his house and trading post he could intercept Indians on their way to and from Albany. Beyond Lydius's post was the fort and settlement of Saratoga. For most of the eighteenth century Saratoga was the northernmost English community, and its vulnerability was revealed in 1745 when a French and Indian force destroyed the settlement and took many of its residents as captives, including Louis Cook, the son of African and Abenaki parents who eventually became a leader at Kahnawake. Indians often arrived at Albany in large numbers. One colonial official counted over two hundred Kahnawake Iroquois during one visit. Eighteenth-century Albany was the perfect counterpoint to Montreal: a small, isolated frontier town and fur-trading entrepôt that was the seat of Indian diplomacy in colonial New York. The continued ties between southern and northern Mohawks "insulated Albany from imperial warfare in the Northeast," just as Kahnawake protected Montreal.

Indian delegations often came to this outpost from near and far for diplomatic meetings with New York officials and were commonly seen in the city's streets and shops.[64]

One of the many Kahnawake Mohawks who made this journey southward to Albany—not to trade, but to settle—was a man named Karighondontee. He and his family resettled in the Schoharie Valley southwest of Albany around 1700. His story and that of the three Mohawk communities at the eastern gateway to the Haudenosaunee Confederacy are the subjects of the next chapter. We will encounter other Kahnawake Indians in subsequent pages: Quainant, who adopted a young German boy named Conrad Weiser, who in turn would become an interpreter for the province of Pennsylvania; Atiatoharongwen, who fought against Gen. Edward Braddock at the Monongahela in 1755; Tontileaugo, who captured a British settler named James Smith and had bad things to say about the Germans; and finally, Mohawk Peter and his wife, a white woman, who peacefully lived with a group of British backcountry squatters in the Ohio Valley in the 1760s. As these life stories suggest, the Iroquois retained an incredible freedom of movement within their territories, but in the Mohawk Valley west of Albany, the Iroquois would confront a major challenge to this freedom as large numbers of European immigrants settled in their midst.

2. Iroquois Communities in the Eighteenth-Century Mohawk Valley

Schoharie, Tiononderoge, and Canajoharie

**Tiononderoge, or Fort Hunter,
the Lower Mohawk Town, January 1745**

"Que! Que! Que!" The sound of Mohawk Indians' plaintive death cries shattered the silence of a wintry January night in 1745. Six Mohawks had just returned from the nearby Dutch town of Schenectady to deliver terrible news to the villagers in the middle of the night. They had just been among "Our Friends among the White People" in Schenectady, who informed them that the "People of Albany, were a coming with Drums & Trumpets with several hundreds to kill the Mohawks." As the report of impending destruction swept through Tiononderoge, "the dead Cry was heard everywhere, Que, Que, Que," as one eyewitness recalled. Villagers slowly recalled that there had been a recent shipment of supplies of gunpowder and bullets to Fort Hunter, a small British fortification that protected Tiononderoge and housed a Protestant chapel named in honor of Queen Anne. Some Mohawks were so alarmed that they fled westward to Canajoharie or the Oneida villages beyond; some were reported to have gone to Kahnawake for refuge. William Barclay, an Anglican missionary living at the fort, attempted to quiet his Tiononderoge flock but was met with "Violence" and accusations that he was "the chief contriver of the destruction intended against them," in league with the devil.[1]

When tempers cooled, all parties recognized the report for what it was: a groundless rumor. Or was it? Why did some Mohawks react to the rumor in such an extremely fearful, even paranoid, manner? After all, the Mohawks were allied with the English. If they could not trust their Anglo-Dutch partners in Albany, whom could they trust? Though a seemingly minor incident in the span of colonial history, this rumor illuminates many important dimensions of European-Indian relations in colonial New York. First, it clearly reveals the deep-seated suspicions and tensions that often lay underneath the surface serenity of intercultural relations. New York claimed to be the most favored colony of the Iroquois, but its diplomatic record was not as clean as that of New France. Second, it demonstrates the complexity—even the confusion—that characterized the daily lives of Mohawks and British colonists. On the one hand, there were fears of imminent military destruction. On the other hand, the Mohawks had "Friends among the White People": the subsequent investigation of the rumor revealed that a Mohawk man had lived for most of the winter at a Dutch settler's house and that the Dutchman's African slave could speak the Mohawk language. Finally, *how* the Mohawks and New Yorkers responded to the rumor reveals just how differently each side viewed the nature of their alliance. Anxious colonial officials sought out the *person or persons* responsible for spreading the rumor, with the end goal of *punishment.* The New York government even enlisted Pennsylvania's official interpreter, Conrad Weiser, to investigate the "Strange Alarm" amongst the Iroquois. But the Mohawks wanted instead to investigate the *source of the bad feelings* and fears, with the aim of restoring *harmony.* The Mohawk leader Hendrick Theyanoguin, who would play a prominent role in diplomacy in years to come, asked the Albany commissioners to "Conceal nothing from us but that we may take counsel together." Again, for the

Natives the leading emotional indicator for a healthy alliance was simply good thoughts between two peoples, who might "go hand in hand as in former times."[2]

By the middle of the 1700s, however, it was more difficult for the Mohawks to muster any good thoughts about their Albany neighbors. In fact, the Tiononderoge leaders expressed a tremendous degree of mistrust for the very individuals in the New York government authorized to negotiate with them—the members of the Albany Commissioners of Indian Affairs. Indeed, the Natives expressed a growing fear that they would soon be overrun or dispossessed by their Anglo-Dutch neighbors at Albany. Aaron Asarageghty, a Tiononderoge Mohawk, had a telling conversation with Conrad Weiser—who as a young man had lived among the Mohawks. When Weiser visited Iroquoia country in 1745, Aaron told him that "the old Cause, That we have been cheated out of Our Lands, stil remains unsetled." Aaron's candid remarks to Weiser reveal that long-standing grievances over land frauds and fears of being dispossessed were at the heart of the Mohawk leaders' remarks. One group of Mohawk leaders from nearby Canajoharie—Hendrick, Abraham, and Arughiadekka—spoke bitterly, remarking that the "Albany People did intend to hurt us,—& have in a manner ruined us." "They have cheated us out of our Land," they told Weiser. They had "bribed our Chiefs to sign Deeds for them—They treat us as Slaves." The three Mohawk leaders went on to list a host of other grievances against the colonists, emphasizing that the Indians "would no more look upon *the [Albany] Commissioners* as their true friends" and threatening to move to New France. They warned that "the Quarrel with Albany will never be made up—They had in a manner made it up by word of Mouth, but on both Sides, only the Tongue Spoke, & not the heart, & we will never be ffriends again with the Albany People." Weiser tried to assuage them by pointing to King George II's eminent sense of justice, but Hendrick was unshakable in his belief that the "Albany people" wished "for nothing [less] than the Destruction of the Mohawck Nation."[3]

Rather than trying to understand Hendrick's extreme statement, New York's colonial officials wanted to find out who was responsible for spreading the malicious tale. But this case was complex. Who were the Mohawks' "Friends among the White People"? Who was this slave woman who could speak a little Mohawk? And were not the French always conspiring to undermine the British? The Albany commissioners believed that the rumor had been "hatched by the French," most likely spread to the Mohawks by the feared French interpreter Chabert de Joncaire, who lived among the pro-French Seneca nation to the west. But John Henry Lydius, a trader with close ties to the Mohawks, correctly reported to the New York government that the man responsible for the rumor "lived between Schenectady and fort Hunter."[4] At a 1745 meeting with Six Nations leaders, Gov. George Clinton himself pressed the matter further, hoping to uncover the rumor's origins and again sidestepping the larger issue of Mohawk lands. In a private conference with Clinton, Hendrick revealed that Andries Van Patten (who may have been one of the carpenters who helped to construct Fort Hunter) was responsible for spreading the report. The Tiononderoge sachem Johannes Canadagaye revealed that he had spent "the most part of the Winter at the House of Andrew Van Patten," as Conrad Weiser interpreted it. Van Patten had heard news that the Mohawks "were to be cut off by their Brethren the Dutch." Johannes could understand a little Dutch, but Van Patten could not speak Mohawk, so they relied instead on Van Patten's "Negro Wench [who] interpreted it into the Indian Language." Greatly alarmed, Johannes went "several times from Van Patten's to the Mohawks, went to Arent [Stevens], and he went down with Johannes to Van Patten's and heard the same from him from his own Mouth . . . and sometimes the Negro Wench put a few Words in Indian." Could those "few Words" from an enslaved African woman have included a greatly embellished report that the Dutch were coming with guns to kill the Mohawks? Van Patten was called before the council, whose members believed his steadfast protestations of innocence. Governor

Clinton and his council summarily dismissed the Mohawks' concerns and concluded that "the Report spread among the Indians at which they pretended to be so much alarmed and uneasy was a device of their own contrivance in order to induce this as well as the neighbouring Governts to give them presents this year."[5] This, in other words, was a charade of their own making.

Unsurprisingly, colonial officials hardened their hearts during that 1745 meeting, while the Mohawks "were resolved to open their Hearts." Hendrick charged that "there were persons that had Deeds in their pockets for five or six lots of land and now he has not a dust of ground to set his foot on." He voiced the Mohawks' concern that "they were become the property of Albany people, they were their dogs," who could be kicked around like their poor and increasingly landless neighbors, the Mahicans, or River Indians. Hendrick even made reference to the past tribulations that Indians had endured in New York, New England, and Maryland, expressing his fear that "we shall be brought to the same pass." What fueled the rumor so powerfully was the Mohawks' very real fear that they would be dispossessed and impoverished—a feeling that had "remained in our hearts for some years." As Weiser recorded, Clinton had rudely spurned the Indians and "went away without fulfilling his Promise to remove the Indians Grievances about Lands." The Indians, "intirely displeased," told Weiser, "Now You see yourself how we are treated."[6]

The British colonists' and the Mohawks' treatment of each other is the focus of the following portraits of three Mohawk communities in the early to mid-eighteenth century. Each place tells a unique story about how and why New York colonists and Iroquois coexisted and contested the Mohawk Valley for most of the eighteenth century. This valley was in fact the primary avenue for European settlement expansion, seen by contemporaries as one of the most important and fertile areas in all of North America. William Johnson boasted that it comprehended "an Extensive Tract of Country which in general in point of Soil Yields to None on the Continent." Surveyor General

Cadwallader Colden explained that the valley's alluvial soils were "exceeding rich, [and yield] large crops of the best wheat and the repeated overflowings of the rivers keep it always in strength." The Mohawk was also the geographical "axis of empire" that provided the British with their only east-west corridor over the Appalachians to the Great Lakes.[7] If New York secured access to the Great Lakes, it could possibly interrupt New France's dominance of the continent's interior waterways and compete for Indian alliances. The Six Nations, however, still occupied the Mohawk Valley and the southern shore of Lake Ontario, and the British had to respect their power, lest the Iroquois align with the French. Given all of these geopolitical calculations, historians might assume that relations between colonists and Indians at a local level could only lead to land disputes, warfare, and inevitable displacement of the Indians.[8]

But unlike the colonial expansion of many other British colonies such as Virginia or Massachusetts, New York's did not inevitably degenerate into open warfare with the Iroquois. Similar to New France, New York had a small colonial population concentrated in the lower Hudson Valley in the seventeenth century that did not significantly intrude onto Iroquois lands.

The Five Nations' abiding prestige and power hindered settlement to a degree, for the New York government could not afford to alienate their Iroquois trading partners. Nor could the government as easily dominate the Mohawks as it did the much-weakened Mahicans, or "River Indians," who lived among the European settlers in the Hudson Valley. The Mohawks also had a reputation as "the most warlike and renowned of all" the Five Nations. Sir William Johnson further heightened the reputation of the Mohawks, writing in 1767, "This Nation tho' at present Weak in Number is the first of the Confederacy in Rank, & as it is called by them, the Door to the Six Nations." The threat of war with New France and its Indian allies also deterred settlement to a degree. Many European emigrants came to America to escape war's depredations and were thus reluctant to live on such an exposed borderland, where their lives and labor would again be in jeopardy; some chose to go to safer colonies. Gov. Benjamin Fletcher believed that "the hardships that this province hath undergone in the defence of the Frontiers and the detaching of our people hath drove many of them thither [to Pennsylvania] to enjoy their ease." For all of these reasons, as geographer Donald Meinig concludes, New York's growth was "relatively slow in pace and constricted in area" for most of the colony's history.[9]

New York's system of land distribution, unlike Pennsylvania's more liberal system, also did little to stimulate settlement expansion. "The distinctive hallmark of New York in the colonial period," writes historian Sung Bok Kim, "was the string of great baronial estates that dominated its landscape." The Hudson Valley, in particular, had many large manors peopled by tenant farmers and dominated by aristocratic landowners. New York's leaders and elites tended to obtain land in "extravagant grants" of tens of thousands of acres, which were then subdivided among their partners. Colden pointed out "how prejudicial these excessive grants have been to the Settlement & improvement of this Colony . . . the true reason why it is not near so populous & well cultivated as the neighbouring colonies." He observed that "the hopes of having land of their own & becoming independent of Landlords is what chiefly induces people into America" and that the opportunity to obtain a freehold was greater in Pennsylvania than in New York. In fact, many concerned New York officials believed that the proprietary colonies, such as Pennsylvania and South Carolina, were draining away potential or actual settlers with the lure of cheap land. Moreover, the process of patenting land was expensive for the applicant but incredibly lucrative for the governor and councilmen, who received the many fees for patenting.[10]

Despite many hindrances, a salient of colonial settlements had begun to bulge westward into the Mohawk Valley by the middle of the eighteenth century. The Mohawks were the first to feel this intrusion and pressure, literally in their own backyards. The decades after the end of Queen Anne's War in 1713 were the most important. These were the years of the so-called long peace between New France and Britain, which lasted from 1713 to 1744. Peace lessened the dangers of settlement in the colonists' minds, as did the establishment of Fort Hunter at Tiononderoge in 1712. Moreover, lands in the Hudson Valley became scarce as manor lords developed and peopled their vast estates, and interest in Mohawk Valley lands soared. When the Five Nations allowed New York to establish a trading post at Oswego on Lake Ontario in 1726, the flames of colonization were fanned even further up the Mohawk Valley. Traders, batteauxmen, teamsters, and settlers began traveling up the valley in ever greater numbers, including the Irish trader William Johnson. Lt. Gov. George Clarke, governor of New York from 1736 to 1743, symbolized the increasingly aggressive British expansion up the Mohawk Valley. From 1730 to 1743 he acquired 57,228 acres, eventually holding 95,997 acres of Mohawk Valley lands (which he either did not improve or settled sparsely). No wonder that shortly after Clarke's governorship, the Mohawks found it believable that their neighbors were coming to destroy them.[11]

By the 1750s British colonists greatly outnumbered the Indians living in the Mohawk Valley. Surveyor General Cadwallader Colden observed that the Mohawks increasingly lived "intermixed with the Christians" and "daily resort to their houses." This geographical proximity caused boundaries between people to blur and made personal interactions a fact of life. Eighteenth-century settlement patterns confirm Colden's description: thousands of Europeans in fact settled in very close proximity to Indian towns. In 1710 Albany and Schenectady remained Dutch enclaves and garrison towns on the exposed northern periphery of the colony; there were very few European farms north or west of these towns. But by 1750 Palatine, Dutch, English, Irish, and African settlers and slaves were living interspersed among Mohawks, Oneidas, and Mahicans. In the Schoharie Valley, for instance, German villages were located on the east bank of Schoharie Creek, within sight of Mohawk settlements. The largely Anglo-

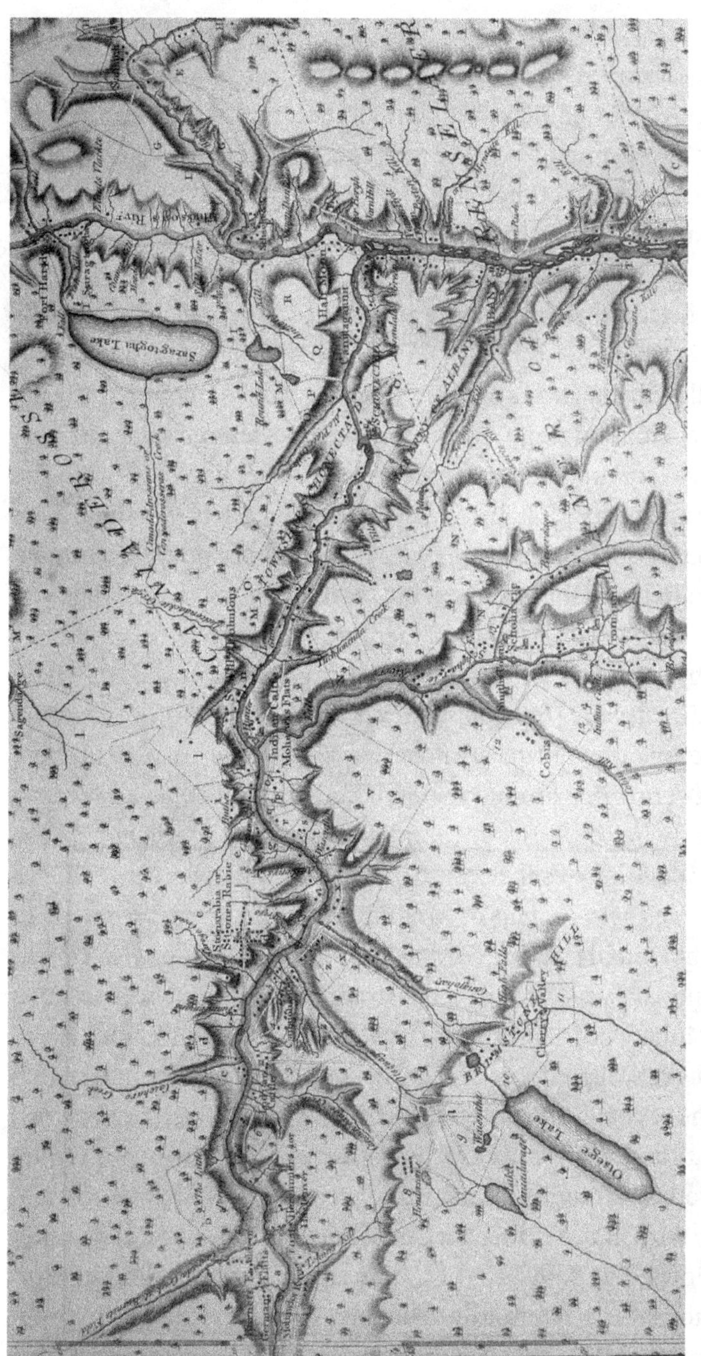

Fig. 4. Detail, the Mohawk Valley, from "A Map of the Province of New York," by John Montresor, 1775. Courtesy of William L. Clements Library, University of Michigan.

Irish plantations at Warrensbush were only a few miles from Tio-nonderoge, the lower Mohawk town. In the upper Mohawk Valley the Germans' closest neighbors were Oneida, Oswegatchie, and Cana-joharie Iroquois, not other Europeans.[12] The Iroquois who were alive in 1745 had always dwelled among Dutch, English, Irish, and German settlers: by 1745 European colonists had inhabited the area for over one hundred years. Was it possible to imagine a world without them?

The following portraits of three different Mohawk communities—Schoharie, Tiononderoge, and Canajoharie—demonstrate just how intertwined colonial and Iroquois communities had become in the eighteenth-century Mohawk Valley. Without reference to the village worlds that framed ordinary peoples' lives and outlooks, it is impossible to understand the texture of individuals' daily lives and the decisions they made. Mohawks and other Iroquois were increasingly surrounded by European settlers, but this did not automatically translate into their irrelevancy or dependency. Rather than being passive victims, Iroquois adapted in very novel ways to the increasing numbers of families crowding around them. As the story of Schoharie reveals, Europeans who settled close to Indian communities did not always arrive in a position of superiority. In fact, the Mohawks viewed these newcomers either as equals or as children who were indebted to them for their hospitable sharing of the land. The European settlers' initial dependence was also reflected in some of the land negotiations that the Mohawks undertook with colonial farmers. At Canajoharie the Mohawks accepted trustworthy colonial farm families as tenants as a means of cementing peaceful relationships. In fact, the Natives' local relationships with nearby European settlers were often more harmonious than their formal diplomatic ties to New York officials entrusted with maintaining the Covenant Chain alliance, as the 1745 rumor shows. The daily lives of Indian and colonial settlers were often characterized by mutually beneficial social, economic, and religious relationships. Perhaps no other person better symbolizes this harmony of interests than the trader and diplomat William Johnson. The Mohawks' adoption of Johnson, and Johnson's common-law marriage to a Mohawk woman, made him a powerful ally and advocate of Mohawk interests in the colonial and imperial governments. For in years to come the struggle for land would become the common denominator among all three communities.

Mohawk Mothers and Palatine Children in Schoharie

The German-speaking Palatine immigrants and the Indian peoples who lived together in the Schoharie Valley in the eighteenth century were all new settlers who had been displaced by larger historical forces. Fittingly, the Iroquoian word *Schoharie*, or *Eskahare*, probably means "driftwood"—perhaps a reference to the flotsam that collected at the junction of Schoharie, Little Schoharie, Stony, and Line creeks. Displaced by the storms of war and the floodtides of disease and privation, a diverse set of peoples—Palatines, Mohawks, Mahicans, Tuscaroras, Delawares, Oneidas, and Oquagans—also drifted into the Schoharie Valley in the early to mid-eighteenth century. This meeting of peoples, then, was not between European newcomers and Iroquois Natives who had lived in the same place since time immemorial. Rather, the Schoharie Valley witnessed two peoples settling the same place nearly simultaneously, but with an interesting reversal of roles: the Iroquois, who had inhabited the valley first, acted as parents to the Palatine children who came to them in the winter of 1709, destitute and desperate. The moral of the Palatines' story is one of coming of age, in which rebellious children defied and ultimately denied their parents' rights. In 1732 a Canajoharie Mohawk sachem named Taraghjories reflected on the time when the Dutch first settled Schenectady. He believed that initially, they "understood one another Innocently & out of Love," which led to misunderstandings. Modern readers so conditioned to believe in inevitable conflict between whites and Indians must struggle to understand this innocence.[13]

The "Schoharie Indians," as they were often called by colonial officials, constituted a third major Native settlement in the area west and south of Albany.[14] They were located about twenty miles south of the Mohawk town of Tiononderoge, where the creek empties into the Mohawk River. The life stories of these Indian settlers reveal a fascinating set of connections to other places and peoples: like Kahnawake, this new people—"a mixture of several nations," according to one colonial report—was very much a creation of early America.[15] One of the first settlers of Schoharie was a Kahnawake Mohawk named Karighondontee, who came with his family sometime around the year 1700. He may have resettled as a result of the growing rapprochement between the Five Nations and the French; perhaps Karighondontee had once hunted in the valley and knew it to be a good location to settle. The valley lay at the intersection of numerous Indian trails radiating outward in all directions; it had long been an extended hunting ground and trade artery for many Indian peoples of the Hudson, Mohawk, and Delaware valleys. Schoharie Indians in the eighteenth century could travel southwestward along the Adageghtinge and Delaware rivers' branches and trade with Indians at Oquaga and Tioga on the Susquehanna. Mahican Indians also traveled westward from the Hudson River to Schoharie to hunt; some bands settled there in the early 1700s and later dwelled among the Mohawks permanently. Both the geography of the valley and the influx of Indian settlers from all points of the compass gave Indian communities in the Schoharie country a multiethnic cast. Seth Tehodoghwenziageghte, the son of Karighondontee and his Turtle-clan wife Marie, married a woman named Catharine in the late 1720s. Catharine was the daughter of Nicolas Etowaucum, a Mahican war leader. Nicolas himself was a world traveler, one of the four Indian "kings" who had visited London in 1710 and stood for his portrait by Jan Verelst. Elisabeth, the daughter of Karighondontee's daughter Catharine, married an Oquaga Indian named Lawrence, the son of Isaac Dekayenensere (Isaac's daughter would become the first wife of the famous Mohawk leader Joseph Brant). Another Kahnawake transplant, Quainant, would later adopt a young German boy, Conrad Weiser, who eventually became an important diplomat in eighteenth-century Pennsylvania. When an English missionary visited Schoharie in 1752, he received provisions from an Indian named Jonah, who had a French mother and a Tuscarora wife. Occasionally, Schoharie Indians captured Catawbas and African slaves in their traditional wars against southern Indians. In 1732 they returned two slaves "belonging to Mr. John Wall of Virginia" to authorities at Albany, but they apparently allowed other runaway slaves to remain. As a result of such marriages, additions, and resettlement, there were one hundred to two hundred Indians living in the upper Schoharie Valley in the early to mid-eighteenth century.[16]

Regardless of its settlers' ethnic backgrounds, Schoharie was a land rich in emotional and spiritual significance for the Natives who lived there. The valley itself was incredibly fertile, although surrounded by broad mountains. On the west side of Schoharie Creek lay three distinct peaks—one of which was called "Onistagrawa," or Corn Mountain. Given its proximity to the lush Indian cornfields in the bottomlands, Onistagrawa probably had the same spiritual meaning for the Schoharies that a similar mountain held for their Cayuga brethren further west. During his 1743 journey to Onondaga, John Bartram recorded an Indian story regarding the supernatural origins of the "three sisters"—corn, beans, and squash—from a distinct hill in the Cayugas' country. Somewhat removed from Anglo-Dutch settlements, the Schoharie must have seemed to the Native settlers a very secure place in which to live.[17]

But across the Atlantic Ocean a migration was under way that would forever change the world that the Schoharie Indians knew. In the early eighteenth century German peasants living in the Palatinate and other upper Rhine Valley regions faced great social and economic hardships. The continued domination of aristocratic rulers, and depredations caused by invading armies, high taxes, and poor harvests, fueled an extensive *auswanderung*, or outmigration, of German peasants. Some of these subsistence farmers, many living on the brink of poverty, migrated to America to become freeholders. The Germans had high hopes of obtaining land because of favorable reports from other German emigrants and cheerful promotional literature on America. And then there came the welcome news that Queen Anne of England would patronize their voyage to America. In 1709 alone more than thirteen thousand Palatine families journeyed to Holland and England. The British government sponsored a plan to settle the "poor palatines" in New York to produce naval stores (tar, pitch, and turpentine) for the Royal Navy. Overseeing the project was the newly appointed governor of New York, Col. Robert Hunter, a British army officer who had served with distinction under the Duke of Marlborough. As he and the Palatines departed for America in April 1710, the four "Indian Kings"—three Mohawks and one Mahican, the aforementioned Nicolas Etowaucum—were approaching England on their diplomatic voyage.[18]

Like many colonial projects at the time, the British government's naval-stores plan ran aground on the shoals of New World conditions. After a hard journey on crowded, disease-ridden vessels in which hundreds died, Hunter and the surviving settlers arrived in New York Harbor in June 1710. The governor had initially planned to settle the Palatines at Schoharie to produce naval stores. Many New Yorkers could still remember a French and Indian attack on the town of Schenectady in 1690, and it was hoped that the Palatine settlement would serve as a frontier buffer against the French (a role that Kahnawake played for Montreal against the English). But Hunter decided against Schoharie because of preexisting land disputes with the Mohawks and the navigational barrier of Cohoes Falls on the Mohawk River near Albany. More important, Hunter discovered that Schoharie did not even have suitable pines for the production of naval stores. Instead, then, he purchased a tract of about six thousand acres on the Hudson River from the wealthy landowner Robert Livingston.[19]

With unfailing accuracy one British politician predicted that under such arrangements "the Palatines will not be the richer." The nearly two thousand Germans living on the Hudson discovered that their new homes bore a disconcerting resemblance to their old ones. Worse still, they were not prosperous farmers owning land, but nearly destitute tar-and-pitch makers who were tenants on the land. Given the Palatines' inexperience in producing naval stores, the project never became solvent and eventually collapsed, leaving Hunter's personal credit exhausted and the Palatines living on "almost barren land." One Palatine representative recounted to Hunter a conversation he had heard among five frustrated Germans sitting around a fire: "We came to America to establish our families," one remarked, "to secure lands for our children on which they will be able to support themselves after we die."[20]

Over time the Schoharie Valley became a promised land in the minds of the Palatines—a "Land of Canaan" flowing with milk and honey that the New York "Pharao," Governor Hunter, had unjustly denied them. But few Palatines knew that Schoharie had once been the object of a land-fraud case involving New York's government. In 1695 Col. Nicholas Bayard, a member of the governor's council, had obtained a patent for Schoharie lands from Gov. Benjamin Fletcher. Like many of Fletcher's land grants, the Bayard patent's size was almost incalculable: colonial officials later reported to the Board of Trade in 1698 that it was twenty-four to thirty miles long, but "its breadth we know not." The Mohawks protested that Bayard, in gaining the patent, had obtained the signatures of three drunken Mohawks who had no authority in land matters. Worried about the possibility of losing its alliance with the Five Nations, the British government instructed Fletcher's successor, the Earl of Bellomont, to rescind some of Fletcher's egregious land grants. Bellomont and the Assembly subsequently negotiated an "Act for Vacating Breaking and Annulling Severall Extravagant Grants of Land made by Coll Fletcher." Colonial representatives informed the Mohawks in 1699 that they were "possessed of said land [Schoharie], as if no such writing had been, and the said writing fully destroyed."[21]

But Schoharie lands again became an object of wealthy colonists' interest as a result of the proposed Palatine settlement there. Powerful persons and interests were arrayed against the Mohawks. A group of Albany commissioners who oversaw Indian affairs in early New York, along with would-be landholders, knew how to make the colony's land laws work in their favor and against the Indians. In early July 1710 the Commissioners of Indian Affairs informed the Mohawks that Governor Hunter had arrived with "a great many familys" to settle at Schoharie, which, they falsely claimed, "is already purchased from you." They further requested that the Mohawks accompany the surveyor general to lay out the tract. But the Mohawks asserted their claims to the area, recalling that Governor Bellomont had voided the deed and that rightful ownership had returned on them. They were distrustful of government surveyors who might, through sleight of compass and chain, steal more of their lands. In one of their first meetings with Governor Hunter, Mohawks told him that they had heard rumors that Queen Anne "had Sent a Considerable Number of People with your Ex.^{ly} to Setle upon the Land called Skohere, *which was a great Surprize to us and we were much Disatisfyd at the news, in Regard the Land belongd to us.*" But true to their sense of hospitality and their care for the poor and indigent, the Mohawks were "willing y^t her maj.^{es} shall have ye Land at Skohere for poor people, & not one foot more, provided it be duely purchased." They reserved most of the fertile flood plains below Onistagrawa for their own planting and requested that all future land sales be public events, with all three clans present, to prevent precisely such land disputes. By setting aside a small amount of land, the Mohawks demonstrated faith in their British alliance and kindness toward the people included in that friendship. Governor Hunter, however, believed that the Mohawks had "resigned their claims to their Lands to the Crown," for in subsequent years he speedily issued land grants to many applicants.

The Mohawks' willingness to provide for the destitute could not have been further from Hunter's interpretation of events: that the Indians had ceded their claims to the king.[22]

The remarkable turn in the story concerns the Germans' determination to negotiate a favorable arrangement between themselves and the Indians: the Palatines did not apply to Governor Hunter for land, but went directly to the original Mohawk settlers. It is unclear how the Palatines came to know the locations of the Mohawk villages and how they established personal ties to them. Perhaps they had read promotional tracts that gave them a favorable impression of Indian character and confidence to approach the Natives. Perhaps some of the Palatines (including John Conrad Weiser) who had participated in the aborted 1711 expedition to Canada had encountered some of their Mohawk allies during their military service. Another possibility is that the Palatines on the Hudson frequently met Mahican Indians, who told them of the Schoharie Mohawks and the Indian path leading to the valley.[23]

During a harsh winter in 1712, during which the Palatines suffered heavily, they were "put under the hard and greeting necessity of seeking relief from the Indians." This decision was "much against their wills," but the Palatines had few alternatives: they had no military strength to vanquish the Indians, no defensive strength to resist the French, and no food. During the Palatines' exodus the "Canaanites," not an invisible God, led the Israelites to the "promis'd land of Schorie." The Palatine faction that advocated moving to Schoharie sent a delegation of "Chiefs" to the Mohawks, including John Conrad Weiser. These delegates were leading officials, or "listmasters," among the Hudson River camps. The Mohawks "kindly" received the Palatine "Chiefs," who told them of "their miserable Condition." During this meeting the Iroquois likely spread out grass mats on which their guests might sit and shared the calumet before proceeding with business. The deputies sought the Mohawks' permission to settle at Schoharie—one indication that the Palatines believed that the Indians were "the true owners of the soil." The Palatine villagers had come to America with an understanding of land and community that was similar to the Iroquois' own. In the Palatine account of the meeting the Indians agreed to the Palatines' settlement among them, remarking that they had long ago set aside the land to Queen Anne for their use, but pledged that "no body else should hinder them of it, and they would assist them as farr as they were able." In the dead of winter in late 1712 about 150 hungry families (perhaps numbering around four hundred or more persons) made a grueling journey through deep snow along the Indian paths leading to Schoharie.[24]

The locations of the Palatine and Mohawk settlements are astonishing for their proximity. The Palatines' agricultural villages—more motley collections of huts—were located on the east bank of Schoharie Creek. The villages' names—Kneskernsdorf, Gerlachsdorf, Fuchsendorf, Schmidtsdorf, Weisersdorf, Hartmanndorf, and Oberweiserdorf (from north to south)—commemorated the six Palatine "Chiefs" who had negotiated with the Mohawks. In plain view of Weisersdorf was Karighondonte's Mohawk village, which was situated near a bend in Schoharie Creek, close to a mountain that the Palatines would also come to know as Onistagrawa. A smaller village of Mahicans or River Indians was located just a few miles south of Oberweiserdorf, on the east side of Schoharie. The Schoharie Indians' principal village, known as "Eskahare," was situated about twenty-four miles south of Tiononderoge on the west side of Schoharie, opposite the northernmost German villages. Collectively, the Schoharie Indians numbered between one and two hundred for most of the eighteenth century, but their numbers were steadily declining due to disease and frequent participation in British military campaigns. By 1713 more than five hundred Germans had settled the valley, far outnumbering the Schoharie Mohawks and imparting a decidedly European cast to the landscape.[25]

Initially, the Palatines were totally dependent upon their Mohawk neighbors for food, shelter, and clothing. They once portrayed themselves as babes suckling at their Mohawk mothers' breasts, a metaphor that suggests how dependent they were on the Mohawks' parental care. Surely, the Mohawks would have appreciated this metaphor, given their own kinship-based understanding of relationships. A 1720 petition acknowledged that due to the Palatines' defenseless condition, "they were oblig'd to keep fair with the friendly Indians amongst Whom, they dwelt, which was the only way to be protected and live in peace." It also revealed that "had it not been for the Charity of the Indians who shew'd them where to gather some eatable roots and herbs, must inevitably have perish'd every soul of them." The Indians showed the Palatines where to gather wild potatoes and strawberries. The Palatines also benefited from the Mohawks' earlier clearing of the Schoharie bottomlands to plant corn and other staples; they were instructed in the cultivation of Indian corn, "the Chief of their subsistence," which they "got of the natives." A second-generation German settler also remembered exchanges of material goods between Indians and colonists: the Palatines "wore moggisins—buckskin breeches and jackets of leather, which they plentifully obtained of the Indians." Adoption of Indian or colonial dress may have occurred while Natives and newcomers hunted together. One settler, who claimed to be "part native," later recalled how a party of Indian and European hunters rescued her from a panther in the hills above the Schoharie Valley.[26]

Peaceful exchanges between the Mohawks and the Palatines, and the creation of kinship ties, reinforced their alliance. When John Conrad Weiser settled along Schoharie Creek, he sent his young son Conrad to live with the family of a Kahnawake Mohawk named Quainant (or Taquayanont), who had resettled in the valley. Conrad was to learn the Mohawk language and act as an interpreter. John Conrad's ultimate goal, to create stronger links between the Palatine and Mohawk communities, came at enormous personal risk: he had already lost one of his sons, Johann Frederick, who had died a few years earlier when Governor Hunter apprenticed him to other New York colonists. During a harsh winter in 1713 young Conrad, along with his Indian hosts, suffered from "severe cold" and was "poorly clothed." To make matters worse, Weiser frequently had to hide from inebriated Indians. His initially traumatic initiation, however, did not cause him to hate Indians. Instead Weiser returned the affection of his adoptive Mohawk family; he kept up with two of his brothers, Jonathan Cayenquiloquoa and Moses, and a Mohawk sister, for the rest of his life. He became fluent in Mohawk, as he recounted in his journal: "One English mile from my father's house lived some Maqua families. Then there were often some of the Maqua on their hunting trips in trouble and there was much to interpret but without pay. There was no one else to be found among our people who understood the language. I therefore mastered the language completely, as much as my years and other circumstances permitted." Weiser's apprenticeship later paid great dividends for the Palatines in their approaching confrontations with New York's well-connected landed interests.[27]

Governor Hunter and the provincial government were determined to squelch the Palatines' defiance (unwarranted and brazen in his view) of repeated orders forbidding them to remove to Schoharie. Colonial officials in 1711–12 were undoubtedly more sensitive to threats from below because the Palatines' insubordination occurred while rumors circulated of a slave conspiracy in New York City. Colonial officials were particularly concerned with what they saw as unsanctioned diplomacy with the Mohawks. In June 1715 the New York government issued a warrant for John Conrad Weiser's arrest, "for Acting and Treating with ye Indians contrary to His Excellencies Proclamation." Hunter presumed Weiser guilty of "several Mutinous Riotous & other disobedient & illegal practices" and accused him of "skulking" on the frontier to avoid capture. But he did not have the power to expel the Palatines by force or arrest the troublesome Weisers. The governor would have to content himself with the hope that the Palatines would be on the receiving end of any future French-Indian attacks.[28]

The absence of central authority was very evident in the settlers' everyday lives. Conrad Weiser observed that at Schoharie "the people lived for a few years without preacher and without government, generally in peace." Mohawk and Palatine villagers were capable of crafting mutually beneficial arrangements over land, establishing boundaries between their communities, and living in peace. For example, since the Germans did not initially obtain land through official measures, they and the Mohawks relied on local landmarks to delineate communal boundaries. Certainly Schoharie Creek, with its east side inhabited by the Palatines and its west side by the Mohawks—was one important boundary. Another landmark, which denoted the southern boundary of Palatine lands, was an old oak stump, along with a pile of stones (which stood into the early nineteenth century), located near the junction of Little and Big Schoharie creeks. The oak stump, with turtle and snake totems carved into it, served the Schoharie Indians as a place to grind their corn. While some Germans carried their wheat and corn to Schenectady for milling, others used the oak stump, imitating Indian technology for producing meal in the early years of settlement. Disputes did arise, as they commonly did throughout the colony, over Indians killing stray Palatine livestock.[29]

When Schoharie was threatened by outsiders, however, both the Indians and the Palatines became allies as they tried to thwart the outsiders' schemes. They found themselves under siege by individuals who had access to the legal weapons of New York's land system—a group of investors called the "Seven Partners" and a Schenectady merchant named Adam Vrooman. The Germans' and Indians' improvements had aroused the interest of these wealthier individuals, who hoped to secure both Schoharie lands and the Palatines as tenants, and in April 1714 Vrooman obtained a license to purchase from the Natives 340 acres of land on the west side of Schoharie Creek.

Vrooman's veracity, however, is doubtful, given that the lands in question were quite close to the Mohawks' planting grounds and that his claims quickly expanded from 340 to 600 acres. When Vrooman attempted to settle on his tract, then, the Palatines struck back with the aid of their Mohawk allies. Vrooman complained to the governor that "Wiser with his Crew" had damaged his property and prevented him from settling lands given to him by the Indians "so long agoe." He particularly denounced "Wiser's Son a Young Lad [who] is very Impudent." Conrad Weiser, he declared, employed his interpreting skills "to Run to Call the Indians that Lives [there] to help Him" drive cattle through Vrooman's cornfield, in what appeared to be a frequent act of defiance. The disgruntled Vrooman warned Governor Hunter that "[Weiser] and his father with some Confederates Conive with the Indians every day . . . and tells them many Lyes."[30]

In November 1714 a more formidable threat to the Schoharie Mohawks' and Palatines' lands emerged when the "Seven Partners" of Albany—a group that included members of the wealthy Livingston and Schuyler families—received a land grant for about 10,000 acres along Schoharie Creek. The grant embraced much of Bayard's defunct claim and enveloped the Palatines' settlements. The Seven Partners served notice to the Palatines that "Wee are King's of this land" and that they should either sign leases or leave. According to the Palatines, the partners also tried to sow "enmity betwixt them and the Indians, and if possible to persuade them (for money or Rumm) to put them in possession of the land and declare them rightfull owners thereof, but in this also they fail'd." The Germans were disgusted at the partners' "extravagant terms," so they pleaded to the Mohawks "that since they had so long sukled them at their breast, not to wean them so soon and Cast them of."[31]

The Palatines' description of themselves as children suckling at the breast of Mohawk mothers is certainly unique in the history of colonial America. Although the Mohawks' response to their plea is not recorded, it is clear that the Palatines increasingly chose to wean themselves from Mohawk care and veer toward petitioning their erstwhile British fathers. For five or six years the Palatines remained squatters in the eyes of the absentee landholders, the Palatine leadership holding out hope that a direct appeal to the British Crown might secure their occupancy of Schoharie. In 1718 John Conrad Weiser and two other leaders sailed for England, where they presented petitions on behalf of the Palatines. These petitions shed light on the Palatines' attitudes toward Indian occupancy and land. They argued that since the area they had initially settled was too small, they were "oblig'd to sollicit all the Indian Kings there adjoyning for more land, which they willingly granted for 33 pieces of Eight." Johannes Wilhelm Schefs's petition emphasized the numerous improvements the settlers had made, including "Hutts, Houses, & some Mills for grinding of Corn." He asked that King George grant the Palatines the lands they occupied in Schoharie, since their residence predated the Seven Partners and Vrooman patents. While these applications did not result in a royal land grant to the Germans, the Board of Trade ordered the new governor of New York, William Burnet, to settle the Palatines elsewhere on the frontier.[32]

In their collective memory of their emigration to New York, Palatine settlers remembered peaceful relations and cooperation with the Mohawks, not existence in a vacant land over which "savages" had no rights. When John Conrad Weiser and other agents petitioned the British government in 1720, they mentioned that the Palatines had decided to settle at Schoharie because "the Indians had given [Schoharie lands] to the late Queen Ann for their use." By the time young Conrad Weiser penned his autobiographical account, this legend had become even more embellished. In Weiser's telling the Palatines had sent deputies to the Mohawks because one of the four "Indian Kings" who visited England in 1710 saw "the German people [lying] in tents on the Black Heath" and set aside some of the Schoharie lands out of pity for the "poor palatines." As Weiser remembered it, "the Indian Deputies were sent to direct the Germans to

Schochary." Shiploads of Palatines, however, had already departed for New York when the "Indian Kings" reached England, so there is no basis in fact for the Palatines' belief. But factuality is not the point: the widely held myth of a shared past suggested the possibility of a shared future on the same land.[33]

The wealthier landholders of Albany, however, foreclosed on that future and the Palatine and Indian farmers' dwelling places by pre-empting their claims through land patents. In this sense the patents were investments in the future, but investments that did not include independent-minded Palatines and Indians sharing the land. The Palatines, who had experience with aristocratic oppression in their own country, seem to have sensed that the game was up in Schoharie. By the early 1720s the Palatine community there had fractured, and the leadership that structured the community's alliance with the Mohawks had dispersed. As Conrad Weiser recalled, "there was no one among the people who could govern them," and Palatines drifted to other areas in New York, New Jersey, Pennsylvania, and Virginia that bordered Indian lands. Ironically, the Palatines' dispersion effectively "Indianized" them, in a sense: when Weiser observed that "each one did as he wished," he pointed out a liberty that virtually all Iroquois possessed. Other Palatines, including Conrad Weiser, migrated westward and southward along the Susquehanna, taking up lands in the Tulpehocken Valley, an area still occupied by the Delawares but nominally claimed by Pennsylvania (the Palatines made no effort to negotiate with the Delawares over land there). Some Schoharie residents decided to stay put and, as Governor Burnet reported, had "actually taken leases from [the absentee landlords] and attorned Tenants to them." Having been defeated in their attempt to bypass New York's procedures for land patenting, some Germans "began to get a little wiser" and applied for licenses to purchase Indian lands themselves. Well-to-do settlers began patenting lands in the Schoharie Valley. Those Palatines who elected to stay in the Schoharie Valley increasingly outnumbered and pressured the Schoharie Indians, whose numbers slowly dwindled until the time of the American Revolution. Other Palatines went on to settle a tract nearly forty miles west of Albany called Burnetsfield. In the early 1720s Palatine leaders such as Johann Jost Petrie, John Conrad Weiser, and Johann Peter Kniskern negotiated with Mohawks and Oneidas for lands further west.[34]

The upper Mohawk Valley, especially the areas that became known as Stone Arabia, Burnetsfield, and German Flatts, was a Palatine haven in the eighteenth century. The Palatines carried with them into these areas the legacy of cooperation and face-to-face negotiation with the Natives they had evidenced at Schoharie. German Flatts inhabitants lived interspersed among Mohawk and Oneida villages. For the second time, then, the Palatines' lives on the frontier would become intricately linked with those of Indian peoples with whom they were obliged to keep on friendly terms. New York officials hoped that the Palatines, allowed to settle the far-western border, would serve as "more immediately a Barrier against the Sudden incursions of the French, who made this their Road" when they attacked Schenectady in 1690. When the Board of Trade wrote in favor of the Palatine emigration in 1709, it noted its belief that the Palatines would "in process of time by intermarrying with the neighbouring Indians (as the French do) . . . be Capable [of] rendring very great Service to Her Majesty's Subjects." As we will see, the Palatine and Oneida communities did indeed create an incredibly complex alliance, bound by personal, economic, and marital ties, that offered both peoples protection from the threat of French attacks on their settlements (see chapter 4).[35]

Tiononderoge Mohawks at the Confluence of Anglo-Dutch Culture

In the early eighteenth century the Mohawk town of Tiononderoge, also called the "Lower Castle," was under particular colonial pressure because it was closest to the principal Anglo-Dutch settlements at Albany and Schenectady. The Iroquoian word *Tiononderoge* signifies "two streams coming together"—where Schoharie Creek empties into the Mohawk River. The Native peoples living at the village of Tiononderoge also increasingly found themselves at the confluence of Mohawk and Anglo-Dutch cultural streams.[36] To the south were Anglo-Irish settlers at Warrensbush, and farther south, down the Schoharie Valley, were the Palatines. Only twenty miles away to the east lived the Dutch settlers at Schenectady. The story of the Tiononderoge community reveals the extraordinary colonial pressures the Mohawks faced and the scope of their struggle against the legal weapons aimed at their lands. The New York officials who administered the law and were responsible for maintaining the Covenant Chain alliance were often most involved in attempts to aggrandize Indian lands. Still, despite the powerful officials arrayed against them, the Mohawks succeeded in gaining a modicum of security for their lands, avoiding total dependency and poverty, and maintaining their prestige for decades to come. Like their Schoharie brethren, the Tiononderoge Mohawks created alliances with local colonists—based upon strong personal relationships—to protect their lands from hostile outsiders who coveted their valuable planting grounds. One such colonist whom the Mohawks befriended was a twenty-three-year-old Irish immigrant named William Johnson, who lived only three miles from the Tiononderoge Mohawks, at Fort Johnson. When Johnson arrived in New York in 1737, he was virtually unknown, but within twenty years he would become an influential person in Iroquois life and a major figure in the British Empire. He would emerge as a vocal advocate of Mohawks' interests, though not always for completely magnanimous reasons. As a result of this relationship, the histories of the Mohawks and of Johnson's family would be intricately interwoven in the eighteenth century.

Tiononderoge, like Schoharie, had only recently been settled by the Mohawks: it looked nothing like a typical seventeenth-century Iroquoian village, with log palisades to protect the longhouses inside.

In fact, an old, abandoned palisaded village called Ogsadaga was visible on a hilltop to the west of Tiononderoge, a reminder that the Mohawks had largely ceased to live in longhouses by the mid-eighteenth century. During a diplomatic mission to Iroquoia in 1677, an English official named Wentworth Greenhalgh had described five different Mohawk villages before this transformation. Four of them were palisaded villages, or "castles"; only one was "withoutt Fence & contayns about ten houses." All of the Mohawk villages were located on the north side of the Mohawk River. But French military attacks against Mohawk settlements in 1693 had forced the abandonment of the four main villages that Greenhalgh saw. By 1712 only three major Mohawk settlements remained in the valley—Tiononderoge, Schoharie, and Canajoharie—and all of them were now located on the south side of the river for added protection. Tiononderoge initially was a series of four distinct clusters near the mouth of Schoharie Creek, but after the construction of Fort Hunter, the Mohawk settlements became concentrated on the creek's eastern shore. In 1713 an English missionary estimated the Mohawk population at Tiononderoge as 360 persons living in forty to fifty houses. Many of the town's inhabitants lived prosperously, as one property inventory made clear: a Mohawk leader named Johannes Crine recorded in 1775 that he had "three Good Dwelling Houses, two Barns, and an Orchard," in addition to furniture, farming utensils, and numerous livestock.[37]

Everyday life at Tiononderoge was punctuated by dangers that imparted a certain fatalism to its residents. "Death follows us everywhere we go," one Iroquois despondently told Governor Hunter in 1719. He might have been referring to the smallpox epidemic that had raged in Iroquois communities in 1716–17, perhaps as a result of their previous participation in British military campaigns. What disease had left undone, the plague of rum finished. The Mohawks' proximity to Dutch traders at Albany and Schenectady virtually guaranteed a torrent of rum that swept away much of the village's peace and health. English missionaries stationed at Fort Hunter regularly reported how drunkenness unleashed violence among the villagers. Some Mohawks were accidentally killed in drunken brawls. The source of the problem, as a 1726 petition makes clear, was that Europeans were coming "to buy the Corn from the Indians there & selling them Rum which has been found by Experience to be very Destructive to them."[38]

Like the rest of the Iroquois peoples after the 1701 treaty with the French, the Mohawks wanted to build a lasting peace from war's ashes. Above all, the Keepers of the Eastern Door needed to maintain their neutral course of action: they balanced their ties with the French through their Kahnawake Mohawk brethren, but they also kept close ties to their English neighbors. For example, Tiononderoge leaders pressed the New York government to build a fort for their protection, believing that it was necessary to "preserve us from our Ennemies for we were surrounded by the French and Dawaganhaes on all hands." In 1712 four local carpenters completed a square-shaped fort with four blockhouses, a chapel, and a parsonage. The complex was called Fort Hunter, in honor of the governor. The chapel was named in honor of Queen Anne, who donated a set of communion silver to the Mohawks, and a missionary named William Andrews was appointed by the evangelical Society for the Propagation of the Gospel to preach the good news of Christ to the Mohawks. Andrews arrived at Fort Hunter in 1712, hoping to convert the Mohawks to Christianity and strengthen their alliance to the English, just as Catholicism had bonded the French and the Kahnawake Iroquois. Many Mohawks had already received Protestant instruction through Dutch Reformed clergy such as Godfridius Dellius. Andrews, however, left the mission in 1719, disheartened that his efforts had not produced more converts. In fact, there was a solid core of Protestant Mohawk converts at Fort Hunter who had fashioned a Mohawk Christianity that Andrews did not recognize. Just as the Mohawks shaped their religious experience, refusing passive acceptance, they shaped the political events unfolding around them.[39]

No sooner had Fort Hunter been established than rumors circulated of potential English threats to Mohawk lands. The Indians accused Andrews of establishing himself among them in hopes of obtaining Mohawk land, not redeeming Mohawk souls. The sachem Decanissorens reported that he had encountered a Mohawk messenger carrying news that an Indian named Johannes had been murdered and another wounded. This report may have originated in a "Drunken Quarrel" between some Mohawks and soldiers stationed at Albany. The Mohawks, according to Decanissorens, were "ready and [making] Bullets . . . resolved to distroy ye Christians and desired ye assistance of the other four Nations." Lt. Charles Huddy at Fort Hunter confirmed that there was a conspiracy afoot among "the four upper Indian Nations to surprise the fort in the Mohocks Country."[40]

Corrupt New York officials, from the Commissioners of Indian Affairs to the commanders of colonial garrisons, consistently used their offices to defraud Mohawks of their lands. Ironically, these officials who were responsible for keeping the peace often jeopardized it the most. The governor's council received word that one officer at Fort Hunter, Lt. John Scott, was "Treating with the Indians to make . . . purchases of them for land without any Lycense from this Board" and ordered him to desist. Hendrick Tekarihogen, who had visited London in 1710, later complained that the Tiononderoge villagers could not practice their devotions "as Long as rum was sold so Publickly in their Country." In particular, four traders named John Scott, Johannes Harmense, Joseph Clement, and Thomas Wildman "sold Rum so plentifully as if it were water out of a fountain and if that Cannot be privinted they Cannot Live Peaceably in their Castle." Scott's rum was probably involved in his land deals, for in 1720 Hendrick Tekarihogen vehemently expressed his resentment that "Capt Scot had bought some Land of the Maquase in a Clandestin way in the Night time and not in a Regular Lawfull way." The Commissioners of

Indian Affairs callously ignored Hendrick's request "that no Patent of any Land in the Mohoggs Country should be Granted [to Scott]"; Gov. William Burnet and the council went on to approve John Scott's patent in 1722.[41]

Land controversies in colonial New York tended to be long, drawn-out affairs lasting for decades. They often involved colonial *claims* to Indian lands: even if colonists received letters patent, they could not attempt actual settlement if Natives still inhabited or claimed the area. Speculating on land was like investing in the stock market, based on the faith that Natives would eventually remove themselves or be removed by settlement pressure. The Tiononderoge Mohawks, for example, faced chronic challenges from the Corporation of Albany for Mohawk Flatts—the fertile bottomlands situated near the junction of Schoharie Creek and the Mohawk River. This land dispute, which persisted into the 1770s, was doubly explosive because it involved two sets of rival colonial claimants: Walter Butler's predominantly Anglo-Irish faction and the largely Dutch claimants of the Corporation of Albany. Butler was a Connecticut man who had relocated to New York and become a lieutenant in the New York militia, commanding the small garrison at Fort Hunter. In 1730 he obtained a license to purchase 12,000 acres at Tiononderoge (also known as Mohawk Flatts) from the Natives he ostensibly guarded from harm. The Corporation of Albany soon filed a petition for a grant of 4,000 acres of Mohawk Flatts, which they claimed the Mohawks had "formerly granted to the city" in 1686. The Albanians also filed a *caveat* against Butler's petition to stop the land-patenting machinery. In response Butler enlisted other officeholders to become his partners, including Governor Cosby and some of his council members. With a larger political base to satisfy, Butler's initial claim for 12,000 acres ballooned into a claim for 86,000 acres of Mohawks' land. Unlike the Palatines, who showed a degree of respect for Indian occupancy, both Butler and the Albanians (some of whom were entrusted with Indian relations) referred to Mohawk Flatts as "vacant land," ignoring Native uses of the area. The controversy lingered until August 1733, when Cosby and the interested councilmen approved Butler's application. At least one of Butler's Indian deeds was produced post factum in 1735, suggesting less than scrupulous methods for obtaining the necessary Indian quit claim. If the Mohawks had full knowledge of that duplicitous conniving for their lands, they might have broken the alliance immediately, but they only knew part of the truth. Or more accurately, Governor Cosby only let them see part of the truth.[42]

In a September 1733 meeting with the Mohawks, Cosby took action to discredit the Albany Corporation's claims and to secure his own. In his historical writings Cadwallader Colden stressed that once Cosby learned of Tiononderoge's value and the "defects" of the Albany deed, he "resolv'd to have it for himself." According to Colden, the governor may have arranged for Butler to incite the Mohawks about the nature of the Albany deed. The Mohawks later protested that the mayor and the Corporation of Albany had by "deceitful and Indirect ways and Means" induced them to sign a deed of trust for Mohawk Flatts. The Indians feared that the Corporation "would Defraud us of the Said land by taking possession of it for themselves." The Mohawks declared that they were "able to take care of our own Land ourselves" and demanded justice. Cosby ordered the mayor of Albany to produce the deed and asked interpreter Laurence Clausen to read it to the assembled Indians. Upon learning that the deed was an "absolute conveyance" of the lands, rather than a deed of trust, the Mohawks "cryed out with one voice that they were cheated" and threatened to "leave their Country, and go over to the French." Cosby turned the deed over to the Mohawks, who in a "great rage" tore it up and burned it. The Mohawks then signed another deed in trust with the king of England and asked for their own copy. Significantly, the name of a principal Mohawk woman, Jacomine, is the first signature to appear on the deed.[43]

The written records do not document the authentic voices of the

Mohawks, just as they veil the role that women like Jacomine played in such proceedings. Why, for example, would the Mohawks, who had just discovered a gross fraud, convey more lands to Walter Butler and directly ask the governor to give Butler a patent? Did the Mohawks truly have "Affection" for Butler, as the minutes declare? Cosby's interest in obtaining other Tiononderoge Mohawk lands and defeating the Albanians' claims meant that he and his associates may have manipulated the Mohawks' speech and actions to bolster their own claims. Cosby's colonial contemporaries were also suspicious of his actions: as Colden saw it, Cosby and "his friends could not avoid the Impression it made on peoples minds that he would stop at no Injustice in order to fill his pockets."[44]

The Mohawk Flatts controversy haunted both the Mohawks and New York political life for years to come. The Tiononderoge Mohawks never fully resolved the conflict with Albany's leaders until 1773, when the British government in London pressured the Albany Corporation to issue a quit claim. In the short term Cosby had a 14,000-acre interest in Butler's Tiononderoge patent. After the governor's death in 1736 Sir Peter Warren purchased this tract of land from his widow and enlisted his young nephew, William Johnson, to develop his new plantation.[45]

Of all the Europeans who settled near Tiononderoge, Johnson would prove to be the most significant in Mohawk history. His life has an inherent drama about it, given that the twenty-three-year-old arrived in New York unheralded and inexperienced. He rose from the ranks of a fur trader on the fringes of the British world to become an aristocratic baronet with immense power. Johnson, however, was not without connections. Born into a prominent Anglo-Irish gentry family in 1715, Johnson emigrated to New York in 1737–38 as a client of his uncle, Peter Warren, a Royal Navy captain. Johnson's task was to profitably manage his uncle's estate—Warrensbush—located only a few miles southeast of the Mohawk town at Tiononderoge. In addition to the twelve Irish families who accompanied him to New

York, Johnson later settled Irish, English, and Palatine families at Warrensbush (including a handful of free blacks called the "Willegee Negroes"). He always took great pride in settling and developing the Mohawk Valley with industrious families.[46]

There was something about William Johnson's character that inclined him to live peaceably with his Iroquois neighbors. He once admonished an acquaintance to "live easy and Peaceable with the Indians" and throughout his life displayed curiosity about Native customs, history, and ancient artifacts. Like the Palatines, Johnson and his "Neighbours at the Mohawks Castle" established a harmonious and symbiotic relationship through close economic and social ties that benefited both communities. Johnson's papers do not shed light on the precise details of his first meetings with the Mohawks: Who visited whom first? How often did visits take place? Did Johnson live among the Mohawks for a short time? What can be said with certainty is that within ten years of his arrival, Johnson was an adept fur trader in colonial New York with wide-ranging contacts. He traded distantly with the Oquaga Indians on the Susquehanna River, and he obtained a lucrative contract to supply the British garrison at Oswego, on Lake Ontario. But Johnson's main local trade was with the Mohawks and Germans. He recognized that his trading store would intercept "all the High Germans passing by that way in the winter, and all the upper Nations of Indians, whose trade is pritty valuable." The Irish trader's relations with his Mohawk neighbors soon made him an important negotiator in Anglo-Iroquois diplomacy, earning him the resentment of the Commissioners of Indian Affairs at Albany and of their interests in the New York Assembly. Johnson, however, proved a quick learner of diplomatic metaphors, as one of his early journals suggests. The Mohawks appreciated his liberality and fairness, naming him "Warrighiyagey" (variously translated as "doer of great things" or "in the midst of affairs"). Johnson once boasted that the Mohawks were "well pleased at my Settleing here, and keeping w.ᵗ necessarys they wanted." Historians typically emphasize Johnson's influence on the Mohawks, but the Mohawks cultivated Warrighiyagey for their own purposes. In future years the Mohawks employed their powerful neighbor to advocate their interests and lands. Because Johnson's influence among the Six Nations rested largely with the Mohawks, he had a vested interest in protecting their rights and promoting their prestige as Keepers of the Eastern Door. In later years he supported the Mohawks in their land grievances over Mohawk Flatts, Kayaderosseras, Livingston, and other smaller patents. At a local level the relationship between Johnson and the Mohawks helped to stabilize the Mohawk Valley world that Iroquois and Europeans would increasingly have to share.[47]

When Johnson spoke of being "first joined in brothership" to the Iroquois, this was more than metaphor: his ties to the Iroquois broadly and to the Mohawks specifically were built on personal relationships with individual men and women. One of his most important relationships was with the Canajoharie Mohawk leader Hendrick Theyanoguin. Johnson and Hendrick together strived to build a stronger Covenant Chain between the Iroquois and the British at a time when it was seriously flagging. But Johnson's ties to the Iroquois went far deeper than one influential Indian sachem: the Irishman fathered a number of children with a Mohawk woman named Elizabeth and with another unnamed Mohawk woman. William and Elizabeth had three children—Brant Johnson, or Keghneghtaga, in 1742; Thomas in 1744; and Christian in 1745—while the unnamed Mohawk woman bore him a son named William Tagawirunte. Johnson's liaisons led to a host of rumors focused on wild speculation about how many Indian "concubines" he kept. Sadly, these rumors not only diminish the Native women but obscure the vital role they played in Mohawk political and social life. Johnson's relationship with Elizabeth, for example, linked him to the most influential matrons and sachems of Tiononderoge. Indeed, his array of partnerships with male leaders such as Brant Kanagaradunckwa and Hendrick Theyanoguin came about as a result of the Mohawks' matrilineal ties.[48] Two crucial relationships emerged through Elizabeth's family tree: Elizabeth's sister, Christina, married the sachem Brant Kanagaradunckwa in 1738, and Elizabeth's uncle Peter married a Tiononderoge Mohawk named Margaret in 1735. Peter's and Margaret's children included Joseph and Molly Brant, both of whom would powerfully influence Johnson's later years. Johnson learned to speak Mohawk (no small feat for an adult European), occasionally acted as an interpreter, and became familiar with Iroquois customs and condolence rituals. As one contemporary observed, Johnson "knew how to react to the Indians' sense of humor," and he complied "with their humours in his dress & conversation with them."[49] Most important, Johnson understood the significance Natives placed on gift-giving and hospitality; his house was almost never without Indian guests. As Johnson's most recent biographer concludes, "What distinguished William Johnson from the run-of-the-mill European trader was that he understood the ritual dimension of exchange in Indian cultures and paid as much attention to it as he did the accumulation of profits. . . . Watching him closely and seeing his ability to operate in part on their terms, Hendrick and other Mohawk sachems began to identify William Johnson as the man they needed."[50]

Given the disingenuousness of New York's official negotiators, the Mohawks had little choice but to cultivate alternative relationships with their "Friends among the White People," who would benefit their communities economically and defend their lands politically. To the Mohawks, William Johnson was the proverbial right man at the right time. At a time when their faith in the Albany Commissioners was at its nadir, Johnson's political fortunes were on the rise. After Johnson acted as Clinton's agent in his disputes with Albany, the governor appointed him "Colonel of the Six Nations" in 1746 and stripped the Albany Commissioners of their powers. The Mohawks now had another outlet through which to raise long-standing grievances and disputes. King George's War cemented this relationship, for Johnson was instrumental in organizing joint war parties of Mohawk warriors and colonial soldiers to defend the valley and scout against the French. In 1746 Cadwallader Colden captured a particularly defining moment in Johnson's career: "When the *Indians* came near the Town of Albany, on the 8th of *August*, Mr. *Johnson* put himself at the Head of the *Mohawks*, dressed and painted after the Manner of an *Indian* War-Captain; and the *Indians* who followed him, were likewise dressed and painted, as is usual with them when they set out in War." From 1746 to 1747 Johnson equipped many "a Regm[t]. of Christians, & Indians," who undertook joint scouting expeditions in the Lake Champlain area. Some Mohawks, like Abraham, "esteemed Colonel Johnson to be a good warriour." Such statements confirmed and promoted his reputation as one who intimately knew and understood the Indians.[51]

But the Mohawks' close relationship with Johnson came at a price. Even their staunch friend contributed to the colonial settlement boom, settling German and Irish tenants on his estates on favorable terms; he always prided himself on being one of the few large landholders who successfully improved frontier lands. He wrote in 1774 that "the settlements in this Country go on very promisingly, I have lately fixed a Number of Industrious people in my Grant . . . which will be a benefit to it as one good Settlement draws another."[52] One wonders whether Johnson sensed the circular irony: the more settlers he brought in, the more he might diminish the Mohawks' power and, in turn, his own. Did the Mohawks, for their part, ever ponder what they gained by their alliance with Johnson?

By peopling the valley as he did, Johnson assured that the Mohawks would be increasingly surrounded by European farmers, not insulated from them. In the year 1747, for example, Johnson wrote to Governor Clinton that "there is another grand villain George Clock lives by Conajoharie Castle, who robs the Indians of all their cloaths &c which they get of me. I had [several] complaints of Hendrick &c. about his behaviour."[53] Klock's farm was indeed located just across the Mohawk River from Canajoharie, and settlers like Klock would increasingly play a major role in the lives of the Mohawk people. How the Canajoharie Mohawks responded to the influx of new settlers like George Klock is the subject of the next settlement portrait.

Christian Mohawks and German Brothers at Canajoharie

In 1753 a remarkable petition written by a literate Mohawk named Paulus came before the colonial government. Paulus's petition concerned the Canajoharie Mohawks' German neighbors who lived near their settlement. Paulus wrote to defend a particular tract of land where Christian Mohawks and Germans jointly used a church, announcing that the Mohawks and the Germans "are grown up together and we intend to Live our Lifetime together as Brothers." He had come of age with the Germans and saw no reason why brotherhood—especially a Christian one—should cease. By the mid-eighteenth century the world that Paulus and other Mohawks knew would increasingly bear a greater resemblance to that of their European brethren. The Mohawks would live "intermixed with the Christians, and the other Indians living near our Frontiers," and would "resort daily to the Christians Houses." By the 1750s the colonial population in the city and county of Albany had risen from around 3,500 in 1714 to over 10,000 by 1749—more than the total population of the Six Nations. Anywhere from 2,600 to 4,550 colonists outnumbered the few hundred Natives living in the Mohawk Valley. The colonists' sheer numbers presented the Mohawks with fundamental questions regarding their status and lands: How could they retain their political and economic independence in the ancestral homelands that they increasingly shared with outsiders? How much of their lands would they retain? How would they prevent colonists from stealing their lands through chicanery? How could they influence the process of colonial settlement in ways that would bring security to their lands and communities?[54]

Writing in 1769, William Johnson declared his belief that the Mohawks were "already sensible that their Children must from being surrounded on all Sides have recourse to Farming of some sort." According to Johnson, they "were always lamenting that they had so little land left," but they took steps to ensure they would continue to live prosperously in their ancestral lands. They rapidly adapted to the changing political, economic, and material currents of the eighteenth century. They did not view these changes as somehow compromising their identity as Mohawks, nor should modern readers. Those who persisted in their old homelands had committed themselves to living in peace with the British and accepted that they would have to share the land; after a century of contact they were not naive about European methods. In 1772 a sachem named Joseph sadly noted the sordid history of land fraud and lack of redress that had left the Mohawks "reduced to very scanty limits." But he acknowledged that this was partly due to "the many sales we have from time to time made of large Tracts to accommodate your people." The Mohawks did not view their decisions to part with land as a zero-sum game in which any diminution of their land base was total defeat, surrender to European expansion. The Mohawks' decisions to allocate lands to the Europeans were intensely emotional and painful, but the Mohawks were determined to construct a peaceful and secure world—to "accommodate" the British settlers, as Joseph remarked. The Mohawks still retained considerable influence as the "Keepers of the Eastern Door" of the Confederacy and had a strong voice in land negotiations, and William Johnson never let anyone in colonial government forget the Mohawk nation's importance.[55]

The story of Canajoharie defies much of our inherited understanding of the place of Indian peoples in the colonial world. It is easy to assume that Natives who became "settlement Indians" would become economically irrelevant and impoverished. If the fur trade was declining in importance, wasn't land the only thing left that the Mohawks could sell? The evidence in the Mohawks' case, however, suggests otherwise. First, Mohawk settlements were among the most prosperous and thriving in the whole valley: lack of resources was not a major motivation for the Mohawks' decisions to share the valley with European colonists. On the whole, the Mohawks acted on very traditional concerns, such as hospitality and the personal relationships they had built with individual European families. It is misleading to characterize the Mohawks' land sales as a sign of "decline" or of their being duped by forces too powerful for them to control or understand. The story of the Natives at Canajoharie does not fit the image of "settlement Indians" who became impoverished and irrelevant.[56]

The Mohawks' land negotiations with local settlers represented a pressured people's striking adaptation to European expansion, an adaptation that had notable successes and failures in a volatile world. At an official level the Mohawks pursued an aggressive diplomacy of resistance against egregious land frauds, such as the Kayaderosseras and Livingston patents. At a local level the Canajoharies protected their property through symbiotic arrangements with local settlers. William Johnson once observed that the Natives "certainly can give preference to whom they like" in land negotiations (including, of course, to himself).[57] The Mohawks tried to accommodate settlers who demonstrated goodwill and hospitality. For example, the Canajoharies had numerous European farmers living as their tenants on the fertile lowlands around their castle.[58] These tenant farmers not only saw the Mohawks as the land's true "owners" but occasionally defended the Indians' rights against colonial outsiders who tried to disrupt their peaceful living arrangements. But the greatest drawback that the Mohawks and other Iroquois faced was the lack of a central authority over land sales; virtually all colonists, by contrast, accepted that formal title to land rested in the colonial government. Some European squatters respected and defended Indian rights and acted in defiance of colonial authority, but other common farmers employed their close ties to the Mohawks to defraud them of lands and gain letters patent. The Canajoharie Mohawks' history demonstrates their tenacious ability to adapt to a changing world and to maintain a modicum of sovereignty. For most of the eighteenth century, until the 1770s, the Mohawks adapted, safeguarded their lands, and became economic partners with their neighbors. Their story provides a particularly vivid glimpse of human beings in relation on a contested frontier.

Canajoharie, or Kanatsyohare, the "Upper Castle" of the Mohawks, got its name from an interesting geological feature in the rocky gorge carved out by Canajoharie Creek as it flows out of the highlands into the Mohawk River. The word Canajoharie means "washed kettle," for among the flat rocks that the creek has washed smooth over the centuries, there is a circular, potlike opening in the sheetrock containing a deep pool of water. In the eighteenth-century the Mohawk presence at Canajoharie frequently shifted in location: it is perhaps best understood as a cluster of settlements on the south side of the Mohawk River, opposite the mouth of East Canada Creek. Like Fort Hunter and Schoharie, Canajoharie was not a palisaded castle, like older Iroquois villages: dispersed settlements stretched for a few miles along the south side of the Mohawk River, from Ostquago Creek westward to Nowadaga Creek. Along the fertile ground near the river were fruit orchards and fields of corn, wheat, peas, potatoes, beans, oats, and other crops. The castle's population fluctuated over the eighteenth century, but it probably held between 200 and 300 persons. As late as 1773 the population was estimated at 221 men, women, and children. After 1769 a small Anglican chapel on the side of a ridge overlooked the community.[59]

Canajoharie would have looked almost indistinguishable from other European settlements nearby, and much different from Iroquois communities westward in Seneca country.[60] Numerous accounts by eighteenth-century observers marveled at the Mohawks' agricultural wealth, depicting the Mohawks as fully capable of living and prospering, though increasingly outnumbered, in "the Heart of [colonial] Settlements." Col. Peter Gansevoort was one of many American soldiers who observed the prosperity of Iroquois settlements in the

1770s: Canajoharie was "abounding with every Necessary so that it is remarked that the Indians live much better than most of the Mohawk River farmers their Houses very well furnished with all necessary Household utensils, great plenty of Grain, several Horses, cows, and waggons."[61] At both Fort Hunter and Canajoharie the Mohawks' material possessions bore the marks of decades of close contact with European settlers. They ate from a variety of Native and colonial ceramics, pewter ware, copper kettles, and expensive china. Many Mohawks adopted domesticated livestock and maintained herds of horses, pigs, and cows. In addition, by 1760 "almost all the Indians have Sleas [sleighs]," as Warren Johnson noted. Horse-drawn sleighs and wagons facilitated easy travel and the transport of wood, pelts, or trade goods. European architectural designs also influenced Mohawk structures. During a visit to Brant Kanagaradunckwa's house Daniel Claus and Conrad Weiser "could not find fault" with it. The house itself was evidence of melding European and Mohawk styles: Claus wrote that Brant "lived in a well built, 2 story house, provided with furniture like that of a middle-class family; there was nothing wanting in our food or drink or in our beds." Claus's evocation of a middle-class family reveals the growing differences between richer and poorer Indians—evident in house construction and furnishings. Wealthier Mohawks' houses had limestone foundations, wood floors, glass panes in the windows, curtains, clapboards, chimneys, and numerous outbuildings such as Dutch barns. But ordinary Mohawk villagers lived in structures similar to the makeshift log houses that European farmers constructed.[62]

While Mohawk material culture had significantly changed, its meanings and purposes were still framed by traditional patterns. Some warriors used a rum keg with a hide covering as a drum when they sang war songs and marched in processional dances. The rhythms of life in the newer Mohawk communities—ceremonies, marriages, births, deaths, warfare—melded with older rhythms. Margaret and Peter Tehowaghwengaraghkwin migrated from Fort

Hunter to traditional Mohawk hunting lands in the Cuyahoga Valley, where some migrant Mohawks were settling; a son named Thayendanegea (Joseph Brant) was born there in early 1743. Margaret returned to Canajoharie in the late 1740s after her husband's death, probably during an epidemic. She married again, but her happiness was short-lived: Catawba warriors killed her second husband, Lykas, during a 1750 expedition. In the early 1750s she married the Tiononderoge sachem Brant Kanagaradunckwa. The couple had evidently violated longstanding Mohawk taboos, for Claus explained that Brant had "ruined himself by marriage, & was forced to leave his place" and move to Canajoharie.[63]

As the lives of Margaret, Peter, Lykas, and others suggest, Canajoharie was in some senses an unchanging world. But as increasing numbers of Europeans settled within sight of the castle, Canajoharie came to be defined as a neighborhood that both Mohawks and Europeans shared. A 1743 petition from "the inhabitants of Canajoharie"—the European ones—reveals that it was equally an Indian and a European place. Beginning in the 1720s Palatine emigrants, who as we have seen were no strangers to the Mohawks, settled on the north side of the Mohawk Valley, opposite Canajoharie. They established a series of settlements called German Flatts, Stone Arabia, and Burnetsfield. But settlers also built homes on the south side of the valley, where the Mohawks lived. Peter Schuyler remembered the proximity of their settlements: he wrote that when his father, David, was a young boy, his house was "one Mile and a quarter below the Indian Castle." Germans, English, Irish, and Mohawks lived in relative peace, and their very human relationships created a network of personal, religious, economic, and political bonds. Many ordinary farmers could speak Mohawk, Iroquoian dialects, and trade pidgins. According to later sources, the newcomers "always were on friendly terms with the Indians they were never sent off empty handed when they needed food." One colonial family's oral tradition hearkened to a time when an ancestor's farm was "a favorite resort of the Indians for fishing purposes, and particularly of the Indian boys," including young Joseph Brant, who "remained several days at a time" with the family.[64]

Small-scale trading and local exchanges between Canajoharie's European and Indian peoples made them economically interdependent. Mohawk Valley farmers sold much of their produce to local Mohawks, Oneidas, and other Six Nations Indians constantly traveling through their neighborhood or attending conferences. From the 1750s to the 1770s Mohawks gathered ginseng and traded it to nearby colonists or traders, such as the widow Sarah Magin (who spoke Mohawk), in return for rum or other necessities. Mohawks also supplied furs and food (e.g., meat, fish, fowl, corn) to colonists in return for various services or goods. Indians had their corn ground at nearby settlers' mills and obtained boards for their houses at nearby sawmills. Mohawks relied on local blacksmiths and gunsmiths to repair kettles, tools, hoes, knives, firearms, and, increasingly, plows. When the Canajoharie Mohawks informed Warrighiyagey that the women were having problems hoeing especially hard ground, Johnson promised that he would direct some German farmers "who live nearest to you, to go up with some Plows to break up your stiff Ground." Mohawks occasionally relied on local farmers to "repair [their] Fences & assist [them] in planting [their] Corn." With such tutelage the Mohawks and Oneidas began to acquire their own plows and "common farming tools" such as scythes and pitchforks. Christian missionaries such as Samuel Kirkland also served as conduits of such equipment to the Iroquois.[65]

Religion also formed part of the common ground between Mohawk and European communities. Rather than taking long journeys to Albany, Christian Mohawks attended local Dutch or Palatine churches for christenings, baptisms, and marriages; these sacred events were meticulously recorded in many colonial church records. In the mid-1720s, for example, the Rev. John Jacob Ehle (or Oel), a Westphalian German, settled in the upper Mohawk Valley and established a log

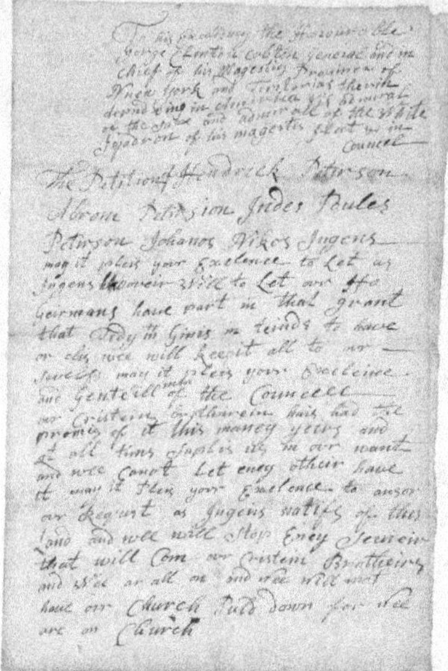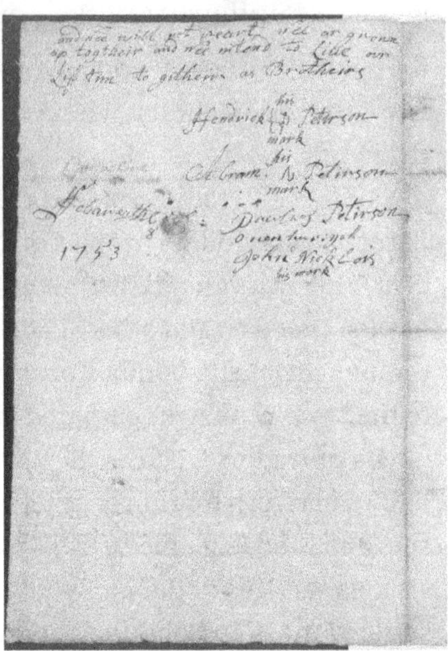

Fig. 5. Petition of Hendrick, Abram, Paulus, and John to George Clinton, February 8, 1753. Courtesy of William L. Clements Library, University of Michigan.

mission house on the north side of the Mohawk River, opposite Canajoharie. The Indians had bestowed this land "in consideration of the love, good will, and affection which we have and bear for the Revd's. Petrus Van Driessen and Johannes Ehle." These two ministers baptized dozens of Mohawk adults and children in the next decades. In June of 1732 a group of Canajoharies appeared before the Albany Commissioners, explaining that "we have now Embraced the Christian Faith." "We are closer united together," they hoped, "since we believe in one Lord & Saviour Jesus Christ." Palatines and Mohawks even worshiped in the same church together, as Paulus's 1753 petition attests. Interceding for local German settlers, Canajoharie headmen asked Governor Clinton to set aside some land from Teady Magin's patent for "our Christian brethren here [who] had the promise of it these many years." Clearly worried that Magin would force the Germans off, the Mohawks declared, "We will not have our Church Pulled down for we [the Mohawks and the Palatines] are one church and we will not part." Paulus added, as noted earlier,

"We are grown up together and we intend to Live our Lifetime together as Brothers."[66]

Brothers, however, were prone to fight. Harmonious relations tended to become dissonant because of property disputes, land-use disagreements, and alcohol. A perennial Native complaint on many British colonial frontiers, including New York and Pennsylvania, involved unpenned European livestock, which trampled Native cornfields and competed with deer for the forest's bounty. But Mohawk leaders were especially concerned that "the bringing [of] rum to our Castle, has made us dwindle away as the snow does in a warm sun shining day." Their grief over the corrosive effects of rum on individual lives was exceeded only by their grief over colonists endangering their collective lives by defrauding them of land. In one of the most hotly contested land cases of the eighteenth century, the 1731 Canajoharie Patent, Philip Livingston and other Albany parties obtained a deed for the Canajoharie area that encompassed the Mohawks' settlements and planting grounds. When the Indians learned of the fraudulent deed, they declared, "If this is true then Mr Livingston has murdered us asleep for our Land is our Life."[67]

Canajoharie sachems believed that land was the "Affair [of] the greatest importance to us, which is concerning the boundaries of our Lands, or the Division between us & our neighbors." The Mohawks were determined to maintain their lands and independence, while accommodating European settlers. It was often a hard, narrow line to walk, fraught with the risk of dispossession and eventual poverty. In 1763 the Mohawk sachem Cayenquiragoa spoke on behalf of thirty-three Mohawk women, who were considered "the Truest Owners being the persons who labour on the Lands, and therefore are esteemed in that light." Mohawk women "unanimously declared" that "they would keep their Land, and did not chuse to part with the same to be reduced to make Brooms." How, then, would the Mohawks preserve their lands and accommodate increasing numbers of European colonists surrounding their settlements? While "lands have often been the Occasion of Quarrels," as one Mohawk speaker believed, they were also the occasion of intricate negotiations between ordinary colonists and Mohawks that enabled both peoples to coexist.[68]

But why were the Mohawks not twice shy about allotting lands to British colonists, having been defrauded so many times in the past? The answer lies principally in how faithful the Mohawks were to the core Iroquois values that informed alliances. The important practices of adoption and hospitality, not a literal and figurative "selling out" of lands, better explain why Mohawks gave land rights to British colonists. Hospitality and reciprocity were crucial determinants in the Natives' dealings with outsiders, since good feelings between neighbors were as important as formal conferences in maintaining healthy alliances. Historian James Lynch argues that the Iroquois adopted outsiders in one of two ways: by assimilation and by association. In the first case war captives and related Indian peoples (e.g., the Tuscaroras) were totally assimilated into Iroquois communities and families. Associative adoption was a status frequently extended to Europeans "who were considered to be trustworthy and had proved their sincere friendship to the Iroquois." Adoptees like William Johnson or nearby colonial farmers like David Schuyler typically received honorary Iroquoian names and were treated as kin. The Mohawks, for example, believed that "one half of Coll°. Johnson belonged to his Excellency [the N.Y. Governor], and the other to them." When David Schuyler was imprisoned for debt in 1732, certain Canajoharie Indians protested, saying that "he is Incorporated among us as one of our Children. We have given him a Tract of Land and he is one of us." David was also the godfather to a young Mohawk girl.[69]

Given abiding Six Nations prestige and the legal requirement of an Indian deed for land patenting, the Mohawks retained considerable leverage in granting land rights and creating a larger framework for peace. Both the Mohawks and the Oneidas were especially receptive to poorer European frontier families. They adopted these families and temporarily allocated planting rights—and in some cases outright ownership—to them premised on future good behavior. Just as alliances had to be renewed at Albany and Montreal each year, renting required that Mohawks and their tenants maintain goodwill with one another. The Mohawks once spoke of Conrad Gondermann, a "very poor man . . . who we took amongst us and gave him a Tract of Land out of Charity." On another occasion three Canajoharie sachems interceded on behalf of a "poor Man" named Conrad Mattys (or Mattice) who lived in their neighborhood. They requested that the government carve out a thousand-acre tract for Mattys from lands they had already sold to David Schuyler and Nicholas Pickerd (Conrad Weiser's brother-in-law). The Mohawks' desire to share the land with Mattys reveals that they had not completely forsaken the land that they had allegedly "sold" to Schuyler and Pickerd. Other beneficiaries of such provisions included one Eve Pickerd of Canajoharie, who was given a "little spot of Land" for her family.[70]

The story of Eve Pickerd illustrates how the Mohawks' hospitable practice of giving selective land grants to favored individuals often backfired, leading to prolonged and heated land disputes and to a reduction in their land base. The problem was with European settlers like Conrad Gondermann, who turned his gift into a land patent legalized by the colonial government, and Eve Pickerd, who used her close ties to defraud the Indians of more land. Later Mohawk sachems lamented, "We hav[ing] given away & Sold the greatest part of our Lands to our Bretheren the White People (whom we could not refuse, on their declaring their poverty & want of them to us) . . . are now surrounded entirely by them." Theyanoguin pointed out that most frauds involved individuals who claimed more land than the Mohawks had originally agreed upon. The tavernkeeper Eve Pickerd, originally from Schenectady, was married to an English immigrant, Bartholomew. Their son Nicholas married Anna Barbara Weiser, the sister of the famed Pennsylvania interpreter Conrad Weiser. The latter's relations with the Mohawks may have provided Eve an entrance to the Mohawk world, for she later relocated to the south side of the

Mohawk River, near Canajoharie, and "understood the Indian language well" enough to become embroiled in land disputes. Under intense scrutiny from Sir William Johnson in 1760, Eve produced a deed for part of Canajoharie Flatts, signed only three days before by "the drunkenest Rascals in yᵉ whole Castle" but deceitfully predated a few months before to make it look authentic. The shady deed signing had begun with another slippery but festive event: Indians and colonists held a "Horse race on the Ice," and Eve's children afterward entertained the unsuspecting Mohawks at "their House wʰ is a Tavern and there made [them] drunk" and forced or cajoled them to sign the deed. When Johnson spoke to the Mohawks, they "declared they knew nothing of it." The Mohawks were galled by the "unbrotherlike behaviour" that their neighbors' actions betrayed. How could peace be maintained when such underhanded plans were being formulated? The Mohawks felt betrayed "by people whom they assisted, and nourished like Children when unable to help themselves." New York authorities finally ejected Pickerd in the 1760s, but the Mohawks did not insist on the removal of all European neighbors.[71]

The Canajoharie Mohawks were successful in creating a symbiotic relationship with a group of Swiss and German settlers that lasted for decades. These farmers became the Canajoharie Mohawks' tenants and "remained in peaceable possession" of agricultural lands without any legal title. As William Johnson affirmed in 1762, "some of them have lived on sᵈ. Land about twenty years, unmolested by any one." The Mohawks apparently initiated this arrangement themselves, in response to increasing numbers of European colonists: "They applied to the Settlers for rent, who accordingly have ever since paid it to them in Corn, or otherwise as they desire it, for wch they gave them regular [receipts] [*considering them as Landlords, & Original proprietaries*]." As the tenants' deposition attests, they initially applied to Philip Livingston for land, believing that he was the legitimate owner. But Livingston knew that his patent was fraudulent, for he feared that developing land would be the "occasion of a quarrell with the Indians."

The Canajoharie settlers, who believed that the Mohawks had undisputed rights to the land, reached a mutually satisfactory arrangement that lasted two decades: "The People liveing on Said Land, have for these Several years past, paid their Rent to the Indians uninterruptedly, and they say they will pay it to no other, until it appears to them clearly that the Indians have no right to it, & indeed I cant see they are to blame." Rents were typically paid with corn and wheat. These tenants were later at the center of a swirling controversy involving George Klock and other colonists, who in 1761 "bought the Pattent whereon the Switzers live, who paid Rent to ye Ind^s. and takes in the whole Canajoharie Castle their planting Lands &^{ca} w^h. causes a verry great uneasiness among ye whole."[72]

While some local colonists such as George Klock and Eve Pickerd betrayed the Mohawks' trust and generosity, not all colonists were the same. The Indians could rely upon other white neighbors to come to their defense in land disputes. Able to wield pen and paper, and knowledgeable about legal processes, the Mohawks' allies proved invaluable. For example, two settlers exposed the illegality of Eve Pickerd's deed by testifying that they were present at its signing: the Indians had never received any consideration, nor was there a justice of the peace present, as required by law. In 1758 the Schoharie headman Seth complained to Johnson of German farmers lately settling on the Mohawks' lands by virtue of an Albany landowner's claim. However, Johannes Lawyer and "many more Inhabitants of Schohary" told the Indians that "it was yet their property." Lawyer even "shewed them a Draught of Schohary & showed the Indians that the Patroon had no right or Title to said Lands." Settlers may have had pecuniary motives of their own, but some were clearly cognizant of justice for the Indians.[73]

The Mohawks frequently resisted what they saw as European intrusions and thus influenced the land-patenting process to their advantage. They intentionally sowed divisions between rival colonial claimants, obstructed suspicious surveyors roaming about, and warned off white trespassers from hunting and planting grounds. They were especially zealous about protecting their main hunting grounds of Kayaderosseras, north of the Mohawk Valley. Kayaderosseras was undeveloped for most of the eighteenth century, given the threat of French invasion and the patentees' fear that the Mohawks would go to war if they tried to develop lands obtained wholly by subterfuge. Small numbers of squatters and hunters, however, began trespassing in Kayaderosseras in the 1760s. Four white farmers who were "well acquainted with the Mohock Language" testified that Mohawks had complained to them "of the great injustice of the patent called Kay-aderosseras." Lewis Davis, a farmer "well acquainted with the said Indians for above forty years," learned of the Kayaderosseras con-troversy when "one Mr Nelson was about running some lines there, but was prevented by the Mohocks who fired upon his horses where upon he desisted." In 1765 the Mohawks "procured a Country School Master to write a few Lines" to squatters at Kayaderosseras warn-ing them off, though the squatters' response that they "would make good their possession" surely did not please the Indians. The Mo-hawks nevertheless demonstrated great patience toward the squatters. They repeatedly warned Cobus Maybe—Eve Pickerd's troublemak-ing grandson—to remove from Canajoharie Flatts before burning his house to the ground. They also repeatedly interfered with sur-veyors or succeeded in having trustworthy surveyors appointed. In 1736 Surveyor General Cadwallader Colden said that the Mohawks "would not suffer [him] to Survey . . . alledging in some cases that they had not sold the quantity of land describ'd in the Deeds of Pur-chase." Mohawks also watchfully followed surveyors to ensure that the boundaries were accurately marked. One "Indian Chain bearer" who went along with a surveying party in 1752 to vouch for accurate boundaries "found out how much [land] was stolen" by the provin-cial interpreter Arent Stevens. Theyanoguin brought this matter to the New York government's attention the following year.[74]

Another stratagem was to sow divisions between rival colonial claimants to delay settlement or to guarantee that settlers whom the Mohawks favored remained in place. This was one of the objects of Paulus's 1753 petition, mentioned earlier. In 1752 Teady Magin, an Oswego trader, associate of William Johnson, and agent of Philip Livingston, applied for a license to purchase 8,000 acres at Burnetsfield, adjoining the disputed Canajoharie patent. (Magin later applied for 30,000 acres in the same area, enlisting Governor Clinton's son as a partner.) Mohawk sachems petitioned the governor, "praying that the High Germans living near them may have a part of the Lands that Teady Magin is taking up, and that his Honour would grant a Lycense to the [Germans] to purchase four Miles in depth joyning to the [lands they] now live on." According to the petition, the land was meant for "our Christian brethren here [who] had the promise of it these many years." After receiving no response to their petition, however, the Mohawks took direct action. In October 1753 Hendrick and other Mohawk sachems refused to allow Deputy Surveyor Alexander Colden to survey Teady Magin's tract "on any other Terms then what is set forth in their Petition" on the German settlers' behalf. By refusing permission to survey, they obstructed Magin's attempt to patent the land on his terms. Instead they "marked owt on the Floor what Lands" they intended to give the Germans to live on.[75]

By 1753 the storms of settlement and land disputes had left the Mohawks angry and uneasy. The imperial pressure coming to bear on the Six Nations was evident in the speech of Sequaresere, or Red Head, an Onondaga sachem: "We don't know what you Christians French, and English together intend we are so hemm'd in by both, that we have hardly a Hunting place left, in a little while, if we find a Bear in a Tree, there will immediately Appear an Owner for the Land to Challenge the Property, and hinder us from killing it which is our livelyhood, we are so Perplexed, between both, that we hardly know what to say or to think." As William Johnson later pointed out, the deep-seated "dread of haveing their Lands snatched from them, as they call it, without the consent & knowledge of the whole, is, by what I can see, the greatest trouble, and uneasiness they labour under."[76]

This silent, invisible dread that welled in Mohawk hearts burst forth in New York City in 1753. Theyanoguin had come to renew the Covenant Chain at a conference with Governor Clinton, the council, and some assemblymen, but he found no chain left to renew or brighten, charging that it was "likely to be broken not from our Faults but yours." Before commencing his speech, he warned, "If you dont endeavour to redress our Grievances the rest of our Brethren the 5 Nations shall know of it and all Paths will be stopped." The Mohawks' chief concern was not just the colonists' "indifference and neglect," but the numerous instances of their duplicitous dealings over land. In the Mohawks' view the colonists' premeditated attempts to cheat them betrayed a callous disregard for the whole alliance. They had intended land cessions to strengthen the Anglo-Iroquois alliance, but "it seems now as if we had no Lands left for ourselves," as Theyanoguin complained. Theyanoquin then provided a list of persons against whom they had grievances, including Eve Pickerd, Arent Stevens, Conrad Gondermann, Philip Livingston, and others. What galled the Mohawks was that these colonists had acted with "stealth and Deceit" in taking up larger quantities of land than what had in good faith been agreed upon.[77]

Hendrick's next move completely stunned and silenced the assembled colonial officials. After the governor casually brushed aside the Mohawks' points and showed little inclination to assuage them, Hendrick simply stated, "When we came here to relate our Grievances about our Lands, we expected to have some thing done for us." He marveled that "all what we have desired to be done for our Good is not granted which makes our hearts ache very much." The colonial officials' hearts also ached after Theyanoguin announced, "As soon as we come home we will send up a Belt of Wampum to our Brothers the 5 Nations to acquaint them the Covenant Chain is broken between you and us." The Indians then left for their homes.[78]

The reality of Mohawk and Iroquois power was made evident in 1753, when Theyanoguin precipitously declared that the Covenant Chain was broken. Hendrick's action could not have been better timed. By the early 1750s the British believed that their influence among the Six Nations and other nearby nations had reached its nadir. French advances into the Ohio Country and consolidation of the French hold over the Champlain Valley had made the British appear weak and defenseless. The Lords of Trade fretted over the "fatal Consequences which must inevitably follow from the neglect" of the Six Nations, particularly New York's "dissatisfactory answers" to the Mohawks' land grievances. The Lords of Trade thus instructed the new governor of New York, Sir Danvers Osborne, to look into the Mohawks' complaints and renew the Covenant Chain upon his arrival. The fact that a single Mohawk sachem, acting on behalf of one Mohawk castle, could cause such trepidation and panic throughout British imperial circles provides tangible evidence of just how much influence the Six Nations commanded in British eyes.[79]

At the Albany Congress of 1754 commissioners from many British colonies met to discuss common defense measures and, in a separate conference, to renew the Covenant Chain with the Six Nations. This was in some small way a moment of justice for the Mohawks, as the New York government tried to resolve some (but not all) of the land disputes that Hendrick had outlined in 1753. For example, Philip Livingston's heirs "declared their Readiness to give up all Right" to the infamous Livingston Patent of 1731, which took in most of Canajoharie itself. Gov. James DeLancey also mediated a compromise between Teady Magin and the Mohawks and the German settlers whom they favored. Upon learning that one-third of Magin's patent, formerly held by Governor Clinton, now devolved upon him, DeLancey compromised the dispute by offering the Germans his parcel of land. Hendrick explained that "we thought the Coven Chain was broken, because we were neglected." "Taking a stick and throwing it behind his back," he warned that "you have thus thrown us behind your back, and disregarded us, whereas the French are a subtle and vigilant people." He turned his face toward the Commissioners of Indian Affairs and announced, "We think our request about Coll: Johnson [that he be reappointed to superintend their affairs], which Gov Clinton promised to carry to the King our Father is drowned in the sea. The fire here is burnt out." The Mohawks' open disdain for the Albany Commissioners meant that their "good trusty friend"—William Johnson—would emerge from the 1754 conference with heightened prestige.[80]

The Anglo-Iroquois Covenant Chain had been renewed and brightened, but its luster was diminished by news of French victories that nullified the Albany Congress's achievements. The British were terrified of the "evident design of the French to surround the British Colonies, to fortifie themselves on the back thereof, to take and keep possession of the heads of all the important Rivers, to draw over the Indians to their Interest." If the French Navy ever appeared in strength, James DeLancey warned, "there is the utmost danger that the whole continent will be subjected to [the French] Crown" and that "slavery" was a real possibility.[81]

By the early 1750s the Mohawk peoples in the St. Lawrence and Mohawk valleys, though closely aligned with their respective French and British allies, continued to maintain their autonomy and their kinship ties with each other. The southern Mohawks, however, were the more hard-pressed of the two groups. In the space of about fifty years British colonists had rapidly expanded in the midst of Mohawk communities: the Palatines who lived within view of the Schoharie settlements, William Johnson's Warrensbush settlement near Tiononderoge, and the colonial villages at German Flatts and Stone Arabia near Canajoharie. Despite the pressure Mohawks accommodated the New York colonists and lived a peaceful, if increasingly tense, coexistence. But the French and Indian War that began in America in 1754 would significantly change the character of human relationships in the Mohawk Valley.

Toward the close of the Albany Congress in July 1754 all eyes shifted toward the Ohio Valley. Over the past decade that strategic valley had been emerging as the next imperial battleground between Great Britain and France. Virginia and Pennsylvania traders, settlers, and soldiers had begun venturing into the Ohio Valley in the 1740s and early 1750s to assert British claims to the region. New France, however, had long claimed the valley and its important Ohio River link to the Mississippi River and Louisiana. In 1753 and 1754 French forces militarily occupied the valley, establishing four forts along the Allegheny River to contain British advances. After diplomatic warnings failed, the royal governor of Virginia, Robert Dinwiddie, sent militia forces to warn away the French from the Forks of the Ohio (modern Pittsburgh). The Commissioners, the colonists, and the Iroquois meeting at Albany began receiving reports of a French victory over a force of Virginia militia under Col. George Washington's command.[82] The British defeat at Fort Necessity in July 1754 elevated French prestige among the Delawares and Shawnees in the Ohio Country. But even greater catastrophe struck the following year when Gen. Edward Braddock's two regiments of British regulars advanced into the Ohio Country to expel the French in June and July of 1755. A predominantly Indian army of Delawares, Shawnees, and other western nations accompanied by French soldiers routed and nearly annihilated Braddock's army. In an isolated mountain valley in Pennsylvania called the Great Cove, frontier settlers braced for the worst, as rumors of impending French and Indian attacks spread across their now defenseless frontier.

3. Dispossessing the Indians

Proprietors, Squatters, and Natives in the Susquehanna Valley

On November 1, 1755, a war party of ninety Delawares, Mingoes, and Shawnees attacked the European settlements in an area of south-central Pennsylvania called the Great Cove Valley (so named because of the steep mountain ridgelines that hemmed in the bottomlands below). Squatters had been seeking safe harbor in the Great Cove as early as the 1730s, but the provincial government did not purchase the lands from the Six Nations until the Albany Congress of 1754, in a fraudulent arrangement that the Indian attackers refused to recognize. Columns of smoke rising up from the valley, the bloating corpses of settlers and livestock, and refugees fleeing eastward were visible signs of the warriors' successful offensive. "The Great Cove is destroyed," one European who surveyed the scene tersely remarked. The warriors also took several settlers captive, including Charles Stuart, his wife, and their two small children.[1] A short distance from the scene of their capture, the triumphant war party halted, and some English-speaking Indians informed Charles Stuart in excruciating detail of the execution that awaited him.[2] But Stuart lived to see another day, largely because the Delaware leader Shingas reminded his comrades that Stuart had "Lived on the Frontiers and that their People had Frequently Call[d] at [his] House in their Passing and Repassing between Aughwick & Fort Cumberland and had Always been supplied with Proviss[ions] and what they wanted Both for themselves & Creatures without Ever Chargeing them anything for it."[3]

Stuart's experience reveals far more than the familiar tropes of encroaching settlers, frontier violence, destructive Indian raids, and grueling captivities. It vividly illustrates the fact that the Seven Years' War in Pennsylvania, like King Philip's War in New England, occurred between neighbors.[4] Throughout the ridge and valley country of the Appalachians squatters had frequently encountered Indians at their homesteads. The Stuarts, for example, began squatting in the Great Cove sometime in the late 1740s, probably after King George's War (1744–48). Their homestead was near the Tuscarora Indian path, and as Shingas remembered, they had extended hospitality to untold numbers of Indian travelers over the years. Such apparently amicable encounters raise the question of how ordinary people on the frontier—squatters, farmers, hunters, and rural artisans—shaped their worlds at a local level. How did the Delawares, Shawnees, Iroquois, and other Natives—many of whom were relatively "new Settlers" themselves—interact with neighboring European families?[5] How did settlers like the Stuarts actually dispossess the Natives of their lands?

A close analysis of ordinary settlers' and Indians' face-to-face meetings reveals an important aspect of the colonial encounter that has largely escaped historians' attention: Pennsylvania colonists' and Indian frontier inhabitants' intense negotiations with each other over land use and possession before and after the upheaval of the Seven Years' War. In spite of their many conflicts and misunderstandings, they uneasily coexisted, communicated, and crafted mutually beneficial relationships through such routine encounters as the small-scale trading of corn, alcohol, tobacco, and wild game. Some squatters acknowledged Indians' occupancy and approached them for permission to remain on the land or tried to purchase it from them without the authorization of proprietary leaders. Natives in the Susquehanna Valley also enlisted European farmers as tenants in an adaptive response to colonial expansion, just as Iroquois settlers did in the Mohawk Valley. In the first half of the eighteenth century squatters paid Indians yearly rents in return for planting rights, perhaps hoping that these extralegal actions (along with their improvements) would bolster their claims when the government actually purchased the lands. Settlers cleverly exploited their local relationships with Indians to resist proprietary attempts to eject them. For many frontier Euroamericans negotiations and trading relationships with the Indians were simply means to landed ends—part of the process of achieving a decent living, building prosperous farms, and asserting patriarchal ideals. In comparison to the St. Lawrence and Mohawk valleys, the Susquehanna Valley saw ties between European and Indian communities that were attenuated and momentary.

The engine driving the struggle for frontier lands in Pennsylvania was a triangular contest among proprietary officials, squatters, and Indians.[6] But often the contest had even larger dimensions, as Pennsylvania, Maryland, Virginia, the Six Nations, Susquehanna Indians, Ohio Indians, squatters, land speculators, and British rulers all battled for control of the same valuable patches of ground. Imperial officials, proprietary agents, and land speculators fretted over the unofficial relationships that squatters and Indians were forging, for these ties threatened interests. Squatters did not pay for land or quitrents, and they blurred the Proprietors' visions of orderly settlement. Colonial officials regarded unlicensed settlers as "mutinous spirits" who "cut & mangle the best parts of the Country and make it impossible for the Proprietors to appropriate . . . good lands for their own use." Thomas Penn envisioned a dark future in which "we shall have the Country intirely over run with people, who will neither pay us our due nor submit to the Laws of the Country." Informal, local, and unofficial negotiations between ordinary settlers and Indians also threatened the government's claims to exclusive jurisdiction over diplomatic negotiations with Indians.[7] The need to extinguish Indian title made it essential that the Proprietors try to maintain rigid control over Indian diplomacy and the purchase of land by treaties. From William Penn to John Penn, Pennsylvania leaders issued stern warnings against private individuals buying land from Indians. Settlers who dared to negotiate with Indians were, from the government's perspective, "intermeddling" or "tampering" with Indians. Colonial magistrates occasionally prosecuted squatters for trespass, burned their cabins, and ejected them, but the expeditions failed to resolve the squatter problem permanently. Moreover, squatters used their local ties with Indians to defeat the 1748 expedition. Commoners' confrontations with colonial authorities are a useful reminder that Pennsylvania's frontier diplomats were hardly neutral "cultural brokers" negotiating between Indian and European worlds. Officials like Conrad Weiser, Richard Peters, and George Croghan were neither reacting to squatters running amok in the backcountry nor magnanimously protecting Indians' rights: they were aggressively negotiating their own economic interests, visions of orderly expansion, and definitions of property. The interpreter Conrad Weiser, whose work had helped to secure peace between the colony and neighboring Indians, also had "a real Love for the Prop[rietors] & cordially & industriously consults their Interest & will spare no pains to advance it," as Richard Peters approvingly noted.[8]

The relationships among the Proprietors, squatters, and Native Americans reveal the permeable nature of eighteenth-century frontiers and yield insights into larger processes that would transform these frontiers into more rigid borders after the Seven Years' War.[9] They shed light on the interplay of local events with imperial developments; on the entire spectrum of cultural contact (from routine encounters between ordinary peoples on the frontier to official diplomacy between colonial and Native leaders); and on the complicated, often indirect processes through which the Proprietors and ordinary settlers eventually displaced Native peoples.

Conflict between Pennsylvania settlers and Native inhabitants belies Pennsylvania's reputation as the "best poor man's country in the world," where one could easily attain landed independence and enjoy religious toleration. To be sure, Pennsylvania's strong ties with the Six Nations sustained an exceptional period of peaceful relations—"the Long Peace," which lasted from the 1680s to the 1750s. Pennsylvania, however, advanced the most expansive settlement frontier in all of British North America, and it could not forever hide from the consequences of its displacement of the Shawnees, Delawares, and multiethnic Susquehanna Indians. Between the 1600s and the 1750s tens of thousands of European settlers—primarily Scots-Irish and Germans but also Swedes, Dutch, English, Welsh, Scots, and Moravians—had immigrated to Pennsylvania. From 1720 to 1750 the colony's population nearly quadrupled because of immigration and natural increase. By the middle of the eighteenth century European settlements had pushed relentlessly into the area southeast of the Blue (or Kittatinny) Mountain, a long, imposing, nearly unbroken ridge running diagonally across Pennsylvania from southwest to northeast. For many Native peoples Blue Mountain was an important demarcation between their lands and Pennsylvania.[10]

Even as the territory occupied by Euroamericans expanded, a revival of old feudal institutions in eighteenth-century America was fast eclipsing Pennsylvania's shining reputation as the "best poor man's country." Between 1730 and 1745 colonial proprietors from New York to Pennsylvania to South Carolina began to revive old land claims that had not initially yielded wealth in the seventeenth century. Thomas Penn arrived in Philadelphia in 1732 after a decade-long legal imbroglio over William Penn's will (an English court finally ruled in favor of Hannah Penn's sons—Thomas, John, and Richard—in 1727). William Penn's sons asserted their proprietary rights to restore their shaky finances and initiated an aggressive policy of

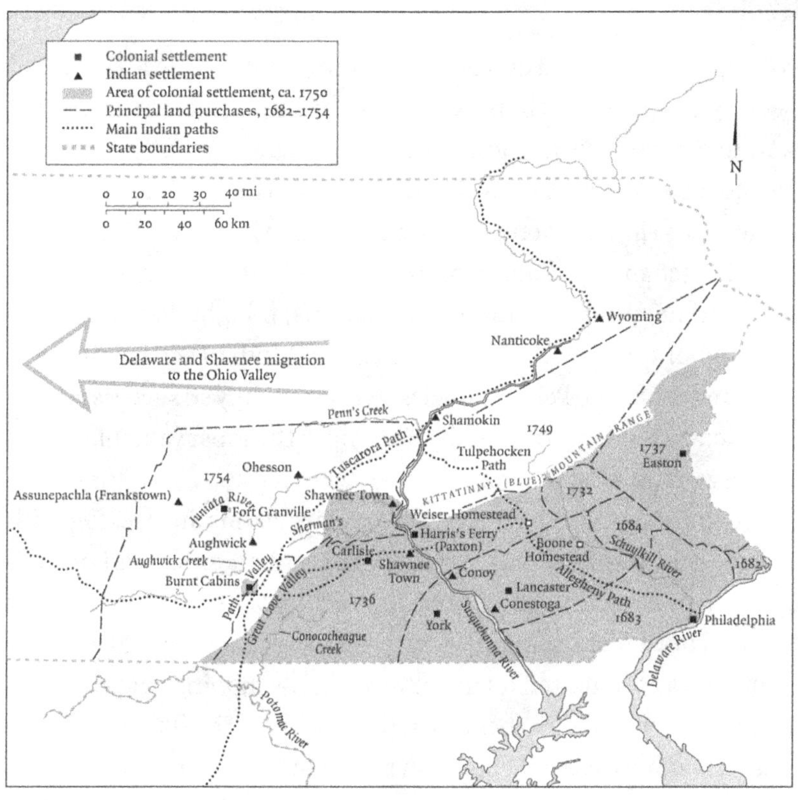

Map 2. Pennsylvania and Indian Communities in the Susquehanna Valley

raising land prices and quitrents, collecting quitrents in arrears, and ejecting trespassers. Thomas Penn, for example, raised the price of land to £15 10s. per 100 acres and the quitrent to a halfpenny sterling per acre. Penn's sons also colluded with the Six Nations to purchase lands that had actually been settled by Shawnees, Delawares, and Susquehanna Indians. Not coincidentally, the Pennsylvania government, negotiating with the Six Nations, bought disputed lands out from under resident Euroamerican and Indian settlers in 1749, 1754, and 1768. The Penns' policies were eventually so successful that proprietary lands were "rapidly becoming the most valuable single holding in the Western world."[11]

Squatters' decisions to ignore proprietary claims and treaties with the Iroquois were prompted in part by the Penns' aggressive land policies and by economic conditions in the colony. Because proprietary title had been uncertain for so long, many settlers ignored quitrent payments and squatted on unsurveyed lands, hoping that their improvements would give them legal possession in the future. One colonist remarked that the Scots-Irish had been "so much oppressed and harrassed under Landlords in our own Country" that they came to America "with the chief and principal view of being, in this foreign world, freed from such oppression."[12] Settlers resented the Penns' brand of "mercenary feudalism" because their claims "divorced the pursuit of profit from any larger sense of community welfare."[13] They also objected to the speculators' practice of buying land cheap and selling dear. One farmer believed that "the removing of them from the unpurchased Lands, was a Contrivance of the Gentlemen and Merchants of Philadelphia, that they might take Rights for their Improvements when a Purchase was made." In a period when economic inequality (in terms of land ownership and proportionate wealth) in Pennsylvania was growing, settlers bristled at tenancy, rising land prices, and rampant land speculation, which drove freeholds further out of reach.[14]

By the late 1740s, then, unsettled lands (especially in older settlements) were generally becoming scarce and too expensive for poor immigrants disembarking at Philadelphia. The Proprietors, meanwhile, saw their wealth dwindling away as many discontented settlers either migrated up the Great Valley into Maryland, Virginia, and the Carolinas or ventured right into Indian country to establish homesteads. The settlers' desire to live free and independent on the land was the most important motivation in their decision to establish themselves in places they found foreboding. Squatters' deeply held belief in the value of their labor and their improvements to the land also sustained their hope of eventually possessing legal title to their properties. Indeed, when unlicensed settlers had an opportunity to apply to the Proprietors for land on good terms in 1754 and 1768, they did so. There were no squatter rebellions in eighteenth-century Pennsylvania and no overt acts of collective resistance against the Proprietors over land policy. Like their accommodations with Natives, the squatters' defiance of the Proprietors was limited and practical.[15]

Squatter families began moving north up the Susquehanna Valley and west along the Juniata Valley as early as the 1730s. Many poorer Ulster emigrants in search of land headed directly to the frontiers after disembarking at Philadelphia. The life of Simon Girty Sr.—whose family appears on a list of squatters compiled by Richard Peters in 1750—illustrates one of the many paths to the frontier for European settlers and the nature of their personal relations with Natives. Girty, who emigrated from Ireland to Pennsylvania in 1735, soon entered into the fur trade and had contacts with the Delawares in the Ohio Country. He undoubtedly grew familiar with the geography of the central Appalachians through the course of his journeys west. After his marriage to an English woman named Mary Newton in the late 1730s, Girty moved to the Path Valley in the 1740s and continued his fur-trading activities without official license. The magistrates expelled the Girty family and burned their cabin to the ground in 1750. Later that year Girty, already in debt, was killed in a duel. Other squatters listed in Peters's report—like Jacob Pyatt (father and son) and Arthur Dunlap—were also Indian traders or had informal connections to the Indians. Such individuals may have occupied frontier land under the pretense of trading, or Natives may have given them permission to establish posts at convenient locations. Indians sometimes bestowed usufruct rights or "gifts" of land to favored individuals (such as William Johnson and Conrad Weiser). Trader George Croghan believed that the Juniata Valley squatters were "a Set of White Men that make their living by trading with the Indians." Many settlers—or "litle Traders," as the Provincial Council called them—"without any Authority from the Government take a few trifling Goods and go into the Woods to sell them." It is likely that some squatters saw a brief stint as traders as a means to a landed end.[16]

A "frontier exchange economy" prevailed for the first few years of the squatters' residence on the frontier. As recent historians have argued, European and Indian settlers' economic goals and organization were similar, at least temporarily. Dauntless European settlers had taken extraordinary risks in moving families, possessions, and livestock over mountains so steep that one traveler had "to hold by the tails of the horses & let them haul us up." "The road was dismal," wrote the Rev. David McClure in 1772, after his ascent of McAllister's Gap through Kittatinny Mountain: "It was a hollow through the mountain about six miles, rough, rocky & narrow." Once ensconced in the mountain valleys, the settlers must have been exceptionally cognizant of their isolation and vulnerability. There were no forts to flee to, no military forces that could mobilize quickly, no roads to facilitate trade with more settled parts. The area resembled an "open-country neighborhood"—a "landscape of dispersed family farms and rural kinship communities." Frontier folk typically lived in temporary log cabins in small, isolated clearings. They subsisted, in Indian fashion, through hunting and agriculture and depended on

Indian generosity. Peaceable dealings with the Natives were therefore a necessity on a frontier that remained an Indian world, albeit one increasingly threatened by French and English imperial rivalry.[17]

Native peoples thus faced a potent combination of zealous Proprietors, ecological changes, and the rapid expansion of colonial settlements, all of which dramatically heightened tensions in Pennsylvania's Indian relations. Many Susquehanna and Delaware Valley Natives had found little evidence of benevolence in the Penn family's actions. The colony's strong alliance with the Six Nations was partly designed to bring the Delawares, Shawnees, and multiethnic Susquehanna Indians (and their lands) under Iroquoia's preponderant power. The Proprietors presumed that "the Five Nations have an absolute Authority over all our Indians" and negotiated with the Iroquois for Delaware, Shawnee, and Susquehanna Indians' lands. Incidents like the Walking Purchase of 1737, the loss of key hunting and planting grounds, ecological changes, unprincipled European traders, and settlement expansion prompted most of the Delawares and Shawnees living in eastern Pennsylvania to migrate to the Ohio Valley in the 1720s. Yet Indians did not simply retire westward when colonial settlements first appeared. Some Delawares, Shawnees, and Conestogas remained *east* of the Appalachians, intending "to live & dye where they are now settled." Other Indian peoples weakened by warfare and disease—Tuscaroras, Nanticokes, Tutelos, and Conoys—migrated northward and settled in the Susquehanna and Juniata valleys in the early eighteenth century.[18]

Europeans moving onto frontier lands did not find vacant wilderness, but an Indian landscape. Multiethnic Indian towns, Indian farms, and Indian families still lined the Juniata and Susquehanna valleys; Native hunters sought game in the same bottomlands that squatters were using. As Conrad Weiser informed the Proprietors, the Juniata was the Indians' "only Hunting ground for dears, because further to the nord there was nothing but Spruce woods . . . and not a single dear could be found or killed there."[19] The Shawnee leader

Kishacoquillas presided over a village of twenty families at the town of Ohesson well into the 1740s; further upstream on the Juniata was the Delaware town Assunepachla, which contained twelve families. Another group of Tuscarora settlers continued to live in the Tuscarora or Path Valley until the 1760s and maintained ties with their kin living in Iroquoia and North Carolina. During his 1747 journey through the Conococheague Valley in Pennsylvania and Maryland, the Rev. Michael Schlatter noted that "in this neighborhood there are still many Indians, who are well disposed and very obliging, and are not disinclined toward Christians." While Schlatter may have misrepresented Indian attitudes, he rightly noted that Natives and newcomers shared the same valley. In fact, some of the new Indian immigrants had previous experience coexisting with white settlers: Nanticoke Indians in Maryland, who later moved northward, told a colonial official that "we live comfortably upon the Rents of our lands."[20]

European settlers had no qualms about living near Indian towns or amid the numerous individual Native families that remained in the area, and some Indians were willing to accommodate limited numbers of newcomers. In the late 1740s Arthur Buchanan and three Scots-Irish families approached the Shawnees at Ohesson and received permission to settle in the Juniata; Buchanan evidently developed a close relationship with the Shawnee leader Kishacoquillas. In 1755 George Armstrong applied for 300 acres of land along Tuscarora Creek, "opposite to the settlement of the Indians called Lakens" (perhaps a Tuscarora settlement). Turbut Francis described his tract as lying "about 3 miles below the place where an Indian lived whose name was Connosque." Even if Francis had no personal dealings with Connosque, it is significant that Indian peoples and Indian landmarks figured so prominently in his mental landscape. He added that the creek running through his tract was "almost opposite to ye place that Jno. Thompson a Delaware Indian formerly lived."[21]

Perhaps Thompson was among those Natives who were dissatisfied over colonial encroachments and removed to the Ohio Country.

Fig. 6. "Early Settlers and Their Visitors," from Frank Reid Diffenderfer, *The German Immigration into Pennsylvania* (1900). Courtesy of the Pennsylvania German Society.

Others relocated closer to Iroquoia. For example, a Nanticoke band that had once lived at the mouth of the Juniata River had established a new settlement in the Wyoming Valley by 1750. Tuscaroras who later settled among the Five Nations "brought forward the subject of the history [of] their land on the Juniata" to three Moravian missionaries in 1752. They told the Moravians that they were "deeply grieved to see white people living on their lands. They wished to have them removed." The Tuscaroras' desire to avoid "dissension in their land" explains why they chose relocation over confrontation. But many Native families could not forget the familiar faces of the farmer-hunters who displaced them. When Indian warriors attacked Pennsylvania's settlements in 1755–58, they frequently targeted the settlers who had earlier invaded their lands. As the Delaware leader Teedyuscung concluded, "The Land is the Cause of our Differences; that is, our being unhappily turned out of the land is the cause."[22]

The experience of the Brandywine Delawares, living closest to the most populated areas around Philadelphia, illustrates the larger processes of displacement and ecological change accompanying European colonization. Hannah Freeman, a Delaware woman who remained in the area, later testified that "the country becoming more settled the Indians were not allowed to Plant Corn any longer [probably because of unpenned livestock and an inability to relocate seasonally to new lands] [and] her father went to Shamokin and never returned." The Brandywines also complained to the government that colonists' dams and gristmills interfered with the seasonal movements of fish. In a 1729 letter to Lt. Gov. Patrick Gordon, the sachem Checochinican complained that "the Land has been unjustly Sold, whereby we are redused to great wants & hardships." He described his people as "greatly disquieted" and complained that new settlers would not even allow them to cut down trees for their cabins."[23]

Other illustrations of ecological change abound in the historical record. As early as 1718 the Commissioners of Property noted that the fields surrounding Conestoga had been fenced "to secure the Indians' Corn from the Horses, Cattle, and Hoggs of those new settlers." The colonists' unpenned livestock trampled Indian cornfields and, running free in the woods, competed with deer for mast. While Europeans saw the trees and livestock as their property, Natives did not give up the right to bark trees for shelter and treated the colonists' roaming livestock as, at best, fair game and, at worst, a source of "dissension" in the land. Gov. William Keith, for example, asked visiting Susquehanna Indians to "not suffer your young People with their Dogs & Arrows to Hunt & kill [the colonists'] Creatures." Declining numbers of deer and other game remained a thorny issue between European and Indian settlers. Like many Delawares, a small band of Conoy immigrants living on the Susquehanna River removed to Shamokin because of declining game. A Conoy sachem named Old Sack asked a resident of Lancaster to inform the governor that "the Lands all around them being settled by white People, their hunting is spoiled." Indicating that relations with the settlers themselves may have remained amicable, Old Sack noted that the Conoys "were under no fear or Apprehension of [the colonists] using them ill."[24]

Still, colonial and Native inhabitants were capable of communicating effectively and creating mutually beneficial relationships with one another. Indian and European settlers lived in a world of tremendous ambivalence: friendship, harmony, trust, understanding, and amity coexisted with antagonism, suspicion, fear, misunderstanding, and enmity. Backcountry settlers often bartered, worked, socialized, and hunted with Indians at their homesteads. The frontier inhabitants could readily communicate, probably with a blend of hand movements, Delaware jargon, and English-speaking Indian intermediaries. Meetings must have been an almost daily occurrence, especially for traders and settlers living along well-worn Indian paths. Native and colonial travelers found lodging and food at one another's cabins. The eighteenth-century journal of a Conestoga settler, Rhoda Barber, noted her family's relationships with the local Conestoga Indians, including her brother's Indian playmate, a Conestoga hoeing her father's field: "[The Indians] made brooms and baskets and exchang'd them for food and often spent the night by the kitchen fire of the farmers round about. They appeared much attach'd to the white people, calling their children after their favourite neighbours." A backcountry settler named Richard Thomas believed that he had entertained and provisioned "the king of the five nations" and other Iroquois; they took up "their Lodging near to his house, whear they Resided about fore days and nights" in July 1727. A Delaware sachem "in want of provisions received ten bushels of meal from a miller on Tulpehocken Creek" in 1730. The missionary David Brainerd complained of Indians who "upon Christmas days" in the 1740s went "to drink and revel among some of the white people." When the Seven Years' War began in 1755, John Bartram captured the sense of betrayal that many settlers felt in light of such past hospitality: Indians destroying "all before them with fire ball & tomahawk" in 1755 had once been "allmost dayly familiars at thair houses eat drank cursed & swore together were even intimate play mates."[25]

Underlying these peaceful interactions, then, was an undercurrent of disagreement. European and Indian settlers competed over crucial frontier resources such as hunting grounds, springs, and alluvial soils for agriculture. Different cultural beliefs about alcohol use, land use, property, and reciprocity made settler-Indian encounters prone to break down into fights, brawls, and, more infrequently, murders. Some squatters were openly hostile to "friendly" Indians. James Patterson, who began trespassing in the Juniata Valley in the early 1750s, carved out loopholes in his log cabin in case of attack. His Native neighbors frequently visited his homestead "on the friendly mission of bartering furs and venison for rum and tobacco." But Patterson—"Big Shot," according to legend—used these visits to gain much-needed food supplies and to intimidate the Indians. He allegedly fired at a target posted on a nearby tree so that visiting Natives could see what might happen to his human targets.[26]

Unofficial meetings between ordinary settlers and Indians, whether peaceful or violent, remained a potent issue for many British colonial governments. As squatters began moving up the Susquehanna and Juniata valleys in the 1730s, they established farms astride major Indian trade routes and north-south war paths that Iroquois parties used to attack their Catawba and Cherokee enemies in the Carolinas. Colonial officials in Pennsylvania, Maryland, Virginia, and the Carolinas feared that the intruders would provoke these war parties and precipitate open conflict. During the winter of 1742–43 this nightmare almost came true when a group of Virginia backcountry settlers inflicted eight casualties on an Iroquois war party. Only the deft diplomacy of Conrad Weiser and Shikellamy staved off war between the Six Nations and Virginia and Pennsylvania, but their efforts did not subdue the nagging fear that such incidents would reoccur.[27]

Squatter encounters with Indian war parties provided occasions for misunderstandings over the meanings of reciprocity and property. Villages in the Susquehanna Valley had long been centers of hospitality for traveling Indians, especially for Iroquois war parties. Well into the 1760s Iroquois warriors expected supplies from European and Indian settlers alike. They would camp near colonists' homesteads and either request or demand food and supplies from the inhabitants. Whether through fear or openhandedness, some squatters routinely gave provisions to the war parties. During a journey to Onondaga in 1737, for example, the provincial interpreter Conrad Weiser encountered a destitute and ragged Iroquois warrior north of Shamokin, a major Indian town in the upper Susquehanna Valley. The warrior's condition was due in part to a raid against southern Indians that had gone awry and in part to the fact that he "had squandered a part of his property drinking with the Irish" at a backcountry tavern or a settler's homestead. An Iroquois warrior imbibing with the Irish is only one indication that squatters frequently socialized with members of war parties. In 1749 George Croghan reported that an Iroquois warrior was killed while drinking with his comrades on the way home to Onondaga. The four Iroquois men stopped at a "Stillhouse," or tavern, along Aughwick Creek, and one of them died from knife wounds inflicted during a scuffle. Croghan promised to "Secure all ye white Men that was att ye plese till I find outt the Truth of ye affair." He believed that such meetings occurred frequently enough to justify a stiff fine on "all Stillers and Tavern keepers . . . for Making ye Indians Drunk, & Espesely warriers."[28]

Squatters routinely used such encounters to engage in unauthorized negotiations for rights to live on Indian land. The Oneida sachem Shikellamy complained of a German squatter named Frederick Star, who moved to the Juniata Valley in the early 1740s and claimed "a Right to the Land meerly because he gave a little Victuals to our Warriours, who stand very often in need of it." Shikellamy desired that Brother Onas (the Native name for the Pennsylvania governor) would "take the Dutchman by the Arm and . . . throw him over the big Mountains [Blue Mountain?] within your Borders." This incident reveals that squatters and Indians were not living isolated lives, but trading, communicating, and negotiating over land issues. It also suggests that some squatters, recognizing Indian possession of the land, attempted to "purchase" it for themselves. In July 1742, for example, a Six Nations delegation at Philadelphia complained of squatters along the Conococheague Creek who brazenly approached some Iroquois warriors "while they were hunting." According to the Iroquois speaker, the squatters "made some proposals about the Purchasing of Land from them," and the Iroquois warriors tentatively agreed to "receive five Duffield Strowds for two Plantations on the River Cohongoranta [the Potomac River]." The warriors, of course, had no authority to give away land and probably thought that the strouds were gifts, not down payments.[29]

Shikellamy's protest represented only one event in a decades-long series of complaints about trespassing in the Susquehanna and Juniata valleys. As the Six Nations' supervisor of the multiethnic Susquehanna Valley peoples, Shikellamy assumed responsibility for representing their grievances to Pennsylvania officials. The Susquehanna Indians, as Conrad Weiser once reported, were "very uneasy about the white peoples Setling beyond the Endless [i.e., Kittatinny] mountains on Joniady [i.e., Juniata], on Shermans Creek and Else where." In 1749 he reported that "above 30 familys are setled upon [their] land this spring, and dayly more goes to setle thereon; some have setled all most to the heads of Joniady River along the path that leads to Ohio." As Weiser's paraphrasing indicates, the Indians' conceptions of frontiers or borders usually involved mountains. Natives viewed the long ridge line of the Kittatinny (Blue) Mountain as a natural divide between their settlements and European settlements. Ogashtash, a Seneca sachem, once argued that "our Boundaries are so well known, & so remarkably distinguish'd by a range of high Mountains." The Iroquois also saw the Susquehanna Valley as an important buffer zone between Iroquoia and Pennsylvania. As their major north-south war paths ran through this zone, Iroquois diplomats and warriors saw firsthand the constant seepage of settlers into the fertile river valleys. As early as 1733 Shikellamy noted his belief that the sight of trader John Harris's farm on the Susquehanna would offend his brethren: "the Warriours of the Six Nations, when they pass that way, may take it ill to see a Settlement made on Lands which they have always desired to be kept from any persons settling on."[30]

Pennsylvania officials usually replied to Indian complaints with official proclamations warning settlers to remove and forbidding them to purchase lands from Indians. But proclamations alone could not effectively stem the rising tide of squatters, and the government finally took direct action in response to Indian complaints. The Proprietors' first major attempt to remove squatters by force occurred in August 1748 in the Tuscarora (or Path) Valley. Set between sharp and rugged mountain ridge lines, such pockets of alluvial soils attracted both Indian and European settlers. During Weiser's 1748 journey to the Ohio Country to conduct treaty negotiations with the Wyandots, the Proprietors ordered him to expel squatters who had taken up residence along the Allegheny path, the main trade route between the Ohio Country and the Susquehanna River. In what might appear at first glance a strange twist of events, Indians and squatters combined to resist these evictions. About fifty miles west of George Croghan's trading post on Aughwick Creek, Weiser and a few local magistrates encountered the Oneida sachem Scaroyady (or Monacatootha), along with a group of Indians who were probably Ohio Country Mingo Iroquois. The squatters had somehow received advanced warning of Weiser's mission and appealed to the Indians for help, lest they "be turned off by the Govern[t]." The Indians did not insist that all of the Europeans be unconditionally removed. Instead, they "desired that at least two familys, to wit, Abraham Shlechl and another, might stay, that they, the said Indians, had given them liberty, and that they thought it was in their power to give liberty to such as they [liked]."

Scaroyady made it clear to Weiser that "if any of the people now living there was turned off, no other Body should setle there, they [the Indians] being informed that as soon as the people were turned off others would be put on the land," who would presumably be more favored by the Government.[31]

Scaroyady's comment reveals that some Natives were willing to accommodate trustworthy European settlers who had demonstrated goodwill and hospitality. His insistence that "no other Body should settle there" reflects the Indians' unwillingness to negotiate with the Pennsylvania government for lands that would be permanently alienated and settled with outsiders unknown to them. Scaroyady clearly established friendly relations with a few squatter families and may have genuinely sympathized with their plight. Weiser reported that "the people used [the Indians] well on their coming by, and Informed them of the design" for their eviction. The squatters feared the authorities' actions, made their predicament clear to the Indians, and lobbied for permission to stay. Like their Indian counterparts, they mostly desired small plots of land for farming, whereas the Proprietors negotiated for hundreds of thousands of acres. Scaroyady may also have perceived the squatters' disaffection from the provincial government and perhaps hoped to forge informal alliances with them to forestall a more wholesale and irreversible invasion of his people's territory. He explicitly distinguished between two kinds of settlers: those the Indians liked and those "the Government [liked]."[32]

But why would Scaroyady and his companions allow certain families to stay, given the Susquehanna Indians' previous complaints? Why did the Oneida sachem believe that he had the authority to decide on this matter? Conrad Weiser himself was at a loss to explain it.[33] Scaroyady was probably granting these people usufruct rights of some kind for farming or hunting. Native peoples in the eighteenth-century Northeast, including Mohawks and Oneidas in Scaroyady's Iroquoian homeland, frequently invited displaced or indigent neighbors to live among them, as was the case with the Palatine immigrants at Schoharie. Algonquians and Iroquoians also bestowed usufruct rights upon favored individuals in instances of "associative adoption," a reflection of the strong hospitality ethic that bound Native societies together.[34] Such complicated and overlapping rights were a major source of controversy between the proprietary government and the Indians over whom it hoped to extend legal sovereignty.

The changing political and military balance of power in the Ohio Country may also have influenced Scaroyady's decision. Keenly aware of English and French designs on the Ohio Country, Scaroyady perhaps hoped to retain trustworthy settlers as sources of information on colonists' intentions. When disgruntled Shawnees and Delawares migrated to the Ohio Country in the 1720s, they soon cultivated closer ties to the French. Both Pennsylvania and the Six Nations fretted over their inability to control the independent-minded Ohio Indians. By the end of King George's War in 1748, however, some far-western Indian nations, such as the Wyandots and Miamis, were breaking ties with the French and entering into alliances with Pennsylvania— hence the warm reception that Conrad Weiser received when he traveled to Logstown in 1748. On that occasion Scaroyady urged Weiser to delay any action on illegal settlement until after the Logstown meeting, at which point the Six Nations would arbitrate the affair. Indians in the Juniata Valley were probably resentful of Iroquois decisions regarding their homes, but as client peoples, they were expected to defer to Iroquois leadership.[35]

The problem of illegal settlement was much on the minds of both Pennsylvanians and the Iroquois delegation represented by Canasatego at the Philadelphia treaty of 1749. As nearly three hundred Iroquois, Tutelos, Nanticokes, and Delawares made their way to Philadelphia in August, they were incensed at the number of squatters on the Susquehanna's eastern bank, beyond the Kittatinny Mountain. On their way down they also saw "Papers which were Interpreted to us to be Orders for these People to Remove." Canasatego delivered a stinging rebuke to Brother Onas: "Notwithstanding your Engagements," he told Governor Hamilton, "many People have settled on the East side of Sasquehanna, & though you may have done your Endeavours to remove them, yet we see these have been without Effect." Canasatego concluded that "white People are no more obedient to you than our young Indians are to us."[36]

Colonial negotiators had hoped that the Iroquois would take notice of the illegal settlements and bring their grievances before the governor. Conrad Weiser urged his employers to refrain from using open force against the squatters until after the conference, "when all proper means ought to be used to make a purchase from [the Six Nations] . . . for some part of that land between the Kititany or Endless mountains & alleghiny Hill." Weiser wanted the Proprietors to purchase "all the Lands on the Waters of Juniata." The canny provincial interpreter correctly anticipated that the Iroquois would be receptive to a land purchase as a way of defusing the growing crisis over colonial encroachment. Gov. James Hamilton went on the offensive and attempted to shift responsibility for the squatters' encroachments onto the Indians' shoulders and proposed a land purchase to diffuse the crisis. Playing Weiser's 1748 rebuff for all that it was worth, Hamilton asserted to Canasatego and his entourage, "We shall not find it difficult effectually to remove all these Intruders if some of your Indians do not give them Countenance." Hamilton warned that "such Lycenses [to remain on the land] must not be given, & that if we turn the People off you must not defend them nor invite them there again." According to Richard Peters, the provincial government, "as an Expedient to quiet them, proposed a purchase of [the Juniata lands] from the Indians." The Six Nations, however, wanted to preserve both the Juniata and the Wyoming valleys from European encroachment. Accordingly, the Iroquois delegates agreed to sell only a small parcel of land on the east side of the Susquehanna. On the Proprietors' maps, however, the purchase became a huge swath of land between the Susquehanna and Delaware rivers, which bordered the Wyoming Valley. Proprietary officials hoped that their 1749 purchase would lure illegal settlers away from the troubled Juniata Valley. Governor Hamilton assured the Indians that squatters would yield to his proclamations to remove, "especially as they may be provided with Land on the East side of Sasquehanna within the new Purchase."[37]

As the 1749 Philadelphia conference shows, squatting increasingly became the ideological pretext for colonial land purchases in the eighteenth century. Controlling the frontier and its white inhabitants was an important corollary of colonial Indian policy. Colonial elites espoused general views of social evolution in which frontier people living outside the law were degenerating into a state of savagery. They argued that lawless and violent settlers would inevitably spark a war with the Indians. Provincial secretary Richard Peters greatly feared that "the lower sort of People who are exceeding Loose & ungovernable from the mildness of the Constitution & pacifick principles of yᵉ Friends [Quakers] wou'd go over in spite of all measures & probably quarrel with the Indians." He worried that "the People over the Hills are combin'd against the Government, are putting in new Cropps & bid us Defiance." He correctly discerned that "it would be impossible to preserve the Peace of the Province" unless the Penns resolved the Indians' grievances over squatters. But the provincial secretary's solution did not include respect for Indian sovereignty: Pennsylvania officials believed that squatters had to be contained and peace preserved by purchasing disputed lands from the Six Nations by whatever means necessary. In 1749 Peters suggestively informed the sons of William Penn that "all mouths were full of the necessity of an Indian purchase" as the only way to forestall a frontier war. In fact, proprietary officials were even willing to fabricate a diplomatic crisis, anticipating that Natives would try to resolve it with a settlement culminating in a land purchase. Even as war loomed in 1754, Conrad Weiser urged the Proprietors that "our people Should be let loose to Set upon any part of the Indian lands upon giveing Sec[urity] for their Complying with the proprietary terms after pu[rchase;] the Indians would Come in and demand Consideration . . . and what Can they Say, the people of pensilvania are their [Breth]ren according too the treatys Subsisting." The only problem with Weiser's plan was that the squatters had never been on the Proprietors' leash.[38]

To contain the threat posed by squatters' and Indians' land negotiations, the Proprietors worked to completely dispossess both groups. Like Southern planters who saw the Appalachians as a possible haven for runaway slaves, the Proprietors considered the possibility that endemic squatting might result in total loss of control over frontier lands. Weiser and other officials feared that illegal settlement, if not "nipt in the bud," might lead to a more lasting accommodation between Indians and colonists. According to Richard Peters, Weiser apprehended "a worse Effect, that is that [squatters] will become tributary to the Indians & pay them yearly sums for their Lycense to be there." Settlers paying tribute to Indians would be a complete disaster for the Penns, who were deeply in debt at the time and dependent upon income derived from land sales and quitrents. Thomas Penn once observed that "the regulation of our Quit Rents is of the utmost consequence to us." And in 1749 Weiser claimed to know "positively" that squatters "are got into this way [paying tribute] on the East side of Sasquehanna' beyond the Hills & receive acknowledgements & are easy about those Lands." Weiser envisioned that Pennsylvania's rulers would "not only have all the abandon'd People of the Province to deal with but the Indians too & that they will mutually support each other & do a vast deal of Mischief." Peters agreed that "this consideration has alarm'd me more than any other."[39]

Colonial officials were never able to discover which Indians had granted rights to colonial farmers—an indication of just how peripheral officials might appear in local negotiations and how elusive and personal such arrangements could be. Thomas Penn believed that the culprits were Delawares at Shamokin, who should be "severely reprimanded"; Peters speculated that Shamokin Indians had given tracts of land to Thomas McKee, who had married a woman from Shamokin, but he reported as certain the fact that Shikellamy, Shamokin Indians, Delawares, and Nanticokes had all "levyd large Contributions" from neighboring colonial farmers. Years later an indebted Andrew Montour, emulating what seemed to be a customary practice, also tried to attract European tenants. Some Indians living around Shamokin, aware of the value Europeans placed on their lands, accepted white settlers as tenants as a way of making them dependent upon Native landlords. Aboriginal conceptions of land tenure had not remained frozen in some primordial state. As an Iroquois speaker asserted in 1742, "We know our Lands are now become more Valuable; the white People think we don't know their Value, but we are sensible that the Land is Everlasting." Periodic famines and food shortages also may have driven some Susquehanna Indians to negotiate land-tenure arrangements in return for payment-in-kind. Eighteenth-century land records confirm that such relationships existed. One squatter named William Smith, who settled below Shamokin in the 1740s, claimed that his improvements were made "with the consent of the Indians." The relationships that some settlers and Indians were forging in the backcountry clearly represented a threat to both the colony's land policy and the social order, as the authorities saw it.[40]

In May 1750 Pennsylvania authorities took forceful action to circumvent any challenges to their authority in a second and even more sweeping ejection of squatters from the Ridge and Valley country. Acting upon the complaints Canasatego had voiced in 1749, Governor Hamilton sent Peters and Weiser to eject squatters "on the Lands beyond *Kittochtinny* [i.e., Blue] Mountains, not purchased of the *Indians*." Peters, Weiser, and eight Cumberland County magistrates assembled at George Croghan's trading post at Aughwick. Five Shamokin Indians accompanied them as observers and "expressed great Satisfaction" with the authorities' mission.[41] Peters conducted this 1750 expedition as a quasi-military operation to suppress a "set of Scoun-drels." Thomas Penn later commended the "Hussar Spirit" that Pe-ters displayed during the expedition as "nothing less than which will do with these People." For the latter half of May 1750 Peters and the magistrates scoured the mountain valleys of the Juniata watershed, ejected squatters, arrested a few of them, and burned log cabins. Al-though Peters's report lists neither the total number of people living in each household nor the number of squatters in areas the expedi-tion left untouched, the number of households Peters counted still as-tounded the officials: five stood along the Juniata, eleven along Sher-man's Creek, eighteen lining the Path valley (including one occupied by "Abraham Slach," probably the "Abraham Schlechl" whom Sca-royady had defended two years earlier), four along Aughwick Creek, and twenty-three in the Great Cove.[42]

Most of the trespassers were submissive and "had nothing to say for themselves but craved Mercy." They readily confessed to Peters that they had "no Right or Authority" to settle there. The provincial secretary magnanimously informed the evictees that "they might go directly on any Part of the two Millions of Acres lately purchased of the Indians" in 1749 and offered large families the chance to live rent-free on his manors until they could support themselves. The mag-istrates entered the trespassers into recognizance for £100 and into bonds to the Proprietors for £500. Then, after "great deliberation," the authorities decided to burn the empty log cabins: "*Mr. Weiser* also giving it as his firm Opinion, that if all the Cabbins were left stand-ing, the [Shamokin] *Indians* would conceive such a contemptible Opin-ion of the Government, that they would come themselves in the Win-ter, murder the People, and set their Houses on Fire." After removing their personal belongings, the indebted squatters painfully watched their labor and improvements go up in smoke.[43]

Although historians often stereotype squatters as outlaws prone to violence, only one violent incident occurred during the expedition. On May 24 Peters, Weiser, and the magistrates approached Andrew

Lycon's log cabin, located along the Juniata. A band of unidentified Indians had "fixed their Tent on [Lycon's] Plantation" the night before—another indication of the frequent social interactions between Natives and squatters. Lycon resisted the authorities and "presented a loaded Gun to the Magistrates and the Sheriff, said, he would shoot the first Man that dared to come nigher." The squatter's militant outburst gave the Indians "great Offence," and members of Shikellamy's family who were present insisted that the authorities burn Lycon's cabin, "or they would burn it themselves." Lycon was "disarmed, convicted, and committed to the Custody of the Sheriff" and "carried to Gaol." Such actions effectively extended the province's legal system into the interior: although the unpurchased lands remained outside Pennsylvania's jurisdiction, squatters were bound to appear before Cumberland County courts.[44]

Lycon's vehement and violent defense of his claim was the exception to the rule. The vast majority of squatters sheepishly acquiesced to the magistrates and acknowledged that they were intruding on Indian lands. Some squatters who lived near the border—perhaps hoping to play off Maryland and Pennsylvania—petitioned Maryland officials for warrants for their lands, but nothing ever came of their proposal. Another group sent a petition to the governor of Pennsylvania that "prayed that his Honour might suffer them to remain there, till the [boundary] Line should be extended [westward], and the Purchase made of the Lands from the *Indians*." Peters even recorded some evictees as saying that "if the *Indians* were determined they should not stay there, it was better to go away directly." In both cases the squatters exhibited an awareness of their role in maintaining peaceful relations with the Natives. Perhaps they had realized for the first time the extent of the Indians' resentment of their intrusions.[45]

Thomas Penn may have commended Peters's "Hussar Spirit," but he was uninformed about the clandestine dealings of his province's frontier magistrates. Indian witnesses had long suspected that colonial officials acted in collusion with the settlers. In 1742 Iroquois speakers interrupted Gov. George Thomas's speech when Thomas pointed out that officials had removed illegal settlers. The Indians insisted that "these persons who were sent did not do their Duty; so far from removing the people, they made Surveys for themselves, and they are in League with the Trespassers." The Natives' accusation was equally applicable to the 1750 expedition. Some magistrates scouted for new lands while throwing off squatters. Benjamin Chambers and James Galbreath, Cumberland County justices involved in the expedition, both engrossed thousands of acres of land in places that they saw in 1750 (lands in the Path Valley, Conococheague, and the Great Cove). Moreover, Richard Peters apparently gave verbal guarantees to many settlers that they would have preemption rights when the government purchased the lands west of the Susquehanna, so long as they agreed to proprietary terms—a fact that went unmentioned in his official report.[46]

Peters's official report on the sixty-one squatter households he counted—incomplete as it is—provides a revealing glimpse of frontier families and their lifelong quests for land and security. Contrary to historians' image of transient and rootless wanderers, most of these squatters persisted on the frontier, despite proprietary expeditions and later Indian wars. Of the sixty-one heads of households ejected in 1750, at least forty-three remained in the area in the 1750s and the 1760s. In theory the Proprietors cringed at the idea of allowing squatters to claim land rights based upon their "illegal" improvements, but in the end most displaced squatters returned to their claims and gained some tenuous hold on the land—if they were not killed in the Seven Years' War or, like Charles Stuart, in Pontiac's War. Very few of these inhabitants ever succeeded in gaining letters patent, but many filed applications to have their lands surveyed (which conveyed a modicum of legal title) and issued *caveats* against one another. For example, the provincial secretary promised William White that he would have preemption rights, and White agreed to remove his family. In February 1755 White warranted 100 acres of land in territory purchased from the Six Nations (but not from its Indian inhabitants) at the Albany Conference of 1754. After White's death his widow, Mary, defended their claim before the Board of Property in the 1760s. In 1782 Mary still occupied their original tract in Cumberland County; she owned an additional 280 acres of land and a few livestock. In such ways colonial legal titles replaced the informal arrangements that had once existed between European and Indian farmers.[47]

Backcountry families like the Whites were generally small, "very poor" (as Weiser reported in 1748), and living in temporary log cabins in small clearings. Although Peters had reason to diminish the worth of the squatters' improvements, he described their cabins as "of no considerable Value; being such as the Country People erect in a Day or two, and only cost the Charge of an Entertainment." It would be a mistake, however, to think that squatters were dirt-poor outcasts. Descriptions of frontier farms in the *Pennsylvania Gazette* during the Seven Years' War reveal extensive improvements. One tract in Berks County had a house with a cellar, a barn, outbuildings, and corncribs in 1756. Settlers at the refurbished village of Burnt Cabins—a name that commemorated the Proprietors' actions—had erected a stone gristmill. Andrew Lycon's farm—he returned to his claim in the early 1750s—contained a sturdy "Dwelling house" and a "Hog house." Even more significant, Lycon had enough wealth to own two African American slaves—a father and son. Richard Peters confirmed that other squatters he encountered on the frontier also employed "servants." Lycon's quest for landed independence as a yeoman farmer was intricately interwoven with the colonists' destruction of Indians' landed independence and, in his case, the use of unfree labor.[48]

The results of squatters' lifelong quests for land and commitment to property rights suggest that their friendly relations with Indians may have been short-term accommodations in order to master the "wilderness" and then the Indians. One dispossessed settler named

Peter Falconer, in Richard Peters's words, believed that "it woud be impossible that Peace coud have Subsisted long" between colonists and Indians. Still, the squatters' relationships with the Proprietors, land speculators, and interpreters and colonial agents doubling as Indian diplomats who used treaties to extract land concessions were just as ambivalent. Proprietors' land purchases in 1749 and 1754, and again in 1768, preempted both Native and colonial inhabitants' claims. At Albany in 1754, for example, the Pennsylvania delegation, primarily Richard Peters and Conrad Weiser, orchestrated a deceitful land deal with the Iroquois for a vast area west of the Susquehanna River, extending clear to the Ohio Country. The Proprietor Thomas Penn ordered that the Juniata Valley be settled "as fast as possible" by settlers who could pay for land and quitrents. The Albany Purchase further alienated both the Six Nations and the Ohio Indians, and war loomed on the horizon. When the Seven Years' War began, Indian war parties from the Ohio Country specifically targeted settlements within the disputed Albany Purchase, including the Great Cove Valley, where Charles Stuart lived. A Delaware war party also targeted Andrew Lycon's homestead in 1756—another indication that Natives did not forget their dispossessors. Lycon was mortally wounded in combat after he and his neighbors killed a few of the warriors: "One of the Indians killed was Tom Hickman, and Tom Hayes, all Delawares, and well known in [those] Parts."[49]

Although the provincial expeditions failed to evict the squatters, their efforts fulfilled vital legal and diplomatic functions that paid off in the short term. First, the Pennsylvania government asserted jurisdiction over frontier lands whose boundaries were disputed with Maryland, Virginia, and Connecticut.[50] Second, Pennsylvania employed its strong ties to the Six Nations to graft Iroquois claims and influence onto Delawares', Shawnees', or Susquehanna Indians' lands. The colony's land purchases from the Six Nations extinguished Indian title, ended squatter occupancy, and secured the areas from colonial competitors, epitomizing what Dorothy Jones has called "colonialism by treaty," meaning the exploitation of intercultural diplomacy to acquire land.[51] Third, provincial expeditions against squatters extended the province's legal system into the interior. Fourth, removing illegal settlers cleared the way for surveyors, land speculators, and legal settlers who could pay for land and quitrents. The dispossession of Native peoples created repetitive crises for Indian and proprietary negotiators and helped to ensure a level of intercultural warfare that dwarfed the sporadic violence that had plagued tense relations between the squatters and Indians who had previously shared the land. Native dispossession was not simply a function of greater numbers of European farmers invading an Indian neighborhood. European and Indian farmers had coexisted in places like Juniata, negotiating land use, possession, and boundaries as they formed temporary alliances based on hospitable social and economic ties. European families occasionally lived as Indians' tenants, without provincial title to the land. Perceiving these relationships as a threat to their interests, the Proprietors aggressively asserted colonial jurisdiction over the disputed areas. Their egregious land purchases from the Six Nations resulted in further dispossession of resident Natives and fueled their desire for retribution.

Great issues hung in the balance in 1755, when the Ohio Indians and their French allies unleashed their military offensive against the Pennsylvania, Maryland, and Virginia frontiers. For decades Native sovereignty had been eroded by the repeated incursions of settlers, livestock, alcohol, traders, and imperialistic colonial officials. The Indian peoples who had inhabited what is now eastern Pennsylvania were often smaller, weakened, and less powerful than the Six Nations to the north. Unlike the Mohawks bordering New York, the diverse Algonquian and Iroquois peoples in the Susquehanna Valley did not have the benefit of five powerful confederate nations to their west that had to be respected by Pennsylvania. As a result Delawares and others were more susceptible to the aggressive combination of Pennsylvania Proprietors, settlers, and—ironically—their erstwhile

Six Nations guardians. But the Native peoples in eastern Pennsylvania did have the advantage of mobility. They were able to seek freedom by moving westward into the Ohio Valley, just as Kahnawake Mohawks exercised independence in moving seamlessly between Montreal and Albany in the Champlain Valley. Both of these groups inhabited regions in between the rival European empires. The Delawares in particular hoped that the Appalachians would prove a lasting barrier to European encroachments. Instead French and English traders, settlers, and armies brought their rivalry to the Ohio Valley. In 1755 the Ohio Indians struck back against the British colonies in a war for independence and sovereignty—a war that would unleash untold horrors and unanticipated consequences.

4. "The Storm Which Had Been So Long Gathering"

Pennsylvanians and Indians at War

Penn's (formerly Mahanoy) Creek, Pennsylvania, October 16, 1755

Marie Le Roy and Barbara Leininger and their families were among the thousands of Europeans who immigrated to Pennsylvania in the early eighteenth century. The Leiningers, from the city of Reutlingen in the Rhine-Neckar region, arrived in the colony in 1748; the Swiss Le Roy family emigrated in 1752. Both families quickly occupied lands in the "new purchase" of 1754, their new homes on the west side of the Susquehanna River located only a few miles from the Susquehanna Indian town at Shamokin. Settlers were willing to risk everything—lives and property—to obtain frontier land: a land rush in late 1754 and early 1755 occurred even as French soldiers occupied *la belle rivière*, George Washington was defeated at Fort Necessity, and isolated Indian attacks began on Virginia frontier settlements. In August 1755 Indian and French forces nearly annihilated Gen. Edward Braddock's army at the Monongahela, and rumors of impending Indian attacks reached a crescendo among ordinary settlers. Some European settlers and anglophile Indian refugees (from the Ohio and Susquehanna valleys) began fleeing eastward. Still, life seemed to go on in its familiar patterns for many families who remained on the frontier in the fall of 1755. Perhaps "Braddock's War" would not affect them after all.[1]

On October 16, 1755, the Le Roys' servant braved a chilly morning to round up stray cows. Mrs. Leininger was at a nearby gristmill, and Indians, who routinely came to trade for rum and tobacco, were coming to the Leininger house. Accustomed to the sight of passing Indian war parties, the hosts perhaps thought nothing of the visit—or did they interpret the warriors' requests as demands? The Delawares had painted their bodies black and their faces red and black, the distinct geometric patterns on their cheeks and the circles around their eyes making them look especially foreboding to the colonists. The eight familiar Delawares who came to the Mahanoy Creek settlement that morning—Keckenepaulin, Joseph and James Compass, Thomas Hickman, Kalasquay, Souchy, Machynego, and Katoochquay—were not intent on trading. The two English-speaking Delawares who had stopped at the Leiningers finished smoking their pipes and announced, "We are Alleghany Indians, your enemies. You must all die." In an instant they shot Barbara's father, Sebastian, and tomahawked her twenty-year-old brother, John Conrad. Barbara and her sister Regina were taken captive. A half a mile away, at the same moment, the other Delawares approached the Le Roy homestead, entered, and split Jean Jacques Le Roy's skull with two tomahawks. Marie's brother Jacob vainly struggled against the warriors, and he, his sister, and a small girl visiting were taken captive. The family stood powerless as the Delawares ransacked and fired their house and placed Jean Jacques's body in the flames, two tomahawks sticking in his skull, so that his lower torso was burned off. They watched the Delawares topple a neighbor, approaching on horseback, with a well-aimed shot and then scalp him. The warriors then led them to an encampment where other captives were located. Unsure of their fates and traumatized from the suddenness of death, they grieved as the warriors flaunted the scalps of their deceased kin and neighbors. The Delawares adopted Marie and Barbara, and they lived together for three and a half years, though the sisters never thought of their new lives as anything but "the yoke of the heaviest slavery." During their captivity they would later witness Pennsylvania soldiers, driven on by a spirit of vengeance, attack their captors' village at Kittanning.[2]

Marie's and Barbara's experiences poignantly reveal the human dimension of a much larger process: how the Seven Years' War fundamentally altered the ways that ordinary colonists and Indians on the Pennsylvania frontier interacted with and viewed one another. Like a fiery crucible the war refined Europeans' and Indians' elemental attitudes toward one another. Despite years of peaceful if uneasy coexistence, colonists and Indians now regarded each other with a deepening hatred—a feeling that Pontiac's War in 1763–64 and the American Revolution only exacerbated. The war set in motion a cycle of vengeful violence—raids and counterraids and a series of individual and mass murders—that endured on the Pennsylvania and Ohio frontiers for another forty years. For a long time Indians were the "savage" villains of frontier wars, and European settlers were the advance troops of civilization. More recently, historians have focused their attention on the rise of racialized "Indian hating" among the European settlers, often negatively portrayed as backcountry "thugs," as Francis Jennings quipped. But "substituting one savage folk for another," as James Merrell discerns, "risks pushing the interpretive pendulum too far in the other direction." Daniel Richter's work rightly suggests that Indians also hated, in an increasingly racialized way, the colonists who threatened their lands. What is lost in cardboard stereotypes is the profoundly human story of warfare in eighteenth-century America and the emotions it produced.[3]

The great irony is that both Indian and European settlers understood the war as a profound betrayal: the Seven Years' War was fought not between total strangers, but between former neighbors who had once shared, and contested, a common world in the Susquehanna and

Delaware valleys. Marie and Barbara's captors, for instance, brought along French and German Bibles as trophies so that unfortunate captives might "prepare for death."[4] Perhaps the most striking feature of the war—a feature that partly explains why colonists and Indians became so alienated from one another—was how violence was so interwoven with the common world that Indians and colonists had previously shared. This chapter explores the social and economic origins of colonist-Indian hatred and violence, the spectrum of their wartime encounters, and how Indians' and colonists' mutual hatred and retributive attacks transformed their relationships.

The character of human relationships among the peoples of Pennsylvania, New York, the Six Nations, and other nations dramatically shifted between 1754 and 1763, in part because of the structural differences between the two British colonies. New York did not suffer the repetitive incursions of French-Indian expeditions that Pennsylvania, Maryland, and Virginia did during the war. The Six Nations' powerful position vis à vis New France and the British colonies, and their wartime neutrality, shielded the New York frontier from most Franco-Indian offensives (the main exceptions being the attacks on Saratoga in 1745 and on German Flatts in 1757). New York maintained both a militia and numerous fortifications in the militarized Mohawk and Champlain valleys, which afforded the inhabitants a degree of protection. Not until the American Revolution did New York experience *la guerre sauvage* in all its destructiveness: Iroquois villagers and New York colonists living in the Mohawk Valley coexisted until the mid-1770s. By contrast, chronic colonist-Indian violence, born of the Seven Years' War, consistently threatened the peace on the Pennsylvania frontier after 1758.

The demilitarized and defenseless structure of Pennsylvania's settlement frontier predisposed its inhabitants to pursue violent retribution against all Indians without distinction. Because the Quaker leadership and population of the colony eschewed violence, there were no militiamen to mobilize, no large caches of arms and ammunition to distribute, few fortifications, and only a few Native communities on the colony's borders. The French-Canadians at Montreal, on the other hand, were shielded by the powerful Mohawk community of Kahnawake and strengthened by their military service. But ordinary people living on the Pennsylvania frontier had mainly encountered Iroquois warriors passing by in their attacks on their southern enemies, and virtually none of them had any experience fighting alongside Indian allies: the Pennsylvania and Six Nations alliance had worked all too well in displacing most Delawares, Shawnees, and Susquehanna Indians from the colonists' advance. As a result, most settlers looked suspiciously upon most Indians as enemies, rather than as potential allies. The method of settlement also created vulnerabilities for the colonial population. The landscape, as we have seen, was one of dispersed farms concentrated in valleys, separated by long mountain ridgelines from the more settled areas near Philadelphia. It would be difficult to imagine a colony more vulnerable to attack and more unprepared for war.[5]

And the Seven Years' War came. It began not in Europe, but in America, in the Ohio Valley. Between 1748 and 1754 imperial rivalry smoldered in the Ohio Valley. Ohio Indians, caught between the rival British and French empires, called the valley home and were determined to keep it free from European encroachment. As British traders moved into the valley in the 1740s, colonial diplomats and settlers alike turned their eyes toward the Ohio Valley, mesmerized by its bountiful resources. When former French-allied nations such as the Twightwees began trading and treating with the British, New France's network of alliances was threatened. Virginians and Pennsylvanians, particularly colonial land speculators and their enterprises, such as the Ohio Company of Virginia, claimed possession of the coveted valley. New France also asserted jurisdiction over the area, recognizing its strategic importance as a communications route to Illinois and Louisiana. Determined to drive out the English traders and to stop the defections of their Indian allies to the English, the French sent an expedition commanded by Céloron de Blainville to assert French sovereignty along *la belle rivière* (the Allegheny River) in 1749. The Ohio Natives, however, were indifferent to Blainville's bluster. Only when French troops militarily occupied the upper Ohio Valley in 1753 did they succeed in cowing the local Natives. Although Delawares, Shawnees, and Mingoes resented the French invasion, they saw the situation as a "marriage of convenience" in which they could deflect British advances, then divorce their French allies. The French established a chain of forts at Lake Erie and along *la belle rivière*—at Presque Isle, Le Boeuf, Venango, and Duquesne—that barred British expansion into the interior.[6]

Virginians—led by a brash young militia colonel named George Washington—precipitated open conflict in the Ohio Country in 1754. The previous year the French had rebuffed a summons written by Gov. Robert Dinwiddie and personally delivered by Washington, warning them to leave the Ohio Valley. Washington, his Virginia militia, and Ohio Iroquois allies returned to the Great Meadows in May 1754 and skirmished with a party of French soldiers on a diplomatic mission; the French commander, Ensign Joseph Coulon de Villiers de Jumonville, and nine French soldiers were killed in the melee. The conflict escalated when a combined French-Indian army forced the surrender of Washington's forces at his aptly named stockade, Fort Necessity. Believing that conflict could be contained in North America without a declaration of war, the British government dispatched two regiments under Maj. Gen. Edward Braddock to eject the French from British territory. But on July 9, 1755, a largely Indian army, accompanied by French-Canadian marines and militia, nearly annihilated Braddock's army along the Monongahela River. One of the warriors there that day was a Kahnawake Iroquois transplant to the Ohio Valley named Atiatonharongwen, also known as Louis Cook because of his Abenaki/African parentage. British military ineptitude also meant that the British had lost all hope of retaining any Ohio Indians as allies. The French, Ohio Indians, and far-western

Indians now enjoyed an open road from Monongahela to Maryland—courtesy of Braddock's army—over which to advance deep into the heart of the British colonies.[7]

From 1755 to 1758 Shawnees, Delawares, Mingoes, Ottawas, Potowatomis, Ohio Iroquois, Caughnawagas, and French-Canadian militia, and marines utterly devastated the British settlement frontiers in Virginia, Maryland, and Pennsylvania. They destroyed farms, crops, and livestock; captured small and large frontier forts; and killed over fifteen hundred frontier settlers and took about one thousand captive. Thousands of colonists became refugees, and large sections of the frontiers were nearly depopulated. At times it seemed that the British colonists were fighting themselves more than the French and Indians, because the colonies were beset by political turmoil and internal dissent. While the French had imperial motives for their attempts to paralyze two of the wealthiest British colonies, the Indians' war aims were to secure their sovereignty and landed independence. These divergent strategic aims were reflected in the two parties' choice of targets: joint French-Indian attacks typically targeted British forts or supply/communication routes; attacks undertaken solely by Indian warriors usually struck colonial settlements. When fighting ceased after the Treaty of Easton in 1758, the Ohio Indians had largely won the war, obtained concessions from the Pennsylvania government concerning prior land frauds, and pushed back colonial settlements. The pejorative terms that colonists and modern historians use to describe their expeditions—"raids" for "plunder" and "booty," "devastations" and "ravages"—detract from the highly organized and successful military campaign that Shawnees, Delawares, Mingoes, and other Natives mounted from 1755 to 1758. The Natives defeated every regular British military force sent against them and their French allies: George Washington's, Edward Braddock's, and James Grant's forces all suffered catastrophic defeats due primarily to Indians' military prowess.[8]

The Ohio Indians' preeminent goal was to drive back the frontier settlers who had betrayed the initial promise of good relations, but they also wanted to reach an accommodation with the British that would bring them territorial security. As historian Matthew Ward argues, "If the inhabitants of Virginia and Pennsylvania, the British colonies that had shown the most interest in settling the Ohio Valley, could be convinced that the cost of continuing a war to gain possession of the region was too high, the Ohio Indians could retain their homelands."[9] With the exception of the Quakers, however, most frontier colonists failed to ask why the Delawares, the Shawnees, and other Natives were fighting in the first place. Instead colonists were determined to avenge what they saw as "massacres" and "atrocities" carried out by "savages" whose actions they thought revealed the instincts of wild animals. Why did ordinary colonial farmers and Indian villagers pursue such extremely violent measures and come to possess an all-consuming hatred of each other? What were, as Charles Thomson inquired, the "causes of the alienation" of Indians and colonists from one another?[10]

In December 1754, on the eve of the conflict, Richard Peters strongly disagreed with the Assembly's suggestion that the trading post of George Croghan be relocated within the colonial settlement for better protection. Croghan's trading post at Aughwick had become a refuge for pro-British Iroquois settlers from the Ohio Valley. Reflecting on previous relations between Indians and settlers, Peters composed an epitaph to the failure of these peoples to coexist: "Will it not be impossible for Indians & White people to live together? Will there not be an eternal Intercourse of Rum and a perpetual Scene of quarrelling?" Although Peters was primarily concerned with keeping the Indians at Aughwick so that they might bear the brunt of any French and Indian attacks on the province, his rhetorical questions were partially prophetic. Not more than a year after Peters wrote this letter, the Ohio Indians and their French allies were waging *la guerre sauvage* on Pennsylvania.[11]

Historians have pursued various explanations for the coming of war. No matter how peaceful and amicable Indian-settler interactions were, the settlement frontier's expansion had been an unmitigated disaster for the Indian peoples living in the Susquehanna and Delaware watersheds. Most historians point to the onslaughts of disease, trade, dependency, liquor, and missionaries; European settlements also ecologically transformed a distinctly Indian landscape. Other historians point to murders and the diplomatic crises that they caused. James Merrell's recent work presents the frontier as official negotiators saw it: "one task, one trip, one crisis at a time."[12] Murders unquestionably alienated colonists and Indians from one another, but they were relatively uncommon before 1755 (the high-profile cases occurred in 1722, 1728, 1743, and 1744).

The mistreatment, misunderstanding, and violence that arose in the context of ordinary colonial farmers and Indians' everyday encounters better explain how and why the seeds of warfare and racial hatred exploded in the 1750s. And hatred in mid-eighteenth-century Pennsylvania was by no means a one-way street: Indians also espoused a growing hatred of the white colonists. While Ohio Valley Natives did not develop an identity as "red" Indians, their attitudes toward Europeans increasingly focused on their whiteness and on their destructiveness to Native societies.[13] Natives had long distinguished Europeans by their ethnic (e.g., German or Irish) and colonial (e.g., New York or Pennsylvania) backgrounds. But as early as 1743 a Shawnee warrior dismissed such distinctions between Virginians and Pennsylvanians: he exclaimed that "the white People are all of one Colour and as one Body, and in case of Warr would Assist one another." During the war many Indians' faces "were quite distorted with rage," as Moravian emissary Christian Frederick Post discovered in his 1758 journey to the Ohio Country. The Delaware warrior Captain Jacobs, escaped captive John Craig reported, said that the Indian allies "would carry on the War against them [the colonists] as long as there was a Man of them alive." John Cox reported that during his captivity "Delaware, Mohiccon, and Minsha" warriors' "whole Conversation was continually filled with Expressions of Vengeance against the English, and Resolutions to kill them, and lay waste their Country." Later, before his captors departed to attack the Scots-Irish at Paxton, "the Indians said they were resolved to kill all the white folks, except a few, with whom they would afterwards make a Peace." Post, a messenger of peace in 1758, recorded in his journal the unalloyed hatred of Euroamericans he experienced. The people of Sankonk, or Shingas's Old Town on the Beaver River, "received me in a very rough manner. They surrounded me with drawn knives in their hands . . . running up against me, with their breasts open, as if they wanted some pretence to kill me. I saw by their countenances they sought my death."[14]

The deep enmity that Post felt was also expressed on the bodies of war captives whom the Indians tortured and put to death. After Armstrong's raid on Kittanning in 1756, the Delawares tortured and killed Mrs. Alexander McCallister, the wife of a Tuscarora Valley squatter, perhaps to vent their frustrations over the defeat and to discourage other captives from running away. They tied her to a small sapling and burned her alive. If she was the same "English woman" that Marie Le Roy and Barbara Leininger saw at Kittanning, Mrs. McAllister suffered an extremely violent and painful death: "First, they scalped her; next, they laid burning splinters of wood, here and there, upon her body; and then they cut off her ears and fingers, forcing them into her mouth so that she had to swallow them. Amidst such torments, this woman lived from nine o'clock in the morning until toward sunset, when a French officer took compassion on her, and put her out of her misery. . . . When she was dead, the Indians chopped her in two, through the middle, and let her lie until the dogs came and devoured her." Hugh Gibson, who witnessed and wrote of the spectacle, recorded that the Delawares "shot her, and threw her remains upon the embers." The Indians' actions were not mindless expressions of racial "savagery," as colonists believed and as older historical narratives conveyed. Historians now like to use culture to explain Indian motivations and actions in war, but they should not dehumanize Indians by ignoring the rage expressed and the pain felt by captor and captive. If the account quoted above is accurate, what did the Indians think and feel as one cut Mrs. McAllister's scalp with a knife, one pierced her with burning wood, or another kindled the fire to burn her alive?[15]

Perhaps some thought of old injustices and slights received at the (now bound) hands of settlers like Mrs. McCallister. The Indian peoples at war had lived in a world in which contact with Euroamerican colonists was a frequent and often unpleasant occurrence. In the first half of the eighteenth century ordinary settlers were the object of Indian complaints both individually and collectively. In 1735 Tagotolessa ("Civility") came to Philadelphia to brighten the chain of friendship, bringing with him a gift of skins and a request that the Proprietors "assist in composing any Differences that may arise between the Irish people, who are come into these parts, and these Indians, who intend to live & dye where they are now settled." Earlier that year Tagotolessa had spoken in behalf of Whiwhinjac, a Conoy sachem, declaring that "they desire that the settlers & young men near Conestogoe & their other Towns, may be directed to treat them with Kindness and Respect like brethren." Individual settlers such as Samuel DuPuy, a well-to-do landowner living near the Delaware Water Gap, infuriated the Indians with their aggressive treatment. Count Zinzendorf recorded that "while at his house, [DuPuy] had some Indians arrested for robbing his orchard." In 1731 the Conestogas complained of a Marylander named Crissop, who was "very abusive to them when they pass that way." He was alleged to have beaten "one of their women who went to Get Apples from their own Trees." Given such treatment, many Indians familiar with the European settlements came to associate them with evil spirits and diseases such as smallpox.[16]

European observers often corroborated the Indians' grievances. Government officials and intermediaries such as Conrad Weiser and Shikellamy were, of course, more cognizant than most of the obstacles to peace. But observant colonists occasionally petitioned the government to reform the Indian trade, limit the flow of rum, and restrict settler/hunters from invading Indian hunting grounds. Rev. Henry Melchior Muhlenberg learned from Conrad Weiser that Natives' attitudes toward Europeans had come to focus on both their whiteness and their destructiveness: "Toward the white people as a whole [the Indians] have a deeply rooted prejudice and secret mistrust and . . . they say that the white people should have remained on their own ground and lived there and not have bothered them. We came over here with no other purpose than to take their land away from them, to decrease their catch of game, fish, and birds, to drive them farther into the wilderness, to make their life more difficult." James Smith, who was taken captive by the Delawares during the Seven Years' War, also gained a new perspective on colonial society. Mohawk émigrés from Kahnawake were among those who captured and adopted Smith in 1755. One Mohawk hunter, Tontileaugo, noted with approval that Smith gave venison to a Wyandot warrior who was visiting Muskingum. Tontileaugo asked Smith whether he had also given the Wyandot "sugar and bear's oil, to eat with his venison." When Smith replied that he had left the condiments in the canoe, Tontileaugo exploded: "You have behaved just like a Dutchman. Do you not know that when strangers come to our camp, we ought to give them the best that we have?" Smith noted that he called German settlers "Skoharehango, which took its derivation from a Dutch settlement called Skoharey [Schoharie NY]." Tontileaugo had apparently never received "the best" that the German settlers had. Perhaps his sharp contrast of the Indians' and the colonists' sense of hospitality was one of the reasons for his departure from Kahnawake to the Ohio Country.[17]

The Seven Years' War represented a *crise de la conscience* for many Pennsylvania colonists, but especially Quakers. Why had the Delawares and Shawnees gone to war against the people of William Penn? One of the first attempts to find the answer came in 1756. The Pennsylvania governor sent the Oneida sachem Scaroyady and the métis interpreter Andrew Montour to the upper Susquehanna Valley to discover from neutral Delawares and Shawnees what the Ohio Indians' grievances were. They brought back disconcerting news. The Indians spoke of fraudulent land deals, traders who had cheated them, and the settlers' inhospitable behavior:

> When we lived among them they behaved very ill to us; they used us like Dogs, they often saw us pinched with want and starving, and would take no Pity of us; sometimes we were in Liquor, a Fault which you are sensible we cannot always avoid, as we cannot govern ourselves when we come where Liquors are; when we were in this Condition they turned us out of their Houses and beat us, so that when we came to be sober we were not able to get up. . . . Now Uncles, can this be called Brotherly Treatment? don't you imagine such Usage must raise Ill Nature in our Hearts?[18]

During and after the Treaty of Easton in 1758 Quakers encouraged the Indians to express the lack of "Brotherly Treatment." The Quakers and other colonists recognized that the Proprietors' dealings with the Indians had been less than fair. They were determined to achieve a just peace with the Ohio Indians and return to the beneficent policies of William Penn. While the Indians most often mentioned being cheated out of their lands, unfair trade practices, alcohol, and corrupt traders, settlers were also singled out as a provocation for war and vengeance. Indeed, some of the Indians' first targets were settler communities at Tulpehocken, Penn's Creek, and newly settled areas west of the Susquehanna.[19]

Recent historians have typically analyzed Pennsylvania's wartime society in terms of its demonstrable violence and its racialized hatred of Indians. Euroamericans' mass killings of Indians at Kittanning (1756) and Conestoga (1763) seem to eerily foreshadow later massacres at Sand Creek and Wounded Knee in the 1800s. In many accounts historians present ordinary settlers as cardboard "Indian haters" committing atrocities upon Indians. Yet as James Merrell recently noted, "The sources of American anger, fear, and hatred that fueled these atrocities are unclear."[20] Preexisting cultural ideas, such as the civilization-savagery dualism, certainly shaped ordinary settlers' thinking about Natives, and travel literature such as Gottlieb Mittelberger's *Reise nach Pennsilvania* (1750) may have given European immigrants an inaccurate and vague impression of Indian society and culture.[21] But most European frontier settlers formed their attitudes toward Natives and their cultural practices through personal experiences with neighboring or traveling Indians. Misunderstandings over property and reciprocity in colonial farmers' meetings with Indians often led to violent clashes and predisposed colonists to despise the Indians once open warfare erupted in 1755.

Thousands of Natives—Iroquois, Delawares, Shawnees, Conestogas, and others—traveled to and from Philadelphia during the first half of the eighteenth century to brighten the "chain of friendship." The Indians habitually passed through innumerable colonial settlements along well-tramped routes like the Tulpehocken Path, which led southeast from the Indian town of Shamokin past Conrad Weiser's house to Philadelphia. Colonists routinely complained to the provincial government about the Native delegations. Farmers were most often angered by offenses such as Indians stealing or killing their livestock, helping themselves to tempting orchards and cornfields, and "barking" the farmers' trees for shelters. Settlers undoubtedly resented the Indians' damage to their property, especially when such offenses seemed chronic. Lt. Gov. James Hamilton warned an Iroquois delegation in 1749 to "Chastise your unruly Indians, . . . or they will certainly draw on them the resentment of the Country People, who will not be restrain'd from taking vengeance."[22]

But what was property? The traveling Indians had a far different perspective on their interactions with backcountry settlers. In a speech to the Provincial Council in 1737 a Six Nations spokesman analyzed two very different views of property and human kindness: "Amongst them there is never any victuals sold, the Indians give to each other freely what they can spare, but if they come among our People they can have none without paying." In reply Conrad Weiser responded that Europeans had "distinct Properties & Interests, & none of us can demand from another Victuals or any thing of the kind without payment." Having spent part of his youth among Mohawk Indians, Weiser had observed and benefited from Indian hospitality, as had many of his contemporaries. The naturalist John Bartram noted as much during his journey from Philadelphia to Onondaga: "[Indian] hospitality is agreeable to the honest simplicity of antient times and is so punctually adhered to, that not only what is already dressed is immediately set before a traveller, but the most pressing business is postponed to prepare the best they can get for him, keeping it as a maxim that he must always be hungry."[23] The Indians expected reciprocal treatment when they came to white settlements. As their diplomatic imagery showed, the Indians were in alliance with Pennsylvania *and* the inhabitants thereof. The Natives' personal interactions with Pennsylvania's inhabitants became crucial indicators of colonists' feelings of goodwill. In addition, many Six Nations embassies had traveled through Susquehanna Indian towns that had long been centers of hospitality. As a Moravian at Shamokin reported, "Many strange Indians pass through the town whom they must feed." The contrast between the hospitality of the Susquehanna towns and the tightfistedness in the Christians' settlements must have been starkly apparent to traveling Iroquois. Farmers jealously guarded "their" trees, orchards, livestock, and crops when Indians tried to "steal" them. The Indians' frustration was clearly evident in the Iroquois speaker's message.[24]

Yet the colonists' misunderstandings of the intricacies of Indian reciprocity customs should not be overemphasized. Neighborliness and reciprocal obligations were also important to European immigrant communities. At best, Indians and colonists were truly hospitable to one another and experienced their common humanity; at worst, disagreements emerged over different conceptions of property and monetary exchange. But colonists did not have a fundamental inability to understand Indian notions of hospitality or sharing the land. When Indians at the 1744 Lancaster Treaty stripped the bark off the walnut trees on John Musser's plantation, the colonist learned "not to oppose or differ with the *Indians* about it, since they wanted the Bark to form their Cabins," and instead petitioned the government for relief. Familiarity often bred understanding.[25]

The combination of alcohol and different hospitality ethics produced violent incidents during Indian-settler meetings along the roads to Philadelphia. When a traveling Iroquois "Struck a White man with his Hatchit and offered to Stick a Nother with his Knife," a gang of colonists returned and pummeled the offending Indian, beating him so badly that "he could hardly walk," Conrad Weiser reported. When an Iroquois warrior was murdered on the way to Philadelphia, the Iroquois delegation believed that the culprits were "the White People at whose House the Indians got Liquors" (Indians were the apparent murderers). Inebriated Natives occasionally staggered into colonial settlements demanding liquor; either they were "with some Difficulty perswaded to leave," or they injured themselves or the residents. The provincial officials were usually quick to attribute any crimes or depredations to "the rude behaviour of the Indians." They in fact contributed to the rash of violent incidents by consistently giving "provisions and Gallons of Rum" to the Indians at the conclusion of every conference to "Comfort them upon the Road." Many colonists, such as the indentured servant William Moraley, thus encountered drunken Indians "in the Fields in their Return, . . . so drunk, that they could not stir from the Place." By acquiescing to Indians' requests for rum on the return journey, provincial rulers failed to appreciate how a trickle of rum could turn into a freshet of hostility and violence.[26]

The written record provides only partial evidence for the frequency of sexual relations or sexual assaults committed by Europeans and Indians in their routine interactions. If a 1707 conference at Conestoga provides any indication, colonists and traders living close to Indian settlements may have had clandestine or open relationships with Native men and women. No sooner had the lieutenant governor and his party returned from Conestoga than the Assembly sent a remonstrance to William Penn in England, complaining that "some who went with thy Lieutenant to *Conestogoe* to visit the *Indians*, committed vile Abominations with them." In 1750 an inebriated Nanticoke Indian named John Toby assaulted Anna Hunter, an eight-year-old girl living at Paxton. When the neighboring Indian came to the house, Elizabeth Hunter sent Anna to "fetch some Tin Vessels from the Suggars trees, Least the Indian might steal them." As she did her chores, John Toby "took hold of her and said that he must lie with her, and so throwed her down and Lifted up her Cloaths, and hurted her very much." Elizabeth testified before Conrad Weiser that "the Child was very much Hurt her Private Parts Being Bloody and Swelled." Weiser succeeded in committing John Toby to the Lancaster jail, but such incidents—certainly in the minds of the Paxton settlers—lingered and fueled their animosity toward their Indian neighbors. Indian peoples were probably victims of sexual assault, but being unfamiliar with colonial legal procedures, they lacked easy access to courts and magistrates that would have recorded their complaints.[27]

Given the record of misunderstanding, harsh words, mistrust, and violence, it is remarkable that in the fall of 1755 many frontier Pennsylvanians did not expect the Indians to attack them. Conrad Weiser reported shortly after the Penn's Creek attack in October 1755,

"The people down here seem to be senseless and say the Indians will never come this side [east] of Sasquehannah River." Daniel Dulany, the provincial secretary of Maryland, remarked that "the people of Pennsylvania flattered themselves that the Indians would spare them, and indeed, it was so late before they attacked, that many people suspected they had some grounds to rely upon the mercy of the savages." While many farmers had fled the frontiers in terror after Washington's defeat and news of Indian attacks in 1754–55, many had stayed on their farms, harvesting crops as fall approached. Mary Jemison, taken captive by a Franco-Shawnee war party from the Pennsylvania frontier in 1755, remembered that her father "knew that the enemy was at no great distance from us" in early 1755. But he decided to remain for another season, believing that when British and colonial forces advanced into the Ohio Country, "the enemy would be conquered and compelled to agree to a treaty of peace."[28]

When Indian attacks began in earnest along the Pennsylvania frontier in late 1755, they terrified, angered, and above all perplexed the European settlers. Historian Paul A. W. Wallace correctly notes that "what gave the invasion a peculiar pall of horror was that local Indians—inoffensive, shiftless, companionable fellows as they had seemed a few weeks before—were among the scalping parties." The naturalist John Bartram, who had explored many of the Pennsylvania frontier settlements before the war, captured a crucial source of the settlers' astonishment: "most of yᵉ Indians which are so cruel are such as was allmost dayly familiar at thair houses eate drank & swore together was even intimate playmates." Bartram had personally observed the frequent interactions between neighboring Indians and colonists in the decades before the war. He correctly discerned the settlers' feelings of betrayal—emotions that rationalized and aroused their desire for harsh retribution against Natives. But what most colonists did not know was that Indians' emotions were also torn over the outbreak of war. A Seneca named Silver Heels remembered that in

1755 and again in 1763 he "saw with deep Concern many of my white friends kill'd and taken, before they got the least notice."[29]

The colonists' bellicosity toward Indians was partly a product of the atmosphere of peace that had existed between Indians and Europeans in the years before the war. What particularly galled the colonists was how Indian warriors used their intimate knowledge of the English language and of the settlements to their advantage. Accounts of frontier raids and most captivity narratives prominently reported the presence of both English- and German-speaking Indians who had at one time been familiar faces among the settlers. In one of many examples Conrad Weiser reported an Indian attack on a group of isolated settlers in which the Indians "spoke to them in High Dutch, *be still we wont hurt you*." Thomas Baird, who was captured in 1758 and escaped soon after, "knew several of the Indians, particularly James Lingonoa, Indian Isaac's brother, who with others, enquired after several People in Marsh Creek." Even as late as 1758, when Frederick Post and a delegation of Indians passed by Chambers' Fort on the Forbes Road, "some of the *Irish* people, knowing some of the *Indians*, in a rash manner exclaimed against them, and we had some difficulty to get them off clear."[30]

After the Paxton Boys' slayings of the Conestoga Indians during Pontiac's War in 1763, the Rev. John Elder remarked that "the storm which had been so long gathering, has at length exploded." This brewing storm was fueled by the settlers' deep desire for retribution and what they saw as self-defense. One incident involving Conrad Weiser and a frontier mob reveals just how powerful the settlers' desire for vengeance was. "Friendly" Indians—diplomats, messengers, and refugee communities—were the most accessible targets. The settlers asked Weiser, "Why must we be killed by the Indians and we not kill them? why are our Hands so tied?" The mob was "so enraged against all the Indians, & would kill them without Distinction. . . . They cried out that so much for an Indian Scalp they would have (be they Friends or Enemies) from the Governor." When Weiser refused to consider this, "some [began] to Curse the Governor; some the Assembly; called me a Traitor of the Country who held with the Indians and must have known this Murder before hand." The mob progressed from lashing out against the Indians, the governor, and then the Assembly, to Weiser himself. Conrad readily emphasized, "I was in danger of being shot to death."[31]

The style of the war also explains why the colonists almost instantaneously turned against Indian enemies and friends alike in 1755. *La guerre sauvage* was a total war waged not against professional armies and elaborate fortifications, but against individual families, their lands and houses, and their identities. Colonists expected wars to be fought between armies; they had never experienced a war where they were the strategic targets. From the Leiningers' and the Le Roys' points of view, the Indians' war methods were completely arbitrary and brutal, their attacks terrifying in their invisibility. Indian warriors slipped through the cordon of frontier forts that the government had erected from 1755 to 1757 and destroyed settlements at will. War parties struck like lightning and disappeared just as quickly. Able to live off the land and elude colonial pursuers with ease, Indian warriors—painted red and black—were literally demonized by the colonists.[32]

Indian warriors struck at the jugular of backcountry society: its close family, kin, and ethnic ties that formed the basis of community. The landscape also ceased to be Euroamerican. In a matter of hours Indians could annihilate entire settlements, killing, capturing, and driving away their residents and laying waste the countryside. Almost the entire population of Penn's Creek was killed or captured in October 1755. The ninety-three settlers who remained in the Great Cove in 1755 suffered forty-seven killed or captured. Families and extended kin networks were destroyed and separated. One representative account noted, "One of the men had a Daughter with him that is yet missing, and the other man had a Wife & three or four children that are also missing." Colonists' great pains to record in letters and newspapers every settler killed or captured reflected a deeper concern about the destruction of families. Stories that seemed particularly tragic—such as those of living infants found in their dead mothers' arms—became the stuff of legend.[33]

The settlers' petitions to the government reveal a profound sense of frustration over their losses and an utter helplessness, which partly explains their desire for retribution against any Indian. Matthew Smith, one of the Paxton Boys, defended his actions in 1763 by pointing out that "no man, unless he were living at that time in Paxton, could have an idea of the sufferings and anxieties of the people." The settlers' perception of the random and arbitrary Indian attacks, along with the provincial government's initially pusillanimous response, only exacerbated their feeling of helplessness and their desire for vengeance. Dispersed homestead locations made defense doubly difficult and led to further feelings of isolation: petitioners from Lancaster knew that they were "in a great degree separate and disunited by means of our distant abodes." Even worse, rumors of impending French-Indian attacks took on a life of their own, leaving panic, hysteria, and a sense of deathly foreboding in their wake. Feelings of helplessness and uncertainty account for much of the settlers' need to blame someone—anyone. As William Trent put it, "How long will those in power by their Quarrels suffer us to be massacred?" Another petitioner was even more blunt: "So many Mouths crying for Vengeance against their Murderers, and yelling at the negligence & insensibility of the Administration, to whose inactivity there are so many sacrifices." The governor, the Assembly, Quakers, Roman Catholics, Moravians, and British Army commanders were all objects of the colonists' wrath.[34]

Indian attacks also struck a nerve among patriarchal frontier families and wounded the male colonists' sense of manhood. Often powerless to stop the Indian warriors, patriarchs were reduced to despair over the "broken remains of our dismembered families." Watching as their families were dismembered, literally and metaphorically, was more than some men could bear. A husband or father might see his wife's or children's bloody scalps stretched over hoops by their captors. Mary Jemison's father, Thomas, was reduced to depression over his powerlessness to stop a French-Indian war party from capturing his entire family in 1758. Mary remembered that he was "so much overcome with his situation—so much exhausted by anxiety and grief, that silent despair seemed fastened upon his countenance, and he could not be prevailed upon to refresh his sinking nature" by eating food. By contrast, Mary's mother, Jane, was a bulwark of strength to the entire family during their hard march back to Indian country. Thomas had "lost all his ambition in the beginning of our trouble, and continued apparently lost to every care—absorbed in melancholy." Frontier families who survived attacks often became refugees, instantly reduced to abject poverty. Once-prosperous farms, which represented bastions of independence to frontiersmen and decades of toil, were now reduced to ashes. The male colonists' inability to provide for their displaced families also wounded them. As one pamphlet emphasized, "Hundreds were reduced from plentiful & independent circumstances to a State of Beggary & Dispair." Another writer queried, "Shall the *free born Subjects of Britain*, the brave and industrious Sons of *Pennsylvania*, be left naked and defenceless—abandon'd to Misery and Want"?[35]

Most British officers would have scoffed at the "brave and industrious Sons" of Pennsylvania. Frontier patriarchs were expected, on the one hand, to ably defend their households and female dependents. But the British Army also expected that hardy American frontiersmen would take "manly steps for defence" by effectively serving as rangers. Given the Indians' all-out war against the settlement frontier, however, frontiersmen could not rightly abandon their destitute or refugee families to join the military. Consequently, British officers and colonial officials cast aspersions on the frontiersmen's manhood, accusing them of cowardice and lukewarm support while others fought their battles. During Pontiac's War, when Pennsylvania settlers' again felt the Indians' wrath, Col. Henry Bouquet disparaged the colony's young men when they did not enlist in great numbers for his 1764 expedition. He wrote to John Harris that even the men who enlisted went as "Pack Horse Drivers and Waggoners, Employ for which a Coward is as fit as a brave man." Particularly denouncing the Paxton Boys as cowards, Bouquet asked, "Will not People say that they have found it easier to kill Indians in a Goal [gaol], than to fight them fairly in the Woods?" He contrasted Virginia's "brave militia," who provided volunteers without pay, to Pennsylvania's cowardly frontiersmen, who "chuse to remain peaceably at home & leave it to others to fight [their battles with] wild Indians." In a world where men were "judged from their Actions and not from Words," British officers deemed the Pennsylvania frontiersmen's deeds lacking from 1755 to 1763. Frontier inhabitants responded in turn by contrasting their steadfastness in the face of extreme cruelty with the complacency of colonists closer to Philadelphia. They characterized themselves as industrious "worthy bleeding Men" who staunchly absorbed Indian attacks while effeminate Quakers refused to bear arms.[36]

Ordinary colonists also pointed out the extreme emotional effects of Indian warriors' common practice of mutilating corpses. Stories of Indian "atrocities" that appeared in colonial newspapers and in later history books cannot be taken prima facie, since their authors may have exaggerated, distorted, or fabricated the accounts to highlight Indian "savagery." Whether accurate or enhanced, stories and rumors of atrocities ran like wildfire through the backcountry; they at once demoralized the colonists and fueled their desire for retribution. Natives' frequent mutilations of their victims' bodies expressed their anger against the settlers, their desire for revenge, and their feelings of loss; they symbolized Indians' "rejection of a common world," as historian Richard White argues. But they also had an intended psychological effect on the captives who survived and on colonial soldiers in pursuit, for they discouraged attempts to escape or pursue. The secretary of the Council noted that colonists' discoveries of mutilated bodies had "struck so great a Pannick and Damp upon the Spirits of the people" that effective defense was inhibited.[37]

Native mutilation of European bodies was doubly disconcerting because it was frequently directed at male and female reproductive organs. As historian Richard White suggests, "fighters who had rejected peace with its images of a common mother and common births now assailed actual mothers." Sheriff John Potter of Cumberland County reported "that a Woman of 93 years of age was found lying killed with her Breast tore off and a stake run thro' her Body." When unidentified Indians attacked and burned the Hoeth homestead in the Lehigh Valley, Frederick Hoeth's wife "ran out thro' the Flames, and being very much burnt she ran into the Water and their dyed. The Indians cut her belly open, and used her otherwise inhumanly." As provincial soldiers near Fort Augusta discovered, male colonists' bodies were not exempt from warriors' pointed disfigurements: one scouting party "found a man lying in the Road shott & scalped his Scull split open & one of the provincial Tomahawks sticking in his private parts." The psychological effects of the Indians' actions on the minds of colonial frontiersmen were apparent in a 1758 article in the *Pennsylvania Gazette*. It recounted a skirmish along the Savage River involving nine Indians and two scouts, John Lane and Griffith Johnson. The two scouts fired on the Indian camp and felled one Indian; "Lane ran in to scalp his Man, but whilst he was stooping down, his backside being towards them, the Indians fired at him." One bullet "went through the Crotch of his Breeches, making two holes in them, and he very narrowly escaped being served as bad as, or worse than, being scalped: for the bullet just grazed—and took off a small Piece of the Skin." But Lane survived this bizarre circumcision and finished scalping the Indian warrior.[38]

Though initially demoralized when they came upon the mangled remains of fellow colonists, frontier people were soon filled with inveterate rage. When frontier crowds marched on Philadelphia in 1755, they insisted that they would "rather be hanged than to be butchered by the Indians." They carried mutilated bodies to illustrate their plight and demanded that the government wage an equally total war against Native populations, beginning with the institution of scalp bounties "for every Indian which they kill." Pennsylvania did institute scalp bounties in April 1756, an act that encouraged animosity toward "friendly" Indians and contradicted the government's expressed desire to protect them. The measure was virtually useless militarily. As James Axtell notes, "English scalping parties could at best make the Indians think twice before leaving their own villages; at worst they could find themselves outfoxed by superior woodsmen and wind up as hairy hoops in those same villages." In practice scalp bounties resulted in brutal slayings of both friend and enemy Indians. In the spring of 1756 one group of New Jersey settlers plotted not only to murder a family of peaceful Indians living in New Jersey but to take them to Pennsylvania to collect the bounties. At Philadelphia they "were to swear that they were enemy Indians, and they had killed them in the Province of Pennsylvania." They killed the mother of the Indian family, named Kate. Scalping enabled the colonists to respond in kind to Indian warriors' mutilations of colonists. When Paxton settlers captured an enemy Indian in 1755, they "brought him down to Carson's House, where they examining him, The Indian begged his Life and promised to tell all what he knew." Conrad Weiser was not shocked when "they shott him in the midst of them, scalped him and threw his Body into the River." When no live Natives could be found, colonists might desecrate Indian remains, as the scout John Lane did after escaping from his Indian captors. Although stripped naked and tied up, Lane escaped and found the remains of an Indian who had recently been buried. He dug him up, "took away his Match coat, and scalped him with a broken Stone." Nearly four years of frontier bloodshed made ordinary people despise and fear Indians. Their hatred, ironically, threatened to compromise the provincial government's 1757 peace negotiations with Teedyuscung and the eastern Delawares. When a woman stormed into town hysterically reporting that "her Husband and some of her Children were killed by the Indians," rumors careered through the town. Conrad Weiser sent out scouts to verify the woman's claims, which turned out to be false. But the rumor and the resulting panic threatened to turn into an ugly confrontation with Easton's inhabitants: "The cry of the common People, of which the Town was full, was very great against the Indians, & the poor People [the Indians] did not know what to do or what to say, finding all the People so enraged and using such Language. . . . . The common People behave very ill, in asking the Indians unbecoming Questions, and using ill Language." In the end Weiser "had the good Luck to pacify both the white People and the Indians."[39]

Visible and invisible reminders of Indian "brutality" kept the memory of frontier wars painfully alive in the colonists' minds for decades. The Pennsylvania countryside was littered with the human wreckage of *la guerre sauvage*. Ann Mary Duck recounted her family's travails to the Board of Property in her 1760 caveat against another settler's survey. The stresses of becoming a refugee during "the first Indian War" may have cost her husband, Henry, his sanity: he was "depriv'd of his Senses and continues to wander through the Country like an Ideot." One young girl, who had been "shot in the Neck, and through the Mouth, and scalped," apparently survived her wounds. In 1766 a widow named Cunigunda Jager sent a petition to the Pennsylvania Assembly seeking relief for her daughter Catherine, a former captive: "that her said Daughter is a very unhappy young Woman, having spent in the Indian Idleness those Days of her Life in which Girls learn to qualify themselves for Business, and is now unable to support herself; and what makes her Misfortune still greater, she has a Child by an Indian Man, for which other young Women look upon her with Contempt and Derision." So great was the community's disdain for Indians that they viewed Catherine Jager as polluted and defiled by what had probably been a consensual relationship with an Indian man. Another young woman, Catherine Smith, a blind, ten-year-old orphan in 1760, had been taken captive in 1756 and freed by Armstrong's men during the Kittanning raid. Along with other war orphans, the Pennsylvania Hospital sheltered and cared for Catherine for three or more years. The managers requested that Catherine, "a child of a mild and tractable temper, and promising genius," should be "placed in some family of reputation, in order that she may be instructed in such business as may be proper for her circumstances." Many colonists' deep wounds—physical and mental—festered with hatred of Indians for decades.[40]

Kittanning, Delaware Indian Town, Allegheny River, September 1756

On Monday, August 30, 1756, seven companies of the Pennsylvania Regiment's Second Battalion, under Col. John Armstrong, left Fort Shirley in the Juniata Valley on a daring mission to attack and destroy the Delaware Indian town at Kittanning. They advanced westward along the Frankstown Path, guided by former English traders who had traveled that route in more peaceful times. The colonial soldiers were determined to exact vengeance for the raids that Pennsylvanians had suffered in 1755 and 1756. For Armstrong the mission was even more personal: his brother, Edward, had died during an unsuccessful defense of Fort Granville against a joint French-Indian force in early 1756. Armstrong's men arrived near Kittanning on the night of September 7, 1756. Amazingly, they had made the trek across the mountains undetected. Guided toward the town by the moonlight and by the sounds of Delawares' dancing and drums, Armstrong deployed his men and prepared for battle at dawn. The colonists, through the reports of escaped captives, had learned that Kittanning was a major staging point for French-Indian expeditions against the Pennsylvania frontier. Destroying Kittanning and its Indian population would alleviate the frontier attacks, perhaps redeem British captives, and restore the soldiers' wounded sense of manhood. Kittanning was also home to two of the most prominent and feared Delaware war leaders: Shingas and Tewea (Captain Jacobs).[41]

Tewea knew the colonists better than most Delawares. He had lived along the Juniata, had been involved in land negotiations with a settler named Arthur Buchanan, and had received the name "Captain Jacobs" because of his resemblance to a German farmer in nearby Cumberland County. Like other Delawares, Tewea had joined in the exodus to the Ohio Country to escape British colonists' intrusions on Delaware lands; he had settled at the town of Kittanning, along the Allegheny River, in the 1750s. When war began on the frontier, he was clearly determined to take revenge upon the Pennsylvanians. In 1755–56 he and Shingas led war parties against colonists in the 1754 "New Purchase" lands. In August 1756 Tewea was largely responsible for leading a joint French-Indian force against Fort Granville and capturing it; this fort was located near his old home on the Juniata. Colonists, who particularly feared Captain Jacobs, had placed a $700 bounty on his head.[42]

The combat at Kittanning on the morning of September 8, 1756, demonstrated the depth of Delawares' and British colonists' mutual hatred after just a year of open warfare. It also suggests that the colonial soldiers' retributions against Indians were interwoven with a desire to prove their manhood. "With great eagerness," the provincials advanced in columns of companies through the cornfields surrounding the town. Dogs barked warnings, and the Delawares stirred from their log cabins and longhouses; one provincial soldier remembered that at "the first house we came to, the Indian came out, and held his hand, as shading the light from his eyes, looking towards us, until there was five guns fired at him; he then ran and with a loud voice, called *shewanick*, which signifies whitemen." Native warriors from the town and across the river rallied; sounded their war cries; and sent away most of the women, children, and elderly. Captain Jacobs was alleged to have cried out, "The White Men were at last come, they would have Scalps enough." Soon Armstrong's men found themselves at a great disadvantage, as superior Indian marksmanship "seldom mist of wounding or killing" the attackers. Firing from loopholes in their log houses, the Delawares inflicted heavy casualties on the provincials. Armstrong and his officers retaliated by burning the Delawares' homes and calling on them to surrender. But this was a fight to the death between mortal enemies. One warrior, perhaps Captain Jacobs, called out that "he was a Man and would not be a Prisoner; Upon which he was told in Indian he would be burnt." The warrior answered that he did not care and mocked the novice provincials for carelessly exposing themselves to musket fire.[43]

Delaware warriors, some with their wives reloading their weapons, continued to fight despite the smoke, flames, and searing heat. One warrior "to show his Manhood began to sing" his battle or death song. Captain Jacobs, according to one captive's report, killed fourteen or more soldiers as his wife reloaded his muskets; he replied to the soldiers' threats to burn his house that "they might if they would; he could eat fire." He continued to fight until seven musket balls felled him. Provincials indiscriminately gunned down men, women, and children who attempted to flee the flames. Most Delawares probably died from asphyxiation or exploding ammunition. As Armstrong reported, "With the Roof of Cap[t]. Jacob's House, when the Powder blew up, was thrown the Leg & Thigh of an Indian, with a child of three or four years old, to such a height that they appeared as Nothing, & fell in the adjacent Corn Field."[44]

Having heard a rumor of the arrival of French troops from Duquesne, Armstrong's forces withdrew and were able to elude the Delawares harassing them. In one last skirmish the provincials shouted at the Delawares, "Your town is on fire, you dogs you." In the burning town the Natives counted anywhere from seven to seventy casualties. Armstrong's forces lost roughly seventeen killed, thirteen wounded, and nineteen missing; they also freed eleven captives. Despite Armstrong's heavy losses, the destruction of Kittanning lifted the flagging morale of the Pennsylvania colonists. It provided the frontier settlements a

Fig. 7. Kittanning Destroyed medal (front and back), 1756. Courtesy of Winterthur Museum.

brief respite from Indian attacks and enabled certain Delaware factions to seek peace with the English.[45]

The Pennsylvanians' attack on Kittanning was a defining moment in the colony's history and a symbol of the Seven Years' War's transforming effect on colonist-Indian relations. It established both a precedent and a paradigm for the future mass killing of Indians and the total destruction of Indian towns and crops.[46] Soldiers came away with twelve Indian scalps and trophies of their campaign, including "Jacobs Horn and Pouch, and many Belts of Wampum." British colonists hailed the Kittanning raid as "the greatest Blow the Indians have received since the War began" and clamored for more Armstrongs, more Kittannings, more dead Indians. A ballad that appeared in the *Pennsylvania Gazette*, "Ode to the Inhabitants of Pennsylvania," reflected changing sentiments about Native peoples on the colony's borders, particularly the need to destroy Indians to prove white manhood:

> Rouze, rouze at once, and boldly chase
> From their deep Haunts the savage Race,
>   Till they confess you Men.
> Let other Armstrongs grace the Field;
> Let other Slaves before them yield,
>   And tremble round Du Quesne.[47]

The deeper significance of the Kittanning raid was evident in a commemorative medal that the Pennsylvania government had struck for Armstrong and his officers, for "signal Proofs of Courage and personal Bravery." This medal, cut by clockmaker Edward Duffield and struck by silversmith Joseph Richardson, was the "first medal (created from dies) awarded by any of the North American colonies or cities to their soldiers for war services." The reverse of the medal shows a provincial officer (probably Armstrong) directing his troops, with the Delawares' log cabins (with window frames and panes) burning in the background. Off to the side a soldier fells an Indian with his musket; the Indian falls lifeless into the Allegheny River. In a colony that had mythologized its founder's friendly relations with the Delawares, leaders and peoples now celebrated the killing of Delaware men, women, and children. John Armstrong later wrote, "Those Barbarians don't in Action stand so close together as the Philistines of Old who fell by the hands of the Hebrew hero." "May the same Almighty hand," he hoped, "fight against those modern Infidels, and extend his Sons heritage from Sea to Sea & from Pole to Pole." This was a significant step toward a destiny that became manifest to Americans in the nineteenth century.[48]

5. "Our Neighbourhood with the Settlers"

Iroquois and German Communities in the Seven Years' War

German Flatts, Oneida Country, November 1757

In late November 1757 nearly two hundred Mississaugas and Canadian Iroquois and around sixty-five French marines and militia embarked on an expedition against New York. Their target was a prosperous settlement called German Flatts in the upper Mohawk Valley. Settled by Oneidas for centuries and the Palatines since the 1720s, it was the far-western periphery of European settlements when the Seven Years' War began in 1755. German Flatts was defended by a substantial star-shaped redoubt called Fort Herkimer and a series of five blockhouses in the surrounding settlements. The French commander, François-Marie Picoté de Belêtre, and the principal Indian war leaders orchestrated a stunningly successful attack that began around 3:00 a.m. on the morning of November 12, 1757. Bypassing Fort Herkimer and its garrison, the French-Indian party fell instead on the Palatine settlement and the five blockhouses. The surprised German settlers' defense was futile. Around 40 settlers were killed, around 150 others taken captive back to New France; many houses, barns, and outbuildings were burned to ashes. German Flatts, once

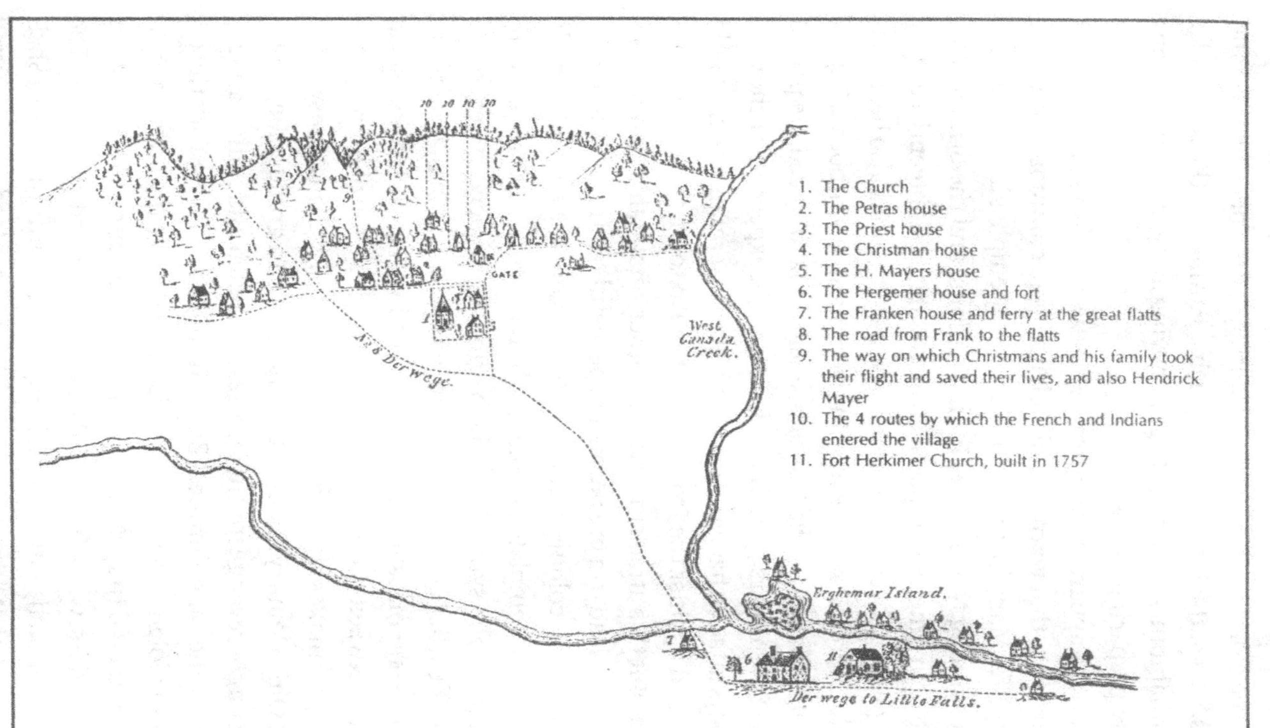

Fig. 8. "Palatines' Village Destroyed by Canadian French and Indians, Nov. 12th, 1757," from Jeptha Simms, *The Frontiersmen of New York* (1882).

a "valuable settlement" with "as fertile a piece of ground as any perhaps in the world," was now a smoldering "scene of desolation and distress." The attack "had Struck such a Pannick in the remainder of the Inhabitants" that they began moving away their possessions and were preparing to flee.[1]

This attack apparently confirms what we have long known about early America: that warfare and violence were common features of everyday life. Many historians today rightly emphasize the chronic conflicts among New France, Indian nations, and the British colonies in North America. Imperial struggles in the eighteenth century defined peoples' lives in fundamental ways. There has also been considerable interest among historians in explaining Europeans' racial hatred of Indians and the frontier violence that plagued the period after the Seven Years' War. Indeed, one might expect, after the German Flatts attack, that gangs of bloodthirsty German settlers would have turned against the Iroquois, as the Paxton Boys did in Pennsylvania. But this attack in 1757, and other small raids against New York, did not lead to a breakdown in peaceful relations between the Mohawk Valley colonists and Indians. Colonial New York simply does not fit the template established by recent historians—the contention that 1763 symbolized the beginning of racial violence and the end of earlier coexistence. There were no Paxton Massacres in New York—no mass murders of Indians by New York colonists at any time between the Seven Years' War and the Revolution. As the next chapter makes clear, the war and its aftermath in Pennsylvania and the Ohio Country involved bloodletting on a grand scale, as colonists sought revenge for the successful French and Indian attacks on their homes and families. But in Iroquoia and New York the incidence of violence, let alone murder, was drastically lower (see table 1). From 1756 to 1774 six Indians were murdered by colonists or British soldiers, while five colonists were murdered by Indians. The New York Council, with minimal exaggeration, informed Lord Shelburne in 1766 that "they knew of no Violence or Murders committed on any Indians bordering on this Government." In fact, everyday relations on the New York–Iroquois frontier remained similar to those in New France, where, as we have seen, relations between French-Canadian and Canadian Iroquois had incredible depth.[2] This chapter explains why the Seven Years' War strained, but did not completely sever, the cultural accommodation that prevailed in the New York–Iroquoian borderlands. The New York colonists and the Indians had forged strong personal, family, economic, religious, social, and military ties that bound their communities together beyond the stresses of two wars. The following discussion reveals, for the first time, just how interwoven European and Indian communities were on the Mohawk frontier. At no other place in Britain's mainland colonies were Indians and settlers as culturally integrated and economically interdependent as along the New York–Iroquoian borderlands.

The attack on German Flatts tells a different story, more complex and more ambivalent. This is a story about possibilities—and limitations—as a European and an Indian community tried to peacefully coexist and create mutually beneficial relationships even as a global war threatened their security. We have seen that once the war began, Pennsylvania's frontier settlers quickly lashed out against peaceful refugee and mission Indians who remained in the colony. But in the Mohawk Valley German Flatts settlers and their Oneida neighbors pursued a different course: they sought a common trading and military alliance that would secure neutrality for both parties during the Seven Years' War. What made it possible for the Palatines and the Oneidas to envision such a framework for peace? Our point of entrance into this story can be found on one seemingly unremarkable page of a Schenectady merchant's account book, where an entry dated October 1756 reads: "To M.ʳ George Weaver of the German Flats 38000 Black Wampon @ 32/6 £61„15„0." Other entries reveal that Weaver also received shipments of wampum in 1755 and 1757. Who was George Weaver, and what was he doing with 38,000 beads of black wampum—enough to make dozens of wampum belts (the

Table 1. Murders and Assaults: New York Colonists and Iroquois, 1756–70

Date	Victim(s)	Assailant(s)	Location	Circumstances	Documentary references
1756 (Aug.)	Jerry or Showonidous (Tuscarora)	British soldiers of the 44th Regiment	Schenectady	Jerry's severed head was found "Stuck upon Pole in Camp"; murderers never brought to justice	SWJP, 2:529, 533–34; 9:495, 499–500, 825; 13:89; DRCHNY, 7:177–78; Way, "Cutting Edge of Culture," 123–48
1757 (Apr.)	Adam Rypenberger	Two Indians, possibly Shawnees, Munsees, or Mahicans from "Jenango" (Venango?)	Near Albany(?)	Rypenberger killed	SWJP, 9:686; NYCMSS, 83:71 (a–b)
1757 (Apr.)	Mahican Indian	Royal American soldier	On the road from Schenectady to Albany	Mahican wounded	SWJP, 2:686
1757 (May)	Unidentified Indian(s) killed, one wounded	Unknown	Albany	Manuscript partially destroyed in 1911 New York State Capitol fire	SWJP, 2:713
1757 (July)	Two Oneidas, possibly one Mohawk	Thomas Smith, Albany trader	German Flatts	Unclear: "The two Indians were helpless & dead drunk when he knocked their brains out with a Setting Pole"; Smith escaped and died at Ft. Niagara in 1761	SWJP, 2:726; 9:796–99, 825; 10:292
1758 (Jan.)	Tiononderoge Mohawks	British regulars	Fort Hunter and Tiononderoge	British soldiers, apparently enlisted men, assaulted several Mohawk men and women with fists and cutlasses; some Mohawks wounded; one attempted rape of an old Mohawk woman	SWJP, 2:772–74; 13:104–7

1758 (Dec.)	John McMichael (trader)	Unidentified Cayugas	Near Fort Stanwix	McMichael was robbed and scalped	*SWJP*, 3:28; 10:82–84, 86, 88, 93–98, 962
1759	Thennewhannega (Cayuga)	Unknown, probably Albany resident	Albany	Possibly revenge for McMichael's murder	*SWJP*, 10:962
1761	Gustavus Frank	Oneida warrior	German Flatts	Twenty to thirty Oneidas came to German Flatts "to have their Children Christened & Likewise to have Some of them Married"; they killed one of Stephen Frank's hogs; when Justice Gustavus Frank approached the Oneida to ask why he had killed the hog, a scuffle ensued in which the Oneida shot and killed Frank and escaped	*SWJP*, 3:407, 430–37, 504–6; 10:292, 297, 312; 13:216
1763	Unidentified blacksmith	Unidentified Senecas	Seneca Country	The Senecas escaped to the Ohio Country	*SWJP*, 10:627–28
1770	British soldiers	Five Senecas	Near Fort Niagara	Senecas plundered traders' canoe, then shot at and wounded British soldiers in a batteaux who had agreed to ferry them across a river; one British soldier died of his wounds	*SWJP*, 7:942–43, 993–94, 1052–54, 1076–77, 1117, 1125

lingua franca of Indian diplomacy)? Other account books show that George (or Urey) Weaver and other Palatine settlers received several shipments of rum (one of which contained 331.5 gallons!), strouds, blankets, linen, ribbon, vermilion, and pigeon shot—all items commonly used in the fur trade and diplomacy. Weaver was one of many farmer-traders at German Flatts who had close trading ties to Oneidas, Tuscaroras, Onondagas, Oswegatchie Iroquois, Kahnawake Iroquois, and other Iroquois (many of whom were women coming to trade). The Germans had also formed connections with Albany and Schenectady merchants, longtime trading partners of the Canadian Iroquois. Weaver, for example, obtained wampum with the help of the Albany merchant David Vanderheyden, who had been involved in the Albany-Montreal fur trade and knew "a great many Indians here abouts." The wampum beads were readily available: Peter Kalm observed that "many people at Albany make wampum for the Indians . . . by grinding and finishing certain kinds of shells and mussels."[3]

Perhaps no other settlers in mainland British North America had such intimate daily interactions with nearby Natives. German Flatts settlers truly lived at a Native, not a colonial, crossroads. The Mohawk settlements at Canajoharie were only a few miles to the south and east, Oneida and Tuscarora settlements to the west, Oswegatchie Iroquois to the north. From their principal towns at Kanowalohale, Ganaghsaraga, and Oriske, the Oneidas controlled a vital strategic area: the Oneida Carrying Place, where traders had to portage their goods between the Mohawk River and Wood Creek, which ultimately led to Lake Ontario. In asserting their control over this vital corridor, Oneida men acted as porters, charged fares, and competed with Palatine carriers. On the whole the Oneidas remained insulated from the direct pressure of colonial settlers before the 1750s, and they maintained a prosperous trading network from New York to Canada.[4]

The Palatine settlers not only participated in this thriving Iroquois trade but conducted their own diplomacy, separate from the British government. Both the Germans and the Iroquois perceived that they were increasingly vulnerable to attack. In 1756 French and Indian forces had successfully cut off the British from the Great Lakes, destroying Fort Bull and capturing Fort Oswego. These victories made German Flatts, and the British Fort Herkimer (or Kouari), the colony's exposed far-western periphery. Both the Palatines and the Oneidas resented the fort's presence, seeing it as an inviting target that would tend to attract, not repel, enemy thrusts. The Palatines communicated to the Oneidas their resentment of "the ill treatment they receive from the English, meaning the Troops, who past and repast that Way, as well as from those posted there." Even village leaders such as Han Jost Herkimer were not immune from marauding soldiers, who "Tieraniece over me as they think proper" and "take a prerogative power . . . Not only by Infesting my house, and taking up my Rooms at pleashure, but takes what they think Nesserarie of my Effects." At least one German, old George Klock of Canajoharie, "frequently called, and held private meetings with the Indians, at which, he and some others of ye. Germans liveing in that quarter, have endeavoured by false tales, & artfull insinuating to create differences, and misunderstandings, between the Army Inhabitants and Indians." Along with Weaver, Klock was deemed responsible for sending "treasonable Belts & Messages" to the Indians and French.[5]

Beginning in the fall of 1756 the Palatine community conducted negotiations on Weaver's wampum with their Oneida neighbors, the Oswegatchie Iroquois, and the governor general of New France, Pierre Rigaud de Vaudreuil. The Palatines sent a letter to Vaudreuil saying that they "looked upon themselves to be in Danger as well as the Six Nations, they were determined to live and die by them, & therefore begged the protection of the French." The Palatine-Oneida alliance came into sharper focus during a December 1756 conference between Vaudreuil and other Iroquois. One of the Oneidas' belts contained this message: "We inform you of a message given us by a Nation which is neither French nor English, nor Indian, and inhabits the lands round about us. . . . That Nation has proposed to

Fig. 9. Johannes Klock House, ca. 1750s. Photographed by the author, courtesy of Fort Klock Historic Foundation.

annex us to itself in order to afford each other mutual help and defence against the English." Vaudreuil responded: "I think I know that Nation. There is reason to believe that they are Palatines." But Vaudreuil would not tolerate such neutrality. He offered the Germans a choice: either "remove to him, [and] he would receive them with open arms and give them lands," or be considered as enemies. The Oneidas and the Palatines stalled for time. For example, the Oneidas told Vaudreuil that they had "not given our answer" to the Palatines' annexation request, although other actions make it clear that they in fact had: the Oneidas had promised that "they would Give them [the Palatines] Notice when Ever they found them in Danger of Being Attacked." In at least one instance the Oneidas redeemed a Palatine captive from the Oswegatchies, who later complained to Vaudreuil about this. The French governor concluded that the German "Nation" had negotiated "with a view only to guarantee its settlements and itself against the incursions of my warriors and children." He warned that "its trick will avail nothing; for whensoever I shall think proper, I will dispatch my warriors to Corlac [the French name for New York]." Vaudreuil's intolerance of Palatine neutrality is reminiscent of British authorities' conduct toward the Acadians in Nova Scotia after 1755.[6]

Strangely, from his seat just a short distance eastward, the British superintendent of Indian affairs, Sir William Johnson, was almost blind to the extent of the Palatine-Oneida alliance in the same valley, and the French attack on German Flatts also caught him by surprise. His battle wounds from 1755 apparently made him unwell in late 1757, which may account for his lack of attention to reports of impending assaults. He was aware of the clandestine German Flatts trade from Indian informants. The British commander-in-chief, the Earl of Loudoun, thought it "a very bad practice," since Oswegatchie and Kahnawake Iroquois might obtain arms and ammunition there. Johnson condemned Urey Weaver as a "very bad Man" for sending "a Quantity of Wampum last Fall to Canada by an Indian in the French Interest," but he never discovered exactly what messages the belts contained. Johnson doubted the Germans' fidelity, but he later admitted to Loudoun that "Justice requires me to declare that I have never discovered anything in the Germans behaviour which would justify the Accusation laid to their charge." Even the wily George Croghan and John Butler investigated the stories and wrote back to Johnson that they could find no evidence of Palatine-French correspondence. Johnson was solely concerned with how the Palatines were "intermeddling" in the superintendent's business.[7]

The Palatine-Oneida alliance cannot be dismissed as a wartime convenience. It was an outgrowth of longstanding economic, linguistic, religious, and personal ties that had transformed the identities of both peoples. When the Oneidas sent four belts of wampum to Vaudreuil, so that he would "restrain his Indians from committing Hostilities any where upon [the Mohawk] River, particularly upon the German Flatts," they emphasized that "it will be in effect destroying of [sic] us, *for we get a great deal of Provisions from the Settlements there, & reap many Advantages from our Neighbourhood with the*

Settlers there." German Flatts was a major source of provisions, rum, and services. Blacksmiths at German Flatts repaired Oneida weapons and metalware; Canajoharie Mohawks had their corn ground into flour at George Klock's gristmill. When one of Sir William's agents met with the Oneidas in 1757, the sachems complained of "the Great Quantitys of Rum Sold them at the German Flatts" and asked Johnson to put a stop to it. But the Oneidas made an exception for rum's use at "Marriges, Christings & Burials" and asked that Nicholas and Urey Weaver and one "Crissman" be allowed to continue sales. The Oneidas and other Christian Iroquois desiring baptism or marriage ceremonies visited Palatine churches, where Palatine settlers occasionally acted as godparents or sponsors. There were also a few intermarriages between Germans and Iroquois: the Palatine leadership sent a letter to the governor general of New France, pleading him "not to due them any hurt *as [they were no more white people but] Oneidas and that their Blood was mixed with [the Indians]."*[8]

This relationship was, on the whole, harmonious and strong enough to outweigh the tensions that beset it. Germans and Oneidas competed as portagers at the Oneida Carrying Place between the Mohawk and Wood Creek. Oneidas objected when a few German squatters began taking up lands at the Carry in the early 1750s. Oneida sachems told Johnson, "As to the Germans who live there its only by our permission, for they have never paid for the land they are settled upon." Like their Mohawk brethren the Oneidas had "received them [the settlers] in compassion to their poverty and expected when they could afford it, that they would pay us for their land." In a familiar cycle the Germans had "grown rich [and] they not only refuse to pay us for our land but impose on us in every thing we have to do with them." The Oneidas warned these Germans "to go about their business and remove from our land."[9]

Why, then, was the Palatine-Oneida alliance ultimately unsuccessful in securing both groups a modicum of neutrality? In part it was because the alliance worked all too well. The Oneidas provided the Palatines with "every piece of Intelligence" that came to them regarding French-Indian strikes on the Mohawk Valley. Palatines and Oneidas even went out on joint scouting parties to bring back intelligence. There were literally dozens of separate rumors, reports, and warnings that the Iroquois passed on to the Palatines; over time the settlers became complacent and discounted the Indians' warnings. For example, the Palatines had advance notice of the November 12 attack from two separate Oneida messengers. The sachem Canaghquiesa had also urged the Germans to "collect themselves together in a Body at their Fort, and secure their Women Children and Effects and make the best Defence they could." But the Germans, Canaghquiesa explained, "laughed at me and slapping their Hands on their Buttucks said they did not value the Enemy." The Oneidas also sent a belt of wampum "to confirm the Truth" of Belêtre's impending attack, but it went unheeded.[10]

The Palatines, according to Cadwallader Colden's later assessment, had "trusted to a private Neutrality entered into between the Mohawks and the French Indians, in which the Inhabitants of the Mohawk river were included." He faulted the Palatines for being "so infatuated under this security that they gave no ear to the repeated intelligence" of Belêtre's approach. Johann Jost Petrie, writing from Montreal after his capture, was angry that "our people have been taken by the Indians and French (but the most part by our own Indians) and by our own fault." Petrie's assessment of Palatine complacency and Iroquois duplicity was accurate. Some of the francophile Oswegatchie Iroquois (among whom were recently settled Oneidas and Onondagas) were trading partners in one breath and attackers the next. Perhaps Onontio's pressure to commit to the French resulted in some Oneidas participating in the attack on German Flatts (though some Iroquois withdrew from the attack when they realized the target). The Oneidas thereafter endured Palatine accusations of being coconspirators.[11]

Of greater significance is the fact that the Iroquois and the German Flatts settlers renewed their long-established trading ties after the Seven Years' War. In fact, Oneidas and Tuscaroras came to the ruins of German Flatts to formally condole the survivors and cover the graves of the dead shortly after the attack. The sachem Canaghquiesa stated that "we have condoled with our Brethren the Germans on the Loss of their Friends, who have been lately killed and taken by the Enemy . . . that Ceremony being over 3 Days ago." Such renewal of local relationships between Indian and European communities was almost outside the realm of possibility in post-1763 Pennsylvania. In fact, when Pennsylvania traders began to reestablish ties with the Ohio Indians after Pontiac's War, a mob of Cumberland County frontier settlers called the "Black Boys" ransacked and destroyed their Ohio-bound goods. During the dozens of Indian conferences that took place in the Mohawk Valley in the 1760s, Johnson relied on German Flatts settlers to provision traveling Indians; he even requested that Rudolph Shoemaker purchase and store wheat for Iroquois use in the winter and spring. These abiding community ties help to explain both the continuance of peace in the 1760s and why the Oneidas sided with the American rebels during the Revolution.[12]

The Palatine and Oneida communities' relations were neither anomalous nor exceptional. When we survey the diplomatic, military, economic, material culture, linguistic, religious, personal, and familial ties between Indian and European communities in the Mohawk Valley, it is easy to understand why a period of coexistence lasted until the American Revolution. The Seven Years' War unfolded along the Mohawk Valley in a far different way than on Pennsylvania's or Virginia's frontiers. The Six Nations were determined to preserve their neutrality in this latest imperial showdown between France and Britain. In Iroquois eyes, as one sachem informed the Canadian governor, "The English your Brothers & you are the common Disturbers of this Country." The Iroquois were, in William Johnson's words, "a People who have never considered themselves as Principals in the present

War, anxious for their own security & courted by both sides." Neither the French nor the British had the power to tip the balance of Iroquois power in their favor. In fact, Vaudreuil's attempts to bring the war to the Mohawk Valley in 1757 may have been counterproductive, as they violated an earlier pledge to refrain from such attacks through Iroquoia. Despite French violations of their territory, the Six Nations as a whole remained neutral until 1759–60, when large numbers of Iroquois warriors advanced with the British armies against Fort Niagara and Montreal. Iroquois neutrality shielded the Mohawk Valley from direct and sustained French or Indian attacks; the destruction of German Flatts was truly the exception to the rule. The hardest-hit areas of the New York frontiers were Orange and Ulster counties, northwest of New York City, whose defenseless western boundaries left them subject to Delaware and Shawnee attacks.[13]

Despite their desire for neutrality, the Six Nations faced intense social and economic stresses from the continuous operations of British and French forces on Iroquoia's periphery. The presence of foreign armies on their lands and increased fort building in the Mohawk Valley–Oswego corridor greatly aggravated many Iroquois, though they had initially requested the forts' construction. The basic chronology of the war can be quickly summarized: Military campaigns began in earnest in 1755 as British forces targeted French forts at Crown Point, Niagara, Duquesne, and Beauséjour. Most of these expeditions failed to achieve their objectives, with the exception of Beauséjour's capture and William Johnson's tactical victory over the French at Lake George in 1755 that significantly raised British morale after Braddock's defeat near Fort Duquesne. But Johnson's Mohawk allies suffered heavy losses, including the venerable Hendrick Theyanoguin, who was felled in battle by Kahnawake Iroquois. The momentum swung to the French, and Governor Vaudreuil orchestrated a stunning offensive against his enemies that maximized New France's strengths. From 1755 to 1757 French regulars, highly skilled Canadian militia, and their Native allies inflicted catastrophic defeats upon the more numerous British colonies and devastated the vulnerable frontiers of Virginia, Maryland, and Pennsylvania. In 1756 Britain's outlet to the Great Lakes—Fort Oswego—fell to a French-Indian force led by the Marquis de Montcalm; British control was further reduced in 1757, when Fort William Henry, at the southern tip of Lac St. Sacrament (Lake George), surrendered after a short siege in 1757. When Belêtre's men fell on German Flatts, it seemed as though the French would triumph in North America. French officer Louis Antoine de Bougainville heard incredible rumors that Pennsylvania "would make itself an independent republic under the protection of France." With so many French military successes, William Johnson was mostly unsuccessful in his attempts to influence the Six Nations from 1755 to 1758, though he had secured the assistance of Mohawk, Oquaga, and Schoharie warriors during the war. It seemed to him, and to other British officials, that "the old Cov^t. Chain was very much rust-eaten & held so loosely by the 5 Nations" that it was in danger "of slipping out of their hands."[14]

Both Johnson and his contemporaries gauged his effectiveness by how well he "managed" the Indians and brought them over to Britain's side. But his true significance as the Indian superintendent rested in his mediation of local disputes between the Iroquois and the colonists. Johnson's authority and status continued to rise during and after the Seven Years' War. In 1755 Gen. Edward Braddock commissioned Johnson to superintend Anglo-Iroquois relations and to command the Crown Point expedition. Johnson's victory over the French at Lake George won him great transatlantic prestige: in 1755 the Crown awarded him a baronetcy and in 1756 appointed him superintendent of Indian affairs of the Northern Department. Sir William regularly communicated with British cabinet ministers, the Lords of Trade, British Army officers, and colonial governors. Both Warrighiyagey's new powers as royal superintendent and the simple fact that he resided in the Mohawk Valley made him an effective mediator of local disputes. He was not a distant colonial official who rarely assuaged Indian grievances or punished recalcitrant colonists. Pennsylvania's Conrad Weiser also, like Johnson, lived on the frontier. But Weiser's employ as an interpreter and his ethnicity lessened his effectiveness in his employers' eyes. Johnson believed that acculturated Mohawks, like the *réserve* Indians in Canada, could live among the settlers as "orderly a people as any of our Lower Class are" and consistently worked toward this end. But Johnson also believed that "the Motion [toward civilizing] must flow from themselves, & that they must fall into it when our increas'd Numbers place them more in our Neighborhood." Through hunting, farming, and Christian teachings Johnson believed that the Mohawks could become "usefull Members of Society." This was a vision of the future that many British colonists did not share, and one that would be overturned in the American Revolution.[15]

Johnson's frequent meetings with the Iroquois—his homes were always filled with Indian guests—enabled him to maintain a rust-free Covenant Chain and to mediate any land or property disputes, murders, or crimes that occurred on New York's frontiers. As demonstrated earlier (see chapter 1), Johnson's generosity and knowledge of the forms of the condolence ceremony enabled him to meet Mohawks' and other Iroquois' material and emotional needs like few British officials of his time. He also advocated Iroquois rights in many land disputes with colonists and New York officials. As he remarked to Colden in 1764, "I am everry day more & more convinced of y[e] necessity there is for a method to do the Ind[s] Justice in a Summary way as well with regard to property."[16]

A 1758 dispute among the Schoharie Mohawks, Oneidas, and Germans provides an excellent example of how Johnson cooled tempers and restored harmony. Some Oneida families had wintered in Schoharie Valley to hunt. They complained to Johnson that they were in "a starving Condition" due to game's scarcity and to "the Sullenness & ill temper of the Inhabitants of that Settlement." The white settlers were angry "on Account of some Pigs &[c] which were killed by some Indians lately"—"so much out of Temper that they will not give an Indian a Morsel of any thing tho ever so much in want, but give them ill language." Johnson provided the Oneidas with money to buy provisions, told them that he would "enquire into the Affair & have it settled," and encouraged the Natives to remain on friendly terms with the settlers. He sent the trader Jelles Fonda with instructions to warn the Schoharie settlers of "the ill consequences of their differing with the Indians," to maintain a "good Agreement" with the Indians, and "to make a collection of Indian Corn &ᶜ. for such as are now in want of Provisions." Fonda convened a meeting of Schoharie and Mahican Indians and other colonists at the house of Josias Swaart. The chief sachem Seth presented three strings of wampum, affirming his village's friendly disposition. A Schoharie warrior named David related that only one pig had been killed and that the colonial family did not vilify the Indians as first reported. The Schoharie colonists later "returned him [Sir William] their hearty thanks for the early Steps he had taken to prevent the late little differences which had happened between them & the Indians their Neighbors from going further." The colonists' use of the word *Neighbors* was evinced by a collection of corn for needy Indians.[17]

Johnson's personal example helped to stabilize the Mohawk Valley in wartime. He fortified his stone house, stockpiling muskets, small cannons, and ammunition there, and sent out tenants to scout the surrounding area. Whereas Pennsylvanians and Virginians deserted the frontiers in droves, many settlers and Indians in the Mohawk Valley felt confident enough to remain in their homes. During King George's War, according to Cadwallader Colden, "this Province remain'd in Peace the Farmers at the plow on their frontiers while New England was in many places desolated with fire & sword & sometimes so near our borders as to be seen from thence." William Johnson confided to his uncle Peter in 1749, "As to Your own Settlements near me, the Mohawks will defend that [& me] I am not afraid of." In 1764, after nearly a decade of war, Johnson boasted to

Colden that he had settled "above 100 Familys dureing the heat of the War, to the North, & North Westward of yᵉ greatest part of it, and they were never molested." Europeans felt safer having the Mohawks as neighbors and allies: Johnson believed that "without the nations in our neighbourhood continue our friends, the Inhabitants will all abandon their settlements."[18]

One reason that colonists and Indians smoothed over their differences was the common military threat they faced: the French and their Indian allies. Both Indian villagers and European settlers participated in joint military expeditions throughout the eighteenth century to defend the valley that they shared. As Johnson told the Mohawks in 1755, "our mutual safety & honour is at stake." Mohawks, Schoharie Iroquois, and Oquagans all requested that forts be built for their protection during the war. Many New York colonists in military service were stationed in Mohawk Valley forts or scouted alongside Mohawk, Oquaga, Mahican, and Schoharie warriors. Pennsylvania's settlers had no history of fighting alongside Indian allies and saw little distinction between friend and enemy Indians. During King George's War Johnson helped organize frequent scouting parties of colonists and Indians; in 1747, for example, a "party of fifty Indians, & as Many Christians" went out against the French. The same pattern was even more evident during the Seven Years' War. In 1755 Mohawks accompanied twenty of Johnson's tenants who "who went & ranged the Woods in his Neighborhood." Leonard Spaulding recorded in his 1755 diary that "I was sent for to go a Skout fort of 4 [forty four?] of us went for five days their being ten Indians with us." As a result, the Mohawk Valley colonists were said to have become "good Marksmen, some used to Indian Fighting."[19]

Increased militarization of the Mohawk Valley meant that forts became important places of cultural contact and contention. By 1756 the British maintained garrisons at Albany; Schenectady; and forts Hunter, Hendrick (at Canajoharie), Herkimer, Bull, Oswego, Edward, and William Henry. These garrisons created many hardships for nearby Indian communities. Given the fact that eighteenth-century armies were cesspools of disease, Indians suffered from epidemics such as the 1757–58 smallpox contagion, which claimed many lives. Armies also threatened the Indians' subsistence. Soldiers and batteauxmen killed Indian livestock and stole corn. British forces drove immense herds of cattle up the Mohawk Valley to Oswego, where they trampled Indian cornfields in the lowlands. As a result, Mohawks and Oneidas suffered crop failures during the war. But war offered opportunities as well: Indians during wartime served as "waggin, battow & sledd men," as well as interpreters and messengers.[20]

The interactions between Iroquois and colonial soldiers, however, reveal a pattern of trust and familiarity that the British regulars lacked. In fact, British regulars were responsible for many of the murders and assaults against Indians that occurred on the New York frontiers during the Seven Years' War (see table 1). British officers' haughty mistreatment of their Iroquois allies mirrored their disdain for colonial militias. Mohawks reported in 1757 that the regular garrison and the commander of Fort William Henry "used them very ill . . . took them by the shoulders & turned them out like Dogs." In one particularly egregious case of British aggression regulars "emptied a chamber pot upon [a Mohawk] and shrew him with snow balls"; they then entered Tiononderoge and assaulted and wounded a number of Mohawk men and women with fists and cutlasses. Indians responded in kind: at Fort Brewerton Indians ransacked the garrison's garden and expressed their dissatisfaction over the fort's presence on their lands. One officer at Fort Herkimer awoke to find his garden plundered and horses stolen.[21]

To prevent further hostilities the Mohawks, Schoharies, and Oquagas came to favor colonial militias—not regular troops—as fort garrisons. Their requests suggest a similarity between French-Canadian and New York militiamen, who knew how to fight alongside Native allies. In their frequent requests for protection the Indians may not have anticipated the disputes and bad feelings that might arise from the British military's presence. But by 1756 Tiononderoge and Canajoharie Mohawks were reported as being "averse to having Red Coats as they call 'em put in their Forts." The Canajoharies told Johnson to send the regulars away and to "order a Number of the Country pople Such as we are Acquainted with to garrison this Fort." A year later the Mohawks specifically requested the appointment of militia officer Peter Schuyler to the garrison. Their trust in the colonial militia was not replicated anywhere in Pennsylvania or Virginia in the 1750s and 1760s.[22]

Beyond the exigencies of war both European and Indian communities on the Mohawk frontier had longstanding social, familial, economic, and religious ties that emerged largely intact from the Seven Years' War. Their ability to forge common bonds depended upon effective communication. Villagers and settlers were not dependent upon interpreters who acted in an official capacity, such as Conrad Weiser and Arent Stevens. There were many farmers, traders, smiths, and artisans who could speak an Iroquoian dialect: one German farmer's daughter, named Sarah Kast, spoke at least two different Native languages. Many others communicated in a trade pidgin, a language described by a French writer as a "jargon whose vocabulary is very short and deals only with trade." The ethnic diversity of the Mohawk Valley necessitated a certain linguistic savoir-faire among Europeans. In 1776 an American officer stationed in the Mohawk Valley, Joseph Bloomfield, remarked that "it is not uncommon here to hear the different English Scotch, Dutch & Indian Languages talked at one time." On another occasion he heard English, German, Dutch, French, Mohawk, Oneida, Seneca, Cayuga, Tuscarora, and Onondaga spoken: "The most of these Tongues I heard daily spoke and one Person in particular a frenchman can speak French, English, Low-Dutch & the five Indian-Languages." The African woman who interpreted Dutch, Mohawk, and English at her master's house at Schenectady in the winter of 1745 could only have acquired Mohawk through habitual conversations with nearby Mohawks. Canajoharie and German Flatts settlers' conversations were sufficiently complex to arrange rent and land-tenure agreements with the Iroquois, and settlers were also well-versed in the uses of wampum.[23]

Taverns and colonists' homes were often scenes of conviviality, exchange, and violence; it was in such intimate settings that colonists and Indians learned each other's languages and manners. As early as 1704 the Albany Common Council ordered constables to fine tavernkeepers for "all Indians & Negros found In any Tavern" on the Sabbath. Warren Johnson described how a party of Indians left Fort Johnson and went to a nearby tavern, where they feasted on bear, wild turkey, and rum. Mohawks imbibed the rum and the music and dance styles of the European tavern-goers: Warren later "heard an Indian playing many European Tunes, & pretty well on the Fidle." In 1751 the Canajoharie sachem Hendrick requested that the governor take action against colonists' liquor sales: Clinton issued orders to the sheriff of Albany to "forbid the two Tavernkeepers living in the Mohawk River selling any Rum or other spirituous Liquors to the Indians on pain of being prosecuted . . . and to charge them to shut up their Houses til the Indians return from Albany." Joseph Clement sold liquor "within 20 yards" of Johnson's house; no sooner did the Indians receive guns, trade goods, and provisions, than they "immediately go to his house & spend all there." Native sachems complained that "our grown people have become so addicted to liquor that unless some stop be put thereto, we shall soon be a ruined people."[24]

Johann Georg Kast's encounters with traveling Indians brightly illustrate both the frequency and the ambivalent atmosphere of social interactions. The Kast family came to New York in the Palatine migration of 1709, lived at Schoharie, and eventually settled at German Flatts in the 1720s. The family lived along the principal east-west Indian path and provided lodging and provisions to Iroquois and colonial travelers. Daniel Claus described it as "the last plantation inhabited by white people" before the Oneidas' country. He noted the

Fig. 10. *Indians and British Soldiers near Montreal*, by John Andre, ca. 1775. Courtesy of William L. Clements Library, University of Michigan.

ordinariness of Kast's meetings with the Natives: "the Indians visited him quite often and never departed emptyhanded." Kast's children literally came of age with Indians in the house. Kast's daughter Sarah, born in the year 1717, was especially well liked. In the 1730s she married an Irishman named Teady, or Timothy McGinnis, an associate of William Johnson. Sarah not only "understood the Language of the Six Nations" but was paid by the New York government in 1746 to interpret the Algonquian tongue spoken by Indians of the Susquehanna Valley. She later traded with the Iroquois for ginseng and became an influential loyalist among the Iroquois during the American Revolution. Moravian travelers once noted Nanticokes, Onondagas, Oneidas, Tuscaroras, and Senecas at the house of "their German host." But the Kast family's hospitality did not mean acceptance of Indian ways. Johann Georg once chided Moravian visitors: "Why did we wander around in the woods, and not live like other Christians? For we would derive no benefit, but be obliged to live like cattle among the Indians, and spend a miserable life." Kast clearly did not like or fully understand Indian manners and lifestyles. As a result, friendly meetings became "unpleasant when they came drunk because they were apt to take whatever they could find; if one hindered them, the evil only grew worse." Kast told his guests of a recent visit during which an Indian took his food cooking on a fire. When Kast pushed him away, the Indian left, returned with a gun, and killed two of Kast's horses. Both the German and his Indian guests were clearly not incapable of communicating and interacting in nonviolent ways—witness Kast and an Indian in the same house, sitting beside a fire, awaiting a meal—but different notions of hospitality and property introduced conflict into their relationship. The food that Kast saw as personal property might have been seen by the visiting Iroquois as food to be shared from a common bowl as brothers.[25]

Routine social and economic interactions produced unmistakable tension, hostility, and occasional violence and crime, especially when alcohol was involved. Mohawk sachems told the Anglican missionary John Ogilvie of a 1754 incident involving two young men who went "to the House of one Jury Klock & there stole a Cagg of Rum." The two men "set down by the Way to drink, & being very drunk, a very smart contention arose, one of them took up a Stone & struck the other on the Temple, upon which he fell down Dead upon the Spot." The nearly ceaseless flow of traveling Indians, traders, batteauxmen, and soldiers also occasioned disputes and confrontations. A group of forty-seven traders who traveled to and from Oswego complained in 1754 of their treatment at the Mohawks' hands: "they board our Battoes, with axes, knives ettc and by force take what Rum they think proper hooping and yelping as if they Gloried in their depredations and threatning Murder to any that oppose them." The traders indicated that the Mohawks and the Oneidas also turned away German laborers who were competing with them to portage batteaux and trade goods at the Great Carrying Place on their way to Lake Ontario. Iroquois making their way to Johnson Hall for formal conferences occasionally killed colonists' livestock or extorted provisions from them. Some Oneidas coming to Albany in 1754 "assaulted, and forced Rum from Daniel M:Michal, and frightned Not

Only his family But Also his Nabors" (the Oneidas, however, called this story "Groundless").[26]

On the other hand, Indians and colonists' interactions produced personal, sexual, and occasional marital ties. Like William Johnson, who counted Indians among his friends and family, ordinary settlers formed friendships with nearby Indians. The exchanging of names also indicates their familiarity with one another. Oneidas and Mohawks alike were known by German or Dutch names such as Hans Ury, Catarina, or Johann Jost; Indians reciprocated with names like "Kouari" (bear) or "Yokum" for Joachim. A small band of Mohawks at George Klock's in Canajoharie were "allways living at his house." William Johnson once spent a sleepless night at Klock's brother's house nearby, for "by their Singing dancing & other noise I was disturbed during the whole night." Joachim Falkenberg, a farmer in the Cherry Valley whom the Indians called "Yokum," thought that the Oquagas were "not troublesome to him tho they often call at his House." While the account is susceptible to memory's manipulation, one early settler family's oral history recorded how their ancestor's farm on the Mohawk River was "a favorite resort of the Indians for fishing purposes, and particularly of the Indian boys." The writer recalled how a young Mohawk boy named "Brandt" "remained several days at a time" with her two brothers.[27]

Such intimate relations became worrisome to British officials when they involved renegade traders, white Indians, army deserters, French settlers, indentured servants, or African slaves who might sway the Indians' minds against them. In 1753, for example, the Albany commissioners listened to Oneida Indians complain about their visit to a fort, where "a gang of Negroes, who had got a fiddle; & probably were all in liquor, quarreled, & lost their Blanketts." African slaves in the Mohawk Valley also forged their own ties with the Indians, which facilitated resistance to their British owners. One slave from Virginia ended up as Abbé François Piquet's servant at the Iroquois mission town at Oswegatchie. He told Piquet that if New France granted land

and provisions for New England's slaves, "these Negroes would be the most terrible enemies of the English"; they would then fight to preserve New France and their freedom. Piquet's Virginia servant was one of many slaves who fled to Indian country or New France hoping to escape bondage.[28]

While the Iroquois and other eastern Natives sometimes returned the runaways, they occasionally adopted and married them. The 1820 New York Supreme Court case of *Solomon Parmalee v. Henry Welch* sheds light on one such intermarriage. Parmalee sued Welch, a black man, for a debt of $16.50. Welch "rested his defence on the ground that he was an Indian within the Statute" (which apparently made him immune from prosecution). Welch offered as a witness "one Hendrick Aupaumut who testified that said Welch was always considered as an Indian descended from the Nanticocke tribe in Maryland—That Welch was regularly admitted. . . . That he knew the Welch family on the Mohawk whilst they were held in Slavery but supposed the mother was a squaw." Solomon U. Hendrick, the clerk of the Stockbridge tribe, testified, with "their book of Records" in hand, that Welch had long been admitted, since July 1800. Bartholomew Calvin testified that "he always considered Welch a member of the tribe— Always understood his mother was a Squaw and thought he must be at least half blood[.] That he had always understood her mother was a squaw and originated from Maryland. That Welch's father was not an Indian." For the plaintiff John Moyer testified that "he had known Welch's father and Mother between fifty and sixty years—That she was not called a Squaw—That they were in servitude to one Klock and he has understood Welch's maternal grandmother was a slave and thinks he has seen her but is not certain—He has heard a report that the Welch family were freed from slavery by proving Indian blood." Discounting the Stockbridge Indians' evidence, the court did not believe that Welch had sufficiently proved his Indian identity and ruled in favor of the plaintiff.[29]

Intermarriage and sexual liaisons, which had the potential to strengthen ties between the European settlers and Indians, occurred with greater frequency on the New York–Iroquois frontiers than in Pennsylvania. The legacy of seventeenth-century Dutch-Indian intermarriage and William Johnson's own example may have made intermarriage more socially acceptable than it was on other British frontiers. Johnson's correspondence makes clear that his colonial guests had sexual relations with Native women. Johnson once promised Goldsbrow Banyar that if he visited, he would "introduce you to a Princess of the first Rank here, who has large possessions, as well as parts, provided I could be assured of your paying her more civility than you did to the lady I shewed you at Albany, and dischargeing ye necessary Duty, wh. men of years and infirmities are seldom capable of." On his return from Philadelphia in 1755, Hendrick, Molly Brant, and other Mohawks traveled by way of Albany, where Molly met twenty-seven-year-old Capt. Staats Morris of the New York militia. According to Daniel Claus, Captain Morris "fell in love with Ms. Mary Brant who was then pretty likely not having had the smallpox." Charles Lee, a British officer stationed at Schenectady, wrote to his sister in 1756 that "I have livd a great deal among the Mohawks and have pick'd up a little of their language." He found the Mohawks to be a "much better sort of people than commonly represented" and favorably noted their hospitality, friendliness, and civility. Lee's sister may have been surprised to learn that her brother also had a "Mohawk wife." Friedrich Rohde, traveling through Oneida lands in 1802, remarked on an Oneida chief who "was bred by a white, a German to boot, and a Negro in Canada; and is consequently a mulatto."[30]

Historians cannot know the full extent of intermarriage among Europeans, Africans, and Indians, because many Mohawk Valley church records were destroyed during the American Revolution, and later families may have kept the marriages a secret. But documentary traces suggest a fair number of cross-cultural unions or individuals who chose to live in Indian communities. After the Revolution at least one Indian-European marriage was recorded at the German Flatts Reformed Church in 1788, between "George Martin (Indian) & Catharin (white)." Other Indians with European names were married in the German Flatts church in the 1780s, but the ethnicity of each partner is not clearly defined in the record (e.g., "Jacob Dachstaeder the Indian & Lea"). The existence of Palatine and Oneida families with the surname "Dachstaeder" shows, at least, great familiarity and intimacy and, at most, a history of intermarriage. Other examples include a German named Peter Spelman, or Owiligaska, who was married to the daughter of the Shawnee leader Paxinosa. Hans Croyn's (or Crine's) nickname, "white Hans," and his description as a "whiteish Indian living at the Mohocks" suggest his European parentage. Captives such as Jemmy Campbell, "an Irish lad who was taken at Oswego, and is married to an Oneida," chose to live among their spouse's people. John Stacey, captured during the British debacle at Sabbath Day Point in 1757, married another white captive from Kahnawake, where they continued to live. Other documentary references do not establish intermarriage but show that Indians accepted and adopted whites such as "one Hamilton, who lives among the Indians," or "a white fellow that Lives here in the Sinachass [Senecas' Country]."[31]

The frontier churches where these marriages were blessed were places of a shared religion—Christianity. It is unclear whether Indians and Europeans worshipped together, or if the European congregations witnessed the Indians' ceremonies, or if the Europeans considered the Indians part of their extended flock. As shown earlier (see chapter 2), Europeans and Mohawks at Canajoharie had strong religious ties. Three Mohawk sachems insisted in a petition that "Our Christian Brothers and We are all one and we will not have our Church Pulled down for We are [one] Church and we will not part we are grown up together and we intend to Live our Lifetime together as Brothers." Also suggestive of joint worship is David Zeisberger's account of an Onondaga man "who spoke to him about the singing in the Low Dutch Church at Albany, imitated it, and asked if we did the same in our Church." Frontier settlers' attitudes toward their Indian neighbors may have been more favorable as a result of Christian Indian baptisms or weddings in their churches. Some Christian Mohawks, such as Theyanoguin's brother Abraham, were held in great esteem by Europeans. Abraham was a lay preacher and spiritual leader to the Canajoharie Mohawks. Europeans uniformly praised Abraham's character and spirituality; the famous evangelical minister Jonathan Edwards described him as "a man of great solidity, prudence, devotion, and strict conversation; and acts very much as a person endowed with the simplicity, humanity, self-denial and zeal of a true Christian."[32]

Well over a thousand Indians were baptized, christened, or married in churches at Schoharie, Canajoharie, German Flatts, Albany, and Schenectady. According to the record books of the Dutch Reformed Congregation at Schoharie, approximately 251 Mohawks, Schoharies, Mahicans, Oquagans, and other Indians were either baptized or married there from 1731 to 1778. Significantly, the majority of the baptisms and marriages had European sponsors or witnesses, usually Palatine or Dutch church members such as Bartholomew Vroman, Hendrick Hagedoorn, Johannes Lawyer, or Josias Swaart. In 1748 Indians (probably from Schoharie or Oquaga) told Albert Van Slyck of Schenectady that "they together with the [Christians]" were willing to pay the Rev. Johannes Schuyler of Schoharie to visit them three or four times a year to "Christen & marry our People." This relationship continued until the late 1750s, when Schuyler apparently abandoned his post. Someone else then filled Schuyler's shoes, for Joseph and Peggie Brant's second child, Christina, was baptized by a German clergyman at Schoharie in 1769. In 1761 Conrad Frank reported that twenty to thirty Oneidas came to the Flatts "to have their Children Christened & Likewise to have Some of them Married." Other extant church records in the Mohawk Valley demonstrate that Indian baptisms and marriages were common occasions in frontier congregations. At the Dutch Reformed Church at Caughnawaga at least seven Indian infants were baptized in the late 1750s and early 1760s. At German Flatts Reformed Church and nearby Stone Arabia Lutheran church twelve Indians were either baptized or married from 1762 to 1792. These numbers, however, do not reflect a full count, since some church records were destroyed during the American Revolution, and some events might not have been recorded at all.[33]

As in its religious life, Mohawks and Iroquois remained central participants in the Mohawk Valley's economic life, despite the overall decline of the fur trade in the eighteenth century. Historians' pronouncements that the Mohawks and Iroquois more generally were economically dependent and diplomatically irrelevant by midcentury are inaccurate. As shown earlier (see chapter 2), the circular argument that Mohawks were forced to cede land because it was their last commodity is specious. Mohawks' and Oneidas' economic adaptations meant that they increasingly made a living in the same ways that European farmers did—by selling their produce in local markets. Their adaptations changed the older familial, economic, and political relationships in Mohawk communities; extremes of wealth appeared in Mohawk villages as individuals or families took advantage of greater access to sources of wealth and status. On the whole most Mohawks lived no worse than poorer European farmers and often had access to trade goods that they did not. It is inaccurate to typecast highly skilled Indian farmers and hunters as abjectly dependent peoples. Revolutionary War soldiers who saw Iroquois communities firsthand marveled at their prosperity and abundance; Iroquois loyalist claims also reveal the general prosperity of these communities on the eve of the Revolution. The economies and material cultures of Indian and European frontier communities merged, as both groups became economically interdependent.[34]

Both the Mohawks' and the Oneidas' example demonstrates that many Iroquois had productively adapted to European agricultural techniques and keeping livestock. By the 1770s Mohawk and Oneida communities were highly prosperous. In his travels through the Mohawk Valley Richard Smith encountered Joseph Brant at Canajoharie. Smith described Brant as "a considerable Farmer possessing Horses and Cattle and 100 acres of rich Land at Canejoharie. He says the Mohawks have lately followed Husbandry more than formerly, and that some Hemloc Swamps when cleared will produce good Timothy Grass." Another traveler noted the "several Indian towns, where they have some cows, cultivate some corn, and imitate the European settlers," though he did not believe the Indians would "make good farmers."[35]

The European settler communities were greatly dependent on the Iroquois as an outlet for their surplus crops and goods. The Mohawk Valley was famous for its wheat production and grain exports, but farmers also sold their produce locally to the Iroquois. They provided innumerable goods and services to traveling and resident Indians, especially during conferences and treaties (for which they were entitled to reimbursement). Table 2 shows the common types of services that settlers provided for the Indian peoples and travelers who were a daily presence in the Mohawk Valley. At William Johnson's home Indians occasionally lived as year-round residents. Moreover, there were dozens of conferences that involved hundreds, if not thousands, of Natives. For example, "near 2400 Indians" attended the German Flatts conference in 1770, in Johnson's estimate, making this one of the largest events of its kind ever held. Basic human needs had to be addressed by British officials, such as housing, food, clothing, and medical care for Indian guests. Johnson spent a total of nearly £3,400 at the German Flatts conference in 1770, some of which made its way to local settlers like Rudolph Shoemaker, for goods and services provided to the Indians. While there is no way to quantify settlers' services, there can be no doubt that their cumulative effect on the local economy was sustained and substantial, given the many conferences in the Mohawk Valley. Moreover, settlers were regularly asked to provide transportation, provisions, crops, and services, such as plowing fields for Mohawk and Oneida communities, outside of formal conferences.[36]

European artisans not only produced various Indian trade goods but often wore their handicrafts. Some of the most common items listed in the ledgers of New York merchants account books are "Indian shoes" or moccasins, "Indian shirts," and "Indian stockings" (leggings). Indian and European women (especially widows needing income) typically sewed Indian shirts for local merchants. William Johnson paid the widow Butler £1.13.6 for making sixty-seven Indian shirts; William Powell's wife earned £1.11.6 for making sixty-three shirts. Shoemakers or leatherworkers crafted "Indian shoes" for Indian, colonial, and army use. Indian shoes were among the most common items listed in merchants' account books, and ordinary settlers acquired them so often that moccasins seem to have been their footwear of choice. European settlers involved in the Indian trade could justly claim to have "spent a great part of their lives in hard Labour amongst the Indians."[37] Frontier settlers not only made items for the Indian trade but avidly participated in it themselves. As George Weaver's example shows, ordinary farmers could be well-versed in Indian diplomacy and the uses of wampum. Eighteenth-century account books' ledgers show that settlers commonly acquired Indian trade goods that they later sold or bartered to local Natives: rum, vermillion, wampum, blankets, powder, shot, strouds, and linen. In 1764 Onondagas were reported to have "Gone Down in Order to sell their [wild ginger] Roots to the Widow Maginnis [Sarah Kast]," who gave them rum and other goods in return.[38]

Natives typically offered furs, agricultural produce, and ginseng and ginger roots in return for necessaries. Ginseng harvesting offers an excellent illustration of the merging colonial and Indian economies. From 1751 to 1753 there was a ginseng "craze" in New York and New France in which colonial merchants wildly speculated. Mohawks and colonists commonly gathered native ginseng roots (*ochdera*) in the woods for export to London and then to China. Ginseng

Table 2. Services Provided to Indians by European Settlers during Conferences and Treaties in Colonial New York

Date	Settler	Type of service provided	Documentary references
1713	Matthias Nack	"For making a Stock to Canagkonie's Gun"	NYCMSS, 78:173 (Oct. 5, 1713, entry)
1714	Gosen van Noord	"For 2 times riding with Waggon & horses to and from Schonectady, the said Canasore, Cajenquieragta & other Sacchems"	NYCMSS, 58:173 (June 2, 1714, entry)
1720	Albany blacksmiths	"They mended kettles, steeled around 200 axes, repaired gun locks, and sharpened awls, knives, and needles"	NYCMSS, 62:149–51 (a–b)
1755	Jacobus Mynderse and Peter Groenendyke	"For the carriage of 200 Bushells of Indian Corn from Albany for the use of the Six Nations"	NYCM, 25:46 (June 15, 1755)
1755	Unknown	"To a Battoe to Caiyougas, Oneidas & Onondagas to carry their Sick"	SWJP, 2:580
1756	Hendrick Fry	"For Prov[isions] for the Ind[ians] coming down"	SWJP, 2:600
1756	Isaac Wemp	"For keeping Brants Horse dur[ing] the Congress"	SWJP, 2:601
1756	Cornelius Smith	"100 Boards of Cornelius Smith for Houses of the River Ind[s]"	SWJP, 2:613
1758	Henry Wendal	"For 8 Tin Kettles, Supplied the Inds. with when going to Cadaraque with Colo. Bradstreet"	SWJP, 3:149
1757	Hannis Eils	"Lodging & Provisions" for four Mohawks	SWJP, 9:595
1770	Rudolph Shoemaker	"To 1 Haffar [heifer] to Saguarisera a Tiscarore"	SWJP, 7:808
1770	Rudolph Shoemaker	"To a Coffin mak[er], Nals & Borts mad for an Intian"	SWJP, 7:808
1770	Rudolph Shoemaker	"To my own Tim & Labour procuring provision for ye Congress [at German Flatts]"	SWJP, 7:809
1770	Margaret and William Fox	"To 24 tb. of butter Del[ivered] to Marg[aret] Brant"	SWJP, 7:865
1772	Hugh Lynch	"17 Meals of Victuals for ye Indians"	Walter Butler Account Book, NYSL, 68

was believed to possess aphrodisiacal and medicinal properties. German immigrant Daniel Claus and Sammy Weiser (Conrad's son), for example, were in the woods with Brant Kanagaradunckwa "all day long," gathering ginseng. Claus reported, "I cannot adequately describe what a Furore there is round here over the famous Roots." The ginseng harvest increased the Iroquois' economic ties to local settlers and merchants. Moravian missionary J. Martin Mack, traveling through the Mohawk Valley in 1752, observed around one hundred Oneidas and Cayugas digging for roots. The woods-savvy Indians gathered ginseng and then sold the roots "to the people hereabouts, or exchange them for goods with the traders." Local colonists such as the widow Sarah Magin bartered provisions or trade goods with the Indians for ginseng and then sold the roots to merchants. One colonist reported that ginseng was gathered at "two pounds, or ten Rhine guilders, per bushel, by the wild inhabitants" in 1752. Oneidas, Cayugas, Mohawks, and Tuscaroras who participated in the ginseng harvest could command the terms of the transaction with merchants. When William Johnson sent a string of wampum saying that he would buy ginseng, the Tuscaroras replied with a long list of goods that they wanted him to bring, excluding liquor.[39]

In 1753, however, "many adventurers or speculators in it were nearly ruined," as Gideon Hawley reported. But what many historians do not realize is that ginseng continued to be a locally marketable commodity between Indian and European communities throughout the 1760s and 1770s. While the main period of speculation was 1751–53, ginseng was still gathered and accepted by Indians and merchants as a common medium of exchange for the next two decades in the Mohawk Valley. For example, in 1774 Jelles Fonda stated his intention "to Buy 10000 Pound of Jensang" at the rate of two shillings per pound. He instructed his agent to employ Mohawks to gather and wash the ginseng roots in return for batteaux-loads of goods that he would send them.[40]

Mohawks and Oneidas were important participants in the cash economy of the Mohawk Valley. Aside from the presents that they received through the Indian Department, they obtained material goods from merchants and traders in exactly the same ways that European farmers did. Sir William's tenants, for example, paid for goods from an Albany general store with potash, peas, wood, butter, cows, and cash. Iroquois paid for their goods in nearly identical fashion, with potash, corn, cranberries, venison, wampum, and cash. They also continued to bring in beaver, muskrat, otter, marten, and deer skins and pelts. Merchants' account books show that Indians paid for many goods in cash, to the extent that they were regular participants in the valley's cash economy. Where did they obtain currency? One source was Sir William Johnson's Indian Department, which frequently dispensed cash to sachems or visiting Indians to enable them to buy and redistribute provisions or other necessaries. In 1772 Johnson distributed £2000 to the Mohawks from various sources (apparently for land purchases and trade balances). Indian warriors often earned wages for their military service. The Natives' produce and goods also commanded market prices, for which they were often given money (though they mostly bartered their furs and produce for consumer goods). The Canajoharie Mohawks' tenants may have paid their rents in cash, though it appears that payment-in-kind (a percentage of the harvest) was most common. Indians also worked as wage laborers on farms and plied the Mohawk and Oswego rivers alongside African and European batteauxmen, hauling goods and produce. Similarly, Peter Kalm noted, during his travels through New France, that Indians living near the Quebec *habitants* were so busy harvesting ginseng that "the French farmers were not able during that time to hire a single Indian, as they commonly do to help them in the harvest." Warren Johnson commented that "An Indian makes 40£ & upwards yearly by hunting Winter, Spring, & Fall," though he neglected to include other sources of income.[41]

The material worlds of Indians and colonists also merged over the course of the eighteenth century. On one level colonial elites collected Indian "curiosities" and artifacts such as ancient pottery. William Johnson often acted as a middleman between British acquaintances and Indians. For example, one Samuel Cramer wrote to Johnson asking him to obtain "a piece of Ingenuity that rested with some of the Indians in your Neighbourhood which was an excellence they Poss[ess]ed in carveing a true representation or figure of themselves in their Proper Hunting Habits & their Bodys &ct Decorated in a Warlike manner both Sexes in their Different Apparells." Johnson himself maintained a collection of Indian artifacts, wampum belts, calumets, and various pelts. The merchant Daniel Campbell acquired a belt of wampum, moccasins, a knife and sheath, leggings, a tomahawk, a beaver coat, and a French trade musket for one colonial collector.[42]

For more practical reasons, too, ordinary Indians and colonists exchanged clothing, foodways, medicines, personal decoration customs, and craft goods. The settlers' acquisition of Indian trade goods, however, was often illicit. William Johnson complained that some colonists sold rum to Indians at treaty conferences in exchange for their newly acquired clothing, tools, and weapons. He said that he was "frequently obliged to Arm and Cloath many Indians three times over on this account." More often material goods were exchanged and customs learned at settlers' homesteads, taverns, or forts. In his Mohawk Valley travels Warren Johnson saw "Several Indians, & Some white People blue their Faces, (in a kind of Ridges) & nick their Breasts, &:C: which is done by pricking the Skin with Pins, till the Blood comes, & then applying Gunpowder to it; which will remain for ever." He noted the merging of Indian and colonial foodways, such as "white People & Indians [who] Eat bears' Flesh." Soldiers also partook of Indian fare, probably to supplement their meager rations. Warren recorded the story of a sergeant stationed at one of the Mohawk villages who "requested as a favour of the Indians not to make their Broth soe very rich having put vast quantities of Lice in it for that Purpose." Similarly, Indian women who visited their colonial counterparts either observed or were treated to a tea service. Kalm recalled that William Johnson had told him that "several of the Indians who lived close to the European settlements had learned to drink tea," especially Indian women. Kalm claimed that the Indian women also imitated European women's custom of drinking the tea hot. Indians adopted the European custom of tea drinking and obtained tea consumer wares such as pots, cups, and tongs. In 1750 an Onondaga sachem named Onechsagerat invited Cammerhof and David Zeisberger to breakfast: he "set out a tea table, consisting of two blocks used for crushing corn, and then he prepared some very good tea, to which he added Indian bread. The tea cups were a very large spoon and a wooden dish. The tea was boiled in a kettle which hung over the fire. . . . It tasted very good."[43]

Settlers may not have assembled vast collections of Native "curiosities," but they did acquire utilitarian items from the Natives, such as traditional crafts (e.g., baskets, bowls, and brooms). They frequently purchased "Indian shoes," "Indian gartering," and on one occasion "an Indian cup" from merchants who also dealt in the fur trade. Rufus Alexander Grider, an antiquarian and artist who lived in the late 1800s, recorded examples of colonial-era Indian goods still in the possession of Mohawk Valley families. He painted, for example, a "Birch bark Knife box & Wooden Sugar Bowl made by the Schoharie Indians when they lived at Vromans Nose [Onistagrawa]." He also documented a Mohawk-made birch-bark box featuring elaborate Native iconography. A powder horn showing a colonist lighting his pipe from an Indian's pipe richly expresses the world that both cultures shared.[44]

Indian medicines, derived from an extensive knowledge of plants, were of even greater interest to European settlers. During his travels in New France and the British colonies Peter Kalm recorded many instances of Europeans learning effective Indian medicinal cures.

In the Mohawk Valley he observed that "both Indians and Europeans, collect the root of the *Geum rivale*, and pound it." The fever-reducing root, derived from a species of avens, was then either boiled or mixed with brandy. The fact that European women often related these detailed cures suggests their close contacts with Indian women or shamans in the course of their social interactions. The wife of Captain Lindsey at Oswego learned of an Iroquois remedy for toothache that used anemone seeds. Mrs. John Henry Lydius was beset by severe pains in her legs and had to use crutches to walk. Then "a native woman came to the house who cured her" by using the medicinal properties of a dogwood tree. Lydius also related Indian medicines prepared from iris root and sassafras. By the 1760s European settlers regularly sought out Native shamans for treatment. Their actions suggest a trust of Indian medicines based on years of demonstrable effectiveness. Traveler J. Hector St. John de Crèvecoeur recorded during his 1774 travels that he was "greatly surprised when I was at Anaquaga [Oquaga] to see several white people from different parts of Pennsylvania who had purposefully come there to put themselves in the hands and under the care of some Indians who were famous for the medical knowledge. Several were cured while I was there." In the upper Delaware Valley he encountered a weaver's family, who "when sick they had learnt of the Indians how to find in the woods the remedies they wanted." This accumulated knowledge of Indian medicinal recipes was eventually published in "powow books" in Pennsylvania during the early nineteenth century.[45]

Collectively, the personal, religious, economic, and cultural bonds between Iroquois and European settler communities enabled both peoples to coexist for most of the eighteenth century. They also suggest that acculturation and dependency were two-way streets in the Mohawk Valley. We have seen that Mohawk, Oneida, German, Irish, Dutch, and English peoples lived out their lives in a very commingled way. Most important, the existence of peace between the British and their Indian neighbors was not something that governments, diplomacy, and alliances alone could accomplish. Peoples who saw one another daily had to work out their problems for themselves. From Natives' perspectives this was how it should be: two independent peoples living side by side, with harmonious relationships at a local level. By the mid- to late 1760s, however, there were many inauspicious signs of future conflict in British-Indian relations.

As Germans and Oneidas recovered from the war and began to rebuild their lives and communities, they would live through a host of changes brought about by Britain's conquest of New France in 1759–60. Many British colonists were hopeful of a new era of prosperity, but the end of the Seven Years' War brought no lasting peace to North America. Britain's economy struggled through postwar debts, the government faced political instability and frequent changes in the ministry, and Britain's colonies began to resist Parliament's attempts to assert its supremacy. Although neither the Mohawk Valley nor the St. Lawrence Valley was beset by a complete breakdown of law and order in the 1760s, the Ohio Valley was different. This area had been a hotspot of conflict before the war, and it was the scene of numerous imperial crises in the 1760s, including Pontiac's War, from 1763 to 1765. As the next chapter shows, peace broke down among frontier communities in the Ohio Country, and distant colonial and imperial officials were seemingly powerless to effect change. Indian nations there increasingly espoused united resistance to British settlement expansion across the Appalachians. The settlers' unrestrained settlement and habitual murders and violence against Indians in Pennsylvania and the Ohio Country threatened to disrupt the whole of British America's Indian relations. In 1769 William Johnson confided to his friend Lord Adam Gordon that "matters seem to be Coming to a Crisis here both with regard to Whites & Indians."[46]

6. Imperial Crisis in the Ohio Valley

Indian, Colonial American, and British Military Communities

Mehmonawangehelak (Monongahela Valley), 1762

Native Americans knew it as Mehmonawangehelak, referring to the rich soil along its steep banks that occasionally broke off and fell into the river.[1] European colonists followed suit with "Monongahela." Perhaps no other spot of rich Ohio Country soil was more notorious and contested in the 1760s than the Monongahela Valley, especially the Redstone Country, watered by the Monongahela's tributary, Redstone Creek (after the Lenape *Machkachsenhanne*). Mohawks, Mingoes, Marylanders, Virginians, Pennsylvanians, and Indian war parties all met and clashed in the Redstone Country. Colonial and Indian hunters, farmers, and warriors bartered, hunted, and planted corn together and occasionally intermarried. But the Redstone Country symbolized how frontier violence undercut such symbiotic relationships: murder and mayhem erupted there in the late 1760s. From an imperial viewpoint the Redstone Country threatened the stability of Britain's new empire in North America: uncontainable illegal settlement, frontier violence that threatened to renew open warfare with powerful pan-Indian confederacies, and combustible intercolonial land disputes between Pennsylvania and Virginia.

Colonial travelers passing through the Ohio Country reflected on the melancholy legacy of war, and some disdained the "Colony sprung from Hell" that seemed to have emerged there in the postwar years. Braddock's old road from Fort Cumberland to Fort Pitt was filled with the vestiges of conflict from the battlefields of the last war: burned-out colonists' cabins, the rotting remnants of Fort Necessity, the rebuilt ramparts of Fort Burd, and bleaching bones at Braddock's field. "Great quantities of broken Bombshells, cannon, bullets, and other military stores [were] scattered in the woods" at the site of Dunbar's camp. Despite rumors of another war, numerous colonists could be seen on the road with their wagons, livestock, and possessions, going to settle in the Ohio Country with or without the requisite military licenses. "The People are going out verry fast to Settle that Country," one Pennsylvanian wrote, astonished to see "above two Hundred Men between Ligonier and Carlisle" going to settle. Always appreciative of good land, travelers took note of the "hilly fertile Lands" of the Redstone Country. Interspersed with meadows and cleared fields were stands of massive forty-foot-high walnut, oak, chestnut, and cherry trees, three feet in diameter. As one traveler marveled, "the Land from the foot of the Laurel Mountain to Fort Pitt is rich beyond conception." The bottomlands along Redstone Creek attracted thousands of squatter families from Virginia, Maryland, and Pennsylvania, who cleared the land, planted corn, and hunted the plentiful game. Their small log huts were the seats of such aptly named plantations as "Extent," "Discord," "Pretention and Contention," "Fear Fax," and "Whiskey Mount." The nearby garrison at Fort Burd, a small British stockade near the junction of Redstone Creek and the Monongahela, was powerless to stop the settlers' encroachments, despite its location in the heart of the Redstone Country. So fast was the process of settlement that a Seneca Indian journeying southward to attack the Cherokees was astonished to find new cabins and farms at every bend of the Monongahela by the time he returned.[2]

The convergence of three rivers, Native trails, and British military roads produced an extraordinary confluence of cultures in the Ohio Valley. Thoroughfares such as Braddock's and Forbes's roads began to overlay an even more complex network of Indian trails (Braddock's Road, in fact, was once Nemacolin's trail). The Catawba Path, which ran from Iroquoia to the Southeast, came through the heart of the Redstone Country and other Euroamerican settlements along the Cheat River. The east-west Mingo Path facilitated daily contact between the Mingoes and the Monongahela colonists. Hundreds of Iroquois, Delaware, Shawnee, and Mingo warriors going to fight their Catawba enemies came through the colonial habitations weekly, bartering with or demanding supplies. Some squatters' homesteads "stood right on the war path, where [Indians] went from about Ft. Pitt to kill Catawbas in the south, often in parties of fifty or sixty." The Redstone Country became a source of corn, whiskey, and provisions for Native and British warriors alike.[3]

Despite cultural, ethnic, and linguistic barriers in the Redstone Country, the Native and colonial inhabitants and passersby communicated, creating what were often amicable relationships. Older patterns of peaceful exchange reemerged after the war. Travelers encountered pack-horse drivers who "can talk ye Indian tongue." Former captives could be found among the settlers and the Indians, "well qualified to speak the Delaware's language" and other Native tongues. Travelers came upon settlements of pacifist Quakers from Pennsylvania and Dunkers from Maryland who "receiv'd them kindly." Lastly, Euroamerican women and men occasionally intermarried with Indian men and women. Most of these unions occurred in Indian communities where Euroamerican captives had been fully assimilated. But some marriages were volitional. One Indian-European couple familiar to the Redstone Creek settlers was Mohawk Peter and his wife. Quaker James Kenny recorded in his journal the close ties

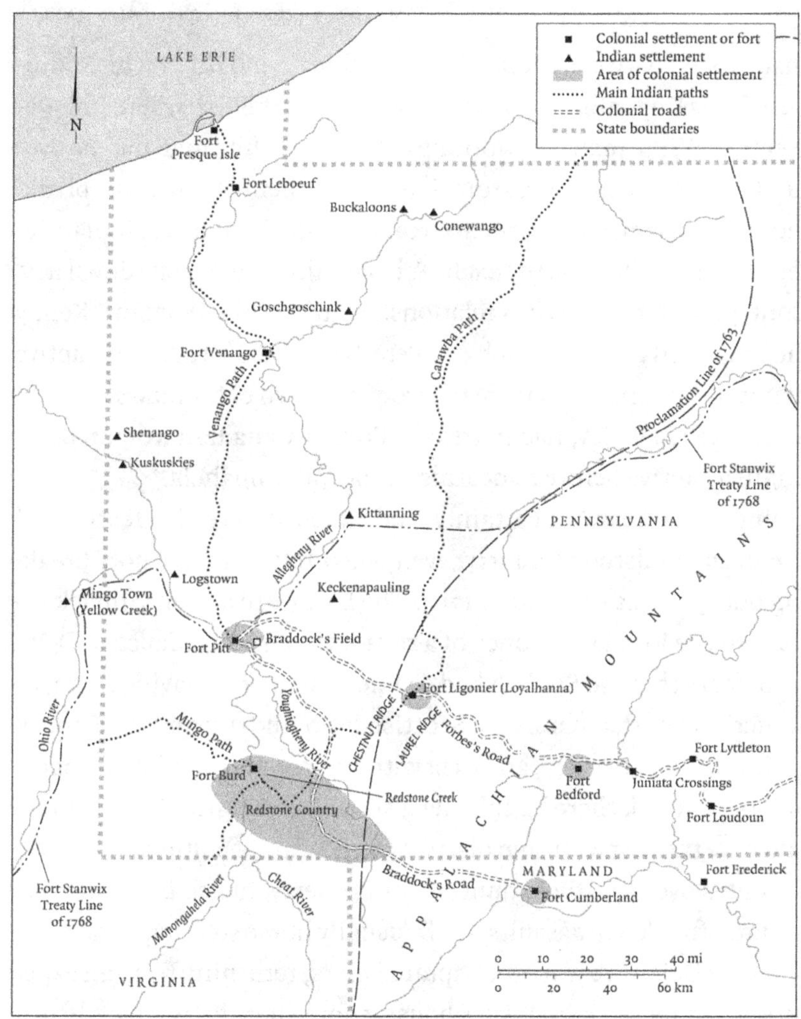

Map 3. The Ohio Valley, ca. 1760s

that existed between Mohawk Peter's family and other white families: "This Day came to yᵉ River opposite yᵉ Fort Burd, where Indⁿ Peter and a White man was working at Corn; yᵉ White man put me over in a Cannoe, Swam yᵉ Creature. I informed them of yᵉ Indians breaking out agin which put them in Great fear; got Breakfast at Indian Peter's House & they talked that he & his family would come down in yᵉ Contry amongst his Wifes relations, being a White Woman." Kenny did not specify whether Mohawk Peter's wife was an adopted captive or not. Peter, originally from the Iroquois town of Kahnawake in the St. Lawrence Valley, had married a French-Canadian woman or an English captive before relocating to the Monongahela.[4]

But "Great fear," uncertainty, and violence were also features of life in the Redstone Country, even when Indians were not "breaking out agin," as they did in 1763. The Delaware leader Killbuck informed the Rev. David Jones of a rumor that gave credence to Delaware fears that the English had "some design of enslaving them, or something of that nature": a Scottish highland officer "took one of their women as his wife, and went with her into Maryland about Joppa: and they heard, there he sold her a slave like a negro." Such rumors laid bare the suspicion and distrust at the heart of cultural meetings. Disputes over livestock, hunting, or property, fueled by ubiquitous liquor, often led to assaults, theft (usually horse stealing), and murder. One Delaware warrior, Captain Peters, returning from an expedition, stopped at John Ryan's house, somewhere between Redstone and the Cheat River. Captain Peters "wanted to take Some Rum from the White Man by the name of Ryan who in the Scuffle shot the Indian, and made his Escape to Virginia." In the spring of 1762 a party of soldiers from Fort Burd came upon a hunting cabin engulfed in flames: Cherokees who had escaped from their Iroquois captors had killed two hunters, Nathaniel Thomlinson and Jacob Aron (a former captive), and taken their long rifles. (The soldiers sent for Mohawk Peter to help mediate the affair.)[5]

Weary travelers who arrived safely at the forks of the Ohio confronted a monumental symbol of British power, Fort Pitt. Comparable in size and design to the British fort at Crown Point, the pentagonal Fort Pitt covered nearly eighteen acres of ground. The British garrisoned the fort beginning in 1759, and it played an important role in their attempts to extend imperial authority over nearby Natives, British frontier settlers, and faraway French posts in the *pays d'en haut*. Fort Pitt was also a military community consisting of soldiers, traders, camp followers, artisans, farmers, laundresses, and Indians. The missionary David McClure recalled that "the first object of our attention was a number of poor drunken Indians, staggering & yelling throughout the Village. It is the headquarters of Indian traders, & the resort of Indians of different & distant tribes, who come to exchange their peltry & furs for rum, blankets & ammunition etc." Outside the fort was an ever-growing colonial village of "40 dwelling houses made of hewed logs." The village was often the scene of encounters between colonists and Indians that commingled intimacy and hostility. Some women at the settlement employed their skills as seamstresses to make ruffled calico "Indian shirts." One traveler noted "an Indian who had a white woman" there. An Iroquois war party passed by Fort Pitt with a Cherokee warrior who "was known by some of the Soldiers here who Spoke to him," because they had fought with him during General Forbes's campaign against the French in 1758. Inside the fort a round of drinks among Iroquois warriors and Virginia militiamen turned violent when "a Difference arose between them," and the Long Knives wounded three of the Iroquois and stole their trade goods. In the commandant's house Col. Henry Bouquet frequently mediated such disputes and addressed Indians' grievances. Shawnees once complained to Bouquet of the increasing numbers of colonists' farms in the Monongahela Valley; Colonel Bouquet promised to have all of them pulled down.[6]

"Redstone" was a name painfully familiar to British officials like the Earl of Shelburne in London and Sir William Johnson in New York.

In 1766 an angry Shelburne had instructed Johnson, "The Violences & Irregularities of the Traders & Settlers cannot & must not be endured: The settlement at Red Stone Creek made as you observe out of the Boundaries of any Province is a striking instance of the Temerity of those Settlers." Illegal settlement and racial violence in places like the Redstone Country became imperial crises in the 1760s, precisely when imperial officials were trying to consolidate the new empire that Britain had won from France. British leaders crafted an Indian policy that tried to accommodate colonial land and commercial interests to the Indians' need for security. The key features of this new policy after 1763 included centralizing colonial-Indian relations in the Indian Departments, preserving peace on the western borders, and regulating land grants and the Indian trade. Controlling illegal settlement by creating a boundary line became the principal focus of imperial agents trying to maintain peace. But as a mortified Sir William Johnson discovered, his "Schemes & endeavours for preserving or restoring tranquility" were frequently defeated by "the gross Irregularities of our worst Enemies the Frontier Banditti." From the perspectives of Whitehall and Johnson Hall, squatters jeopardized the whole edifice of empire. Throughout the mid-to late 1760s British elites were terrified, as Sir William Johnson was in 1765, of a war "more [General] than the last [Pontiac's War]," due to the colonists' "ungovernable passion" for land.[7]

Warfare, violence, rebellions, and rumors of war marked the decade of the 1760s as one of the most chaotic in colonial American history. No sooner had Quebec fallen, than the Cherokee War erupted in South Carolina, followed by Pontiac's War across the Great Lakes and Ohio Country, the Stamp Act riots in port cities, the North and South Carolina regulator movements, tenant resistance in the Hudson Valley of New York, and the series of white-Indian murders that plagued Virginia and Pennsylvania. Rumors of wars and slave rebellions kept people on the mental precipice of conflict. Historians have become accustomed to thinking of imperial crises in terms of the build-up to the American Revolution. Long before 1776, however, imperial administrators and colonial governors were gravely concerned with the crisis that was unfolding primarily in the Ohio Valley. The estimated "500 Families" in the Monongahela and Cheat valleys, who, as one British officer assured Gage, "defy any Force civil or military sent against them," were as serious a threat as Stamp Act rioters. Additionally, in the very same year that the Stamp Act riots unfolded, British authorities became aware that Maryland militia had murdered Shawnee warriors near Pittsburgh; Virginia settlers had waylaid a party of Cherokees, killing five; and a mob of Pennsylvania settlers called "the Black Boys" had destroyed convoys of Indian traders' goods and fired on British regulars at Fort Loudon. One of the reasons for this surge in conflict was the militarization of colonial and Indian societies over the course of the eighteenth century's many imperial wars. But the Seven Years' War itself created the structural conditions for a "hollow British Empire," as historian Fred Anderson argues.[8]

The hollowness of Britain's American empire became fully apparent in the mid-to late 1760s, as squatters from Virginia, Maryland, and Pennsylvania breached the Appalachian barrier—using British military roads—and settled and hunted by the thousands on Indian lands in the Monongahela, Redstone, Youghiogheny, and Cheat valleys. Elites, like later historians, believed that squatters encroached on Indian lands; threatened orderly frontier development; imperiled the Indian trade; committed murders and violent acts upon Indians; and exhibited a disaffected, lawless, even rebellious spirit. Colonial officials in general were fearful that law and authority among the common people were breaking down. As the Pennsylvania Assembly asked in the aftermath of the grisly Frederick Stump murders in 1768, "Where can these Things terminate, but in Tumults, and a total Abolition of the Powers of Government?" In most cases magistrates were unable to apprehend, let alone prosecute, the perpetrators of crimes and murders against Indians. "There is a manifest Failure of

Justice somewhere," the Assembly continued. "From whence can it arise?" British ministers' and imperial agents' worst nightmare was that ordinary settlers would spark another Pontiac's War with another powerful Indian confederacy. Cognizant of their military weakness, British leaders also wished to avoid renewed warfare with the Indians, for it would mean wide-scale deployment of British troops, more expenses added to Britain's staggering postwar debt, and more confrontations with colonial legislatures jealous of their rights of taxation. In short, frontier developments fundamentally shaped British elites' most basic perceptions of colonists and the nature of law and authority in the colonies.[9]

Why and how, then, did the imperial crisis develop out of the struggle for Ohio lands among imperial officials, colonial governments, British garrisons, squatters, and Indians? What were the Ohio Indians' perspectives, and how did they respond differently to the colonization of the Ohio Valley? Most historians would argue that the imperial crisis was ultimately fueled by a burgeoning colonial population freed of French restraint and seeking opportunity and land on the frontiers and that a vicious cycle of violence between local settlers and Indians exacerbated matters. But it is all too easy to reduce these questions to numbers—to the notion that more European settlers came into the western lands than either the Natives or British proclamations could restrain. It is even more inaccurate to characterize all white settlers as racist killers, especially when the historical evidence is closely inspected. Despite the memories of Pontiac's War, peace did return to the frontier, and ordinary Natives and Euroamericans continued to peacefully interact with each other. Their interactions form part of a complex story that will be revealed here. What previous historians have not realized is that the British Army—more so than the squatters, with whom Natives often peacefully dealt—was the touchstone of conflict because of its military colonization of the Ohio Valley. Alfred James, writing in the 1930s, was one of the first historians to suggest that there was a direct relationship between the British Army and settlement expansion in the early West, but neither he nor any subsequent historians have explained how this process actually worked. The historical evidence reveals that the British Army explicitly encouraged and planted colonial settlements on Natives' lands. The Seven Years' War, as Stephen Brumwell argues, "witnessed an unprecedented allocation of redcoats to North America." Paradoxically, this unprecedented deployment of British troops greatly facilitated settlement of western lands that the Empire wanted to preserve from settlers. The British army's military colonization of the Ohio Valley, the Euroamerican settlement expansion that followed, and intercultural violence were crucial developments in the Ohio Valley in the 1760s. These three legacies of the Seven Years' War would set in motion the fundamental processes shaping Indian-colonist relations in the Ohio Valley for the next fifty years.[10]

After two devastating conflicts within ten years British leaders believed that establishing a clear boundary line between the colonies and Indian nations would stave off any impending war. They did not object to colonial expansion per se, but they desired orderly expansion led by men like themselves. From 1763 to 1774 the British governed the trans-Appalachian West as an unorganized area nominally subject to military authority and the superintendents of Indian affairs. British policy held that title to lands that they had wrested from the French rested with George III (Indians had only rights of occupancy) and that the commander-in-chief of British forces in North America could grant rights to settle in the new lands. The temporary Proclamation Line of 1763 forbade settlement west of the Appalachian Mountains until a new boundary could be negotiated. Knowing that a new purchase would occur in the foreseeable future, Virginia and Pennsylvania maintained claims to Ohio Valley lands through their charters, trading operations, and stalled ventures like the Ohio Land Company. A boundary line would prevent not only distended colonial settlement in the trans-Appalachian West but also the rash of Indian-colonist murders that imperiled the peace. In 1765 Sir William

Johnson and Six Nations sachems negotiated a tentative line. John-son informed an Iroquois assembly in 1765 of "the Plan of a Bound-ary between our Provinces and the Indians, (which no White man shall dare to invade) as the best and surest method of ending such like Disputes, & securing your property to you beyond a Possibility of Disturbance." An Onondaga speaker concurred, saying that "such a thing will be very necessary, provided the white people will abide by it." As efforts to iron out the boundary gained momentum, the Lords of Trade argued in 1767 that "the Establishment of this [boundary] Line will, in all probability, have the Effect to prevent the fatal Con-sequences of an Indian War that seems at present to threaten the Middle Colonies."[11]

The Ohio Indians hoped for a lasting peace, based upon Britain's honorable fulfillment of the terms of the 1758 Treaty of Easton, which helped end the fighting in the Ohio Valley. Natives had demonstrated an "acute awareness of strategy and tactics" in their war to restore a just and accommodating peace. They had not only won the war against Pennsylvania but secured key concessions from the colony's Proprietors. Delawares and Quakers had exposed the Penns' deal-ings with the Indians, particularly the infamous Walking Purchase of 1737. Ohio Indians secured a degree of territorial integrity when the Proprietors agreed to renounce most of the dubious 1754 Albany Purchase; British officials promised to reopen trade and prevent colo-nial settlement west of the Appalachians. The commander-in-chief, Gen. Jeffrey Amherst, assured the Ohio Natives, "I mean not to take any of your lands . . . they shall remain your absolute property." But his rhetoric belied the reality of the problem.[12]

In contrast to modern historians' interpretations, most Ohio In-dians did not think of the British Empire as a "restraining force": they viewed the British Army as a powerful instrument of imperial and colonial expansion. As historian Daniel Richter argues, the his-tories of Indians and colonists in the 1700s "moved along parallel paths." Stationing thousands of British troops in America after 1763 provoked protest and conspiratorial notions among colonial Americans; in a parallel way Native Americans also experienced the British presence as an unwanted standing army that threatened to destroy their basic liberties. In 1759–60 the British Army consolidated its control over the valley's waterways to guard against French counterattacks and to support operations against New France's outposts in *le pays d'en haut*. The Delaware leader Tamaqua urged the British to "go back over the mountain, and to stay there." Promising only to drive off the French and to protect trade, Col. Henry Bouquet assured the Ohio Indians that the army would not dispossess them. But the Delawares gave credence to private reports from traders, "many runaways," and captives, who told them that the English and French "intended to join and cut all the *Indians* off." Shingas, Tamaqua, and Pisquetomen had told the Moravian emissary Christian Frederick Post in 1758 that they did not understand why the English did not bring "the news of peace [the Treaty of Easton] *before* your army [Forbes's] had begun to march." Residual anger over the army's continued presence became apparent when Pisquetomen stormed into the Quaker James Kenny's store in 1761, wanting to know "what ye English or ye General meant by coming here." Kenny quickly learned that the Natives were "very jealous of ye English coming here with an army." Keekyuscung, a sage Delaware sachem at Kuskuski, warned Post that "if the English would draw back over the mountain, they would get all the other nations in their interest; but if they staid and settled there, all the nations would be against them; and he was afraid it would be a great war, and never come to a peace again."[13]

Unhappily, Keekyuscung's prophecy was fulfilled. Instead of peace, the Ohio Indians found themselves moving toward renewed hostilities. British neglect in the Indian trade, privation in Native communities, renewed settlement expansion, and news of the Anglo-French peace terms turned many Ohio Natives toward war. The Indians could also deduce from Fort Pitt's size alone that the British Army would not withdraw and sensibly feared that the army might be turned against their villages. The Ohio Indians "pointed out the Forts *Pitt* & *Augusta*, as the greatest Eyesores" from their vantage point. Fort Pitt's garrison ranged anywhere from three hundred to seven hundred during the 1760s, not counting the other regulars stationed at a dozen other outposts in the Ohio Valley and the Great Lakes region. Natives wondered whether the English "designed to Build another Philadelphia on their Lands." Increasingly, the Ohio Indians were "jealous of the growing power of the English in this Country" and "seem^d as if they would be too Strong for God himself." But many Indians, inspired by nativist prophets such as Neolin, held a "Vission of Heaven where there was no White people but all Indians"; they wanted a "total Separation" from whites.[14]

From 1763 to 1765 Indian nations all across the Ohio Valley and Great Lakes waged war against the British, besieged their garrisons, and attacked their settlements in what became known as Pontiac's War. The network of British garrisons in the west fell like a house of cards, with the exceptions of Detroit, Fort Pitt, and Niagara. Pennsylvania's and Virginia's frontier settlers again suffered tremendous losses, which deepened their hatred of Indians. After a series of early reversals the British Army launched a two-pronged foray into the Ohio Country in 1764, but these expeditions did not militarily crush a "rebellion." Stalemate ensued as the exhausted parties made peace. Shortly after Pontiac's War an Onondaga sachem reminded Sir William Johnson that "the chief cause of all the late wars was about Lands, we saw the English coming towards us from all Parts, and they cheated us so often, that we could not think well of it." Native peoples had forcefully united across ethnic lines around the main issues of land and sovereignty; as one Iroquois man told the commander at Fort Niagara, "they still commanded the Lands." Keekyuscung was a casualty of the great war that he had prophesied, falling in the Battle of Bushy Run in 1763. He and his people's land would never come to peace again.[15]

Neither boundary lines nor the threat of war deterred the thousands of ordinary settlers, who believed that "y Land on this side y Alegheny Mountain will be made a King's Governm & that in 2 years or less time, there will be encouragement from y King to Settle these Lands to this place, Viz Pittsburgh." No sooner had the ink dried on the Treaty of Easton than ordinary farmers and hunters began to settle and hunt across the mountains. Maj. Gen. Frederick Haldimand characterized the *Zeitgeist* as a "spirit of emigration" that seemed to possess ordinary people. One descendant of an early settler recalled a common saying: that "land was to be had here for taking up." As early as 1761 Bouquet complained to Robert Monckton that "several Idle People from Virga and Maryland made it a Practice to hunt along the Mononghehela, which gives umbrage to the Indians. Their scheme Seems to be to reconnoitre the Land, & I am told that several of those pretended Hunters intend to settle above & below Redstone Creek." The two migration streams running into the Ohio Country of the 1760s originated primarily in Pennsylvania and Virginia. While it is difficult to estimate precisely the numbers involved, the scale of illegal settlement was enough to confound contemporaries. Travelers in the 1760s and 1770s always commented on the large numbers of colonists heading west on the major wagon roads. George Croghan marveled in 1770, "What number of families has settled since the congress, to the westward of the high ridge, I cannot pretend to say positively; but last year, I am sure, there were between four and five thousand, and all this spring and summer the roads have been lined with waggons moving to the Ohio." By the early 1770s there were perhaps twenty thousand or more colonists living in the Ohio Country.[16]

Euroamericans' determination to obtain land is a major reason why the Ohio Indians found themselves again facing colonial encroachments after fighting two wars designed to prevent them. Despite their horrific experiences in the Seven Years' War and Pontiac's War, Pennsylvania and Virginia settlers were neither disinclined to return to their ruined plantations nor more respectful of Indians' territories. John Struthers's family, for example, migrated from Cecil County, Maryland, to the Ohio Country in 1773–74 despite fears of impending war with the Shawnees. Colonial land papers provide a glimpse of the settlers' unquenchable thirst for land. Some of these land applications contain stories of incredible persistence in the face of adversity. Cumberland County residents William and Mary White, for example, were turned off their property three times between 1750 and 1763: once by Richard Peters in 1750 and twice during wartime. Yet they and other settlers always returned to their tracts. Josiah Records's experience provides another example of how ordinary farmers undertook settlement of the western lands. Records and his brothers-in-law migrated from the Antietam Valley in Maryland to the Redstone Country in the spring of 1766. Traveling on Braddock's Road, they began clearing ground and planting corn and then returned to move their families over the mountains in time for the fall harvest. Josiah was, in addition to being a farmer, an "expert hunter" who took his furs back to Hagerstown, Maryland, to barter for much-needed supplies.[17]

Hunters like Josiah Records were among the most troublesome colonists to flood the Ohio Valley. Sgt. Angus McDonald, commanding the minuscule garrison at Fort Burd, complained to Bouquet that "Here Comes Such Crowds of Hunters out of the Inhabitence as fills those woods at which the Indians seems very much disturbed and say the white people Kills all there Deer." The hunters simply avoided the British garrisons, and McDonald had to content himself with seizing the hunters' horses. In the woods they encountered angry Indian hunters who relied on the Monongahela Valley for wild game. Warriors passing through the area unable to subsist on game were forced to seek provisions at settlers' homesteads, where disputes might arise. Native hunters either warned away the hunters themselves or complained "bitterly" to British officers that "a Number of

White Men have been out the Whole season and Distroyed a Great quantity of game."[18]

Most colonial farmers and hunters crossed the Appalachians with little thought of accommodating Indians, because they envisioned no place for Natives in colonial society. In 1750 Virginia trader Christopher Gist conversed with two Delawares, Beaver and Captain Oppamylucah, who "desired to know where the Indian's Land lay, for that the French claimed all the Land on one side the River Ohio & the English on the other Side." What place, they asked, did Indians have? Reflecting on the conversation, Gist admitted in his journal that "I was at a Loss to answer Him as I now also was." Was it the first time he had ever thought of "where the Indian's Land lay"? He told the Delawares that "We are all one King's People and the different Colour of our Skins makes no Difference in the King's Subjects; You are his People as well as We, if you will take Land & pay the King's Rights You will have the same Privileges as the White People have." But very few ordinary settlers, after two horrendous wars, believed that Indians were equally the king's subjects. With the French threat eliminated, they had even fewer reasons to see the Indians as allies. Many colonists, especially veterans, probably saw the western lands as theirs by right of conquest. In short, the British settlers believed that the edenic Ohio Valley "wants Nothing but Cultivation to make it a most delightfull Country"—a statement that presumed a "natural" landscape devoid of all Indian inhabitants.[19]

But colonists did not simply find a new Eden in the Ohio Country: they had to make one by driving Indians off the land. The series of revenge killings and indiscriminate murders that had begun in the Seven Years' War and Pontiac's War continued unabated from 1763 to the Revolution and beyond. Historians have long emphasized settlers' violence and racial animosity, as exemplified in the Paxton Massacre of 1763. No historian, however, has ever methodically charted violent incidents to understand the nature and frequency of intercultural murders. Almost all of the violence was localized on the Virginia and Pennsylvania frontiers. New York and New France did not experience anywhere near the same degree of violence: peaceful relationships between Natives and colonists continued there until the 1770s and beyond. Table 3, however, demonstrates that a definite increase in violence fueled the flames of the imperial crisis. From 1760 to 1774 (excluding Pontiac's War) there were approximately thirty-nine incidents of murder in the greater Pennsylvania region, in which at least one hundred Indians and colonists died. Colonists committed approximately twenty-six murders of Indians, while there were thirteen cases of Natives murdering colonists. Many historical accounts portray the Virginia and Pennsylvania settlers as bloodthirsty murderers, but much of this portrayal is exaggerated. According to the homicide statistics for Pennsylvania during the same period, whites were more likely to kill whites than they were to kill Indians. In comparison to the twenty-six murders of Indians from 1760 to 1774, there were well over one hundred homicide indictments of whites and others.[20]

It is clear that using the Paxton Massacre as a convenient explanatory device for the beginnings of racial violence will not work. To be sure, repeated incidents of violence kept Indians and Euroamericans on the precipice of open conflict. Despite the formal cessation of hostilities, many colonists and Indians continued their revenge killings. The violence produced "universal uneasiness and discontent" among most northeastern Indian peoples. Further, a large number of murders—ten—were committed between 1766 and 1767, when imperial officials' perception of crisis was especially acute; the officials were especially fearful of another war with a pan-Indian alliance (fueled by rumors of a confederation forming at Scioto). And Thomas Gage sent letters to the western post commanders in July 1766 warning them to prepare for hostilities. Nevertheless, the violence in the Ohio Country was intensely personal in character: killings often occurred in the context of social or economic interactions such as drinking or trading. This understanding challenges recent portraits of racialized Euroamerican settlers. As Elizabeth Perkins observes in her study of Kentucky, "It is tempting to view these brutal incidents as early evidence of Indian dehumanization and racially based Indian hating among white borderers. Yet their context here seems too personal, too immediate, too *intimate* to represent the categorical racialism that would gain respectability by the 1840s." As the portrait of the Redstone Country demonstrates, Indians and settlers continued to interact in nonviolent ways, establish mutually satisfactory trading relationships, and negotiate over land just as they had before the wars. But the new ingredients in these encounters were the mutual distrust, hatred, and vengeful feelings that some—but not all—Indians and colonists held. The desire for vengeance often led colonial assailants to commit indiscriminate mass murders of Indians and their families, often while expressing vengeful anti-Indian sentiments. From the gallows in 1766 James Annin declared that "he thought it a duty to extirpate the Heathen," even if this meant raping and killing a pregnant Indian woman who was "near the Time of Delivery." By contrast, Indians typically murdered individual colonists because of alcohol's influence, colonists' ill-treatment, or pecuniary motives. Indians destroyed colonial families only in wartime or to avenge the colonists' mass killings. The greater incidence of colonists' murdering of Indians reflects the "desire for revenge [that] burned deeply in the backcountry after the fighting in the *pays d'en haut* had ended," as Richard White observes.[21]

A murder at Braddock's Field in the cold of early November 1767 represents one of the most revealing examples of the context in which violence occurred. A white hunter covered in blood stumbled into Fort Pitt, informing Capt. Charles Edmonstone of a shocking murder. The night before the hunter had come to Braddock's Field and found lodging in a tent with an Indian and a local settler, Mr. McDonald, both of whom had been hired at a plantation to watch over the corn crops and livestock. Just past one o'clock the nameless hunter was awakened from his sleep by the sound of gunfire: the Indian had shot

Table 3. Violence in the Ohio Country, 1760–74

Date	Victim(s)	Assailant(s)	Place of murder	Circumstances	Documentary references
1760	Doctor John, wife, two children (Delawares)	John Mason, James Foster, William George, and sons of Arthur Foster	Conodoguinet Creek near Carlisle	At Doctor John's hunting cabin	MPCP, 8:455–56, 709, 712; PA, 1st ser., 3:731
1760	Unidentified Virginia soldier	Corp. Jonathan Swain (Virginia)	Bushy Run	George Croghan believed that the assailant was "some Indian who has been Abused here in his Liquor by the Soldiers."	BP, 4:572
1761	Unidentified Indian	Unidentified Indians (perhaps Mingoes)	Near Venango	A British soldier later reported Swain's "Rifld Piece . . . [was] found upon One of the Mingos."	BP, 5:294–95
1761	Thomas Hickman (Delaware interpreter)	Unidentified; probably Path Valley settler(s)	Path Valley	Hickman, traveling through the valley alone, died of gunshot wounds.	PA, 1st ser., 4:65
1761	Mingo man	Lt. James Piper, Pennsylvania Regiment	Near Fort Ligonier	The Mingo was accused of stealing horses.	BP, 5:575–76, 588–89, 594–95
1761	Unidentified Indian man	Unidentified Easton resident	Easton	The Easton resident claimed the act "was in defence of his Wife and Children, whom the Indian was about to murder . . . after coming several times to his House in the night time, disturbing him & using him very ill."	MPCP, 8:657–58
1761	Seneca warrior	British soldier	Fort Vengence	Another Seneca later "complained of his brother being killed by some of the garrison at Venango without any cause."	SWJP, 3:453, 459, 494; 13:227–28, 233, 255

1762	Nathaniel Thomlinson and Jacob Aron	Cherokees	Redstone Country	Cherokees who had escaped their Iroquois captors burned Thomlinson and Aron's hunting cabin and stole their rifles.	BP, 5:74–75, "Journal of James Kenny, 1761–1763," 152, 158; SWJP, 10:452, 543
1763 (Oct.)	John Stinton	Renatus or Schonqueh (Mahican)	Northampton County	Stenton was a tavernkeeper; Renatus, a Moravian, was tried and acquitted in 1764.	Wallace, Thirty Thousand Miles, 72–82, 434
1763 (Dec.)	Twenty Conestoga Indians	Paxton Boys	Conestoga and Lancaster, Lancaster County	The Paxton Boys suspected the Conestogas of collaborating with enemy Indians; some Conestogas were "gone towards Smith's Iron Works to sell brooms"; others "lodged at one Peter Swar's." The Paxton Boys killed and butchered some of the Indians at Conestoga town; other Indians were killed in the Lancaster jail on a Sunday morning while in protective custody.	MPCP, 9:88–110; Dunbar, The Paxton Papers; Vaughan, "Frontier Banditti and the Indians"
1765	One to three Shawnee warriors	James Bow and William Dice, Maryland militiamen	Near Pittsburgh	Bow wanted to "obtain the reward" for a scalp and openly flaunted it to others.	PA, 1st ser., 4:217; BP, 6:738–39; SWJP, 11:540, 569, 586, 603, 796
1765	Unidentified trader	Unidentified Seneca Indian	Near Pittsburgh (?)	The Seneca man's jealousy over his wife's relationship with the trader sparked the murder.	John Reid to Thomas Gage, June 18, 1765, Gage Papers, AS 38, WLCL
1766	Two British soldiers	St. Joseph Potawatomies	Near Red River	Potawatomie warriors killed two British soldiers for allegedly raping two Indian women.	George Croghan Journal, May 1766, Gage Papers, AS 51, WLCL

continued

Table 3. Violence in the Ohio Country, 1760–74 (continued)

Date	Victim(s)	Assailant(s)	Place of murder	Circumstances	Documentary references
1766	Oneida Indian	Robert Simonds (Seamon)	Sussex County NJ	The Oneida had come to trade and was robbed and murdered by Simonds; a mob of twenty-five men freed Simonds from jail, but he was recaptured about nine months later, tried, convicted, and executed. Witnesses said that Simonds said "he would destroy any Indian that came his way."	*Pennsylvania Gazette,* Apr. 17, 24, 1766, Jan. 1, 1767; SWJP, 5:419
1766	Hannah and Catherine (Delawares?)	James Annin and James McKinzy	Moorestown NJ	Annin and McKinzy had been "on the Western Frontiers of Pennsylvania and Virginia"; McKinzy "gave them abusive Language," and the men "went to the Indians with Intent to ravish them, if they should refuse their Offers." Both were convicted and hanged; Annin declared "he thought it a Duty to extirpate the Heathen." One of the women was "near the Time of Delivery, and had Marks of shocking Treatment."	*Pennsylvania Gazette,* July 10, 17, 1766, Aug. 7, 1766
1766	Mohawk warrior	Samuel Jacobs	Between Forts Cumberland and Bedford	Mohawk warrior returning from the southeast	*MPCP,* 9:304–6, 352; *Papers of Francis Fauquier,* 3:1340–41; Croghan to Gage, Mar. 23, 1766, Gage Papers, AS 50, WLCL

Year					
1766	Karaghiagigo and four other Iroquois	Unknown	Near Fort Pitt	This incident was only a rumor: Iroquois alleged that Karaghiagigo's party, returning from the southeast, were murdered, but they returned a few weeks later.	*SWJP*, 12:115, 123; *DRCHNY*, 7:864
1766	"Captain Peter," Delaware warrior	John Ryan	Between Redstone and Cheat valleys	"The Indian named Captain Peters wanted to take Some Rum from the White Man by the name of Ryan who in the Scuffle shot the Indian, and made his Escape to Virginia."	*SWJP*, 5:540, 12:296, 308; *Papers of Francis Fauquier*, 3:1435–39; Murray to Gage, Feb. 27, 1767, Gage Papers AS 38, WLCL
1766	Four to five Delawares and Shawnees (men)	Two unidentified white men	Near Fort Pitt	An Indian hunting party was "robbed and murdered" by the two white men, who killed the men while they were sleeping but spared an Indian woman and child.	*MPCP*, 9:479; *Papers of Francis Fauquier*, 3:1369; *SWJP*, 12:91–92; William Murray to Gage, Apr. 24, 1766, Gage Papers, AS 50, WLCL
1767	Henry O'Brian, Peter Brown, and eight traders	Unidentified Indians	Ohio River west of Pittsburgh	Two batteaux, loaded with £3,000 in trade goods, were "attacked and Pillaged" near the Falls of the Ohio	*MPCP*, 9:469, 521
1767	Thomas Mitchell (trader)	Shawnees	Shawnee villages	Unknown	*MPCP*, 9:469, 521

continued

Table 3. Violence in the Ohio Country, 1760–74 (*continued*)

Date	Victim(s)	Assailant(s)	Place of murder	Circumstances	Documentary references
1767	John McDonald	Delaware Indian (perhaps métis)	Braddock's Field, near Pittsburgh	McDonald was murdered by a man of Delaware and Euroamerican parentage; both were working on a farm at Braddock's field; the Indian complained of ill treatment by McDonald and another white hunter who survived the assault.	Extract of a letter from Capt. Edmonstone to Lt. Col. Wilkins, Nov. 11, 1767; Report of Ensign [Thomas] Batts, Nov. 10, 1767, Gage Papers, AS 72, WLCL; MPCP, 9:470, 521; SWJP, 9:524
1767	Virginians and Indians killed and wounded in a skirmish		Virginia backcountry	"After the Indians were entertained and fed, they robd the Man at whose house they were received, set fire to his Stacks and wantonly kill'd his Cattle. Upon this eleven young fellows persued them and came up with them when the fray began."	*Papers of Francis Fauquier*, 3:1435
1768	White Mingo (Seneca), Cornelius (Mohican), John Campbell (Mohican), Jonas Griffy (Stockbridge or Jersey Indian), three women (White Mingo's, Cornelius's, and Campbell's wives), two girls, and a child	Frederick Stump and John Ironcutter	Middle Creek	The Indians were drunk and allegedly threatened Stump while they were at his house. Stump and his indentured servant, John Ironcutter, killed the Indians at his house and the Indians' nearby hunting cabins. Stump and Ironcutter killed and scalped their victims, threw some of the bodies into ice-choked Middle Creek, and burned the rest of the bodies.	MPCP 9:414–90; Rowe, "Frederick Stump Affair"

Year	Victim	Assailant	Location	Notes	Source
1769	Seneca George (younger)	Peter Read	Middle Creek	A canoe full of colonists fired upon a party of Indians fishing from the shore; Read was incarcerated, tried, and acquitted.	*MPCP*, 9:603; *PA*, 1st ser., 4:294; *SWJP*, 7:62–65; *Pennsylvania Gazette*, Dec. 14, 1769; Merrell, *Into the American Woods*, 302–15
1769	Jacob Daniel (Delaware) and two male children	Charles Hanigan, James Booth, and two others	Cheat River	The murder occurred at the Indians' hunting cabin.	Edmonstone to Gage, Sept. 10, 1769, Gage Papers, AS 87, WLCL; *Pennsylvania Gazette*, Oct. 5, 1769
1769	Unidentified Indian	Cornelius Dogherty	Pittsburgh	"As there had been, some Time before, a white Man killed by an Indian, there was but little said on either Side, only advising each other to keep fast Hold of the Chain of Friendship, and giving some Tobacco and Provisions."	*Pennsylvania Gazette*, Oct. 5, 1769
1769	Unidentified white man	Seneca Indian	Fort Pitt	Unknown	*SWJP*, 7:79
1770	Two Indians	Unidentified assailant(s)	Fort Pitt	Unclear whether assailants were Indians or colonists	*SWJP*, 7:853
1770	Iroquois (probably Mingo)	Virginia settlers	Cheat River	An altercation over property occurred at a hunting camp at which the Iroquois and Virginians were trading and drinking	George Croghan Journal, 1770, Gage Papers, AS 94, WLCL

continued

Table 3. Violence in the Ohio Country, 1760–74 (continued)

Date	Victim(s)	Assailant(s)	Place of murder	Circumstances	Documentary references
1771	Two unidentified Indians	Matthew Haley	Monongahela Valley	Haley was a runaway indentured servant; he fell in with the two Indians on the trail and killed them in camp	PA, 1st ser., 4:430–32
1771	Delaware warrior	Unidentified	Redstone Creek	Unknown	PA, 1st ser., 4:349
1774	Bald Eagle	Jacob Scott, William Hacker, Eliza Runner	Monongahela Valley (Redstone Country)	Bald Eagle hunted with Monongahela settlers and was well known by them.	Veech, *Monongahela of Old*, 88; Sipe, *Indian Wars of Pennsylvania*, 489
1774 (Apr.)	One trader killed, one wounded	Three Cherokee warriors	Ohio River	Cherokees waylaid the traders' canoe, belonging to Richard Butler, and stole the traders' goods.	PA, 1st ser., 4:499, 569
1774 (Apr. 16)	Delaware man and Shawnee man	Michael Cresap and party of Virginians	Ohio River near Wheeling Creek	Cresap's party ambushed a canoe piloted by a trader named Stephens who employed the Shawnee and Delaware men. According to Stephens, Cresap boasted that "he wou'd put every Indian he met with on the river, to death." The canoe's goods were taken.	DRCHNY, 8:462–63; PA, 1st ser., 4:512
1774 (Apr. 27)	Unidentified Indian and Virginian	Michael Cresap and party of fifteen Virginians	Grave Creek near Great Kanawha River	Cresap's party pursued five canoes containing fourteen Indians and skirmished with them.	DRCHNY, 8:463; PA, 1st ser., 4:511–13; James, *George Rogers Clark Papers*, 8:3–9

1774 (Apr. 27)	Nine to ten Mingoes killed (mainly kin of Mingo leader Logan), others wounded	Daniel Greathouse and party of Virginians	Ohio River and Yellow Creek	Greathouse's Virginians lured a group of Mingoes across the Ohio River under the pretence of trade (the Mingoes and Virginians had traded before). The Virginians then killed the Mingoes and their kin who came to search for them; one victim was a trader's pregnant wife.	DRCHNY, 8:464–65; PA, 1st ser., 4:495–500, 511–13; James, *George Rogers Clark Papers*, 8:3–9
1774 (May)	Joseph Wipey (Delaware)	John Hinkson and James Cooper	Westmoreland County	Wipey was an interpreter and messenger well known to the local settlers.	MPCP, 10:199
1774 (June–July)	Capt. Francis McClure, Lt. Samuel Kinkade (wounded)	Logan and Mingo war party	Ten Mile Creek, Westmoreland County	Mingoes ambushed a party of Virginia rangers pursuing them.	PA, 1st ser., 4:517; Sipe, *Indian Wars of Pennsylvania*, 495
1774 (June–Oct.)	William Speir or Spicer, wife, four children on Ten Mile Creek; two men on Dunkard Creek; man at Old Fort Redstone; Matthew Gray; Colman Brown on Simpson Creek; John Robertson's family in Holston valley	Logan and Mingo war party	Monongahela, Holston, and Clinch valleys	Revenge for killings at Yellow Creek	Force, *American Archives*, 4th ser., 1:405; Sipe, *Indian Wars*, 595–97

McDonald through the head point-blank and then had come at the hunter with an axe, seriously wounding him. Somehow the hunter managed to recover his senses, escape, and walk twelve miles to Fort Pitt, though weakened from blood loss. Edmonstone soon received a report that a bloodied Indian had come to trader William Powell's house, two miles from Fort Pitt, so he ordered a young Irish ensign, Thomas Batts, to investigate. The Indian had since left, and Batts was angered that Powell had not secured him. But Powell was only protecting his nephew: "this Indian," Ensign Batts reported, "is supposed to be the Son of Powel's Sister, by a Delaware Indian, with whom she Cohabited some Years." In conversations with his nephew the old trader learned that he had "Rec'd Ill treatment from the two Men with whom he had worked," perhaps because of his mixed parentage. Batts proceeded to the place where the murder occurred and found McDonald's brains in Braddock's Field.[22]

For every instance of murder there were many more cases of attempted murder, assault, and verbal harassment. The violence and maltreatment that Indians received at the hands of soldiers and settlers provided them with powerful evidence of true British sentiments and a lack of good faith in the larger alliance. As a result Delaware and Shawnee warriors increasingly favored war, as George Croghan reported in 1769: "the Worrars Say they May as well [Die] Like Men as be Kicked about Like Doggs" and put into the Fort Pitt guardhouse for "Trifling Reasons." Natives who traveled through colonial settlements often felt the inhabitants' blind rage and verbal jabs. Sir William Johnson wrote in 1766 that Tuscaroras traveling through Pennsylvania "had been well used, by the Inhabitants, during their whole journey 'till they came to *Paxton*, the people of which Settlement have not only used them ill, but also robbed the Chief and others of sundry horses, &c." The prevailing anti-Indian sentiment often made it impossible for some colonists to tolerate the presence of Natives. In a 1767 petition to the Assembly a group of Bucks County residents complained that they had been "much Burdened & disturbed" by a group of forty Indians who had wintered in their neighborhood. The Natives were "a heavy Expense to Us in furnishing them with Provisions, but have given Occasion of great fear and Terror . . . by their Extream insolence & rudeness in & about some of Our Houses, when Intoxicated." The colonists hoped that the Assembly would prevent the Indians from returning to the area; the whites warned that they were so infuriated that "We Apprehend their [the Indians'] return would be Dangerous."[23]

Colonial and imperial officials felt completely besieged in the 1760s. Pennsylvania's Proprietors and elected leaders struggled to prevent open warfare, as an epidemic of squatting, chronic violence, and challenges to the colony's boundaries in northeastern and southwestern Pennsylvania seemed to spiral out of their control. New Englanders poured into the Wyoming Valley, and Virginians and Marylanders predominated in the upper Monongahela Valley, making Pennsylvania claims seem superfluous. The Proprietors desperately wanted to control these illegal settlers who trespassed on their claims and eject them if necessary. Colonial officials were more perplexed about the rash of colonists' murders of Indians. After two especially grisly murders in New Jersey, Gov. William Franklin wrote to William Johnson in 1766, "It grieves me to hear that our Frontier People are yet greater Barbarians than the Indians, and continue to murder them in time of Peace." Johnson was stupefied that ordinary farmers "were determin^d to bring on a new War tho' their own ruin may be the consequence."[24]

The British commander-in-chief, Gen. Thomas Gage, personified the "dilemma of British policy" in the 1760s. Disdainful of colonists and especially frontier people, Gage penned letters that put into sharp relief his deep fears of mounting disorder on the frontiers, illuminating the sense of increasing chaos that haunted many colonial leaders in that decade. Gage argued that "the Same Causes will have the same Effects": as colonial expansion caused the wars from 1755 to 1763, it would inevitably start another. Gage pointed out that royal authority in the colonies was very brittle: he lamented the "Weakness of the Governments" and their impotent attempts to enforce proclamations against illegal settlement and trade. How, Gage wondered, could governments expect to obtain any more coercive power by extending their boundaries further westward? Gage feared a vicious cycle in which speculators would engross the newly purchased lands and squatters "would have the same Temptation as they have now, to emigrate beyond the Boundary." He concluded that "unless the Hands of Government are strengthened . . . the more the Provinces are extended the weaker they would be." The general and other colonial elites feared that the Ohio Valley would become "the Asylum of fugitive Negroes, and idle Vagabonds escaped from Justice, who in time might become formidable, and subsist by Rapine, and plundering the lower Countrys." The conclusion that Gage had reached by 1770—that "America is a mere bully, from one end to the other"—had its origins in his experience with unruly frontiersmen, not with colonial militiamen at Lexington and Concord.[25]

Gage's schooling on the frontiers of the British Empire predisposed him toward a greater use of military power against recalcitrant American colonists. Governors, however, were reluctant to accept his "Offers to assist with the King's Troops," even though "they own that nothing but a Military Force could enforce obedience." The commander-in-chief proposed that the Crown should finalize the boundary line and create a new colony and that a "Military Government" should administer the colony "as the only Expedient of having either Laws or Rules and Regulations duely observed, or the King's orders obeyed." In a letter to William Johnson, Gage announced that if the Indians destroyed only illegal settlements in a war, he would not immediately intervene, "tho the killing of People must be shocking to Humanity." In a 1764 letter to Henry Bouquet, Gage proposed a "Military Establishment" near Fort Pitt that included land grants of 100 to 150 acres "on Military Tenures," strategically situated for defense of the frontiers. Bouquet concurred that Gage's plan was "the best that can possibly be formed for the Support of advanced Posts, and a Barrier impenetrable to savages." Neither Gage nor Bouquet mentioned ancient precedents, but their ideas roughly mirrored the Roman Empire's frontier defenses, where civilian militias and soldier-farmers could readily be mobilized against barbarian incursions. In 1768, for example, Capt. Charles Edmonstone listed "169 Men able to Bear Arms" who were ready to defend the Town if necessary.[26]

Gage's anxiety apparently confirms prevailing historical interpretations that assert that the British Empire restrained colonial expansion in the 1760s. While there is no question that British officials favored restraint in theory, they were unable to practice it in fact. The British military, and the empire it represented, were ultimately ineffectual in controlling the frontiers, because the military was itself so deeply responsible for the problem: the British Army facilitated a military colonization of the Ohio Valley more than it contained the spread of settlement therein. The evidence challenges the reigning interpretation—that the British Empire and Army were a "restraining force on the activities" of Ohio Valley colonists and that the Revolution broke the restless colonies' chains. As Gregory Dowd has written, the Seven Years' War "did not, as some scholars have hinted, . . . reshape the imperial authorities into potential buffers between Indians on one side and an Indian-hating colonial populace on another."[27]

Just as Ohio warriors and headmen had feared, the British military presence was like a Trojan horse rolled into the Ohio Country, though not perhaps with the intentional deception of the original. Apparently a symbol of goodwill and peace, the British Army instead unleashed legions of Euroamerican settlers into the Ohio Country. The British military facilitated colonial settlement in three ways: by constructing improved roads, by maintaining military garrisons on Indian lands, and by deliberately planting selected colonists near these armed outposts. First, the British Army had opened two roads—Braddock's and Forbes's—during the Seven Years' War that enabled colonists to breach the Appalachian barrier that so many Ohio Natives

hoped would forestall British encroachments; both roads were improved in the years after 1758, thus permitting the movement of colonists into the Ohio Valley. The heavy traffic of families, supply wagons, couriers, and livestock on these roads astounded travelers in
the 1760s and 1770s. Matthew Clarkson, an associate of the trading
firm Baynton, Wharton, and Morgan, recorded in his diary a nearly
constant flow of wagon traffic on Forbes's Road in 1766, carrying
pork, victuals, trade goods, and flour going west, and peltry returning east to Philadelphia merchants. Second, the army planted colonial communities—in the form of military garrisons—on the Ohio
Indians' lands. In the early 1760s the British Army maintained a
network of garrisons at Fort Loudoun, Juniata Crossings, Fort Bedford, Stony Creek, Fort Ligonier, Fort Pitt, Venango, Presque Isle,
Fort Burd, and Fort Cumberland. As archaeological evidence from
Fort Ligonier suggests, many of these places came to resemble colonial towns rather than military garrisons. In 1760 there were already
146 men, women, and children living outside of Fort Pitt's walls; by
1761 the colonial population had swelled to 332 inhabitants. Over
two hundred houses covered the "upper town" and "lower town" of
Pittsburgh. By 1766 a British captain reported "very considerable"
numbers of settlers building "good Houses" in the well-designed
town lots. Finally, British officers explicitly and implicitly encouraged colonial settlements at both forts and along Braddock's and
Forbes's roads. The strong correlation between army and civilian
settlements is also demonstrated in the fact that Native warriors in
Pontiac's War specifically targeted settlers who "lived along crucial
British supply lines."[28]

Why was there such a discrepancy between British officials' rhetoric
and the reality of illegal settlement in the Ohio Country? Military and
imperial officials saw colonial settlements associated with the army
as perfectly legitimate and wholly necessary; such colonists were exempt from the torrent of official proclamations forbidding hunting
and settling. Uncertain boundaries and land titles, especially before

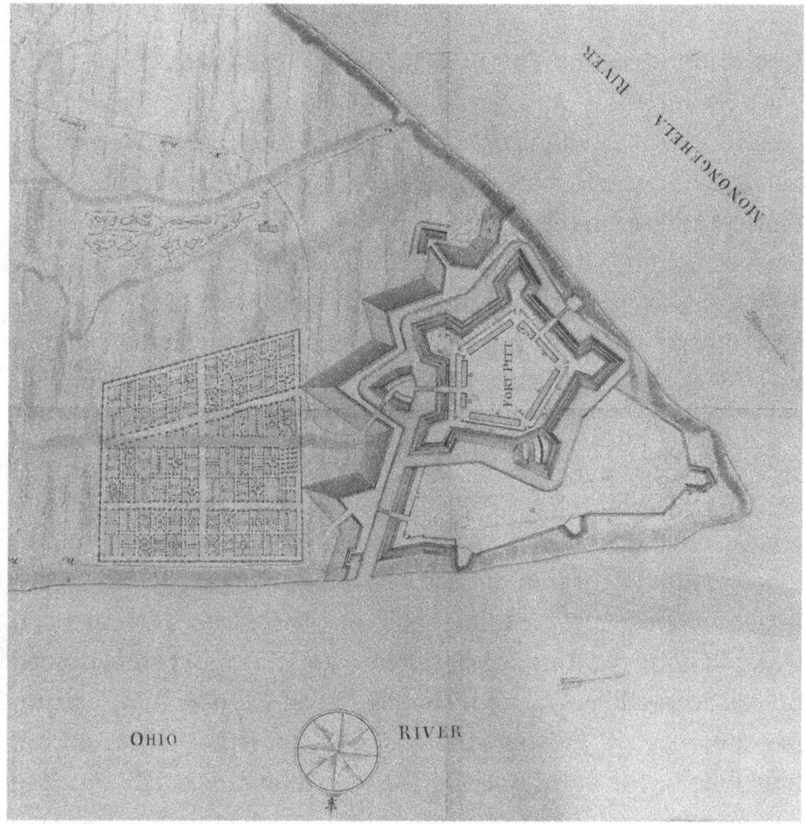

Fig. 11. Map of Fort Pitt and the early settlement of Pittsburgh, 1761. Surveyed by Lt. Elias Meyer, an engineer in the Royal American Regiment. MR 1/518, Public Record Office, The National Archives (UK).

the Proclamation Line of 1763 and the Treaty of Fort Stanwix of 1768, contributed to British vacillation over colonial farmers and hunters crossing the Appalachians. The secretary of the Land Office in Pennsylvania, James Tilghman, observed, "It hath been the fate of several Colonies in America that the People have settled up to and even beyond their bounds before they have been ascertained." Moreover, British commanders' views must be distinguished regarding what they believed constituted illegal versus legal settlement. Virginia governor Francis Fauquier wrote to Henry Bouquet in 1761, shortly after the latter issued a proclamation forbidding colonists settling and hunting across the mountains. This proclamation, Fauquier complained, had given rise "to some Uneasiness in this Colony [Virginia]," especially the threat of prosecution by courts-martial. Bouquet reassured Fauquier that his proclamation applied only to those lacking "legal authority" and that he never intended to "invalidate *the just right* of any Person" holding prior grants to Ohio lands.[29]

The sprawling settlements that soon flourished outside of British ramparts sprouted from small seeds. British officers throughout the 1760s explicitly encouraged colonial settlements, insisting that some were necessary to support the army in the field and its communication and supply lines. Col. Henry Bouquet, who oversaw British consolidation of the upper Ohio Valley from 1758 to 1765, played an instrumental role in the process of military colonization. In 1761 Bouquet argued that building way stations on the road from Fort Le Boeuf to Presque Isle "could give no just Jalousie to the Indians, if we build upon the Ruins of the French settlements." He envisioned farmers and soldiers raising "Horses, Cattle, Corn, & Oats." But unlike the French forts, where Indians could boast that they could still hunt outside the walls, British posts soon attracted small, bustling villages. By 1767 Pittsburgh was large enough for inhabitants to petition General Gage for a stockade to be erected "round the Improved part of the Town" to help their defense.[30]

Military officers in the Ohio Country explicitly encouraged the planting of three types of colonists: farmers/tavernkeepers, artisans, and army veterans. Bouquet knew that the British Army could not depend solely on shipments of supplies from the east and looked for local sources of supply. In a memorandum entitled "Articles necessary for the Western Department in 1760," he declared it necessary to "establish Farmers at Bedford, Ligonier, Wetherhold, Cumberland, [Stewart's] Crossing, Guest, [and] F[t] Burd, and Pittsburgh, to raise oats, Indian corn, Wheat, and Rye, &[a]," citing the "Power vested in the Command[g] officer to grant such Lands." Bouquet intended that licensed farmers occupy land only within view of the forts, but in practice farmers began creating plantations throughout the surrounding countryside. At Fort Bedford Lieutenant Lewis Ourry noted that the country people brought flour, oats, and corn to sell, as "many People about here will have good Crops." When war threatened in 1769, British captain Charles Edmonstone procured large shipments of grain from "Neighbouring Farmers" in case of an enemy siege.[31]

Many of these licensed farmers, doubling as tavernkeepers, eventually became permanent residents in the trans-Appalachian West. Taverns or way stations along Braddock's and Forbes's roads not only provided basic needs to travelers but secured British communications from the western posts to the seaboard. Bouquet early saw the need for "Some Taverns . . . along the Road at the Several Stages West of Bedford" to provide lodging and food for couriers, soldiers, and teamsters and fodder for their horses and livestock. Accordingly, tavernkeepers farmed large tracts of land to provide a steady supply of fodder. Bouquet blindly believed that Ohio Indians could not possibly object to taverns and would recognize the distinction between licensed colonists and unlicensed ones. His superior Gen. Robert Monckton concurred: "There can be no Objection to People Setting up Taverns on the Road between Bedford and Pittsburgh." Individuals like Margaret Stewart, who probably ran a tavern, applied for land in 1769 based on military license: Stewart claimed 300 acres "on each side of the great Road including the eleven mile Spring above Fort Legonier & an improvement made in 1762 by order of the Commander at Fort Pitt." While most colonists solicited the army, Bouquet in 1762 prevailed upon John Metcalfe, a former salt master at Fort Pitt, to establish a tavern at Nine Mile Run on Forbes's Road, "purely for accommodating the Army and travelers." Metcalfe's tavern evolved into a sprawling plantation that included more than sixty acres of crops and herds of livestock. Metcalfe claimed a whopping £1,474 in damages to his plantation sustained during Pontiac's War.[32]

Skilled artisans and tradesmen were another group of colonists whom British officers licensed to settle in the Ohio Country, for their expertise was needed to maintain the army in the field. Every artisan or tradesman necessary for the functioning of a nonmilitary community could be found among the British garrisons: teamsters, wheelwrights, coopers, blacksmiths, gunsmiths, carpenters, millwrights, bricklayers, masons, batteauxmen, tanners, and traders. Anthony and Jane Thompson operated a tannery near Fort Pitt and cultivated around twenty acres of land. After Anthony's accidental drowning, Jane continued to operate the tannery and filed for losses of £1,351 in hides and twenty acres of crops after Pontiac's War. Batteauxmen and ship's carpenters were particularly indispensable, for the British Army principally relied on rivers for communication and supply between posts. The main trading firms operating from Fort Pitt—Trent, Simon, and Franks, and later Baynton, Wharton, and Morgan—sent hundreds of teamsters, ships' carpenters, and boatmen to the Ohio Valley to facilitate trade with the Illinois Country. Twenty-three-year-old Jehu Eyre, a Philadelphia shipwright, took a party of sixteen boat builders to Fort Pitt in 1760; many eventually stayed in the area and obtained land.[33]

Veterans, camp followers, and wives who colonized the Ohio Valley imparted a distinctly military character to the early settlement population. Land grants were also given to Scottish Highlander veterans to settle in the Champlain Valley in the vicinity of Ticonderoga and Crown Point. Virginia, Maryland, Pennsylvania, and the British Regular Army all instituted land bounties, with varying degrees of success, as incentive for provincials to serve in the Seven Years' War. Most important, soldiers came to expect that they would receive grants on French lands by right of conquest. Veterans like Scottish sergeant Angus McDonald often settled in the areas with which they had become familiar, or where they had traded among the Ohio Indians. After commanding at Fort Burd and farming bottomland along the Youghiogheny River from 1760 to 1763, McDonald obtained title to 295 acres near the fort in 1769. Upon leaving the service soldiers sometimes brought their wives and children to settle; single men often met and married the many laundresses, cooks, seamstresses, and camp followers who were integral members of the military community. Vivandiere Martha May, married to a British soldier, testified, "I have been a Wife 22 years and have Traveld with my Husband every Place or Country the Company marcht too and have workt very hard," carrying water in the "Hottest Battle." In his 1772 journey the Rev. David McClure encountered veterans who had married during their terms of service and settled in the area. He attended the marriages of two couples living on the Monongahela: the grooms were "soldiers, who for want of some one to marry them, had lived with their women, several years." During times of conflict with Natives the veterans quickly returned to the ranks. At Fort Bedford, during Pontiac's War, Capt. Lewis Ourry noted that many of the farmers who took refuge there "have been in the Service of the Province, and are ready to engage in the Same now, if call'd upon." Sgt. Angus McDonald's long military career would span the Seven Years' War, Pontiac's War, and Dunmore's War.[34]

Maintaining a distinction between settlers supporting the king's forces and illegal settlers proved immensely difficult in practice. In theory the metropolitan government's imperial policymakers tried to restrain colonial expansion. But in practice, at a local level, British sergeants, lieutenants, captains, majors, and colonels frequently gave licenses to colonial families to settle in the trans-Appalachian West, provided they could establish their usefulness to the king's troops.[35] Once word of the British Army's need for logistical support filtered back to Virginia, Maryland, and Pennsylvania, colonial families began pouring into the Ohio Country. Many came under the pretence of operating taverns or growing crops to support the army. Others simply applied to British officers for permission to build houses and farms: Lt. Archibald Blane, commanding at Ligonier, explained, "Every Day I have a number of People soliciting for Plantations." Other individuals attached themselves to families that did have military licenses. One hunter killed by Cherokees in 1762 had come to the Ohio Country and "went and Joynd himself, to 2 men that had a permit, to hunt for the officer at fort Pitt." A befuddled Sergeant McDonald at Fort Burd wrote of the Redstone settlers coming to plant corn in 1761: "Some Says they had Leave from your honour Some from General monckton Some others from Sir Jn° st Clair." By the time McDonald had learned of Bouquet's opposition to unauthorized farmers coming to plant corn, there were already "people who has been Clearing Ground all winter." Moreover, some officers were indifferent toward the colonists' encroachments and ineffectually executed their orders to warn off trespassers. Capt. Lewis Ourry, Bouquet's close friend, commanding at Fort Bedford, wrote that "there are a great many People Settled all around me, within 3, 4–6, 8–10 Miles, and I never concern myself with them at all."[36]

Imagine how Ohio Indians responded when "authorized" settlers informed them that "they had the Kings orders for making settlements there, and that they would not suffer any Indians whatever, to pass over or hunt *on them.*" How were Ohio Indians to know which settlers in the Redstone Country were authorized by the British Army? Had the king allowed hunters to swarm their hunting grounds? In official diplomatic meetings at Fort Pitt and Philadelphia, Indians were told that the king had never sanctioned *illegal* settlements on their lands. Not surprisingly, Ohio Indians found these distinctions specious, and many deemed the rumors that the British military was conspiring to destroy them and take their lands eminently believable. At a 1767 conference, during which George Croghan tried to explain British logic, the Indians appeared "as if they thought that all which was said to them, was intended *only to amuse them* & they declared plainly that they could not believe, but if it had been the King's desire to prevent his Subjects from making Settlements, in their Country," that it would be done.[37]

To assuage Natives' fears and to contain a problem of their own making, the British occasionally took military action against illegal colonists in the 1760s. Proclamations warning the intruders to remove themselves were routinely issued by officers at Fort Pitt. Squatters' local relationships with Indians, however, drove the British officers to frustration. Only a year after the cessation of hostilities in 1764, squatters on Redstone Creek had befriended Mohawk Peter, his European wife, and his children who were also settled there.[38] The squatters had taken up residence near Mohawk Peter's cabin, where, as James Kenny witnessed, "Indn Peter and a White man was working at Corn." At Fort Pitt in June 1765 the Seneca sachem Ogista informed Col. John Reid, an officer of the Forty-second Regiment, that "several white Families are settled on Redstone Creek, and have planted Corn, with *Peter*, a Mohawk Indian." Ogista distinguished between the hunters and the farmers invading the Ohio Country. The Seneca told Colonel Reid that he did not wish to see the farmers "lose their Labour"; he would allow them to remain until they had harvested their corn, and then they should be removed. But Ogista wanted the hunters removed immediately.[39]

In the summers of 1766 and 1767 Gage authorized Maj. William Murray, the commandant at Fort Pitt, to send out detachments of British regulars from Fort Pitt to expel squatters from the Redstone Country. The first, in August 1766, completely backfired, because it was "prevented by some of the Indians" (Mingoes). When Murray later chided Kiasutha, the White Mingo, and other Indians at a meeting encouraging the squatters to stay, they agreed to accompany another detachment of British regulars. In 1767 Murray again marched a small contingent of regulars to the Redstone country. A few Indian sachems who accompanied him successfully persuaded the squatters to remove (at least the hundred or so who answered Murray's summons). The British commander also sent out parties to destroy as many of their cabins as possible. Murray obediently reported his success to General Gage, but his success was fleeting. The pattern of local diplomacy between Mingo and Redstone settlers continued. In 1770, for example, a backwoods altercation between hunters led the Mingoes to "send for the People who live at Redstone & Cheat River that we may see them and our People together that we may find out who is in the Fault of these differences." The two communities' representatives met in August, and the Indians appealed that "we are now become too near Neighbours to Quarrel if we could help it."[40]

Such confrontations complicate our understanding of Indian-Euroamerican relationships after Pontiac's War. Clearly, the postwar period did not entirely undermine the peaceful patterns of co-existence in the early eighteenth century. Some Indians (primarily Mingoes) still permitted some farmers to live in the Monongahela Valley, and Euroamerican farmers were not all racist thugs. Yet many records indicate that Ohio Indians complained incessantly over illegal settlers. Why, then, would they want to encourage any colonial families to remain? One British officer complained that all too often Indian warriors came into Fort Pitt and treated him as though he "was sent here only to take care of them." Similarly, Natives *wanted* trustworthy colonial farmers along the Catawba path to provision their war parties and enjoyed local trading ties with certain families. The Mingoes who accompanied Murray in 1766 stipulated that at least four settlers were to be left untouched, "to furnish their young men and warriors with corn as they pass and repass." James Kenny noted the presence of "Sutling Inhabitants" in Fort Pitt's environs who traded alcohol. George Croghan wrote simply that "every Farmer is a sutler," particularly of whiskey readily distilled from corn. Licensed traders at Fort Pitt complained that squatters in the Redstone Country were trading with Indians and undercutting them. They averred that "a Number of Lawless persons have lately forced a Settle[ment and opened] a Trade at one half the Rates agreed upon by the Com[missary of] Indian Affairs and the chiefs of the Indian tribes at this [post]." The Redstone's reputation for close colonial-Indian relations was remembered well into the nineteenth century.

Either a freed slave or an Irishman, "Ready Money Jack" was a Red-stone settler who later migrated to Kentucky. One Kentuckian who knew him informed ethnographer John Dabney Shane that Ready Money Jack "was from Monongahela country . . . [and] was less afraid of Indians. People in that country were more accustomed to them." Such familiar trading ties may have benefited Indian communities in the short term, but like pigeons, a few European settlers coming to roost soon attracted larger flocks.[41]

By the end of 1767 imperial and colonial elites recognized that proclamations and parties of soldiers had completely failed to accomplish their aims. Not only had Indians interfered with the expeditions, but the human tide of settlement seemed unstoppable. No sooner had the burned cabins' embers died down than squatters returned to rebuild. George Croghan remarked to William Johnson in October 1767 that "not withstanding all the trouble that has been taken [to re]moove the People settled on Redstone Creek, & Cheat [River] I am well assured there are double the Number of Inhabi[tants] in those two Settlements that ever was before." The British military could do little to coerce the colonists militarily: using military force against civilians in peacetime was a recipe for political disaster. Thomas Gage warned Sir William Johnson that "if a Skirmish happens, and Blood is shed, you know what a Clamor there will be against the Military Acting without Civil Magistrates." Moreover, Gage was increasingly incapable of taking decisive action against illegal settlement by the 1770s, for he was preoccupied with unrest along the seaboard. Indeed, after the Stamp Act riots Gage spoke of evacuating smaller posts in the west as a means of saving Crown finances. He informed a subordinate officer that the "seditious Spirit now reigning in the Provinces, and the open Declaration, that they will oppose the Execution of the Stamp Act, with their Lives & Fortunes, requires my attention to the support of the Kings service in the Inhabited Country." The British were beginning to curtail their influence in the Ohio Country.[42]

Pennsylvania's Proprietors, however, were more than eager to eject illegal settlers from lands that they claimed. Two developments in late 1767 and early 1768 gave Lt. Gov. John Penn and the Pennsylvania government added impetus. First, the home government authorized the Indian superintendents, Sir William Johnson and John Stuart, to negotiate a new boundary line for all of the British colonies. The interests of expansionists in New York, Pennsylvania, Maryland, and Virginia, along with renewed assertions of Iroquois power over the Ohio Valley, were brought to bear on the Ohio Indians. Pennsylvania's Proprietors, who enjoyed close ties to Johnson, hoped that the superintendent would negotiate a boundary favorable to their interests. They looked to a traditional solution to solve disputes: a land sale from the Six Nations. As fears of Indian disaffection grew in 1767, George Croghan asserted that "Nothing now, will in my opinion prevent a War [but] taking a Cession from them [the Six Nations], & paying them for their Lands." But just when British leaders seemed so close to finalizing a permanent boundary, room for colonial growth, and possibly a lasting peace, one of the most vicious murders of the colonial period occurred in the Pennsylvania settlements.[43]

The actions of Frederick Stump and John Ironcutter, two German settlers living on Middle Creek in the Susquehanna Valley, threatened to turn colonists' and Indians' worlds upside down. On January 10, 1768, six Senecas and Mohicans came to Stump's house and traded for liquor. It was said that Stump, who had been the subject of land disputes with Indians and Proprietors, was "apprehensive" that the inebriated Indians "intended to do him some mischief." Stump tomahawked the White Mingo, John Campbell, Cornelius, Jonas Griffy, and two of the men's wives. After throwing their bodies into ice-choked Middle Creek, Stump and his indentured servant John Ironcutter went to the Indians' hunting cabins a few miles away. There they butchered another four Indians and burned the bodies and the cabins to hide their crimes. Over a month later one of the corpses washed up downstream on the Susquehanna. Local magistrates discovered that

Stump had scalped this victim with such ferocity that "a large Scalp [was] taken off his Head, which took both his Ears."[44]

It is impossible to exaggerate just how thunderstruck both Native peoples and colonial officials were when news of Stump's actions reached them. Alexander McKee reported that Indian peoples in the west were angered; he knew that scalping the victims, a declaration of war in Native eyes, was "worse than murdering them." Because Senecas, Mahicans, and Delawares were among the slain, British America stood on the precipice of an apocalyptic war with Indian nations from Iroquoia to the Ohio Valley. A mortified John Penn wrote to Gage, "I am under the greatest Apprehensions that this unhappy affair will, at this Juncture, when the Indians are so much discontented by the Injuries already done to them, be productive of the most Calamitous Consequences." He assured Gage that "nothing on the part of this Government shall be wanting to remove all the Causes of their Complaints." But Stump and Ironcutter were never brought to justice. Briefly incarcerated in a Carlisle jail, Stump was freed by a sympathetic frontier mob that thereafter concealed him from local magistrates. From the Native point of view the government's inability to bring the murderers to justice betrayed great insincerity.[45]

In the aftermath of the Stump murders the Pennsylvania government initially condoled the affected Indian peoples through letters and speeches. The Assembly also allotted the incredible sum of £3,000 for gift-giving during formal condolence ceremonies at Johnson Hall in New York and Fort Pitt. It further enacted draconian measures to redress the Natives' grievances over settlers' intrusions. In January and February 1768 Governor Penn and the Assembly worked out an "Act to remove the Persons now settled, and to prevent others from settling on Lands in this Province, not purchased of the Indians." The Assembly passed the legislation (which had actually predated the Stump murders), and Penn announced it in an official proclamation. This unusual law authorized the penalty of "Death without the

Benefit of Clergy" for illegal settlers who failed to remove after thirty days of receiving notice of the proclamation and were convicted. Exemptions were made for settlers with military licenses and for those whom George Croghan had settled on his lands upriver from Fort Pitt. Because the temporary law was intended more as a carrot than as a stick, no one was ever convicted or executed for trespass—but the law's severity and singularity demonstrate the sense of crisis that its framers felt. Lieutenant Governor Penn commissioned the Rev. John Steel, John Allison, Christopher Lems, and Capt. James Potter, all of Cumberland County, to travel to the Ohio Country "with all possible Expedition" and inform the squatters of the proclamation. Focusing primarily on Redstone, Monongahela, and Youghiogheny, the commissioners were to gather the squatters together, read the proclamation, and explain to them "the Folly and injustice of their settling upon the Indian Lands."[46]

Steel and his companions arrived at Redstone Creek on March 21, 1768. The settlers, having received advance warning of the party's coming, had planned a meeting to decide what to do. Steel addressed the meeting, read the proclamation, and tried to persuade the settlers that removal was their best option. The squatters replied that they would petition the Proprietors for preemption rights, rightly assuming that they would purchase the lands soon. But they also maintained that the Indians were "very Peaceable, and seemed sorry that they [the settlers] were to be removed." Steel must have been baffled when local Indians, probably Mingoes, encouraged the squatters to remain and "apprehended the English intended to make War upon the Indians, as they were moving off their People from their Neighborhood." Given Natives' longstanding suspicions that the British Army would one day be used against them, their fears of an impending attack after their colonial neighbors had been moved out of harm's way were logical. The squatters nonetheless indicated that they would be willing to remove and promised that they would give the commissioners an answer on the following Sabbath.[47]

On March 27, 1768, the commissioners, squatters, and Mingoes met in the Redstone Valley. Steel preached a sermon to the crowd that undoubtedly touched on obedience to magistrates. Hearing that eight Mingoes had come to Mohawk Peter's homestead, he requested that they witness the squatters' ejection. Steel had entertained the hope that the squatters were preparing to remove; he told them that "a few straggling Indians" might have encouraged them to remain at their plantations, but that most Natives resented their settlements. Steel hoped that the Mingoes would support his mission, but instead "they greatly obstructed our design," he later wrote. The Mingoes presented a string of wampum and announced their satisfaction with the commissioners' goals, but essentially deferred any final action until the next conference at Fort Pitt. Sachems and colonial negotiators could then decide which course to pursue. All hope of removing the squatters evaporated when they heard of the Indians' remarks.[48]

The commissioners noted an abrupt change in the squatters' demeanor once they knew that the Mingoes had declined to support their immediate ejection; they "drop't the design of Petitioning" and were "confirmed that there was no danger of War" with the Indians. They concluded that "the removing of them from the unpurchased Lands, was a Contrivance of the Gentlemen and Merchants of Philadelphia, that they might take Rights for their improvements when a Purchase was made." The commissioners returned to Carlisle. Another proprietary expedition had ventured into the backcountry, only to be frustrated by the strange relationship between squatters and Indians.

Indians and colonists met at Fort Pitt in April and May 1768 so that Pennsylvania could conduct condolence rituals for the Stump murders. Unfortunately for the Delawares and Shawnees most immediately threatened by settlement growth, the Fort Pitt conference was a prelude to yet another sale of lands without their consent. As many as fifteen hundred Iroquois, Delawares, Shawnees, Munsees, Mohicans, and Wyandots gathered at the fort, but the dialogue was dominated by George Croghan and Six Nations representatives, particularly the Iroquois "Half King" Guyasutha. The long-established collusion between Pennsylvania and the Six Nations meant that Ohio Indians' voices were again suppressed. Guyasutha, a close ally of Sir William Johnson, "thought it most proper for the English themselves to compel their own people to remove" and deferred any action until the upcoming treaty conference in New York.[49]

The Treaty of Fort Stanwix, signed in the summer of 1768, was the culmination of Britain's efforts to regulate the colonial frontiers after the Seven Years' War. With over three thousand Natives in attendance at the Mohawk Valley fort, the conference was one of the largest Indian councils ever held in North America. Despite Ohio Indians' objections, but with Sir William Johnson's support, the Six Nations relinquished their "claims" to most of the Ohio Valley (including Kentucky). Johnson collaborated with speculators, Proprietors, and impoverished Indian traders to secure large tracts of Natives' lands. The boundary line in Pennsylvania, for example, ran from the Delaware River westward along the Susquehanna's west branch to the old site of Kittanning, then southwest along the Ohio River—most of the area that the Proprietors had secured in the 1754 Albany Purchase but later renounced. This treaty was the culmination of a long pattern of proprietary land grabs designed to preempt squatters' and Indians' land claims and to secure new lands for settlement and speculation: Pennsylvania officially obtained rights to the disputed Monongahela Valley, including Redstone Creek. Despite the methods used to secure the purchase, British officials and colonists and Indian peoples hoped that the Stanwix line would bring peace. Well-qualified to judge the prospects of peace, George Croghan wrote in May 1768 that "if the Boundery Line be settled with them this Summer and the Frontier Inhabitants observe a Friendly intercourse between them and such Indians as may go into the Settlements I am of opinion a Long and Lasting friendship may be kept up between them and his Majesty's subjects."[50]

But the treaty failed to resolve permanently the problems besetting Anglo-Indian relations in the Ohio Valley: it greatly stimulated colonial settlement and again precipitated conflict with the Natives. Sir William Johnson disobeyed the Board of Trade's instructions to fix the end of the line at the mouth of the Great Kanawha River (where the boundary for the southern colonies terminated). The final line instead stretched all the way down the Ohio River to the mouth of the Tennessee River. While the British government was initially furious over Johnson's indiscretions, it eventually acquiesced to his *fait accompli*. In the explosive land rush that followed the treaty, from 1769 to 1773, settlers moved into southwestern Pennsylvania, western Virginia, and Kentucky by the thousands. Land-company representatives, speculators, surveyors, and ordinary farmers gleefully scouted out new tracts of land and poached on Indians' hunting grounds. Like the squatters whom Richard Peters confronted in the Juniata Valley, those who lived in the Monongahela Valley were also remarkably rooted and intransient. While Proprietors may have objected to trespassers claiming rights to land based on their improvements, the idea of "squatter's rights" seems to have been a customary practice established over the course of the eighteenth century. Of the fifty-two households listed in John Steel's 1768 report, at least thirty-four persisted in the area, the majority obtaining either a survey or letters patent for their lands.[51]

British actions between 1765 and 1774 constituted, as Richard White argues, an "abdication" of the "diplomatic middle ground" in the trans-Appalachian West. The imperial crisis on the Ohio Valley frontier unfolded simultaneously with the imperial crises over taxation, representation, and British subjects' rights. As Michael McConnell points out, Britain's fiscal problems, ministerial instability, the colonial resistance movement, and British regulars' movements from the frontiers to the seaboard all combined to produce "paralysis in British-Indian relations." Retrenchment led British military leaders to abandon many frontier outposts in the trans-Appalachian west, including Fort Pitt in 1772. From Thomas Gage's perspective Fort Pitt was merely an "expensive and troublesome" entrepôt between the colonies and the Illinois Country. The general also seemed to take delight in the thought that "If the Colonists will afterwards force the Savages into Quarrells by using them ill, let them feel the Consequences, we shall be out of the Scrape." The British cannily represented their withdrawal to the Ohio Natives as a redress of their objections to the fort; some Indians, especially warriors, were "exceedingly well pleased" over the British Army's departure and demolition of the fort. As George Croghan observed, "The 18th Regm[t] has been obnoxious always to them & no wonder from their Conduct." But Ohio Indians now faced hordes of defenseless settlers who were "greatly alarmed" and full or "Fears and apprehensions" regarding Indian attacks. A "people dependent heretofore and subject to the military," as one group of memorialists represented themselves, now faced the future without "this post as a Barrier between them and the Indians."[52]

On the eve of the Revolution, then, the Ohio Valley was utterly decentralized, unstable, and verging on anarchy. It was, in Eric Hinderaker's words, "a kind of Hobbesian world, where only sheer force could effectively determine the outcome of events." Not only had the British Army departed, but Pennsylvanians and Virginians remained to squabble over land, authority, and allegiance. Sir William Johnson despaired of ever containing settlements, because "these People are not to be confined by any Boundaries or Limits." The territorial dispute between the two colonies threatened to erupt into a small-scale civil war as rival magistrates, courts, and land offices competed for or enforced allegiances. In 1774 Virginia colonists, with the support of Virginia's royal governor, Lord Dunmore, seized what remained of Fort Pitt, organized their militia, and claimed the region for Virginia. But the threat of Indian war and the colonists' commonly held hatred of Indians again glossed over their many differences. War came to the Ohio Country in 1774, long before British regulars and the Lexington militia exchanged shots.[53]

Shawnees informed Alexander McKee in early March 1774 that "We have had many disagreeable Dreams this Winter" about the explosive potential for conflict between Indians and whites. They were convinced that "constant assembling of our Brethren with Red flags" meant that "war is still apparent in their minds." The Shawnees' dreams were nightmarish indeed. In April 1774, in a bloody prelude to the warfare that was coming, a gang of Virginia ruffians began killing individual Indians and massacring Indian families; many of these Virginians believed that a state of war existed between the British and Indians. On April 16 Michael Cresap and a group of Virginians waylaid a trader's canoe and killed a Delaware and a Shawnee. The most egregious murders occurred on April 27, when Daniel Greathouse and other Virginians enticed a group of ten Mingoes into their settlement and then massacred them, including a trader's pregnant wife. Many of these Mingoes, whose village was located across the Ohio River from the Virginians' village, had frequently traded with the colonists. A cycle of revenge killings began, as the Mingo sachem Tachnedorus (or Logan) led warriors against settlements in the Monongahela Valley. Collectively these killings supplied the pretext for Virginia's war of conquest, known as "Lord Dunmore's War." The British waged war against the Shawnees, not the Mingoes, who had launched the revenge attacks. Dunmore personally commanded the small army that attacked the Shawnees in 1774. After the battle of Point Pleasant the Shawnees sued for peace and essentially ceded Kentucky to the Virginians. Dunmore's War inaugurated thirty more years of warfare for Ohio.[54]

It has become almost a cliché that the American Revolution unleashed the floodgates of settlement in the Ohio Valley. But under the British Empire's oversight the fundamental processes affecting Indian-colonist relations for the next fifty years were set in motion during the pivotal decade of the 1760s: inexorable settlement expansion, maintenance of military garrisons in the trans-Appalachian West, a vengeful cycle of violence, and use of the army to force treaties that served the proprietary and trade interests of British elites. Unable to contain settlement, regulate trade, or impose order on its North American frontiers, the British Empire abandoned the Ohio Country in 1773, leaving behind an enormous power vacuum. If the American Revolution struck the valley with notable ferocity, this was due to the area's decades-long instability and decentralization, conditions that the British occupation had helped to create.

Epilogue

The Tree of Peace Uprooted

In early December 1773 a somber Sir William Johnson sent urgent letters to the governor of New York, William Tryon, and to Gen. Frederick Haldimand in New York City. He alerted the government to intercept a German farmer named George Klock, "a fellow of notorious bad Character who has long by various Artifices continued to defraud the Indians in Land Matters, and create Divisions amongst them." Johnson had just learned that Klock had "lately gone to New York, or Philadelphia, with three Stragling indians originally of Conajohare, but Persons of no consequence, with a design to carry them to London on some mischevious purpose." Johnson described Klock as "an old German farmer in this Country who speaks the Mohawk language a little." He denounced him as "the most troublesome, and worst man that I ever knew" and even went so far as to say that Klock was "on[e of the g]reatest Villains on this Continent."[1]

Johnson was even more piqued when Klock and his Canojoharie companion set sail for England in the vessel *Sir William Johnson*, a two-masted, square-sailed snow launched in 1772 and owned by the London merchant John Blackburn. Both Klock's voyage and his choice of sailing vessel were intentional acts of defiance against Johnson's authority as the royally appointed superintendent of Indian affairs. The German farmer had either cajoled or shanghaied a Mohawk from the village of Canajoharie, located across the Mohawk River from his own farm. But this Mohawk individual was probably from the small band of Canajoharie Mohawks and Oneidas who had become permanent residents at Klock's house. The German farmer's voyage to London was but the latest round in his decades-long dispute with British authorities. This conflict concerned land, legitimacy, and the meanings of community. Who would ultimately possess Mohawk Valley lands in a contest that involved the original Mohawk and Oneida inhabitants, European frontier settlers, and the British colonial officials who controlled the legal machinery of land patenting? The journey of Klock and the Mohawk on the *Sir William Johnson* perfectly symbolized the interwoven histories of Iroquois and Europeans in the eighteenth-century Mohawk Valley: two inhabitants of the land—a German farmer and a Mohawk villager—traveled to London in a ship whose name honored William Johnson's office in the British Empire and his political power in New York. Yet the *Sir William Johnson* carried the two travelers safely across the Atlantic on a journey aimed at flouting that authority and resolving a conflict that had long divided the Iroquois and European communities.

Because Klock's journey occurred during the intensifying imperial crisis between Britain and its colonies, it reveals the local origins of the American Revolution in the Mohawk Valley and the growing fault lines between European and Indian communities. The Revolution provoked not one but three civil wars: within the British Empire, between the colonies and the home government; within each of the thirteen colonies, among rebels, loyalists, and the disaffected; and within certain Indian nations.[2] The war ripped apart families, friendships, churches, and communities all across America. The ancient unity of the Iroquois Confederacy was also fractured, as Iroquois sided against other Iroquois. There was nothing inevitable about the Revolution and the violent direction it took, but by 1780 a total war was raging along the entire Stanwix border line, from New York to Kentucky.

The Revolution did not affect all of the Iroquoian frontiers equally. The children of Pennsylvania settlers and Ohio Indians who had come of age after the Seven Years' War knew nothing but violence. In the Ohio Valley the Revolution was simply the latest intensification of widespread fighting in a conflict that had raged nearly unabated since the 1750s. It exacerbated the already established patterns of vengeance killings, hatred, and relentless settlement expansion that were evident before the 1770s.[3] In the Mohawk Valley, however, the Revolution did much to end the cultural accommodation that had once prevailed. British and Iroquois loyalists decimated the New York frontier settlements, killing or capturing hundreds of their former neighbors and burning their homes and crops to ensure their total privation. Jelles Fonda, a Mohawk Valley trader who knew the Iroquois well, confided that he was "mostly affraid of our former Neighbours the Mohawk Indians, who are now in Canada and are our worst Enemys." The destructive border conflicts resulted in the loyalists' and the Mohawks' dispossession from their homes and lands. By war's end many Euroamerican and Iroquois communities had been shattered, and coexistence had become a more tenuous possibility. The St. Lawrence Valley was not visited by the same destructive warfare during the Revolutionary War: Kahnawake and other Iroquois communities were able to maintain their lands throughout the conflict, in which they stayed largely neutral. The former French colony of Canada in fact became a haven for Iroquois refugees during and after the conflict.[4]

A growing torrent of European settlers was primarily responsible for the steady erosion of Iroquois territories in the 1760s and 1770s. On the eve of the Revolution the Mohawks, Oneidas, and Tuscaroras living closest to European settlers believed that they were "threatned to be Dispossessed of our just Property, by those whom we always considered as our Children, and who have had all their possessions from us." Settlers swarming like locusts and the Mohawks' mosaic of land sales meant that by 1770 there was only a "mere trifle of Property remaining in [the Indians'] hands." But Iroquois anxiety over land was only one of the cumulative pressures they felt. The activities of missionaries such as the Anglican John Stuart among the Mohawks and the Presbyterian Samuel Kirkland among the Oneidas and Tuscaroras had also created religious schisms that made the Iroquois more susceptible to political disunion. Kirkland's overt support for the American cause, for example, swayed his Oneida and Tuscarora followers. Events elsewhere also undermined Iroquois accommodation of the New York colonists. The Paxton Massacre, the Stump murders, and other assaults on the Iroquois sharply demonstrated that most British colonists would not maintain the peace. The Paxton Massacre particularly haunted the Mohawks, who believed "it would be their own fate one day, or another." Another hot spot of trouble was the Wyoming Valley on the southern frontiers of Iroquoia: conflict among Pennsylvania, New England, and Delaware settlers had begun there as early as the 1750s, despite the Six Nations' objections to the settlement of Wyoming. British officials established a boundary line between Indian nations and the mainland colonies in the 1768 Fort Stanwix Treaty, but colonists violated this border by moving onto Iroquois lands in the Susquehanna Valley. Had the American Revolution not occurred when it did, it is likely that some kind of conflict or war would have erupted as the Iroquois dealt with the incredible population expansion of the British colonies after 1750. Between 1755 and 1775 the colonies' overall populations grew from about 1.5 million to 2.5 million.[5]

George Klock presents a human face in this conflict, his incredible story personalizing the seemingly relentless expansion of these millions of British colonists. The Klock family and other Palatines had settled in the upper Mohawk Valley in the 1720s or 1730s. George's father, Hendrick Klock, immigrated to New York in 1709 with other

Palatines—a group, as we have seen, with a long history of negoti-ation with Mohawks over land in the Schoharie Valley and of con-flict with large colonial landholders in Albany. Klock and other Pal-atines were initially on good terms with their Canajoharie neighbors across the river and regularly traded with them. It was during these routine encounters that George learned to speak Mohawk and nego-tiate with Indians over rights to the land. Liquor, ginseng, wampum, and other trade items were in his inventory. Klock also constructed a gristmill where Indians came to have their corn ground; he later provided boards for the construction of a Mohawk church at Cana-joharie (the present-day Indian Castle Church). By 1747 Klock's trad-ing had caught the attention of William Johnson, a fur trader and the newly appointed "Colonel of the Six Nations." Johnson wrote twice to Klock, telling him to stop selling liquor. But the German trader replied that Johnson could go hang himself.[6] Johnson probably did not perceive the irony of this situation: Klock had simply replicated what Johnson himself had done to the Albany Commissioners for Indian Affairs in the late 1740s—both men entering the fur trade from their frontier homes, gaining access to land through personal relationships with the Iroquois, and thus undermining the author-ities in colonial government responsible for diplomacy. Some Mo-hawks had great "regard" for Klock and the other "poor Germans our Neighbours." Hendrick, for example, was one of the most in-fluential Mohawk leaders, a vital ally of William Johnson and a key player at the Albany Conference of 1754, a meeting of representa-tives from several British colonies to discuss joint defense against the French. During the conference Hendrick specifically mentioned Klock and requested that the New York government "give the Ger-mans Writings for these Lands" that the Mohawks had promised to them (an area of about 12,000 acres between East Canada and Ga-roga creeks in modern Fulton County). Without naming names, Hen-drick also noted that "there are people who want to do him [Klock] some harm, but we will not agree to it." Klock's family eventually settled near the junction of East Canada Creek (or Caiharon) and the Mohawk River, within plain view of the Canajoharie Mohawk settlements on the south side of the river. Klock was also one of the traders implicated in German Flatts's negotiations with the Oneidas and Vaudreuil from 1755 to 1757.[7]

Klock's notorious land deals are superficially known to historians, but none has fully investigated one of the most heated land disputes in eighteenth-century North America. Earlier studies of the New York frontier, emphasizing land and patent disputes, have created a sense of inevitable conflict between Indians and Europeans. Historians have usually dismissed Klock as representative of most European frontier settlers—an unscrupulous, violent, and land-hungry rogue bent on dispossessing Indians.[8] Condemnations of Klock are not difficult to come by: the correspondence of Sir William Johnson and the records of his diplomatic meetings with Iroquois are teeming with scathing denunciations of the German farmer. Klock was also the object of two prosecutions by the New York government that left behind a considerable legal paper trail. Klock's main offenses were his resurrection of a deed that many Mohawks deemed fraudulent, his use of alcohol in land negotiations, his brusque dealings with his German and Iroquois neighbors, and his overall combativeness toward Johnson. But no jury found enough unequivocal and overwhelming evidence to convict him of defrauding the Iroquois. The German farmer's actions may have been no more or less fraudulent than Sir William's transformation of a Mohawk deed of gift into a royal grant by George III in 1769. Why did George Klock draw so much attention at a time when other European settlers also liberally used alcohol to lubricate land deals? Klock never had any official capacity in colonial government, but he emerged as a persuasive, influential, and skilled frontier trader and negotiator who fluently spoke the Mohawk language and understood Iroquois diplomatic rituals; he communicated with Mohawks, Oneidas, Oswegatchies, fellow Palatines, and French officials and formed personal relationships with

Mohawks and Oneidas, such as the sachems Hendrick and Hanyery. But there are fewer surviving documents that fully relate the perspectives of George Klock and the Mohawks and Oneidas who supported his claims and opposed Johnson. The Mohawk sachem Hendrick keenly observed in 1754 that the "the Germans are poor and have no Writings," compared to one of Sir William Johnson's allies, whom he described as "Rich" with "Writings and Friends."[9] Despite the evidentiary pitfalls this controversy speaks volumes about the everyday lives of ordinary European and Iroquois settlers during the tumultuous era of the American Revolution and its aftermath.

In 1761 Klock had escalated a conflict with the Canajoharie Mohawks when he and his partners became involved in a land dispute with them. One of the most hotly contested land deals of the eighteenth century was over the 1731 Canajoharie Patent, which encompassed the Canajoharie Mohawks' settlements and planting grounds on the south side of the Mohawk River. Philip Livingston, Abraham Van Horne, and other wealthy partners had obtained an Indian deed through a scandalous survey conducted clandestinely, by moonlight. Royal Governor George Clinton wrote in 1746 that Livingston was "the principal occasion of all the Disaffection" among the Six Nations, despite Livingston's office as secretary of Indian affairs. The dispute festered until the Albany Conference of 1754, when Livingston relinquished his claim, due to Mohawk protests. But by 1761 the conflict burst open again when Klock and his partners purchased from Livingston the quit claim, or release, to the original 1731 deed. Because of its questionable legitimacy, the quit claim "carrie[d] with it a bad look," as Johnson observed, and did not impart clear title to the land.[10]

Why Klock became involved in this controversial patent is unclear. Certainly, the end of the Seven Years' War signaled to many British colonists, including both Klock and Johnson, an opportunity to expand into the continent's interior. But in 1761 Johnson and Klock came to blows over the lands surrounding Canajoharie. Sir William

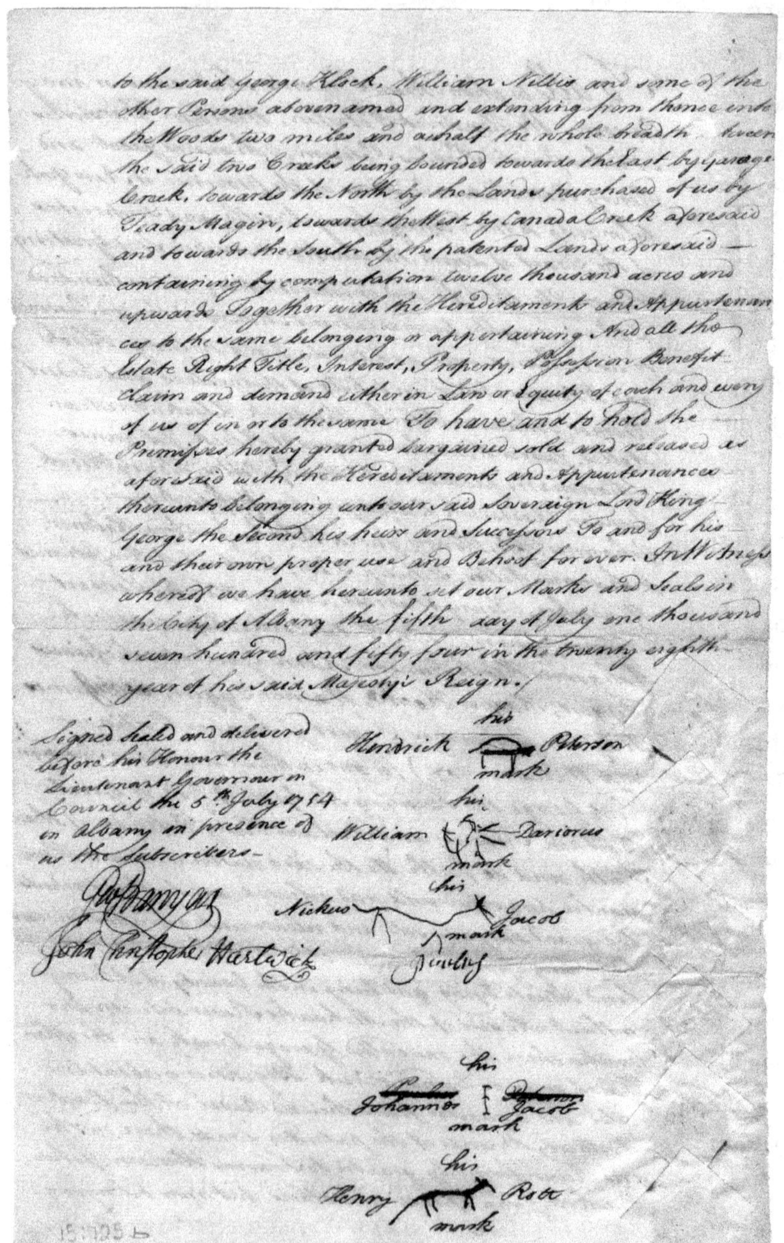

Fig. 12. Indian deed to George Klock and William Nellis, July 5, 1754, in Applications for Land Grants, vol. 15, fol. 125b. Courtesy of New York State Archives, Albany NY.

had excluded Klock from his efforts to obtain lands north of the village, which eventually became his royal grant. He also specifically blocked Klock's attempts to patent a smaller, eight-hundred-acre tract on the north side of the Mohawk River. The Canajoharie area may have captured Klock's attention because of his previous role in negotiating leases between Mohawk landlords and German tenant farmers on the south side of the river. Did Klock hope to interpose himself as landlord and receive rents himself? Regardless of Klock's exact motives in reviving the 1731 deed, Johnson remarked that "in all my life I never saw a People so enraged as they [the Mohawks] were at it." To impart greater legitimacy to his quit claim, Klock needed to obtain requisite Indian deeds affirming the original purchase of Canajoharie lands. His modus operandi in these purchases was to get individual Mohawk men or women drunk and then coax, bribe, or force them to sign deeds affirming land sales over which they had no individual authority. On one occasion he met with three or four young Mohawk men out hunting and invited them to his house; after getting them drunk, he pressed the men to sign his deed. According to one eyewitness, George and his son Jacob "keep each of them a tap in the same house, where they have a resort of many Indians to whom they give plenty of liquor."[11]

From the Mohawks' perspective it seemed that they were "threatned to be Dispossessed of our just Property, *by those whom we always considered as our Children*, and who have had all their possessions from us." Some of these colonial children had rebelled against their Native guardians after establishing themselves under the shade of the Great Tree of Peace. The Iroquois also believed that their alliance and military participation with the British during the Seven Years' War would strengthen the peaceful accommodations that prevailed in the valley and "preserve our Lands." Only ten years after the war, however, the Mohawk leader Abraham lamented, "we could [not] expect from our Brethren that after we had rendered them such Services in those wars that you would take our Lands from us." The Canajoharie Mohawks were particularly aggrieved because Klock's actions threatened to overturn the harmonious and symbiotic relationships that they had forged with other German farmers: their tenants who had "lived on s^d. Land about twenty years, unmolested by any one." Mohawks had occasionally invited trustworthy colonists—usually families like the Klocks, who came to them in poverty—to use and farm their lands. A number of Germans had become tenants and paid rents such as corn or wheat to Indian, not colonial, landlords. Klock, in fact, had been a leader in initially helping "to Settle the Rent w^h. The Tenants pay to the Ind^s," and he "kept Rent Rool thereof." Klock's assertion of Livingston's claim threatened to overturn a mutually beneficial arrangement in the Canajoharie neighborhood, for the Mohawks emphasized that "none of the rest of the Germans have used us as Geo. Klock." The Canajoharies were furious when Klock served ejection notices on some of their tenants in the winter of 1761–62 and informed the rest that they should thenceforth pay rents to him (the ejections were also a way of asserting a claim). The Mohawks defended their European tenants through vigorous protests to Johnson. Facing prosecution for trespass, the tenants defended the Mohawks' ownership. Three Canajoharie Germans petitioned Sir William to induce Klock to sign a release so that the lands would revert to the Mohawks. They also testified against Klock in lawsuits that the New York government brought against him in the 1760s.[12]

What was it about George Klock that made him a magnet for conflict? Johnson's characterization of him as "so designing [and] letigious a Rogue, that there is not a man in the Country would chose to have a penny dealings with him" may contain a small kernel of truth. Klock seems to have been a litigious and disputatious person: his actions created schisms not only among the Mohawks but among his European neighbors, his church, and his own family. Klock's name surfaces in many deeds, court cases, and legal records. His brother Jacob swore an affidavit that exposed Klock's fraudulent practices and affirmed that the Indians would not part with the lands that

George claimed. Jacob also complained that he was "frequently troubled, and Disturbed, day & night, and Obliged to get up at all Hours of the night to let in the Drunken Indians" coming from his brother's house. These strands of evidence, along with the court cases and the collected writings of Sir William Johnson, seem to confirm one historian's characterization of Klock as "the black sheep of a respectable Palatine family." But how much of these negative pronouncements stem from Johnson and other British elites' cultural disdain for the "boorish, nay brutish disposition of the country people"? Did Johnson fear the rise of a German landlord with great influence among the Iroquois?[13]

Klock was without question a persuasive, knowledgeable, and skillful negotiator who had some support among the Iroquois. A small band of around twenty Iroquois men and women—"the Conajohare Ind.s who are Ury [George] Klocks Party"—thought enough of Klock to separate from the main settlements at Canajoharie and move to his farm on the river's north side. The Natives who were "allways living at his house" also supported his claims, resented Johnson, and bickered with their kin at the main settlements. Most of the Native residents appear to have been Mohawks and Oneidas, though a few may have been relative newcomers or recent adoptees; the father of one of the Mohawks living at Klock's house was a Catawba or Cherokee adoptee from the southeast. Another Mohawk named Cobus, "alias Negroe a Creature of Klocks," resided "in an old house belonging to Klock, & near his present place of residence." Archaeological work and the written record confirm that there was a discernible Indian settlement at Klock's house, along with large quantities of trade goods such as wampum and pipes. William Johnson once spent a sleepless night at Klock's brother's house nearby, for "by their Singing dancing & other noise I was disturbed during the whole night." There was something more effective to Klock's diplomacy than simply the way he brandished liquor bottles, as the presence of this small band and the support of Iroquois leaders suggest. The

Oneida sachem Hanyery, or Tehawenkaragwen, sided with Klock in his dispute against Johnson and even made threats against certain Mohawks. Born around 1720, Hanyery grew up in a world of interconnected Oneida and Palatine villagers; Hanyery may have had a Palatine father named Dockstader. The Mohawks and Oneidas asserted conflicting claims to the very lands north and west of Canajoharie that Klock and Johnson vied for. In the early 1750s Oneida sachems spoke of Germans whom they had received "in compassion to their poverty" and who "live there . . . only by our permission." Klock himself had negotiated over land directly with the Oneidas, perhaps including Hanyery.[14]

The Mohawks expressed a profound sense of betrayal, which frequently surfaces in the accounts of William Johnson's diplomatic meetings in the 1760s and 1770s. But the Canajoharie Mohawks' own lands, homes, and agricultural grounds were directly threatened by Klock's actions and the encroachments of other European settlers. Iroquois speakers typically presented strings or belts of wampum with every statement to solemnize and strengthen their points. In 1763 an Onondaga speaker dispensed with presenting wampum and instead "gave a Bottle"—one of Klock's empty rum bottles—to punctuate his request that the liquor traders' traffic be stopped. "Brother," he stated, "Liquor hath been always our Ruin, for whenever any of our people go over to the house of Geo. Klock, and we send for them from thence, he fills them more." Because the Iroquois believed that peace was sustained not by treaties alone, the lack of good feelings between local communities betrayed an infirmity in the larger alliance. What caused the Natives concern was the "unbrotherlike proceedings of George Klock" and the "unbrotherlike behaviour of the white people towards them . . . who seemed to aim at their entire extirpation,—which they added, was a most cruel, and unchristianlike return for their adherence to the English, and charitable conduct towards their Neighbours, when they were unable to assist themselves." Despite these feelings of betrayal, the Mohawks were incredibly long-suffering toward Klock, "that old Rogue, the old Disturber of our village," and toward the New York officials who claimed to be able to render them justice. Despite years of government inaction and near indifference, the Mohawks patiently pressed Klock to sign the release of his Canajoharie claim, and he repeatedly refused.[15]

William Johnson was an erstwhile ally of the Mohawks, supporting their attempts to undo colonists' egregious land patents at Kayaderosseras, Canajoharie, and Mohawk Flatts at Tiononderoge. Johnson's personal ties to Mohawk leaders such as Theyanoguin (Hendrick) and Joseph Brant, and his marital ties to Mohawk women such as Molly Brant (after 1759), undoubtedly strengthened his resolve to see justice done for the Mohawks. But as a land owner, developer, and broker, Johnson also contributed to the Mohawks' diminishing land base. As early as 1750 Johnson was interested in patenting ten thousand acres of land around Canajoharie and solicited Governor Clinton's involvement and approval. In 1761 the Canajoharie Mohawks entrusted Johnson with a large tract of their remaining lands on the north side of the Mohawk River, between East and West Canada creeks. They intended this gift as a deed in trust, to protect and preserve their lands from colonial encroachments. In Sir William's words, the Mohawks believed that the gift was "proof of our friendship, which we fear, will not be long, as our White Brethren are getting all our Lands from us." Johnson, however, made it possible for his white brethren to get Indians' lands when he made it clear to Cadwallader Colden that "we are determined to Settle a Number of People on the Land directly." The superintendent's gift conflicted with the efforts of Klock and his partners to obtain lands between the two creeks, most of which became Johnson's royal grant. Sir William and George also sparred over a smaller, eight-hundred-acre tract on the north side of the Mohawk River, directly opposite Canajoharie.[16]

Sir William used every means at his disposal to block the German settler's attempt to patent land and encouraged the New York government to prosecute Klock. Johnson affirmed to Goldsbrow Banyar in 1761 his "desire that no Pattent Pass to him [Klock] either for the 800 acres he has a Lycense to purchase, or for any other quantity or Tract of Land," and vowed that he would "make it appear that [Klock's] method of proceeding, is not only very villanous, but if allowed of, will be productive of a great deal of trouble." Johnson explained that his interest in the eight-hundred-acre tract was "on Acc[t]. of a report propagated by y[e]. Country People that there was a Mine on it, or rather what they call *Cobalt*, but more so to disapoint *Klock* who was taking verry unfair Steps to obtain it from y[e]. Ind[s]." Johnson also offered land to colonial officials like Goldsbrow Banyar and surveyor Alexander Colden, while insisting on "excluding [Klock] from this [land], as the Condition upon which" they agreed. Before the American Revolution Klock was never able to receive letters patent for tracts that he had legally licensed, purchased, and surveyed between 1754 and 1760.

Johnson, by contrast, petitioned the Crown directly and lobbied New York officials to approve his gift from the Mohawks (which Johnson had to treat as a sale in order to obtain letters patent). In this way Johnson's gift from the Mohawks was transformed into a royal land grant from George III in 1769, which encompassed some one hundred thousand acres of prime Mohawk land. Johnson and the thirty-eight other grantees then subdivided the land and began settling it with Europeans.[17] While the Indian superintendent genuinely believed that Klock had grievously wronged the Mohawks, he also hoped to eliminate rival claims to the lands he had received. In response to his Mohawk allies' frequent complaints of fraud, Johnson strenuously urged royal officials to take legal action. The New York government brought two separate suits against Klock in 1763 and 1768, but both prosecutions were unsuccessful. These legal proceedings against Klock demonstrate the "many Difficulties in the Way to Justice" in cases involving Indian rights. In the 1763 case *The King v. George Klock* the defendant was acquitted by the jury, and the court ruled that "a Pattent however fraudulently obtained is a Claim superior to all Justice and reason." In 1768 Klock pleaded not guilty to the charge of barratry, or "being a Common Sower of Dissentions & Discord," but he apparently did not contend a "presentment fyled for being a dangerous person" and was fined ten pounds plus the costs of the suit by an Albany County court.[18]

In all of his proceedings in his own land dealings and in his attempts to thwart Klock, Johnson seems to have been largely unconscious of the great similarity between himself and the German settler. Each man chafed at the other's political clout. Johnson complained of Klock's unfair dealings, even while offering colonial officials shares of land. Johnson accused Klock of villainous dealings with the Mohawks, even as he subdivided the royal grant among his partners and allies and made plans to settle it with other Europeans. Both Johnson and Klock had permanently and legally alienated large tracts of land from Mohawk and Oneida possession for their "Sole Use and only proper use Benefit and Behoof forever," as the text of Johnson's 1769 royal grant made clear. By the early 1770s the Mohawks had a "mere trifle of Property remaning in their hands" and were "surrounded on all Sides," but Johnson took immense pride in his legacy of peopling the Mohawk Valley with European tenants. A closer look at land dealings in the Mohawk Valley at this time reveals a picture more complex than that of a rivalry between Johnson, great man and friend to the Indians, and the disreputable Klock, their enemy.[19]

Sir William was disgusted at how the German farmer was "Supported and Encouraged by a Powerfull Sett of People at New York" who were really "Creatures of Klock" and his partners in Mohawk Valley land deals. With encouragement from like-minded land speculators, Klock was emboldened to defy the royal governor, Sir Henry Moore, in a face-to-face encounter in 1768, during a meeting with the Mohawks at Johnson Hall. Klock defended his actions, saying that the Mohawks had sold him the land for £45 and fifty shipments of corn and that they had accompanied his sons during the survey.

He refused Moore's repeated requests to sign the release and allegedly "made use of every rude expression to the Speaker of the Indians." The superintendent recognized that New York common law and chancery courts were wholly ineffectual venues for redressing Mohawk grievances. Until his death in 1774 Johnson pressed the New York Assembly to vacate the patent by a legislative act and brought the matter to the Crown's attention. The Mohawks also realized that a petition directly to the king was their last resort. George Klock, too, sought a transatlantic solution to his grievances.[20]

Klock's voyage to London with his Mohawk associate occurred in 1773, amid the imperial crisis brewing over the Tea Act. His trip and its aftermath thus reveal some of the internal tensions in New York that shaped the American Revolution's origins. Klock may have undertaken his voyage for both principle and profit, by "Exhibiting [the Mohawk] as a Show" in London's coffeehouses and taverns. In 1764 Klock had sponsored a similar voyage of Mohawks to London. Johnson's mercantile agent in London, John Blackburn, believed that Klock had "impos'd on Lord Dartmouth," the secretary of state for the American colonies, with a petition to the king. Klock wished to present his claims and also complain of political issues such as the "Division of Tryon County" and Johnstown's establishment as the county seat. In a 1775 meeting of the Palatine District's Committee of Safety the rebellious settlers complained that the county had been "Ruled by one family the Different Branches of Which are still strenuous in disuading people from Coming into the Congressional Measures." Like other Germans in the area Klock chafed at the preponderance of power held by Johnson's coterie in their Tryon County fiefdom. A hostile reception, however, prevented Klock from laying his grievances before the Crown: the Earl of Dartmouth held no audience with Klock, instead investigating his whereabouts with the intention of punishing him. Dartmouth believed that "the enquiries I made concerning him created such an apprehension in him of being proceeded against" that he returned to New York in the spring of 1774.

Regardless of Klock's intentions, his trip was made at the expense of the Mohawk whom he had either cajoled or kidnapped. According to Johnson, the Indian later complained "bitterly of y.[e] Imposition put upon him." But the Mohawk made the most of his situation, for he returned to New York City in May with cash and other gifts he had received in England, all of which Klock absconded with. When the Canajoharie Mohawks found out about Klock's thefts, Joseph Brant, leading about twenty men, "broke into Klocks House, Abused him verry severly, and [took] back the money." They also killed some of Klock's sheep and threatened him and his family with similar destruction. They insisted that Klock officially sign away his claim, and the battered man finally relented. But by the time the Mohawks later returned with a local justice of the peace, Klock had fled to Albany, where he petitioned the governor to prosecute the Mohawks for assaulting him.[21]

The intertwined histories of the Oneidas, the Mohawks, the Palatines, and leading New York officials like Johnson prefigured the destructive civil war that erupted in the Mohawk Valley during the American Revolution. The longstanding relationships between the Oneidas and the Palatines, for example, are a major reason why many Oneidas sided with the rebellious Americans. The kind of household diplomacy that Klock conducted was later evident in the 1775 meetings between the Iroquois and revolutionary Committees of Safety at the homesteads of Jacob Klock and Frederick Bellinger, near German Flatts. A staunch opponent of the colonial resistance movement, Sir William did not live to see Klock punished or the American Revolution destroy the patriarchal, patronage-based society over which he presided. On July 11, 1774, as he listened to Indians' rumors of war over the mass murders of Ohio Indians, violations of the Fort Stanwix boundary line in New York, and Klock's aggressions, Johnson collapsed. He died a few hours later. His funeral procession was led by New Jersey's royal governor William Franklin, New York Supreme Court justices, and other gentlemen; around two thousand local settlers and Iroquois were also present. This was one of the last unified acts of the Mohawk Valley's inhabitants. Another foreshadowing of the impending fractures came when some of Klock's European neighbors sided with the Mohawks in late 1774. During a meeting with Canajoharie settlers the Mohawks pleaded with their neighbors, "among whom we have so long lived in an uninterrupted friendship," to help them put an end to Klock's attempts to dispossess them. In delivering the settlers' reply, magistrate Hendrick Frey affirmed that they "cannot but acknowledge the justness of your observations and claim" and delivered a petition supporting their Native neighbors. According to Guy Johnson, the petition requested that the government "satisfy the Indians or that some steps be taken for freeing the Neighborhood from the apprehensions occasioned by his quarrel." Klock was particularly concerned when he got wind of a rumor that Frey (a magistrate and a militia leader) would turn a blind eye if Brant and the Mohawks happened to kill Klock and his family.[22]

But Joseph Brant did not resort to violence against Klock. In 1775 and 1776 he journeyed to England with Guy Johnson, the acting superintendent of Indian affairs, to present the Mohawks' grievances in an audience with Lord George Germain, who had replaced Dartmouth as colonial secretary. Had the Revolutionary War not intervened, the Mohawks might have received a favorable resolution from the British Crown. In 1775 Lt. Gov. Cadwallader Colden mentioned the possibility of "adequate Punishment upon that mischivous fellow [Klock]" by royal authority. But ultimately, Joseph's answer would come not from the New York government or the king, but from George III's rebellious colonial children. For when Brant returned to his homelands in 1776, they were soon to be engulfed in bloodshed. The Mohawks thus experienced the destructive Revolutionary War and their dispossession as an American betrayal of Iroquois generosity and the ties of reciprocity that had once bound them together in a common alliance.[23]

Both the American rebels and the British initially sought only the Six Nations' neutrality when the conflict opened. The Iroquois were more than happy "not to take any part, but as it is a family Affair to sit still and see you fight it out." Abraham, of Tiononderoge, also stated that the Mohawks "want nothing to be but Brothers with us, and to be entirely unconcerned" with the confrontation. Again, local communities' negotiations confirmed larger arrangements. In June 1775 Whigs from German Flatts met with their Oneida and Tuscarora neighbors to reaffirm their commitment to peace. They maintained that their reason for calling the meeting was "purely on [Account] of the old frindship which has so long kept up between us; it is that friendship we want to Mentain, it is that frindship which will be an Equall Benefit to us it is as much wanted on your side as ours." The settlers feelingly declared that "our meaning is for our Joynt peace and frindship: in which we and our Children may Continue to the end of time." Like many other conflicts, however, the Revolutionary War evolved into a contagion of destruction that no one at the time anticipated.[24] Sir William's nephew Guy Johnson, the acting Indian superintendent, and Sir John Johnson (Sir William's son and heir) were unable to contain growing revolutionary activity in the Mohawk Valley. In the face of growing Whig pressure they abdicated their Mohawk Valley homes and took their families and loyal tenants to Canada in 1775 and 1776. The Tryon County Committee of Safety seamlessly and bloodlessly assumed control of the mechanisms of county government.[25]

As the fighting intensified and the stakes became higher, Indian nations were increasingly drawn into war. The British and Americans conducted parallel negotiations to secure the Indians' military assistance and loyalty, especially after the failure of Gen. William Howe's campaign to crush the rebellion in 1776. The Iroquois, as Joseph Brant observed, were caught "between two hells," as the British and Americans demanded absolute loyalty. In 1776 Col. Elias Dayton marched a force of American soldiers up the Mohawk Valley to contain the loyalist activities of Sir John Johnson. Along the way he presented the Mohawks with an ultimatum that revealed how Americans would enforce loyalty: if they resisted his march, he would "burn all their houses, destroy their Towns & Cast the Mohawks with their Wifes & Children off of the face of the Earth." If they were passive and "let us alone in a Family Quarrel," Dayton promised, they would be free from harm. One of Dayton's officers approvingly noted that "the only way is to strike Terror into them."[26]

During the Seven Years' War Iroquois warriors had also been under intense pressure to join French and British armies whenever they passed through Iroquoia. The factional nature of Iroquois politics made it possible for limited numbers of Mohawks and Senecas, for example, to fight with the British or French without endangering the confederacy's larger commitment to neutrality. What changed during the Revolution is that most Oneidas and Tuscaroras sided with the Americans, while most Mohawks, Onondagas, Cayugas, and Senecas remained true to the British alliance. In 1777 the British launched a campaign to reclaim New York and to isolate New England from the rest of the colonies. Around one thousand Iroquois warriors (mainly Mohawks, Senecas, Onondagas, and Cayugas) fought with the British generals Burgoyne and St. Leger; the Oneidas and Tuscaroras committed themselves to the opposing American armies.[27]

During the Revolution the Iroquoian borderlands from the Mohawk to the Monongahela valleys became an extended battleground in a war increasingly characterized by intense racial antipathies. The 1777 Battle of Oriskany, fought in the upper Mohawk Valley during the British siege of Fort Stanwix, inaugurated the three civil wars and the slaughter that followed. The British and their Iroquois allies orchestrated a gruesomely successful ambush of the Tryon County militia (in which many Klocks served) and their Oneida allies. The Seneca warrior Blacksnake marveled at the carnage, with over five hundred dead and wounded on both sides: "I thought at that time the Blood Shed [was] a Stream Running down on the Decending ground." After Oriskany the New York–Iroquois frontiers were finally plunged into the total war in which Indians and Pennsylvanians had already been subsumed twenty years earlier. The heavy casualties that the British-allied Iroquois suffered at Oriskany (over sixty) prompted them to seek revenge against the American rebels and their Oneida allies.[28]

Because the war was fought between kinsfolk and former neighbors, it fueled feelings of betrayal and vengeance and justified extreme brutality. One rebel soldier, for example, fought "Tories he had been acquainted with before the war." British loyalists such as John Butler sought to destroy the American rebels who had dispossessed them and vowed that "our revenge shall be in proportion to our former loss." This was a war in which Senecas, under a métis warrior named Cornplanter, attacked Fort Plain, New York, and captured Cornplanter's white father, John Abeel, a blacksmith who had once lived among the Senecas and married a Seneca woman. Frontier warfare pitted white settlers and Indians against other whites. In early 1777 loyalist European farmers living in the Delaware and Susquehanna valleys flocked to Joseph Brant at nearby Oquaga and put themselves under his command (without pay). Brant's Volunteers, as the force was known, was a multiethnic company whose members had names such as Middagh, Johnston, Ziely, and Deckert. From their base at Oquaga, Brant and his men began extorting supplies from local communities aligned with the rebels. At Unadilla in 1777 Brant and his volunteers confronted American troops under the command of Brant's old neighbor Nicholas Herkimer and his adversary Ebenezer Cox, who had married George Klock's daughter. Nicholas Herkimer later fought against both Joseph and his loyalist brother Jost at Oriskany.[29]

In 1778 loyalist and Indian forces launched an even broader campaign to destroy the New York and Pennsylvania settlements, rescue family members, and win back their homes and lands. The loyalist-Indian offensives also tied down large numbers of rebel troops, forced thousands of settlers to abandon their farms, and denied precious supplies to the rebel armies. Brant's forces, for example, destroyed Cobleskill, Andrewstown, Springfield, and German Flatts in the late summer and early autumn. Expeditions from Fort Niagara also struck the Pennsylvania settlements in Westmoreland, Bedford, Northampton, and Northumberland counties. In the Wyoming Valley in 1778 Walter Butler's loyalist-Indian force inflicted more than three hundred casualties on the Americans and pillaged the settlements there. Butler and Joseph Brant's multiethnic force also decimated the Scots-Irish settlement of Cherry Valley that same year; in the chaotic action the attackers indiscriminately killed dozens of civilians. While Wyoming and Cherry Valley went down in American memory as "massacres," they were representative of the total war that both sides practiced, in which hundreds of Americans, British, and Iroquois were killed, scalped, mutilated, starved, or captured. An American lieutenant recorded in his 1779 journal that a scouting party "skinned two [dead Indians] from their hips down for boot legs: one pair for the Major the other for myself." When the militia colonel Peter Bellinger surveyed German Flatts in 1778, he saw a smoldering, six-mile swath of destruction along the Mohawk River in which sixty-three houses, fifty-seven barns, and four mills had been burned and numerous cattle destroyed.[30]

The British and Indian offensives invited American counterattacks that also focused on utterly destroying Indian villages, crops, and peoples. As Col. Peter Gansevoort believed, "we shall this campaign have it in our power to Oblige the cruel and inhuman Savages to make peace with us on our own terms." In September 1778 a Pennsylvania officer named Col. Thomas Hartley led two hundred militia members up the Susquehanna River and destroyed the villages of Sheshecunnunk and Tioga before withdrawing. In October Lt. Col. William Butler led detachments of the Fourth Pennsylvania Regiment from Schoharie to the Susquehanna to destroy Unadilla, Oquaga, and a small Tuscarora settlement. The timing of these attacks was crucial, since destroying fields ready for harvest guaranteed wintertime deprivation, if not actual starvation. The Americans visited the Six Nations with even greater destruction in 1779, when Gen. George Washington coordinated a three-pronged invasion of the Iroquois homelands. In western Pennsylvania Daniel Brodhead's small force moved up the Allegheny River and burned eight Seneca and Delaware towns; John Sullivan advanced northwestward from the Delaware Valley to attack Iroquois towns in the upper Susquehanna and Genesee valleys. Col. George Clinton's army advanced up the Mohawk Valley to link up with Sullivan. One of Sullivan's soldiers summarized the expedition's goal: "As I informed you in my last," he wrote his wife, "we are to accomplish the total extirpation & destruction of our enemies amongst the Six Nations." The Americans looted and burned some forty Iroquois villages; destroyed over one hundred thousand bushels of corn; desecrated Indian burial grounds; and cut down fields ripe with corn, squash, beans, pumpkins, and potatoes and orchards of peach trees. George Washington became known as "town destroyer" among the Iroquois. Many Onondagas, Senecas, Cayugas, and Mohawks, who offered ineffective resistance to Sullivan, huddled as refugees near Fort Niagara during the terrible winter of 1779–80. Death from disease, starvation, and the cold claimed more Iroquois lives than combat during Sullivan's invasion.[31]

The Seneca leader Sayenqueraghta told a group of Wyandots visiting Fort Niagara in 1779 that the rebels "wish for nothing more, than to extirpate us from the Earth, that they may possess our Lands, the Desire of attaining which we are convinced is the Cause of the present War." Determined to protect these lands and to seek revenge, the Iroquois and their British allies renewed their onslaught against the New York, Pennsylvania, and Kentucky frontier settlements in 1780. Guy Johnson's journal for the 1780 campaigns reveals that sixty-three different war parties, totaling 2,419 warriors, went out against American frontiers. It reports American losses as 170 killed, 211 taken prisoner, and 81 women released; at a cost of 18 Indian losses, nearly four hundred homes, granaries, and mills had been destroyed, along with hundreds of livestock. The Schoharie Valley remained largely untouched for most of the war. But in 1780 Sir John Johnson led a force of loyalists and Iroquois and laid waste to hundreds of homes there; Canajoharie, German Flatts, Harpersfield, and the Oneida town of Kanonwalohale were also gutted by Sir John's forces. The 1780 Battle of Klock's Field, which pitted Sir John Johnson's loyalists and their Iroquois allies against Jacob Klock and other American rebels, was particularly symbolic of old divisions between the Klocks and the Johnson family. When the fighting ceased on the New York frontiers in 1781–82, a Continental Army officer noted, "Everything except the soil is destroyed from Fort Hunter to Stone Arabia." Gov. George Clinton admitted that "Schenectady may now be said to become the limits of our western Frontier." By 1782 the Iroquois and their British allies had largely won the war on the northern frontiers.[32]

While the Iroquois had maintained their status as a free and independent people, the Revolution and its aftermath greatly diminished their power, population, and lands. The United States thus achieved a preponderance of power over the Iroquois that neither the French nor the British had ever possessed. No Indians participated in or were represented at the 1783 Treaty of Paris, which ended the Revolution. As the French had in 1763, the British abandoned their Native allies and transferred to the United States their claims to North America's interior. American officials assumed the mantle of conqueror in their postwar negotiations with the Iroquois. They were able to enforce punitive treaties upon the Iroquois, such as the 1784 Treaty of Fort Stanwix, which extorted thousands of acres from the Natives as a condition for peace. The lands of the Americans' Oneida and Tuscarora allies also went unsecured, as Euroamerican settlers (including some of Sullivan's veterans) expanded westward. With so many Iroquois living on Lake Ontario, the metaphorical longhouse now straddled Upper Canada and the United States. And because many Mohawks had taken refuge in Canada, the Revolution also resolved many of the long-standing land disputes between Mohawk and European frontier communities in the Americans' favor. Many Iroquois communities became, in Anthony F. C. Wallace's words, "slums in the wilderness," where poverty, anomie, alcoholism, and violence were rampant. Under such conditions the Natives' land base further eroded. Some New York petitioners in 1800 asked for restraints on the liquor trade, because local Oneidas "render themselves very uncomfortable neighbors."[33]

The Iroquois Confederacy would also lose the peace after 1783 because of the continued growth and expansion of the American population. When Indians and Euroamericans returned to their ruined settlements in the Revolution's aftermath, any commitment to accommodation had been swallowed up in animosity and land hunger. Small groups of Mohawks persisted at their settlements during the war years but were "threatened by the Inhabitants," who distrusted them. Rebel and Oneida troops also plundered or destroyed Tiononderoge and Canajoharie in 1778. The Fort Hunter chapel, where Mohawks had once worshiped, was "turned into a tavern by the Americans and a keg of rum stored in the reading desk." Joseph and Molly Brant's personal belongings were stolen, their homes occupied by local settlers. Individual Mohawk families returned to their old settlements in the 1780s and 1790s, but the majority rejoined their kin in Canada or elsewhere in the Iroquois' remaining homelands, now claimed by the state of New York.[34]

The Mohawks were not alone in their banishment, for thousands of American loyalists left New York and resettled in Canada or other British possessions. The Schoharie Reformed Church, built in 1772, displayed the names of its builders on the stone walls near the doorway. In a war that divided congregations, legend has it, the loyalists' names were later chiseled out—a potent act of excommunication from the church and the new American republic. But Euroamericans' most brutal statement that they would never coexist with the Indians, even if they were Christians, was made at the Moravian mission town of

Gnadenhütten in the Ohio Country in 1782. Suspicious that the Moravian Delawares were in league with Delawares allied to the British, a force of Pennsylvania militia confronted the villagers and confined them. Then macabre killings began, as the militia bludgeoned to death more than ninety Delaware men, women, and children with cooper's mallets. Gnadenhütten's carnage did not mark an end to conflict. Fighting on the Ohio frontier continued largely unabated; the United States had conquered and dispossessed most of the Natives living in the Ohio Valley by the time of the War of 1812.[35]

In certain locales, however, Indian and Euroamerican communities continued to interact socially and economically after the war ended. At Cornplanter's Tract on the Allegheny River in northwestern Pennsylvania, for example, Senecas had frequent contact with poorer white settlers living downstream. Oneidas continued to lease lands following the war. But in a visit to Schenectady in 1780 the French officer François-Jean de Beauvoir observed that the deep hatred the Indians' attacks had generated made it "impossible for the Americans to consent to have them longer for neighbors." But he did hold out hope that the Oneidas would eventually become civilized and integrate with the Euroamericans. A decade later Edward Walsh observed in his travels the same feeling: "The Red & white people cannot co-exist in the same place." Thomas Proctor, a veteran of the Sullivan expedition, retraced his steps years later and rejoiced at the signs of grape shot and shell damage still visible on the trees. During his journey he encountered a minister at Tioga, a former Indian settlement, who thanked him and Sullivan "for opening a way into the wilderness, under the guidance of Providence, to the well doing of hundreds of poor families." The minister's comments reflect the sentiments of historians and poets in the early Republic, who defined a national mythology about Indians that erased the ambivalent aspects of cultural contact that settlers themselves remembered.[36]

The Americans' victorious War for Independence enabled George Klock to gain full legal rights to some of the lands around Canajoharie so long in dispute. After the dispossession and exile of loyalists like Sir John Johnson, Guy Johnson, and Joseph Brant and other Mohawks, the state of New York authorized the sale of both confiscated estates and unappropriated lands. In a 1785 petition to the New York government Klock maintained that he "took every legal step to obtain a Patent" for the 800-acre tract north of the old Mohawk village and detailed every step of his "Regularly Executed" deed: his initial petition, license, and survey still survive in the New York Land Papers. He had formerly been unable to obtain final letters patent, due to the "Influence, and Intrigues of Sir William Johnson." Klock appealed not only to "the firmest Foundation in Point of Equity" but also to his "Large Family who have all manifested a Steady and zealous Attachment to American Liberty in the Late war with Great Britain." (Klock had served in the New York militia.) Klock and his offspring also leased or sold parcels of the Canajoharie patent to other Euroamericans. Along with four other associates, Klock had a 48,000-acre tract surveyed in 1786, located northwest of Johnson's old royal grant, in an area claimed by Oneidas. But Klock's history of negotiation with the Iroquois did not end after the American Revolution, and his family's experience, at least, challenges the general sense, common in current histories, that frontier violence during the Seven Years' War and the American Revolution foreclosed on the peaceful relations between Indians and Europeans. In the 1790s Oneidas attempted to protect their land base by enlisting trustworthy Euroamericans as tenants. In 1794 Klock's descendants signed a lease for 300 acres of land from the Oneidas for a term of twenty-one years, indicating that their personal relationships continued well into the postwar era. In 1792 Oneida sachems made a request to William Colbreath, a New York sheriff: that "old Mr. Clock & his family" "may be suffered to remain on our land where he now is during our pleasure." According to the Oneidas, Klock was a "cleaver harmless old man" who was of "service to us especially when we are out that way hunting he supplies us with milk and such things as we want." The Mohawks' "old

Antagonist" ended his days supplying milk to Oneida hunters after settling his family securely on the lands that were the object of his lifelong quest and struggle.[37]

The Tree of Peace that had briefly flourished in the eighteenth century contained the hope and possibility that two peoples could meet and coexist together. Over the course of the eighteenth century, however, the fertile river valleys that Europeans and Indians had once inhabited together were completely transformed. By 1790 American citizens occupied the sites of Canajoharie, Tiononderoge, Schoharie, Kittanning, Shamokin, and other formerly Native communities. Nevertheless, many vestiges of this shared world are evident even today. While the Pennsylvania settlers' dispossession of Natives was so thorough that there are presently no Indian reservations in Penn's woods, in New York even the American Revolution did not completely displace the Iroquois peoples from their homelands. Senecas, Oneidas, Onondagas, and Tuscaroras maintained possession of some of their lands in upstate New York after the Revolution, and they are still there. So too are families of German, Mennonite, and Dutch ancestry, living in the Mohawk and Schoharie valleys. The descendants of Presbyterian Scots-Irish in the valleys of western Pennsylvania are yet another mark of continuity from the colonial period. Of all the communities surveyed, however, only one—Kahnawake—has remained unchanged in its location since colonial times. In another sense modern Iroquois living in New York and Ontario continue to cross the United States–Canada border with the same ease with which their ancestors crossed French and British imperial claims. What is remembered, of course, is less the similarities and more the differences between European and Indian communities: the legacies of warfare, prejudice, displacement, and different views of the land. But European and Indian settlers did not initially believe that their relationships were destined to end in warfare and animosity. Therein lie the tragedy and the continuing challenge. In 1775 the Continental Congress sent an address of hope to the Iroquois

Confederacy that speaks to our time with continuing power: "We live upon the same Ground with you, the same Island in our common Birthplace, we desire to sit down under the same Tree of peace with you, let us water its roots and cherish its growth till the large leaves and flourishing Branches shall extend to the setting Sun and reach the Skies."[38]

Abbreviations

<table>
<tr><td>AIHA</td><td>Albany Institute of History and Art, Albany NY</td></tr>
<tr><td>AN</td><td>Archives Nationales (Paris)</td></tr>
<tr><td>BP</td><td>Sylvester K. Stevens, Donald H. Kent, and Louis M. Waddell, eds. The Papers of Henry Bouquet. 6 vols. Harrisburg: Pennsylvania Historical and Museum Commission, 1951–94</td></tr>
<tr><td>DCB</td><td>George Brown, et al., eds. Dictionary of Canadian Biography. 14 vols. to date. Toronto: University of Toronto Press, 1979–98</td></tr>
<tr><td>DHNY</td><td>E. B. O'Callaghan, ed. Documentary History of the State of New-York. 4 vols. Albany: Weed, Parsons & Co., 1849–51</td></tr>
<tr><td>DRCHNY</td><td>E. B. O'Callaghan and Berthold Fernow, eds. Documents Relative to the Colonial History of the State of New York. 14 vols. Albany: Weed, Parsons and Co., 1855</td></tr>
</table>

ERNY Hugh Hastings, ed. *Ecclesiastical Records of the State of New York.* 7 vols. Albany: J. B. Lyon, Co., 1902

HSP Historical Society of Pennsylvania, Philadelphia

IIDH Francis Jennings, William N. Fenton, Mary A. Druke, and David R. Miller, eds. *Iroquois Indians: A Documentary History of the Diplomacy of the Six Nations and Their League.* 50 microfilm reels. Woodbridge CT: Research Publications, 1984

ISHLC Clarence Walworth Alvord and Clarence Edwin Carter, eds. *Collections of the Illinois State Historical Library.* 32 vols. Springfield: Illinois State Historical Library, 1915–40

JAH *Journal of American History*

JR Reuben Gold Thwaites, ed. *The Jesuit Relations and Allied Documents: Travels and Explorations of the Jesuit Missionaries in New France, 1610–1791.* 73 vols. New York: Pageant Book Co., 1959

MCDHA Montgomery County Department of History and Archives, Fonda NY

MPCP Samuel Hazard, ed. *Minutes of the Provincial Council of Pennsylvania.* 16 vols. Harrisburg: Theophilus Fenn & Co., 1838–1853. Reprint, vols. 1–3, Philadelphia: Jo. Severns and Co., 1852

NAC National Archives of Canada, Ottawa

NYCM New York Council Minutes, 1668–1783 (A1895), New York State Archives

NYCMSS New York Colonial Manuscripts, 1638–1800 (A1894), New York State Archives

NYHS New-York Historical Society, New York City

NYPL New York Public Library, New York City

NYSA New York State Archives, Albany

NYSHA New York State Historical Association, Cooperstown

NYSL New York State Library, Albany

PA *Pennsylvania Archives*, 9 series, 138 vols. Philadelphia and Harrisburg, 1852–1949

PMHB *Pennsylvania Magazine of History and Biography*

PSA Pennsylvania State Archives, Harrisburg

RSPG *Society for the Propagation of the Gospel in Foreign Parts: The Letter Books, Series B, 1701–1786.* Microfilm. London: Micro Methods, 1964

SHSW State Historical Society of Wisconsin, Madison

SWJP James Sullivan, et al., eds. *The Papers of Sir William Johnson.* 14 vols. Albany: State University of New York, 1921–63

VMHB *Virginia Magazine of History and Biography*

WLCL William L. Clements Library, University of Michigan, Ann Arbor

WMQ *William and Mary Quarterly*, 3rd series

WPHM *Western Pennsylvania Historical Magazine*

Notes

Introduction

1. "Petition of the Sachems or Chiefs of the Schoharie Mohawk Indians [1734?]," Applications for Land Grants, 1643–1803 (A0272), 11:106, NYSA; SWJP, 11:368. Cf. the 1734 map to another Iroquois map from the colonial period in Brandão and Starna, "'Some Things May Slip.'" Please note throughout that I have modernized spellings in cases where the original seemed particularly difficult to read.

2. See Armitage, "Everyday Encounters." In his review of James Merrell's *Into the American Woods*, Alan Taylor also points out the need for an investigation of ordinary settlers' relations with Natives. See A. Taylor, "Bad Birds."

3. See, e.g., Fenton, *Great Law and the Longhouse*; Aquila, *Iroquois Restoration*; Richter, *Ordeal of the Longhouse*; Jennings, *Ambiguous Iroquois Empire*; Jennings et al., *History and Culture of Iroquois Diplomacy*; Parmenter, "At the Wood's Edge."

4. Jennings, *Ambiguous Iroquois Empire*, 374–75.

5. For a useful introduction to backcountry studies see Nobles, "Breaking into the Backcountry." For exceptions see, e.g., Hinderaker, *Elusive Empires*; Moyer, *Wild Yankees*; Aron, "Pigs and Hunters"; Aron, *How the West Was Lost*, chaps. 1 and 2; Perkins, *Border Life*; Hatley, *Dividing Paths*; Hofstra, "'Extension of his Majesties Dominions.'"

6. For interpretations that emphasize "Indian-hating" settlers see Jennings, *Empire of Fortune*, chap. 9; Merrell, *Into the American Woods*; Calloway, *American Revolution in Indian Country*; White, *Middle Ground*; Vaughan, "Frontier Banditti and the Indians."

7. Piker, *Okfuskee*; K. A. Jordan, "Archaeology of the Iroquois Restoration"; Calloway, *American Revolution in Indian Country*; O'Brien, *Dispossession by Degrees*; Merrell, "Shamokin."

8. Faragher, *Daniel Boone*, 35.

9. Fenton, "Concept of Locality."

10. The Hudson, Wyoming, and Delaware valleys are also strong candidates for closer inspection, and I include analyses of and evidence from those areas. But I am focusing on areas where Indian and European communities coexisted for long periods (and areas that typified the experiences of most frontier inhabitants). While the land disputes over the Wyoming Valley were crucial developments, New England and Pennsylvania colonizers never coexisted with the resident Indians for any substantial length of time. I include references to the insular religious Moravian mission communities in the Delaware Valley that were established much later in the colonial period. But I wish to capture the broader patterns of European-Indian encounters, in both space and time.

11. White, *Middle Ground*, 14–20, 366–67 (quote at 14); Calloway, *American Revolution in Indian Country*, xvi. Faragher, "Americans, Mexicans, and Métis," has informed my understanding of community as a "system of ecological relations," a "system of reproductive relations," a "field for collective action," and a "set of affective bonds" (94).

12. J. P. Reid, *Better Kind of Hatchet*, 10, 16; MPCP, 3:319 (Sassoonan); Richter, "Ordeals of the Longhouse," in *Beyond the Covenant Chain*, 18; Cardy, "French Officer among the Iroquois," 152. For Fenton's commentary on the complex workings of the Iroquois Confederacy at a local and factional level, see *Great Law and the Longhouse*. My study will echo a theme in Shoemaker, *Strange Likeness*: "Indian and European similarities enabled them to see their differences in sharper relief and . . . construct new identities that exaggerated the contrasts between them while ignoring what they had in common" (3).

13. For the importance Indians placed on local settlers' attitudes see SWJP, 12:371, 453, 10:220, 225–27, 365, 13:104–7, 4:54; MPCP, 3:216–17, 395, 4:64–72, 8:198–99, 247.

14. Richter, "Cultural Brokers and Intercultural Politics," 41; Merrell, *Into the American Woods*; Szasz, *Between Indian and White Worlds*; Grumet, *Northeastern Indian Lives*; Hagedorn, "'Friend to Go Between Them.'"

15. Cadwallader Colden Papers, 4:412.

16. NYCM, Mar. 3, 1722, May 13–14, 1746, 12:250, 21:91–92.

17. NYCM, Dec. 24, 1745, 21:68–69.

18. Long, *Voyages and Travels*, 65; DRCHNY, 10:187; Thomas Gage to William Johnson, Oct. 7, 1772, Thomas Gage Papers, WLCL.

For proof of this point interested readers should examine the George Clinton Papers, the New York Council Minutes, the New York Colonial Manuscripts, and the various minute books of the Albany Commissioners for Indian Affairs (see NAC, WLCL, and AIHA). Even a casual reading of these sources will reveal just how anxious British officials were regarding their strategic position.

19. DRCHNY, 10:294, 9:984, 1030. For French commentary on the alleged British claims in the Treaty of Utrecht see DRCHNY, 9:703, 960–61, 984–86, 988, 10:187, 228, 294. On the French policy of preserving peace with the Five Nations see DRCHNY, 9:736–39, 755, 766, 763, 780, 814, 816–18, 823–25, 855, 869, 878, 936, 951, 984. For French suspicions and fears regarding Indian loyalties see DRCHNY, 9:1068–73, 1095–98, 10:83, 102, 105. Biographies of two governor generals also yield insights onto this insecure strategic view: Zoltvany, *Philippe de Rigaud de Vaudreuil*, 46, 169–70; Groulx, *Roland-Michel Barrin de La Galissoniere*, 29–30.

20. Brewster, *Pennsylvania and New York Frontier*. On the debate over the Middle Colonies as a region see Bodle, "'Myth of the Middle Colonies' Reconsidered"; Bodle, "Themes and Directions in Middle Colonies Historiography"; Bodle, "Fabricated Region"; Landsman, "Roots, Routes, and Rootedness."

21. Stephen D. Feeley's important work "Tuscarora Trails" also demonstrates how Native population movements gave definition to colonial frontiers. See also Adelman and Aron, "From Borderlands to Borders"; G. Taylor, "Ruled with a Pen."

22. Parmenter, "At the Woods' Edge," viii; Dickinson and Grabowski, "Populations amérindiennes de la vallée laurentienne."

23. Richter, *Ordeal of the Longhouse*; Trigger, *Natives and Newcomers*; Dennis, *Cultivating a Landscape of Peace*.

24. A. F. C. Wallace, "Origins of Iroquois Neutrality"; Haan, "Problem of Iroquois Neutrality"; Richter, *Ordeal of the Longhouse*, chaps. 9–11; Kelsay, *Joseph Brant*, 37.

25. Richter, *Facing East from Indian Country*, 8.

26. Engelbrecht, *Iroquoia*.

27. Here I would make an important modification to Adelman and Aron's model, cited above, which traces the process of borderlands becoming borders. The problem with this approach is that it diminishes the historical reality that Native peoples had clearly defined borders and vociferously defended them; those borders were of course not rigid lines on a map, but to argue that Natives defended amorphous fluid borderlands while Europeans advanced rigid borders might unintentionally lessen the reality of Natives' conceptions of borders in the colonial era.

28. I follow Lamar and Thompson's classic definition of a frontier or borderland as an intermediate "zone of interpenetration between two previously distinct societies" (*Frontier in History*, 7). For borderlands scholarship see Brooks, *Captives and Cousins*; Adelman and Aron, "From Borderlands to Borders"; the responses in AHR 104 (Oct. 1999): 1222–39; Weber, *Spanish Frontier in North America*, 1–13; "John Francis Bannon and the Historiography of the Spanish Borderlands"; Poyo and Hinojosa, "Spanish Texas and Borderlands Historiography in Transition."

29. DRCHNY, 8:607.

30. This book does not argue for a revival of a modified "Iroquois Empire." The areas that I define as the Iroquoian frontiers or borderlands were not necessarily controlled by the Six Nations, but they remained predominantly Native spaces and were preponderantly influenced by the Iroquois and their allies.

31. Havard, *Great Peace of Montreal of 1701*; Fenton, *Great Law and the Longhouse*, 103, 127, 184–86, 201, 249, 308, 315; Jennings et al., *History and Culture of Iroquois Diplomacy*, 17, 122. See also chap. 1 below for a more detailed treatment of the uses of the Tree of Peace in the colonial period.

32. DRCHNY, 9:716.

33. Post, quoted in Tiro, "People of the Standing Stone," 50.

34. Parker, *Constitution of the Five Nations*, 97–113. For Iroquois population movements see Parmenter, "At the Wood's Edge"; Dickinson and Grabowski, "Populations amérindiennes de la vallée laurentienne."

35. Very little work has been done specifically on Indian conceptions of borders. For references to the eighteenth-century borders and territories of the Iroquois see Brandão and Starna, "'Some Things May Slip'"; Alfred, *Heeding the Voices of Our Ancestors*, 28–29; Konrad, "Iroquois Frontier," 129; Konrad, "Iroquois Return to Their Homeland"; Adams, "Iroquois Settlement at Fort Frontenac"; Blanchard, "Seven Nations of Canada."

36. For methodological approaches to comparative history see Axtell, *Invasion Within*; Faragher, "Americans, Mexicans, and Métis"; Gitlin, "On the Boundaries of Empire"; Lamar and Thompson, "Comparative Frontier History," in *Frontier in History*; Guy and Sheridan, *Contested Ground*.

37. For better or worse, I use the terms *French and Indian War* and *Seven Years' War* synonymously, while recognizing the limitations of the former. I will use *Seven Years' War* to emphasize the global dimensions of that conflict.

38. Grabowski, "Common Ground," viii; Greer, *People of New France*.

39. Parkman, *Montcalm and Wolfe*, xxii.

1. The Tree of Peace Planted

1. Havard, *Great Peace of Montreal of 1701*; Beaulieu and Viau, *Grande Paix*; Brandão, "Your Fyre Shall Burn No More"; Brandão and Starna, "Treaties of 1701"; Dawson, *Saint Lawrence Basin and Its Borderlands*, xxviii.

2. Ratification de la Paix, 1701, AN, ser. C11A, Correspondance générale, Canada, vol. 19, ff. 41–44. To aid reader accessibility I cite DRCHNY if a French colonial document is available therein, but readers are encouraged to consult the originals in the Archives Nationales (Paris) to ensure accurate translation.

3. Havard, *Great Peace of Montreal of 1701*, 144. For the setting of the conference see Beaulieu and Viau, *Grande Paix*.

4. Aquila, *Iroquois Restoration*, 55–70.

5. Fenton, *Great Law and the Longhouse*, 330–48, at 331; Wraxall, quoted in Richter, *Ordeal of the Longhouse*, 206; Aquila, *Iroquois Restoration*, 55–70.

6. On French foreign policy see Eccles, *Essays on New France*, 169. For the neutrality agreement and French fear of renewed war see DRCHNY, 9:1040; Norton, *Fur Trade in Colonial New York*, 128; Zoltvany, *Philippe de Rigaud de Vaudreuil*.

7. DRCHNY, 9:716. For other references to the Tree of Peace in diplomacy see DRCHNY, 4:804, 8:39, 9:716, 718, 768, 1063–64, 1066–67, 1073–1081, 10:22–23; Havard, *Great Peace of Montreal of 1701*, chap. 8; Johnston, "Onontio"; Jennings et al., *History and Culture of Iroquois Diplomacy*, 17, 122.

8. The literature on the so-called domiciled Indians in the St. Lawrence is scattered but vast: see Jetten, *Enclaves amérindiennes*; Delâge, "Iroquois chrétiens des reductions, 1667–1760"; Delâge, "Iroquois chrétiens des reductions, 1667–1770: Rapports"; Sawaya, *Fédération des Sept Feus*. On La Présentation see Hough, *History of St. Lawrence and Franklin Counties, New York*.

9. Benson, *Peter Kalm's Travels*, 462–63; E. P. Hamilton, *Adventure in the Wilderness*, 75–76. For Native populations see Havard and Vidal, *Histoire de l'Amérique Française*, 136; Dickinson and Grabowski, "Populations amérindiennes de la vallée laurentienne"; Harris, *Historical Atlas of Canada*, plates 33, 47.

10. "Saint-François Xavier de Caughnawaga"; Devine, *Historic Caughnawaga*; Béchard, *Original Caughnawaga Indians*; Blanchard, "Patterns of Tradition and Change"; Green, "New People in an Age of War"; Demos, *Unredeemed Captive*, chaps. 6–7; Alfred, *Heeding the Voices of Our Ancestors*; G. F. Reid, *Kahnawa:ke*; Greer, *Mohawk Saint*, chap. 4.

11. JR, 68:225–35; Campeau, "Luc-François Nau." For references to the names of Kahnawake and its peoples see DRCHNY, 4:87 ("praying Castle"), 9:540 ("Christian Iroquois"), 747 ("praying Indians"), 10:159 ("Iroquois of the Sault"), 810 ("domiciliated Indians of the Sault St. Louis").

12. MPCP, 4:732; Alfred, *Heeding the Voices of Our Ancestors*, 28–29; DRCHNY, 4:747; SWJP, 1:596; Minutes of the Commissioners of Indian Affairs (AIHA), vol. 1, Feb. 25, Apr. 14, 1746; Jetten, *Enclaves amérindiennes*, 140–41. See also Green, "New People in an Age of War," 72, 165–69, 226–27.

13. Axtell, *Invasion Within*, 277. John Demos terms the Jesuits' version a "legend" (*Unredeemed Captive*, 120–22). Blanchard, Greer, and Alfred minimize doctrinal adherence to or the attractiveness of Christianity. None of these works significantly challenges or overturns the evidence that Axtell puts forth in *The Invasion Within* and in his essay "Were Indian Conversions Bona Fide?" (*After Columbus*, 100–121).

14. Richter, *Ordeal of the Longhouse*, 102–4; Fenton, *Great Law and the Longhouse*, 253, 283–84; Green, "New People in an Age of War," 24–28.

15. Béchard, *Original Caughnawaga Indians*, 5–55. Cf. Demos, *Unredeemed Captive*, 121–24; Béchard, "Tonsahoten"; Béchard, "Gandeacteau"; Monet, "Garreau, Léonard"; Jaenen, "Bruyas, Jacques."

16. JR, 55:35, 63:179.

17. DRCHNY, 9:541, 882–84; JR, 66:205; DRCHNY, 4:692; SWJP, 12:172; Demos, *Unredeemed Captive*, 121–24.

18. Béchard, *Original Caughnawaga Indians*, 23; Demos, *Unredeemed Captive*, 128; DRCHNY, 4:747; Greer, *Mohawk Saint*, chaps. 5–6; Richter, *Facing East from Indian Country*, 79–90; Béchard, "Togouiroui." On memorials to martyrs see Gallup, *Memoir of a French and Indian War Soldier*, 40. European visitors from Charlevoix, Lafitau, Kalm, Franquet, Bougainville, and John Long all expressed admiration of the mission Indians' devotion.

19. JR, 63:175; Demos, *Unredeemed Captive*, 125; JR, 66:171–73, 67:38–41, 64:131. See also Béchard, *Original Caughnawaga Indians*, 81; Devine, *Historic Caughnawaga*, 43; Green, "New People in an Age of War," 24–31; Lavallée, *La Prairie en Nouvelle-France*.

20. Vaudreuil et Bigon au Ministre, Apr. 1, 1716, AN, CIIA, vol. 36, ff. 223–34; JR, 67:24–27; Duquesne to Machault, Oct. 31, 1754, DRCHNY, 10:267; Gelinas, *Role of Fort Chambly*, 4; DRCHNY, 9:543, 744, 1018; Charlevoix, *Journal of a Voyage*, 1:218.

21. Lahontan, *New Voyages to North-America*, 2:219; Benson, *Peter Kalm's Travels*, 418, 401; Dawson, *Saint Lawrence Basin and Its Borderlands*, xxxv. This and subsequent descriptions of Kahnawake and Quebec are partly based on my studies of colonial-era historic sites in Canada in 2000, 2002, and 2007.

22. Richter, *Ordeal of the Longhouse*, 128. For evidence of continuity with the Iroquoian past see JR, 67:24–27 (relocation); François Lafitau, *Customs of the American Indians*, 2:69–71 (farming and hunting); Long, *Voyages and Travels*, 90 (lacrosse); Green, "New People in an Age of War," 38–39, 54–56 (kinship and government).

For population estimates see Fenton and Tooker, "Mohawk"; Green, "New People in an Age of War," 194; other references in note 9, above. For English fears that Mohawks near New York would all resettle in Canada see DRCHNY, 4:337, 648, 6:281–82 (Livingston); JR, 63:179; Green, "New People in an Age of War," 170.

23. Greer, *Mohawk Saint*, 98; MacLeod, *Canadian Iroquois*, 1–2; Devine, *Historic Caughnawaga*, 248, 268 (houses); Franquet, *Voyages et Memoires*: "Ces sauvages sont dans le goût de bâtir des maisons à la française, en charpente équarrie, et même en maçonnerie. A cet effet, ils ont attiré des ouvriers français de toute espèce" (38); E. P. Hamilton, *Adventure in the Wilderness*, 124–25 (horses); Lafitau, *Customs of the American Indians*, 2:70–71 (horses); Long, *Voyages and Travels*, 38 (stone houses).

24. E. P. Hamilton, *Adventure in the Wilderness*, 124–25 (trading); Benson, *Peter Kalm's Travels*, 435–37 (ginseng); "Journal of Lord Adam Gordon," in Mereness, *Travels in the American Colonies*, 431 (gristmill); Fenton, "Joseph-François Lafitau"; Devine, *Historic Caughnawaga*, 170–72 (ginseng).

25. Les Missionnaires du Sault St. Louis, May 24, 1721, AN, CIIA, vol. 43, ff. 250–56; DRCHNY, 10:86; Devine, *Historic Caughnawaga*, 186–89, 243–44.

26. DRCHNY, 9:539; Charlevoix, *Journal of a Voyage*, 1:218; Bougainville, *Adventures in the Wilderness*, 124–25; JR, 29–39 (mass), 68:271–75, 279. On the crucial role

of music in catechism and worship see Dubois, *De l'oreille au coeur*; Axtell, *Invasion Within*, 120; Devine, *Historic Caughnawaga*, 181, 185.

27. JR, 68:39, 269, 286 (Nau); "Memoir of Father Lafitau," JR, 67:38–41; Campeau, "Luc-François Nau"; Devine, *Historic Caughnawaga*, 224 (Hateriata); Lavallée, *La Prairie en Nouvelle France*, 235–37 (Desauniers sisters); Stanley, "Indians and the Brandy Trade."

28. JR, 68:267, 277–79 (diversity), 69:59 (Chickasaws); DRCHNY, 10:110, 214–15 (English, Dutch, and German prisoners); Fenton and Tooker, "Mohawk," 470; Devine, *Historic Caughnawaga*, 245–47.

29. DRCHNY, 10:215–16 (Delisle); Graymont, "Atiatoharongwen"; Coleman, *New England Captives Carried to Canada*, 1:324–27 (Rice), 293–94 (Tarbell), 2:87–88 (Harris); Frisch, "John Tarbell"; Forbes, "Iroquois de Caughnawaga": "aujourd'hui, à cause de ces mélanges, il n'y pas une seule famille purement Iroquoise à Caughnawaga, bien que chez presque toutes on ne parlé guere qu'iroquois; il n'y a qu'une couple d'invidus qui se réclament iroquois sans mélange de sang blanc" (117). Informative studies of captives among the Canadian Iroquois include Axtell, *Invasion Within*; Demos, *Unredeemed Captive*; Vaughan and Richter, "Crossing the Cultural Divide."

30. JR, 69:37; Lafitau, *Customs of the American Indians*, 2:30; Intendant Antoine-Denis Raudot, quoted in Moogk, *Nouvelle France*, 42, 287n62.

31. Charlevoix, *Journal of a Voyage*, 1:264; E. P. Hamilton, *Adventure in the Wilderness*, 51. For interpretations of Canadian identity see Moogk, *Nouvelle France*, chaps. 2, 6; Havard and Vidal, *Histoire de l'Amérique Française*, chaps. 6, 9.

32. Greer, *People of New France*, 5; Eccles, *Canadian Frontier*, 6.

33. Moogk, *Nouvelle France*, 85; Greer, *People of New France*, 12; Choquette, *Frenchmen into Peasants*; Harris, *Historical Atlas of Canada*, plate 45; Moogk, "Manon's Fellow Exiles."

34. Lahontan, *New Voyages to North-America*, 1:34, 38, 52 (côtes); F. Grant, "Journal from New York to Canada," 308; Benson, *Peter Kalm's Travels*, 416–17; Moogk, *Nouvelle France*, 176 (pièce-sur-pièce); Harris, *Historical Atlas of Canada*, plates 55–56; JR, 69:61 (wheat harvest). For references to the quality of life among Canadian habitants see Charlevoix, *Journal of a Voyage*, 1:263 (necessaries); Lahontan, *New Voyages to North-America*, 1:36 (nobility); Benson, *Peter Kalm's Travels*, 376 (climate), 437 (farmers); Gallup, *Memoir of a French and Indian War Soldier*, 20, 38. For general treatments of agricultural life see Greer, *People of New France*, chap. 2; Eccles, *Canadian Frontier*; Douville and Casanova, *Daily Life in Early Canada*.

35. Rolle des cabaretiers de Montréal, July 3, 1720, AN, CIIA, vol. 42, ff. 156–58; Grabowski, "Common Ground," 208–9, 280–81. On the population and fur-trade activities see Lavallée, *La Prairie en Nouvelle-France*, 43, 230–38.

36. JR, 68:271–73, 65:32–33; Gallup, *Memoir of a French and Indian War Soldier*, 40. For additional evidence of French and Indians seeking Kateri Tekakwitha's intervention see Greer, *Mohawk Saint*, chap. 7.

37. Dawson, *Saint Lawrence Basin and Its Borderlands*, xxxv–xxxvii; Eccles, *France in America*, 153–54; Benson, *Peter Kalm's Travels*, 411; Harris, *Historical Atlas of Canada*, plate 49; Rushforth, "'Little Flesh We Offer You'"; Robert, *Atlas Historique de Montréal*; Dechêne, *Habitants and Merchants*; Lachance, *Vie urbaine en Nouvelle-France*.

38. Adair, "Montreal under the French Regime," 39; Lahontan, *New Voyages to North-America*, 1:95; Moogk, *Nouvelle France*, 10, 26, 39; "Lettres de Mère Marie-Andrée Duplessis de Sainte Hélène": "on voit a Monreal ou les sauvages abondent de toutes parts, des hommes grands and bienfaits qui se promenent dans les ruës dans cet équipage aussy hardiment que s'ils etoient bien vetus, d'autres portent une chemise seulement, quelqu'uns ont une couverture jettée negligeamment sur une épaule" (42); Demos, *Unredeemed Captive*, 85; Dechêne, *Habitants and Merchants*, 13 (cider). On different taverns see "Rolle des cabaretiers de Montréal," 1720, AN, CIIA, vol. 42, ff. 156–58.

39. Denonville, quoted in Eccles, *Canadian Frontier*, 90; Charlevoix, *Journal of a Voyage*, 1:221 ("coureurs de bois"); Podruchny, *Making the Voyageur World*, 4, 27–28, 55–63, 72 (quote at 63); Podruchny, "Werewolves and Windigos"; Aubry, *Magic Fiddler*. For the lives and travels of the coureurs de bois and voyageurs see Dechêne, *Habitants and Merchants*, 117–24; Henry, *Travels and Adventures*; Jacquin, *Indiens Blancs*, esp. chap. 7.

40. Balvay, "Relations entre soldats français et Amérindiens"; Havard, "Postes français et villages indiens."

41. Moogk, *Nouvelle France*, 45–46; Benson, *Peter Kalm's Travels*, 456–57. See also Olive Patricia Dickason's concise survey of Franco-Indian intermarriage in *Canada's First Nations*, 167–73, and her classic essay "From 'One Nation' in the Northeast to 'New Nation' in the Northwest." Other examples of intermarriage can be found at SWJP, 1:210, 8:235; A. D. Hirsch, "'Celebrated Mme. Montour.'"

42. For cooperation and cultural exchanges between the French-Canadian militia and Native allies see Brumwell, *White Devil*; Parmenter, "After the Mourning Wars"; Nicolai, "Different Kind of Courage"; Delisle, *Equipment of New France Militia*; Eccles, *Canadian Frontier*, 76–77, 101–2.

43. On the Canadian nobility and its experience in war see Moogk, *Nouvelle France*, 168–69; Eccles, *France in America*, 73, 117–18.

44. Douville, "Jacques Hertel de la Fresnière"; Douville, "Joseph-François Hertel de la Fresnière"; Douville, "Jean-Baptiste Hertel de Rouville"; Zoltvany, "Louis-Thomas Chabert de Joncaire," 125–27; MacLeod, "Philippe-Thomas Chabert de Joncaire"; Baker, *True Stories of New England Captives*, 307–15.

45. Benson, *Peter Kalm's Travels*, 511, 573.

46. White, *Middle Ground*, chaps. 2–4; Parmenter, "L'Arbre de Paix"; Havard and Vidal, *Histoire de l'Amérique Française*, chap. 5; Eccles, "The Sovereignty Association, 1500–1783," in *Essays on New France*, 156–81; Dumouchel, "Calumet de paix."

47. Vaudreuil à Nicholson, Jan. 14, 1711, AN, CIIA, vol. 31, ff. 32–39: "elles ne sont

pas assez dans notre dependenance pour leur faire changer leurs coutumes et leurs moeurs"; Beauharnois and Hocquart to Maurepas, Oct. 1, 1731, DRCHNY, 9:1030, and AN, CIIA, vol. 54, ff. 14–19v (quote at 15v); DRCHNY, 9:1030; E. P. Hamilton, *Adventure in the Wilderness*, 170, 259; Johnston, "Onontio" (cf. DRCHNY, 9:1073–80).

48. Eccles, *Canadian Frontier*, 7, 24; Desbarats, "Cost of Early Canada's Native Alliances," 610, 629; Eccles, "Fur Trade and Eighteenth-Century Imperialism," in *Essays on New France*, 79–95.

49. Gilles Hocquart, quoted in Gelinas, *Role of Fort Chambly*, 36; Minutes of the Albany Commissioners for Indian Affairs (NAC), RG 10, Aug. 2, 1749, vol. 2, f. 276 (subject); Beauharnois to Maurepas, Oct. 31, 1740, and Beauharnois to Maurepas, Sept. 21, 1741, both DRCHNY, 9:1068, 1071. See E. P. Hamilton, *Adventures in the Wilderness*, 32, for Bougainville's suspicions of Sault Iroquois loyalty, and Parmenter, "After the Mourning Wars," for Iroquois warfare in the eighteenth century. See Green's conclusions on Sault independence in "New People in an Age of War," 300–301.

50. Grabowski, "Common Ground," 89–90; Delâge and Gilbert, "Amérindiens face à la justice coloniale française . . . I"; Delage and Gilbert, "Amérindiens face à la justice coloniale française . . . II." French officials celebrated the occasions when they could assert colonial laws: see "Lettre de M.de Vaudreuil au conseil de Marine."

51. La Jonquière au ministre, Oct. 19, 1751, AN, CIIA, vol. 97, ff. 127–28v; Lunn, "Illegal Fur Trade"; Grabowski, "Amérindiennes domiciliés et la Contrabande des Fourrures"; Miquelon, *New France*, chap. 9. Roberts, "Samuel Storke," examines a single merchant's involvement in the trade. On the general superiority of French goods see Eccles, *Essays on New France*, 85. For blankets and textiles as the most common items in the fur trade see Miquelon, *New France*, table 4, 152–53; White, *Middle Ground*, 136–40.

52. La Jonquière au minister, Oct. 19, 1751, AN, CIIA, vol. 97, ff. 127–28v; "Memoire de l'état présent du Canada," 1712, AN, CIIA, vol. 33, f. 268 (Chambly); DRCHNY, 9:145–46 (entrepôt); Green, "New People in an Age of War," 233 (estimates); Norton, *Fur Trade in Colonial New York*, 141 (300 packs); Gelinas, *Role of Fort Chambly*, 16, 33–36.

53. Eccles, *Essays on New France*, 87–88; Lunn, "Illegal Fur Trade," 75.

54. DRCHNY, 9:1019–20, 6:569–70; E. P. Hamilton, "John Henry Lydius"; Moogk, "John Hendricks Lydius," 488–90.

55. E. P. Hamilton, "Unrest at Caughnawaga"; Igartua, "Pierre Trottier-Desauniers"; Le Blanc, "Jean-Baptiste Tournois"; Cossette, "Pierre de Lauzon." The best narratives of the Desauniers affair are Hamilton and Lunn, "Illegal Fur Trade"; Lavallée, *La Prairie en Nouvelle-France*, 230–38; Green, "New People in an Age of War," 269–75; Devine, *Historic Caughnawaga*, 236–38.

56. Lettre de Ramezay à Mademoiselle Desauniers, June 12, 1750, AN, CIIA, vol. 97, f. 382.

57. DRCHNY, 9:1071.

58. La Jonquière au ministre, July 26, 1750, AN, CIIA, vol. 95, ff. 163–73v; Paroles de Teganagouassen et Beauvais, May 18, 1750, AN, CIIA, vol. 95, ff. 174–75; Paroles des Iroquois du Sault St. Louis en presence de leur missionnaire, Aug. 18, 1751, AN, CIIA, vol. 97, ff. 58–59; DRCHNY, 9:1071.

59. Paroles de Tegariogrin chef du Iroquois du Sault St. Louis du 5 Juin 1750, AN, CIIA, vol. 95, ff. 181–82.

60. For the sisters' defense of their actions see Placet des demoiselles Desauniers à ministre Rouille, 1751, AN, CIIA, vol. 97, ff. 378–79: "elles y ont fait un commerce qui les a fait subsister honorablement, sans que personne dans la Colonnie ait pû leur rien reprocher"; Requête des demoiselles Desauniers aux syndics et directeurs de la Compagnie des Indes, 1751, AN, CIIA, vol. 97, ff. 380–81; Devine, *Historic Caughnawaga*, 237 (Jesuit testimony).

61. La Jonquière au ministre, Nov. 1, 1751, AN, CIIA, vol. 97, ff. 173–78: "mais je ne suis que trop certain de l'Empire qu'elles avoient pris sur les Iroquois du Sault, des sentiments d'independance même de rebellion qu'elles s'empressoient de leur suggerer" (173v).

62. La Jonquière au ministre, Oct. 17, 1751, AN, CIIA, vol. 97, f. 118.

63. Calloway, *First Peoples*, 146; E. P. Hamilton, *Adventure in the Wilderness*, 65, 129; Benson, *Peter Kalm's Travels*, 400 (supply road); Calloway, *Dawnland Encounters*, 83–85, 162–63. See also Coolidge, "French Occupation"; Steele, *Betrayals*, 3–10.

64. On colonial Albany see Shannon, *Indians and Colonists at the Crossroads*, chap. 4 (at 64); Benson, *Peter Kalm's Travels*, 332–48.

2. Iroquois Communities in the Eighteenth-Century Mohawk Valley

1. NYCM, Apr. 6, May 10, July 29, 1745, 21:14–15, 20, 32–40; Henry Barclay to D. Bearcroft, Mar. 12, 1745, RSPG, 13:314–15; P. A. W. Wallace, *Conrad Weiser*, 227, DRCHNY, 6:275, 292–93 (Jean Coeur); Sivertsen, *Turtles, Wolves, and Bears*, 137–38; Parmenter, "At the Woods' Edge," 199–200; Fenton, *Great Law and the Longhouse*, 439–42; Benson, *Peter Kalm's Travels*, 332, 342–44 (Albany traders).

2. Minutes of the Commissioners of Indian Affairs (AIHA), vol. 1, Jan. 6, 1747; P. A. W. Wallace, *Conrad Weiser*, 217–18.

3. "Extract of the Subscribers Journal" ("Conrad Weiser Journal" hereafter), in Daniel Horsmanden Papers, Extracts Relating to the Six Nations, f. 20; cf. P. A. W. Wallace, *Conrad Weiser*, 217–18.

4. Albany Commissioners of Indian Affairs to George Clinton, May 4, 1746, Minutes of the Commissioners of Indian Affairs (AIHA), vol. 1; Deposition of John Henry Lydius, Apr. 6, 1745, p. 15, and Deposition of Peter Magrigorie, May 9, 1745, both in Daniel Horsmanden Papers, Addenda; "Conrad Weiser Journal," f. 20.

Cf. P. A. W. Wallace, *Conrad Weiser*, 217–28; Henry Barclay to D. Bearcroft, Oct. 21, 1745, RSPG, 13:316–17.

5. "Memorandums taken by Conrad Weiser in Albany," Penn Manuscripts, Indian Affairs, vol. 1 (also printed as "Conrad Weiser's Journal During the Albany Treaty of 1745," in J. P. Boyd, *Indian Treaties Printed by Benjamin Franklin*, 309–11); NYCM, 21:51–52; RSPG, 13:314–15. Barclay called Van Patten an "Honest Farmer" in his letter of Oct. 21, 1745 (13:316–17); Sivertsen, *Turtles, Wolves, and Bears*, 172.

6. "Memorandums taken by Conrad Weiser in Albany," Penn Manuscripts; NYCM, Oct. 9, 1745, 21:50–52; DRCHNY, 6:293–95; Conrad Weiser report, Oct. 6, 1745, in Daniel Horsmanden Papers; P. A. W. Wallace, *Conrad Weiser*, 230–31; Sivertsen, *Turtles, Wolves, and Bears*, 140. See also Conrad Weiser to Thomas Lee, Oct. 25, 1742, Native American History Collection.

7. Shannon, *Indians and Colonists at the Crossroads*, 17.

8. SWJP, 6:27–28; DRCHNY, 6:123.

9. SWJP, 6:27–28; DRCHNY, 6:123; Fletcher to the Lords of Trade, June 10, 1696, DRCHNY, 4:159, 183, 6:960; Meinig, "Colonial Period," 137; Meinig, *Atlantic America*, 119–29. For studies of New York's elites see Kierner, *Traders and Gentlefolk*; Lustig, *Privilege and Prerogative*.

10. Kim, *Landlord and Tenant*, vii; Colden Papers, 4:124, 2:35; Colden, "The State of Lands in the Province of New York, in 1732," DHNY, 1:377–88; Benson, *Peter Kalm's Travels*, 142; Spencer, "Land System of Colonial New York"; Bonomi, *Factious People*, 179–228. Wyllys Terry's "Negotiating the Frontier" must be used with caution due to a number of factual and interpretive errors.

11. Fox, *Land Speculation in the Mohawk Country*, x, 9, 49–50; Higgins, *Expansion in New York*, 33–69; Richter, *Ordeal of the Longhouse*, 236–72.

12. SWJP, 11:368; Snow, *Iroquois*, 131–57; Merwick, *Possessing Albany*; Burke, *Mohawk Frontier*.

13. Minutes of the Albany Commissioners for Indian Affairs (NAC), vol. 2, June 26, 1732. For Taraghjorees see Sivertsen, *Turtles, Wolves, and Bears*, 120–23. For place names see Beauchamp, "Aboriginal Place Names," 202, though in deference to linguists, the exact meaning of such place names may be impossible to decipher.

14. Simms, *History of Schoharie County*, 3, 25–35. The Schoharie Mohawks are not listed anywhere in the articles on Iroquoian peoples in Trigger, *Northeast*. For additional references to the multiethnic Schoharie Mohawks see Ferguson, "Reported Missing"; Ferguson, "Schoharie Iroquois?"

15. Minutes of the Albany Commissioners for Indian Affairs (NAC), Apr. 26, 1727, RG 10, vol. 1820 (reel C-1220).

16. Simms, *History of Schoharie County*, 3, 25–35. See Brasser, "Mahican," esp. 206–8, for Mahican migrations in the eighteenth century. See also Roscoe, *History of Schoharie County*, 1:23; Sivertsen, *Turtles, Wolves, and Bears*, 64–66, 76–77, 186–87, 151, 190–91; [Hawley], "Letter from Rev. Gideon Hawley," 53. For evidence of

Southern Indians and slaves among the Schoharies see Minutes of the Albany Commissioners for Indian Affairs (NAC), vol. 1, Feb. 11, 1732, vol. 2, May 28, 30, 1732; Albany Commissioners' Minutes (WLCL), Mar. 20, 1754.

17. Simms, *Frontiersmen of New York*, 1:76–77; Bartram, Evans, and Weiser, *Journey from Pennsylvania to Onondaga*, 54; Sivertsen, *Turtles, Wolves, and Bears*, 79.

18. Much of the primary source material on eighteenth-century Palatines has been translated into English, including Conrad Weiser's autobiography and certain journals. See Otterness, "Unattained Canaan," chap. 1, esp. 32, 39, 55–57, 62 (cf. Otterness, *Becoming German*); P. A. W. Wallace, *Conrad Weiser*, chap. 1; DHNY, 3:542 (Board of Trade's plan), 543 (German migration of 1708). See also McGregor, "Cultural Adaptation in Colonial New York"; Hinderaker, "'Four Indian Kings.'"

19. DRCHNY, 5:166, 175, 290 3:559–60, 560, 638, 644–51. See also Lustig, *Robert Hunter*.

20. DHNY, 3:657 (Clarendon), 708 (land), 658 (campfire scene), 659 (Canaan), 660 (population), 683 (Hunter's credit), 553 (apprenticing), 168–69 (instruction in naval stores production), 707–14 ("Pharao" at 710). For other references to Palatine unrest in the Hudson camps see DRCHNY, 5:212–15 (Cast's letters), 238–42.

21. DRCHNY, 4:345–46 (Mohawk protest), 391 (extent of Bayard tract), 565–66 (land reverted to Mohawks), 5:284, 915 (Vacating Act); Nammack, *Fraud, Politics, and the Dispossession*, 13–18; Higgins, *Expansion in New York*, 24–25, 48–53.

22. Leder, *Livingston Indian Records*, 215–16; "Propositions made by the Maquase Indians, owners of the Land called Skohere and divers other Sachims of the said Nation to his Excellency Robert Hunter 22nd of August 1710," Miscellaneous Manuscripts, Indians, folder 3; DRCHNY, 5:553. See also DRCHNY, 5:171; NYCM, July 13, 20, 1710, 10:528–29; NYSA.

23. Otterness, "Unattained Canaan," 225–29; DHNY, 2:571–72.

24. DHNY, 3:709–10; Bartram, Evans, and Weiser, *Journey from Pennsylvania to Onondaga*, 49; J. M. Brown, *Brief Sketch*, 32 ("true owners"); Weiser, *Johan Friederich Weisers Buch Containing The Autobiography of John Conrad Weiser (1690–1760)* (Weiser Autobiography hereafter); Knittle, *Early Eighteenth-Century Palatine Emigration*, 191–95; Roeber, "Origins and Transfer," 122–24.

25. For the location of Eskahare see Snow, *Mohawk Valley Archaeology*, 1:481–83; *Weiser Autobiography*, 27–29; Sivertsen, *Turtles, Wolves, and Bears*, 75; P. A. W. Wallace, *Conrad Weiser*, 18.

26. DHNY, 3:711–13; *Weiser Autobiography*, 25; J. M. Brown, *Brief Sketch*, 10; Roscoe, *History of Schoharie County*, 1:30–32; Simms, *History of Schoharie County*, 89–90.

27. *Weiser Autobiography*, 21–23, 29, 33; P. A. W. Wallace, *Conrad Weiser*, 18, 579; DHNY, 3:566–67 (Johann Frederick).

28. DRCHNY, 5:239, 552, 346 (slave conspiracy), 347; Council Meeting Minute, June 15, 1715, and Robert Hunter Letter to Justices of the Peace of Albany and Dutchess Counties, July 22, 1715, both NYCMSS, 60:9, 26.

29. *Weiser Autobiography,* 29; J. M. Brown, *Brief Sketch,* 5; Roscoe, *History of Schoharie County,* 1:30; Simms, *History of Schoharie County,* 48, 52. For disputes over livestock see Minutes of the Albany Commissioners for Indian Affairs (NAC), Apr. 26, 1727, Mar. 10, 1729, Feb. 24, 1744.

30. NYCM, Feb. 28, 1715, 11:288–89; Memorial of Adam Vrooman, June 9, 1711, NYCMSS, 60:3A; DHNY, 3:711–13; Knittle, *Early Eighteenth-Century Palatine Emigration,* 200–201; Higgins, *Expansion in New York,* 52–58; O'Callaghan, *Calendar of N.Y. Colonial Manuscripts,* 6:12–13, 34–36; Hagan, "Adam Vrooman."

31. DHNY, 3:711–13; Knittle, *Early Eighteenth-Century Palatine Emigration,* 200–201; Higgins, *Expansion in New York,* 52–58; O'Callaghan, *Calendar of N.Y. Colonial Manuscripts,* 5:70, 144, 173 (Bayard), 6:24–25, 78–80 (Seven Partners); Fox, *Land Speculation in the Mohawk Country,* 10–11.

32. DRCHNY, 5:554, 575, 582, 634; DHNY, 3:710; Roeber, *Palatines, Liberty, and Property,* 13.

33. DHNY, 3:708; *Weiser Autobiography,* 17.

34. *Weiser Autobiography,* 29, 36–37; DRCHNY, 5:634, 561; Brown, *Brief Sketch,* 14; Higgins, *Expansion in New York,* 62–66; O'Callaghan, *Calendar of N.Y. Colonial Manuscripts,* 8:138, 159, 168, 9:7, 22, 37, 58, 75–76, 81, 89, 95–96, 104, 122, 139, 151–54, 172–4, 10:1–3, 89, 135, 11:24–25, 88 (German Flatts and Burnetsfield), 88, 99, 139, 143 (Schoharie Valley), 14:81, 114, 123 (Petri, Weiser, Wagoner, Frank petitions). See also NYCM, Sept. 9, 1721, Jan. 17, 1723, Mar. 7, 1723, June 28, 1723, 12:162, 14:81, 114, 188. See also minutes of the Sept. 2, 1721, meeting regarding settling the Germans in Onondaga Country: NYCM, 12:143–44. For the dispersal of Palatines to other areas see Otterness, "Unattained Canaan," chaps. 4–5.

35. DHNY, 3:716; DRCHNY, 5:88, 656.

36. Beauchamp, "Aboriginal Place Names," 126–27; Fenton and Tooker, "Mohawk," 15:474.

37. "Observations of Wentworth Greenhalgh," 189. For Crine's inventory see Petition of the Mohawk Indians, Feb. 6, 1786, in Minutes of the Commissioners of Indian Affairs (AIHA), vol. 2. For background on the settlement see Fenton and Tooker, "Mohawk," 474; Snow, *Mohawk Valley Archaeology,* 1:449–81; DRCHNY, 4:802 (Ogsadaga); Guldenzopf, "Frontier Demography"; Richter, *Ordeal of the Longhouse,* 173–74, 255–62; Moody and Fisher, "Archaeological Evidence."

38. NYCMSS, 61:54 (A–B), Minutes of Albany Conference, Sept. 4, 1718 (death follows); Minutes of the Albany Commissioners for Indian Affairs (NAC), vol. 1, Oct. 30, 1724 (corn); John Ogilvie letter, June 29, 1752, RSPG, 20:55; DRCHNY, 5:485–86, 491–93, 565–69; Hart, "For the Good of Our Souls," 160–67 (Indian Kings), 203 (epidemic), 175, 199–200 (alcohol); Richter, *Ordeal of the Longhouse,* 225–29 (campaigns).

39. DRCHNY, 5:224–27, 271 (enemies); "Contract to build Forts in the Mohawk and Onondaga Countries, [1711]," DRCHNY, 5:279–81. See also DRCHNY, 5:249, 271, 278, 358; Richter, *Ordeal of the Longhouse,* chaps. 10–11 (forts). For Dutch and English

missionary efforts among the Mohawks see Letters of Rev. Henry Barclay, box 7, St. Peter's Episcopal Church Records, 1708–1915; Records of Mohawk Indians at Fort Hunter; Axtell, *Invasion Within*, 254–63; Hart, "For the Good of Our Souls," chap. 3.

40. NYCMSS, Jan. 24, 1713, 58:87; NYCM, July 3, 17, 1712, Aug. 3, 1713, 11:115–17, 207. For other rumors see DRCHNY, 5:372–73, 383, 485–86.

41. NYCM, May 30, 1716, Sept. 9 1720, 11:352–53 12:169; DRCHNY, 5:569 (rum). See also DRCHNY, 5:217, 662–63, 863–64 (rum); O'Callaghan, *Calendar of N.Y. Colonial Manuscripts*, 7:185, 8:188, 197, 200, 9:1 (John Scott's patent).

42. The rival claims of Butler and Albany are documented in O'Callaghan, *Calendar of N.Y. Colonial Manuscripts*, 10:122, 132, 155, 11:61, 65–66, 12:86 (Butler's 1735 deed); Colden Papers, 9:304 (Albany deed). For Butler's other land speculation see Colden Papers, 11:83, 138, 155, 179, 182–83, 12:15–16, 31, 131, 13:23. For Butler's background see Sivertsen, *Turtles, Wolves, and Bears*, 117–18, 124–25.

43. Cadwallader Colden, "History of Governor William Cosby's Administration and of Lieutenant Governor George Clarke's Administration Through 1737," Colden Papers, 9:304–5; NYCM, Sept. 12, 1733, 16:253–54; Council Minutes, Apr. 1, 1734, Daniel Horsmanden Papers; DRCHNY, 5:960, 6:15–16 (deed in trust).

44. NYCM, 16:254; Colden Papers, 9:305.

45. O'Callaghan, *Calendar of N.Y. Colonial Manuscripts*, 11:162, 165, 174, 12:79; Colden Papers, 2:188 (Mrs. Cosby's sale of land). For the politics of Cosby's administration see Katz, *Newcastle's New York*, chap. 4; Bonomi, *Factious People*, chap. 4. See DRCHNY, 6:16 (footnote), for the resolution of the Mohawk Flatts land dispute.

46. Henry Barclay, quoted in Sivertsen, *Turtles, Wolves, and Bears*, 125–26; M. W. Hamilton, *Sir William Johnson*, 3–22; Guzzardo, "Sir William Johnson's Official Family," chaps. 1–2; SWJP, 1:4–7, 14, 13:1–3. On the "Willegee Negroes" see SWJP, 1:8, 13:3; Snow, Gehring, and Starna, *In Mohawk Country*, 263.

47. SWJP, 1:172 (peaceable), 10:17 (neighbors). See also SWJP, 1:5–7, 18–19, 22–23, 50; Colden Papers, 4:273 (Oswego); M. W. Hamilton, *Sir William Johnson*, 8–124. SWJP, 8:936–1121 (passim) contains much of Johnson's correspondence aimed at settling the Mohawk Flatts controversy. See SWJP, 3:762, for investigation of the John Scott patent. On the meaning of "Warrighiyagey" cf. Fenton, *Great Law and the Longhouse*, 449; "Journal of Warren Johnson," 258. For Johnson's use of Iroquois metaphors see "Journal of William Johnson, April 24 to 26, 1748," in the George Clinton Papers.

48. "Journal of William Johnson, April 24–26, 1748." See also Shannon, *Indians and Colonists at the Crossroads*, 30–51, 144, 149–52, 220–25; Shannon, "Dressing for Success"; Fenton, *Great Law and the Longhouse*, 448–49, 738–42 (Johnson's mastery of condolence ceremonies); Danvers, "Gendered Encounters."

49. Doblin and Starna, *Journals of Christian Daniel Claus and Conrad Weiser*, 32; Cadwallader Colden to Clinton, Aug. 8, 1751, Colden Papers, 4:272; Sivertsen, *Turtles,*

Wolves, and Bears, 83, 127–35, 143, 170–72, 180–82 (Sivertsen's speculation that Johnson's second Mohawk liaison was with one of Brant Canagaradunckwa's daughters); SWJP, 1:5–7, 351 and 453 (Johnson as interpreter), 126, 342, 365 (Indian views of Johnson), 9:386 (Johnson's Indian "concubines"); Fenton, *Great Law and the Longhouse,* 448–49; Huey and Pulis, *Molly Brant,* 13–23, 127–32. See also Mullin, "Sir William Johnson," 49–53 (mastery of Mohawk language); Shannon, *Indians and Colonists at the Crossroads,* 30–45.

50. O'Toole, *White Savage,* 57.

51. Cadwallader Colden, quoted in M. W. Hamilton, *Sir William Johnson,* 53; SWJP, 9:5 "Answer from ye Sachims to the Honorable His Excellency George Clinton," Aug. 10, 1747, George Clinton Papers (Abraham). Johnson was appointed a justice of the peace in 1745, a colonel of the militia in 1748, and a member of the governor's council in 1751 (SWJP, 1:60, 167).

52. SWJP, 5:412 (tenants); William Johnson to Thomas Gage, Apr. 20, 1774, box 1, folder 6, Guy Johnson Collection (Gen. MSS 494). See also SWJP, 1:411, 3:561, 6:473, 9:54–55, 10:397 (pride as developer).

53. Petition of Hendrick, Abram Peterson, and Others, to George Clinton, Feb. 8, 1753, vol. 14, George Clinton Papers; William Johnson to George Clinton, May 7, 1747, DRCHNY, 6:362. See SWJP, 1:19, for the Albany commissioners' response.

54. SWJP, 11:368; DHNY, 1:695–96, 3:905; Guldenzopf, "Frontier Demography," 83.

55. SWJP, 7:201–2; DRCHNY, 8:305.

56. Shannon, *Indians and Colonists at the Crossroads,* 25–27, 30, 163–65; Merrell, "'Customes of Our Countrey,'" 137, 153. See Guzzardo, "Sir William Johnson's Official Family," for Mohawks as mere clients of Johnson's.

57. SWJP, 12:302.

58. See Preston, "Squatters, Indians."

59. DRCHNY, 8:458 (1773 population); SWJP, 10:49–51 (population estimates derived from numbers of Mohawk women and children); Beauchamp, "Aboriginal Place Names," 120–21; Fenton and Tooker, "Mohawk," 15:475; Guldenzopf, "Colonial Transformation," 45, 169; Kelsay, *Joseph Brant,* 46–54; Lenig, "Archaeology, Education"; Lord, "Taverns, Forts, and Castles"; Snow, *Mohawk Valley Archaeology,* 1:460–70, 485–93.

60. Kurt Anders Jordan's work "The Archaeology of the Iroquois Restoration" presents many interesting contrasts between Seneca and Mohawk communities in the 1700s.

61. Gansevoort, quoted in Graymont, *Iroquois in the American Revolution,* 219, 181. See also the description of Iroquois prosperity in the Continental Army proclamation dated May 8, 1779, in Albany Revolution War Papers, 1775–1779; the multiple depositions on the plundering of Canajoharie during the Revolutionary War in the Philip Schuyler Papers, Indian Papers, 1710–1797, box 14, reel 7 (Apr. 20, 1778,

depositions of Martin Tillebach, Elisabeth Haberman, Hendrick Moyer, Johannes House, George Harkeman, and Jacobus Pickett), NYPL; the Mohawk Revolutionary War Loss Claims, in Haldimand Papers, ser. Q; and the transcriptions in Guldenzopf, "Colonial Transformation," 190–208, and Wonderley, "Oneida Community in 1780." For Oneida prosperity see Samuel Kirkland to Jerusha Kirkland, June 5, 1773, Samuel Kirkland Papers.

62. For details of Canajoharie see Doblin and Starna, *Journals of Christian Daniel Claus and Conrad Weiser*, 35; "Journal of Warren Johnson, 1760–1761"; "Journal of Joseph Bloomfield, 1776," 257, 285; Guldenzopf, "Colonial Transformation," 75, 197–98. For the use of boards in houses and sleighs see SWJP, 2:579, 9:649.

63. SWJP, 10:852 (keg), 9:61 (Lykas's death); P. A. W. Wallace, *Conrad Weiser*, 339 (Claus); Kelsay, *Joseph Brant*, chap. 2; Sivertsen, *Turtles, Wolves, and Bears*, 165–66.

64. Minutes of the Albany Commissioners for Indian Affairs (NAC), Oct. 8, 1743, vol. 2, f. 259A; Peter Schuyler petition, ca. 1780s, box 181, Gansevoort-Lansing Collection, NYPL; Doblin and Starna, *Journals of Christian Daniel Claus and Conrad Weiser*, 10–11, 38; Rufus Alexander Grider Scrapbooks, 1:45–46; Simms, *Frontiersmen of New York*, 1:96–97; Higgins, *Expansion in New York*, 18–19, 60; Vrooman, *Forts and Firesides of the Mohawk Country*, 133–35; Jeff N. Clyde to Lyman Draper, Feb. 11, 1878, Brant Papers, Draper Manuscript Collection, ser. F, 5F74, SHSW.

65. For Indian-European agricultural exchanges see Guldenzopf, "Colonial Transformation," 197–99 ("common farming tools"); DRCHNY, 7:92 (Germans), 105, 109; SWJP, 2:569, 572, 582, 625, 640, 3:167, 9:689, 11:188, 12:286–87, 625. For reliance on local blacksmiths, gunsmiths, and millers see NYCM, Sept. 13, 1726, 15:106; SWJP, 2:579, 4:54, 7:666–68, 9:646–47, 11:985–86. For ginseng and ginger-root trading see SWJP, 4:578, 11:398. For Samuel Kirkland's missionary efforts and imports of agricultural tools see, e.g., "An Account of some Extraordinary Charges," Oct. 1770–Oct. 1771, Samuel Kirkland Papers.

66. Sivertsen, *Turtles, Wolves, and Bears*, 119–21 (quote at 121), 147–48; Minutes of the Albany Commissioners for Indian Affairs (NAC), June 26, 1732, vol. 2; Petition of Hendrick, Abram Peterson, and Others, to George Clinton, Feb. 8, 1753, vol. 14, George Clinton Papers (spelling modernized). On Petrus Paulus's literacy see Albany Commissioners' Minutes (WLCL); SWJP, 9:52. For references to Germans and churches see Rufus Grider Scrapbooks, 1:27–30; O'Callaghan, *Calendar of N.Y. Colonial Manuscripts*, 11:6, 38, 45, 49; Simms, *Frontiersmen of New York*, 1:101–2; Vrooman, *Forts and Firesides of the Mohawk Country*, 1137–40. Ehle's ministry is obscured because so many church records were lost during the Revolution: see ERNY, 4:2535.

67. DRCHNY, 6:315; McIlwain, *Abridgement . . . by Peter Wraxall*, 185. For livestock complaints see Petitions of Hans Helmer and Thomas Davis of Canajoharie, 1733, in O'Callaghan, *Calendar of Historical Manuscripts*, 2:519; SWJP, 4:832 (Baxter's letter was destroyed by fire in 1911); DRCHNY, 5:221, 385–86, 965, 968, 6:302; SWJP, 10:58, 11:817.

68. Canajoharie Indians to Sir William Johnson, Feb. 25, 1760, DRCHNY, 7:434; SWJP, 4:56, 58, 8:967, 10:58.

69. Lynch, "Iroquois Confederacy" (Lynch's dualistic interpretation is probably overschematized and should more properly suggest a range of behaviors); SWJP, 1:342; Minutes of the Albany Commissioners for Indian Affairs (NAC), Apr. 24, June 26, 1732, vol. 1 and vol. 2, respectively (Schuyler). For adoption see also Fenton, *Great Law and the Longhouse*, 29–31, 396–97; Engelbrecht, *Iroquoia*, 162–63, 166–67. On land see Snyderman, "Concepts of Land Ownership," 20–22; A. F. C. Wallace, "Political Organization and Land Tenure."

70. DRCHNY, 6:784; NYCM, July 24, 1754, June 12, 1753, 23:210, 23:73; SWJP, 3:339 (Pickerd).

71. SWJP, 11:767 (poverty); DRCHNY, 6:783–84 (Theyanoguin); SWJP, 13:276–77 (Pickerd); Johnson to Colden, Feb. 20, 1761, Colden Papers, 6:12. Cf. SWJP, 3:339, 10:220, 225 (unbrotherlike behavior). On Gondermann see O'Callaghan, *Calendar of N.Y. Colonial Manuscripts*, 14:123, 145, 157, 176; Indian Treaties and Deeds (A0448), 2:15–16. On Eve Pickerd see Hart, "Black 'Go-Betweens'"; Doblin and Starna, *Journals of Christian Daniel Claus and Conrad Weiser*, 10–11; the Maybee Society's genealogy at http://wc.rootsweb.ancestry.com/cgi-bin/igm.cgi?op=GET&db=mabie-maybee&id=I4775 (accessed Oct. 2007).

72. SWJP, 3:356 (Switzers), 619–20 (peaceable possession), 649 (twenty years) 364 (paid uninterruptedly) 4:116, 667 (original proprietors; brackets original, my emphasis), 144–46 (Klock); Colden Papers, 6:18. For the Canajoharie tenants' side of the story see Deposition of John Diffendorf, Solomon Miers, Jacob Keller, and Henry Miers, Jan. 14, 1762, Duane Papers, Legal-Misc. Box, 1666–1770. See also the John Tabor Kempe Papers, Misc. Microfilms (reel 49) (Case of *The King v. George Klock*); James Alexander Papers, box 48 (Court Papers); references in the index to SWJP (vol. 14), under the headings "Klock" and "Canajoharie Patent." For references to Lappius and his congregation see Colden Papers, 6:19; SWJP, 3:341–42, 365, 602, 606, 619, 651, 4:50, 84, 280–81.

73. SWJP, 4:890 (Pickerd), 657 (Klock), 8:466–67 (lawyer), 10:59–60, 488–89 (Schoharie); see also 4:311–13.

74. Colden Papers, 6:371–75 (Davis); SWJP, 4:652 (Kayederosseras), 11:625 (warning), 926, 12:288 (Maybe), 4:478 (Oneidas); Colden Papers, 2:158–60 (survey); DRCHNY, 6:783 (Indian chain bearer); SWJP, 4:233 (Duncan). See also Alexander Colden's letter to his father, Nov. 7, 1753, Colden Papers, 9:129–34, for Mohawks' obstructions of surveyors; Representation of Cadwallader Colden and Alexander Colden, NYCM, Aug. 9, 1754, 23:212; NYCMSS, July 27, 1754, 79:1–16 (full text). William Johnson was one of Arent Stevens's partners in the land dispute involving the "Indian Chain-bearer" and received one-sixth of the lands. See SWJP, 1:394–95, 411–12, 565; O'Callaghan, *Calendar of N.Y. Colonial Manuscripts*, 15:18, 24, 37.

75. SWJP, 1:97, 287, 368, 9:9 (Magin's background); O'Callaghan, *Calendar of N.Y. Colonial Manuscripts*, 14:149, 15:49, 112 (Indian deed); Colden Papers, 9:124 (Clinton's son); NYCM, Nov. 7, 1753, 23:125–26; Paulus Petition, Feb. 8, 1753, vol. 14, George Clinton Papers; Colden Papers, 9:132 ("marked owt"). For Magin's connection to Livingston see Philip Livingston to Colden, Jan. 3, 1737–38, Colden Papers, 2:188.

76. SWJP, 9:117; Johnson to Colden, Feb. 20, 1761, Colden Papers, 6:12.

77. DRCHNY, 6:781–783, 787.

78. DRCHNY, 6:788.

79. DRCHNY, 6:799–801.

80. MPCP, 6:93; DRCHNY, 6:818, 850, 879. For Mohawk support of the Germans see O'Callaghan, *Calendar of N.Y. Colonial Manuscripts*, 15:77; Shannon, *Indians and Colonists at the Crossroads*, 141–73. For Hendrick at Albany see DRCHNY, 6:867, 869–70, 876.

81. DRCHNY, 6:887–88.

82. DRCHNY, 6:852.

3. Dispossessing the Indians

1. Exactly when the Stuart family settled in the Great Cove is unknown. Most likely the Stuarts arrived there in the late 1740s, following King George's War. When Richard Peters's expedition reached the Great Cove in 1750, the Stuarts were listed among the squatters: see MPCP, 5:444. Shingas's remarks (see p. 2) also suggest that the family had been living on the frontier for a number of years. Stuart was apparently killed during Pontiac's War (see *Pennsylvania Gazette*, Dec. 16, 1763).

2. MPCP, 6:675; Bond, "Captivity of Charles Stuart."

3. Bond, "Captivity of Charles Stuart," 61–62.

4. See Salisbury, introduction.

5. SWJP, 10:645.

6. See Hinderaker, *Elusive Empires*, 244.

7. Thomas Penn to James Hamilton, July 31, 1749, Thomas Penn Letterbooks, 2:272–73, Thomas Penn Papers; Richard Peters to the Proprietors, Apr. 26, 1749, Richard Peters Letterbooks, 1737–1750, 348.

8. NYCM, Mar. 3, 1722, May 13–14, 1746, 12:250, 21:91–92; Richard Peters to the Proprietors, Feb. 16, 1750, Richard Peters Letterbooks, 1737–1750, 393.

9. Adelman and Aron, "From Borderlands to Borders."

10. The best account of settlement patterns in early Pennsylvania remains Lemon, *Best Poor Man's Country*. See also Meinig, *Atlantic America*, 131–44. For immigration to Pennsylvania see Roeber, "'Origin of Whatever Is Not English among Us'"; M. Jones, "Scotch-Irish in British America"; Fogleman, *Hopeful Journeys*; Leyburn, *Scotch-Irish*, 157–200; Simkins, "Growth and Characteristics of Pennsylvania's Population."

11. Berthoff and Murrin, "Feudalism, Communalism," 267; Lemon, *Best Poor*

Man's Country, chap. 2; Illick, *Colonial Pennsylvania*, 130–31, 178; Jennings, *Ambiguous Iroquois Empire*, 316, 318.

12. James Anderson, quoted in Griffin, "People with No Name," 593.

13. Berthoff and Murrin, "Feudalism, Communalism," 272, 267.

14. MPCP, 9:509 (contrivance). For work on tenancy and rising economic inequality in eighteenth-century Pennsylvania see Simler, "Tenancy in Colonial Pennsylvania"; Lemon and Nash, "Distribution of Wealth."

15. R. M. Brown, "Back Country Rebellions." Stephen Aron explores the lack of settler rebellions in Kentucky and the settlers' acquiescence to speculators and nonresident owners in *How the West Was Lost*, 79–81. Aron's arguments are also applicable to Pennsylvania's experience.

16. PA, 1st ser., 2:14 (Girty as unlicensed trader ca. 1748), 8th ser., 4:3325 (Girty's name in Peters's report); MPCP, 6:218–19 (Croghan), 4:445 (traders). For biographies of Girty's early years see Hoffman, "Simon Girty"; Butterfield, *History of the Girtys*, 1–9; T. Boyd, *Simon Girty*, 29–40.

Other known Indian trader-squatters include Jacob Pyatt Sr., Jacob Pyatt Jr., and Arthur Dunlap, all of whom appear in Peters's report (see PA, 8th ser., 4:3325–26). Jacob Pyatt's homestead in the Path Valley appears on Nicholas Scull's 1759 "Map of the Improved Parts of Pennsylvania." See PA, 3rd ser., Appendix, Map: Nicholas Scull, "Map of the Improved Parts of Pennsylvania," 1759. Hanna, in *Wilderness Trail*, reports that Jacob Pyatt was "a Trader at Allegheny in 1734 and 1745; at Logstown in 1751; settled in Path Valley in 1748" (339). He was also present at the 1751 Logstown council. See Hanna, *Wilderness Trail*, 1:364, 2:331, 339.

17. Dexter, *Diary of David McClure*, 38–39. On the merging of Indian and settler economies see White, *Middle Ground*, 341; Aron, "Pigs and Hunters"; Aron, *How the West Was Lost*, chaps. 1–2; Faragher, *Daniel Boone*, 19–23. On the concept of a "frontier exchange economy" see Usner, *Indians, Settlers, and Slaves*. See Hofstra and Mitchell, "Town and Country," for a discussion of the term *open-country neighborhoods* (quote at 628).

18. Pennsylvania Council Minutes, Sept. 1, 1728, IIDH, reel 10; MPCP, 3:599 (settled); Jennings, "Miquon's Passing; Jennings, "Incident at Tulpehocken"; Jennings, "Scandalous Indian Policy of William Penn's Sons"; Richter, *Ordeal of the Longhouse*, 238–44, 273–75. On the Tuscarora migration see Feeley, "Tuscarora Trails."

19. PA, 1st ser., 2:24.

20. Amos Ogden Letter, Aug. 12, 1767, in Sir William Johnson Manuscripts, #658. For Tuscarora settlements see Landy, "Tuscarora among the Iroquois"; MPCP, 8:722–23. For locations of other Native settlements see Kent, Rice, and Ota, "Map of 18th Century Indian Towns" (for references to Ohesson and Assunepachla see 8–9, 12); Harbaugh, *Life of Rev. Michael Schlatter*, 172–73. For analyses of this forgotten colonial frontier see Rice, "Old Appalachia's Path"; Porter, "From Backcountry to County."

21. For settlers' descriptions of Indian families or towns see George Armstrong, Warrant No. 40, Feb. 3, 1755, Original Warrants, Cumberland County, Records of the Land Office (RG-17), PSA (microfilm reel no. 3.46); New Purchase Register, entries 3793 and 2179, Records of the Land Office, PSA (microfilm reel no. 1.9); J. W. Jordan, *History of the Juniata Valley*, 1:30–31.

22. For the Nanticokes' resettlement in Wyoming see MPCP, 5:544; "Diary of J. Martin Mack's, David Zeisberger's and Gottfried Rundt's Journey to Onondaga in 1752," in Beauchamp, *Moravian Journals*, 151 (also 179); MPCP, 7:676.

23. Becker, "Hannah Freeman"; PA, 8th ser., 2:1701 (fish) 1st ser., 1:239. For the provincial government's response to the Delawares' complaints see PA, 8th ser., 2:1710, 1713; MPCP, 3:269.

24. PA, 2nd ser., 19:626; MPCP, 3:48–49, 4:656–58, 8:198–99, 247.

25. Rhoda Barber, "Journal of the Settlement at Wright's Ferry," 1831, HSP; Pettit, *Life of David Brainerd*, 347; MPCP, 3:507 (Sassoonan); PA, 1st ser., 1:205–6 (Richard Thomas); Berkeley and Berkeley, *Correspondence of John Bartram*, 400.

26. U. J. Jones, *History of the Early Settlement*, 64–65.

27. For an excellent account of the skirmish see Merrell, "Shikellamy."

28. Cassell, "Notes on the Iroquois and Delaware Indians." Cassell compiled letters from Conrad Weiser to Christopher Saur that appeared in Saur's German-language newspaper. See George Croghan to ?, July 3, 1749, PA, 1st ser., 2:31–320. For additional evidence of warriors' interactions with settlers see also Rice, "Old Appalachia's Path."

29. MPCP, 4:648, 561. For Frederick Star see PA, 8th ser., 4:3327.

30. PA, 1st ser., 2:24 (Indians uneasy/Joniady); MPCP, 5:389 (boundaries), 3:503 (Shikellamy). See MPCP, 5:391–92, for other references to Kittatinny Mountain as the Indians' preferred boundary ("your side of the Blue Hills").

31. PA, 1st ser., 2:15. See MPCP, 5:394–95, for a governor's proclamation. For context see P. A. W. Wallace, *Conrad Weiser*, 277–79; P. A. W. Wallace, *Indian Paths of Pennsylvania*, 49–53, 168–70. For an account of Weiser's activities at Logstown see McConnell, *Country Between*, 74–77.

32. PA, 1st ser., 2:15.

33. PA, 1st ser., 2:24. Weiser later informed the Shamokin Indians that Scaroyady "had given liberty (with what right I could not tell) to setle."

34. Lynch, "Iroquois Confederacy," 83–99, distinguishes between assimilative (e.g., adoption of peoples such as the Tuscaroras) and associative (individual or honorary) adoption. Scaroyady's actions fall into the category of associative adoption—"a historical adaption to a new set of political realities, in which assimilative adoptions were not necessary nor even desired by either party, but where symbolic identity was still ritually required" (89). For conceptions of land tenure and usufruct see Bragdon, *Native People of Southern New England*, 43, 137–39; A. F. C. Wallace, "Woman, Land, and Society."

35. McConnell, "Peoples 'In Between.'" For biographies of Scaroyady see P. A. W. Wallace, *Indians in Pennsylvania*, 181; Sipe, *Indian Chiefs of Pennsylvania*, 213–54.

36. MPCP, 5:395–410, at 400. See also Starna, "Diplomatic Career of Canasatego."

37. Conrad Weiser to Richard Peters, May 8, 1749, Conrad Weiser Correspondence, 1741–1766, HSP; MPCP, 5:407–8; P. A. W. Wallace, *Conrad Weiser*, 277–85 (quote on Juniata at 279); MPCP, 5:477 (expedient): 408 (Hamilton on new purchase). See MPCP, 5:406–7, for the Proprietors' description of the real extent of the 1749 purchase. See also Fenton's concise account of the 1749 conference in *Great Law and the Longhouse*, 455–57.

38. Richard Peters to the Proprietors, July 5, 1749, Richard Peters Letterbooks, 1737–1750, 363 (also quoted in P. A. W. Wallace, *Conrad Weiser*, 297); Conrad Weiser to Richard Peters, Feb. 7, 1754, Berks and Montgomery Counties, Misc. Manuscripts, 1693–1869.

39. Richard Peters to the Proprietors, May 16, July 5, 1749, Richard Peters Letterbooks, 1737–1750, 357, 363; Thomas Penn to James Tilghman, Nov. 7, 1766, WPHM 57 (Apr. 1974): 239–48, at 242.

40. Thomas Penn to James Hamilton, Oct. 9, 1749, Thomas Penn Letterbooks, 2:390, Thomas Penn Papers; Richard Peters to the Proprietors, Richard Peters Letterbooks, 1737–1750, 381; Richard Peters to the Proprietors, May 5, 1750, Penn Manuscripts, Official Correspondence, 5:9; Conrad Weiser to Richard Peters, Feb. 7, 1754, Berks and Montgomery Counties Manuscripts; MPCP, 4:570 (land value); "Account of the Famine among the Indians." For Indian-settler tenant relationships see New Purchase Applications, 1769, Records of the Land Office, PSA (microfilm reel no. 1.9) (Arthur Auchmuty, no. 46). See also Thomas Penn's letters to Richard Peters, Oct. 9, 1749, Aug. 27, 1750, in Thomas Penn Papers, 1729–1832. For a different interpretation see Merrell, "'Cast of His Countenance.'"

41. "The Report of Richard Peters," PA, 8th ser., 4:3321–32. For other narratives of Peters's expedition see P. A. W. Wallace, *Conrad Weiser*, 277–78, 294–97; Blessing, "Upper Juniata Valley"; and J. W. Jordan, *History of the Juniata Valley*, 1:30–41. See MPCP, 5:435, 479, for Indians' expressions of approval of the Proprietors' expedition.

42. Richard Peters to the Proprietors, July 12, 1750, Penn Manuscripts, Official Correspondence, 5:29; Thomas Penn to Richard Peters, Aug. 27, 1750, Thomas Penn Letterbooks, 3:20, Thomas Penn Papers. Abraham Slack (or Schlechl) never applied for a survey of his tract of land in the Path Valley. He may have continued to live there into the 1760s. In 1762 one of his neighbors, John McClelland, applied for fifty acres of land "in the Great Cove about a mile above Abraham Slack's improvement (Original Warrants, No. 167, Cumberland County, Records of the Land Office, PSA [microfilm reel 3.51]). Slack apparently had relocated to the Wyoming Valley by the late 1760s. In 1769, after the Treaty of Fort Stanwix, he applied for

three hundred acres in the "new purchase" (New Purchase Register, 1769, application no. 2580, Records of the Land Office, PSA [microfilm reel 1.9]).

43. "Report of Richard Peters," 4:3321–32 (quotes at 3323, 3331, 3324).

44. "Report of Richard Peters," 4:3324–25. See D. H. Fischer, *Albion's Seed*, 765–71, for an interpretation of backcountry violence. An "Andrew Lycan" is listed as having warranted 250 acres of land in Lancaster County in 1737, but it is not clear whether this is the same "Andrew Lycon" who lived along the Juniata (see PA, 3rd ser., 24:458).

45. PA, 4:3326, 3331. For squatters' petitions to Maryland and Pennsylvania see MPCP, 5:452–55, 468–69.

46. Thomas Penn to Richard Peters, Aug. 27, 1750, Thomas Penn Papers ("Hussar Spirit"); MPCP, 4:572 ("in league with the Trespassers"). For examples of settlers who later referred to Peters's promises in their caveats, see *Minutes of the Board of Property*, PA, 3rd. ser., 1:140, 152, 234 (Mary White), 241, 346, 2:248–49; Warrant Registers, Cumberland County, Records of the Land Office, PSA (microfilm roll 1.3), warrant numbers 21–22, 31, 51–53, 64–66 (Chambers and Galbreath).

47. Using the households in the Peters report as a sample, I was able to identify definitively forty-four of the sixty-one squatter households using the Records of the Land Office, PSA, and Cumberland County tax lists from the 1750s and 1760s. See Fralish, *Index of Names in the Tax Lists*; Schaumann, *Transcriptions of Original Tax Records*. For references to William and Mary White see PA, 3rd ser., 24:776 ("Warrantees of Land: County of Cumberland, 1750–1874"), 20:567 (Mary White on 1782 Cumberland County tax list).

Settlers often did not receive letters patent because of the fees associated with the land-patenting process and their great distance from the Land Office; some of them also died in the Seven Years' War or Pontiac's War. Possession of a warrant for survey, however, conveyed a modicum of legal title and a basis for possession. I thank Jonathan Stayer of the PSA for explaining the fine points of the land-patenting process to me. See Jordan and Kaups, *American Backwoods Frontier*, 1–7, for the most recent interpretation of the squatters' alleged "compulsive mobility" (3).

48. PA, 1st ser., 2:15 ("very poor"), 8th ser., 4:3325–26, 3331 ("improvements" and "servants"); *Pennsylvania Gazette*, Nov. 11, 1756 (Berks County), Mar. 18, 1756 (Lycon). Elizabeth Lycans—apparently some relation to Andrew—applied for 250 acres of land along the Juniata River in 1766 (West Side Applications, No. 2305, Records of the Land Office, PSA [microfilm reel 1.8]).

49. Richard Peters to the Proprietors, July 20, 1750, Penn Manuscripts, Official Correspondence, 5:39; Thomas Penn, quoted in Jennings, *Empire of Fortune*, 104; *Pennsylvania Gazette*, Mar. 18, 1756 (Delawares). For the Albany Purchase see P. A. W. Wallace, *Conrad Weiser*, 350–63; Jennings, *Empire of Fortune*, 101–6; and Shannon, *Indians and Colonists at the Crossroads*, chap. 5.

50. On the Pennsylvania-Maryland dispute see PA, 2nd ser., 2:683–84; Dutrizac, "Local Identity and Authority."

51. D. V. Jones, *License for Empire*.

4. "The Storm Which Had Been So Long Gathering"

1. Petition, 1767, Miscellaneous Manuscripts, 1570–1938, box 6.

2. "Narrative of Marie Le Roy and Barbara Leininger," 408, 412; P. A. W. Wallace, *Indians in Pennsylvania*, 24–25 (face painting); Sipe, *Indian Wars of Pennsylvania*, 204–9.

3. Jennings, *Invasion of America*, 150; Merrell, review of Calloway, *American Revolution in Indian Country*, 639; Richter, *Facing East*, chap. 6. For examples of historians who emphasize "Indian hating" see works by Jennings, White, and Merritt. See also Peter Silver's penetrating and well-researched study of white identity, *Our Savage Neighbors*.

4. "Narrative of Marie Le Roy and Barbara Leininger," 409.

5. Ward, *Breaking the Backcountry*, 31–32, 92–97, 102–4; Richter, *Facing East*, 185–86.

6. McConnell, *Country Between*, 128. On the Seven Years' War see recent and classic works by Anderson, White, Steele, McConnell, Ward, and Frégault. See also D. H. Kent, *French Invasion of Western Pennsylvania*; Waddell and Bomberger, *French and Indian War in Pennsylvania*.

7. Anderson, *Crucible of War*, prologue and chaps. 4–6, 8–9; Kopperman, *Braddock at the Monongahela*; Sargent, *History of an Expedition*; Russell, "Redcoats in the Wilderness." On Atiatonharongwen see MacLeod, *Canadian Iroquois*, 50–51.

8. Ward, "La Guerre Sauvage"; Ward, "Fighting the 'Old Women.'"

9. Ward, "Fighting the 'Old Women,'" 301.

10. Thomson, *Enquiry into the Causes of the Alienation*. A Presbyterian schoolmaster, Thomson wrote a rare and humane work for its times, based in part on his conversations with the Delaware sachem Teedyuscung.

11. PA, 1st ser., 2:214.

12. Merrell, *Into the American Woods*, 40; Hsiung, "Death on the Juniata"; Smolenski, "Death of Sawantaeny."

13. See Shoemaker, "How the Indians Got to Be Red"; Vaughan, "From White Man to Redskin: Changing Anglo-American Perceptions of the American Indian," in *Roots of American Racism: Essays on the Colonial Experience*.

14. MPCP, 4:633 (Shawnee); *Pennsylvania Gazette*, Apr. 1, Sept. 8, 1756; Post, "Two Journals of Western Tours," 200; Richter, *Facing East*, 190, 199 (Indians and race).

15. "Narrative of Marie Le Roy and Barbara Leininger," 410; [Gibson], "Account of the Captivity of Hugh Gibson," 144. White's classic *Middle Ground* is one example of this emphasis on culture as a motivational reflex.

16. MPCP 3:597, 216–17; Reichel, *Memorials of the Moravian Church*, 1:50; PA, 1st ser., 1:295; MPCP, 5:478 (evil spirits).

17. Muhlenberg, *Journals*, 1:167; Barsotti, *Scoouwa*, 58–59. For colonists' petitions for reform see PA, 8th ser., 6:5097, 5121.

18. MPCP, 4:64–72.

19. MPCP, 8:198–99, 247; Jennings, "Brother Miquon," 207–10; Jennings, *Empire of Fortune*, 253–81, 323–48, 369–404.

20. Merrell, review of Calloway, *American Revolution in Indian Country*, 639. For the Paxton Massacre see Vaughan, "Frontier Banditti and the Indians"; Schock, "'Cloven Foot' Rediscovered."

21. Mittelberger, *Journey to Pennsylvania*.

22. MPCP, 5:401, 408–10. For settlers' complaints see PA, 8th ser., 4:2938, 3085, 3257, 3261, 3466, 3508, 3759; MPCP, 3:219–215, 4:86–87, 5:409–11.

23. Bartram, *Observations*, 16.

24. MPCP, 4:93–94; Bartram, *Observations*, 16; "Missionary's Tour to Shamokin." See also Mancall, *Valley of Opportunity*, 51–57.

25. PA, 8th ser., 4:2938; Heal, *Hospitality in Early Modern England*. See also Griffin, *People with No Name*.

26. P. A. W. Wallace, *Conrad Weiser*, 283; MPCP, 4:280–81 ("perswaded"), 3:311, 4:583 (government providing rum); Klepp and Smith, *Infortunate*, 99–101. See also PA, 8th ser., 3:24; MPCP, 5:409 (alcohol).

27. See PA, 8th ser., 1:770; MPCP, 2:300; depositions of Conrad Weiser, Lancaster County, Feb. 15, 1750, Elizabeth Hunter, and Elizabeth Bethy, all in Conrad Weiser Correspondence, 1741–1766. The definitive work on this case is Waddell, "Justice, Retribution."

28. MPCP, 6:647; Daniel Dulany, quoted in Latrobe, "Military and Political Affairs," 22; Seaver, *Narrative of the Life of Mrs. Mary Jemison*, 5.

29. P. A. W. Wallace, *Conrad Weiser*, 403; Berkeley and Berkeley, *Correspondence of John Bartram*, 400; Silver Heels to Capt. Charles Edmonstone, [1769?], Gage Papers, AS 87.

30. PA, 1st ser., 2:511–12; *Pennsylvania Gazette*, May 10, 1756; Post, "Two Journals of Western Tours," 238.

31. John Elder, quoted in Cavaioli, "Profile of the Paxton Boys," 81; Weiser, quoted in P. A. W. Wallace, *Conrad Weiser*, 414.

32. See Ward, "*La Guerre Sauvage*," chaps. 3, 5, 8; Ward, "Fighting the 'Old Women,'" 297–320; Lepore, *Name of War*, 71–83 (landscape).

33. MPCP, 6:668; Sipe, *Indian Wars of Pennsylvania*, 217. On wartime frontier society see PA, 1st ser., 2:503–4, 511–12; Ward, "*La Guerre Sauvage*," chap. 11; Ward, "Fighting the 'Old Women,'" passim; Franz, *Paxton*; Lepore, *Name of War*, 74 (landscape).

34. Matthew Smith, quoted in Cavaioli, "Profile of the Paxton Boys," 85; William Trent, quoted in P. A. W. Wallace, *Conrad Weiser*, 396; Ward, "*La Guerre Sauvage*," 135–40; PA, 1st ser., 2:450. For other petitions see PA, 1st ser., 2:385, 461, 656–57,

758–59, 3:151–54, 159, 174, 284–85, 357–58, 361. For backcountry rumors see MPCP, 6:649, 655–59, 675–76, 704–5; PA, 1st ser., 2:463, 474, 503–4. Krista Camenzind, in "Violence, Race, and the Paxton Boys," explores gender and racial aspects of violence in the 1760s.

35. Petition of Cumberland County Inhabitants, Mar. 1765, in Stevens, Kent, and Waddell, *Papers of Henry Bouquet* (BP hereafter), 6:778; Seaver, *Narrative of the Life of Mrs. Mary Jemison*, 10–11; Dunbar, *Paxton Papers*, 186, 293 (families).

36. *Pennsylvania Gazette*, Dec. 25, 1755; Henry Bouquet to John Harris, July 9, 1764, Aug. 24, 1764, BP, 6:594–95, 620; Dunbar, *Paxton Papers*, 177 (worthy), 182 (industriousness). For frontier attacks on Quaker complacency see Dunbar, *Paxton Papers*, 179–82, 185–87, 190, 212; BP, 6:778–79. On conflict with British authority see Ward, "La Guerre Sauvage," chap. 11. For manhood see Camenzind, "Violence, Race, and the Paxton Boys."

37. White, *Middle Ground*, 388; MPCP, 6:768. See also Knowles, "Torture of Captives."

38. White, *Middle Ground*, 388; MPCP, 6:707, 759; [Shippen], "Military Letters," 396; *Pennsylvania Gazette*, Mar. 2, 1758. See also Merritt, *At the Crossroads*, 178–84.

39. MPCP, 7:78–79, 88–90 (scalp bounty act); *Pennsylvania Gazette*, July 1, 1756; MPCP, 6:763; *Pennsylvania Gazette*, Mar. 2, 1758; PA, 1st ser., 2:511, 3:221–22; Axtell, "Scalping: The Ethnohistory of a Moral Question," in *European and the Indian*, 227.

40. *Minutes of the Board of Property*, PA, 3rd ser., 2:592; *Pennsylvania Gazette*, Apr. 1, 1756; PA, 8th ser., 7:5883 (Catherine Jager); *Pennsylvania Gazette*, May 8, 1760.

41. See W. A. Hunter, "Victory at Kittanning"; Myers, "Pennsylvania's Awakening." John Armstrong's official report is in PA, 1st ser., 2:767–75.

42. W. A. Hunter, "Victory at Kittanning," 378; Sipe, *Indian Chiefs of Pennsylvania*, 269–74. See Captain Jacobs's boast in MPCP, 7:232.

43. "Robert Robison's Narrative," in Loudon, *Loudon's Indian Narratives*, 162; PA, 1st ser., 2:769.

44. [Gibson], "Account of the Captivity of Hugh Gibson," 143; PA, 1st ser., 2:769–70.

45. "Robert Robison's Narrative," 162; W. A. Hunter, "Victory at Kittanning," 390–93.

46. Myers, "Pennsylvania's Awakening," 399, 407, 414–16.

47. *Pennsylvania Gazette*, Oct. 14 (plunder), Sept. 23 ("greatest Blow"), Sept. 30, 1756 ("Ode").

48. C. C. Dann, "Kittanning Destroyed," 2, 7–9, 15–17; *Pennsylvania Gazette*, Feb. 17, 1757 ("courage"); Armstrong to Bouquet, Aug. 26, 1763, BP, 6:370.

5. "Our Neighbourhood with the Settlers"

1. DRCHNY, 7:341; SWJP, 9:826, 856, 2:759, 802; "Journal de la Campagne de M. de Bellestre"; Frégault, *Canada*, 155–56; Pouchot, *Memoirs on the Late War in North*

America, 128, 132, 403–4, 516; E. P. Hamilton, *Adventure in the Wilderness,* 94, 110–11, 185, 194; Tousignant and Dionne-Tousignant, "Picoté de Belestre, François Marie." For the settlement of German Flatts see *Herkimer County at 200;* Hardin and Willard, *History of Herkimer County.*

2. NYCM, Nov. 6, 1766, 25:65–66. See chap. 1 for comparisons to New France.

3. For account book entries concerning Weaver and other Palatines, see Unidentified Account Book, Schenectady NY, 1756–1764, box 16, Campbell Family Papers, 1707–1907 (EP 11062); John Sanders Account Book, 1752, BV Sanders, NYHS. Also see SWJP, 9:871, for the German Flatts mayor's ties to merchant Robert Sanders. For Vanderheyden see William Hare to Jelles Fonda, Mar. 8, 1766, Jelles Fonda Papers, 1750–1791, coll. 157 (NYSHA). For a brief biographical sketch see Stefan Bielinski, "David Vanderheyden," Colonial Albany Social History Project, http://www .nysm.nysed.gov/albany/bios/vd/davdh5677.html (accessed July 26, 2007). On other evidence of Palatine-Iroquois trade see SWJP, 1:579, 2:664, 673, 9:691 (Oneida emigrants living at Oswegatchie), 696, 699, 825–26 (Oneidas at Oswegatchie), 856 (women traders), 871, 10:478; NYCM, July 3, 1753, May 4, 1757, 23:85, 25:168; MacLeod, *Canadian Iroquois,* 115–17. On wampum production see Benson, *Peter Kalm's Travels,* 129, 343. Neither of the two classic works on the fur trade in New York mentions the German Flatts trade: see Armour, *Merchants of Albany;* Norton, *Fur Trade in Colonial New York,* 201 (David Vanderheyden). On the extensive rum trade in Albany see DiVirgilio, "Rum Punch and Cultural Revolution."

4. For the Oneidas see Campisi, "Oneida"; Tiro, "People of the Standing Stone," 23–24, 39–47; Campisi and Hauptman, *Oneida Indian Experience;* SWJP, 3:631; DRCHNY, 6:857–58 (porters).

5. SWJP, 2:679 (ill treatment), 526–27 (Herkimer), 534–35, 3:443, 453, 8:1009 (treasonable belts), 9:676, 679, 681 (fort not a defense), 919, 10:338 (Klock); DHNY, 2:509–15 (Fort Bull); Steele, *Warpaths,* 199–200.

6. SWJP, 2:679–80 ("live and die"), 692, 707, 709, 723, 9:661 (give notice), 699, 725–26, 778, 803, 832, 857; "Conferences Between M. de Vaudreuil and the Indians, December 1756," DRCHNY, 10:513–15, 562; Hamilton, *Adventure in the Wilderness,* 94–95, 110–11, 113 (Oneidas rescue captive). See Frégault, *Canada,* 156, for the comparison of German Flatts with Acadia.

7. SWJP, 2:723 (bad practice), 9:676, 679, 681 (Justice requires), 699 (wampum), 720–21, 725, 854–55 (Johnson's illness), 857 (Croghan's ignorance), 13:95.

8. SWJP, 9:832 ("many Advantages"; my emphasis), 2:664 (rum), 692 (blood mixed; my emphasis); John Butler Account Book, 1755–1775, box 3, item 75, Willis T. Hanson Colonial Manuscript Collection (see June 1766 entry for blacksmith work); SWJP, 4:54 (Klock's gristmill).

9. DRCHNY, 6:985 (permission), 857–58 (Oneida-German portagers); SWJP, 6:412 (Germans as laborers); Albany Commissioners' Minutes (WLCL), June 18, 1754 (portage).

10. SWJP, 9:860–61 (Canaghquiesa), 778 (Palatines discount intelligence). For rumors and reports of French-Indian attacks on German Flatts or the Mohawk Valley in the late 1750s see SWJP, 2:676, 696, 698, 703, 707, 756, 9:424, 449–50, 534–35, 613, 627–28, 634–38, 643, 663–65, 670, 675, 681, 701, 768 (joint scouting), 803, 817, 820, 833, 854–57 (warnings), 860, 865–67.

11. Cadwallader Colden to Peter Collinson, Dec. 31, 1757, Colden Papers, 5:212–13, 9:870–71. On Oneida-Oswegatchie-Onondaga ties see SWJP, 9:458, 460, 516, 598, 825 (Oneida contrivance), 856 (one hundred Oswegatchies turn back). One Palatine female, whom the Indians mutilated, later escaped and testified that she saw Onondagas among the war party (DHNY, 2:523). On the Oneidas' accusations see SWJP, 9:860, 10:338. According to Nathaniel S. Benton, William Johnson tried to deflect any culpability from his office: see Benton, *History of Herkimer County*, chap. 4. For Canadian Iroquois see MacLeod, *Canadian Iroquois*; Green, "New People in an Age of War," chaps. 6–8.

12. SWJP, 9:860 (see 3:430–31 for 1761 condolence ritual and 10:674 for another similar example); DRCHNY, 10:881–84 (German Flatts captives returned). On the postwar German Flatts trade and provisioning of Indians see John Butler Account Book; Schenectady Merchant Account Book, 1756–1764, box 16, Campbell Family Papers; SWJP, 10:644, 647, 834, 844, 894, 915–16, 4:648, 7:832–33, 836–38, 844, 894, 11:595–96, 12:286–87, 545, 617, 667, 690 (Rudolph Shoemaker), 802–3, 852, 856–58, 866–67, 868. On the "Black Boys" see Cutliffe, "Sideling Hill Affair."

13. SWJP, 9:669, 904; NYCM, vol. 25 (passim). On the earlier agreement regarding Iroquoia and New York see chap. 1.

14. Bougainville, *Adventure in the Wilderness*, 191; SWJP, 9:838; Steele, *Warpaths*, chap. 10. Indicative of his flagging prestige, a rumor circulated among the Iroquois in 1757 that Johnson was going to step down from his position as superintendent (SWJP, 9:836).

15. SWJP, 5:530, 6:618, 7:597, 599–600. On Johnson's political connections see M. W. Hamilton, *Sir William Johnson*, 113–200; Anderson, *Crucible of War*, part 2. For colonial officials' views of interpreters, see Merrell, *Into the American Woods*.

16. Johnson to Colden, Dec. 11, 1764, Colden Papers, 6:397. For examples of Johnson's mediation see SWJP, 5:274, 9:767, 10:501–2 (Condolence Ceremony), 9:803, 10:49–51, 60, 87 (provisions), 9:596 (dream fulfillment), and the index (vol. 14).

17. SWJP, 10:63–65, 79–80 (Schoharie dispute).

18. Colden Papers, 9:34, 6:375–76; SWJP, 1:240; DRCHNY, 7:527. See also SWJP, 1:200, 9:921; NYCM, 25:221; Guzzardo, "Sir William Johnson's Official Family," 124–25.

19. SWJP, 1:147, 638, 640, 847; Leonard Spaulding Diary, 1755–1782, 8. For joint war parties composed of colonists and Indians see Jonathan French Journal, 1757; DRCHNY, 4:247 (1696); NYCMSS, Jan. 9, 1712, 57:56; SWJP, 1:60, 64, 72–73, 78, 80, 116, 146–47, 525, 638, 882, 2:295, 575, 816, 9:473, 645, 724, 774, 780; NYCM, Sept. 4, 1747, Feb. 18, Mar. 28, 1748, 21:267, 289, 296; John Henry Lydius Correspondence,

Miscellaneous Manuscripts, L, NYHS (esp. John Henry Lydius to John Stoddard, Sept. 19, 1747, which mentions a party of 317 Christians and 390 Indians scouting near Crown Point). For Mohawks, Schoharie, and Oquaga requests for forts see SWJP, 1:276, 484, 513, 603, 630, 2:382, 9:338, 354, 392, 416, 438, 498, 527, 568–69, 620; NYCM, Sept. 27, 1746, 21:192–93.

20. "Transporting Provisions Baggage and Warlike Stores," Oct. 3, 1747, box 17, George Clinton Papers; Jehu Hay Diary, 1763–1765 (messengers). On Indian batteauxmen see SWJP, 3:631, 7:32, 9:430, 463, 10:175, 180–85; DRCHNY, 6:857–58.

21. For hostilities between British garrisons and Indians see SWJP, 2:7, 554, 560–61, 614, 3:165, 218, 870, 882, 4:595, 626, 9:544–45, 591, 617, 704, 10:56, 62–63, 512, 13:104–7 (chamber pot); NYCM, Nov. 12, 1755, 25:97–98. For Mohawk wartime grievances regarding prisoners held by the French, disease, and deprivation, see SWJP, 1:149, 233, 322 (prisoners), 9:800, 813, 820 (1757–58 smallpox epidemic), 11:817, 718, 813 (crop failures). See also Way, "Cutting Edge of Culture."

22. NYCM, Oct. 14, 1755, 25:92–93; SWJP, 9:392, 461 (Red Coats), 548 (Country People), 600, 626, 11:40–41.

23. "Journal of Joseph Bloomfield, 1776," 281, 289; Lafitau, *Customs of the American Indians*, 2:261–62. For Indian and colonial linguistic proficiency see SWJP, 1:112, 624, 2:660, 786, 3:833, 4:61, 145, 7:59, 8:1008–9, 13:276; NYCM, Mar. 21, 1763, 25:478; NYCMSS, 58:30, 62:2, 79:15–16, 34; DRCHNY, 6:867–68; DHNY, 2:521; Colden Papers, 6:371–75, 9:105; McAnear, "Personal Accounts of the Albany Congress," 742; Pilkington, *Journals of Samuel Kirkland*, 3; J. C. Dann, *Revolution Remembered*, 269. See also Nancy Hagedorn's work, including her 1995 *New York History* article ("Brokers of Understanding") and her 1995 dissertation ("'Friend to Go Between Them'"); Axtell, "Babel of Tongues: Communicating with the Indians," in *Natives and Newcomers*.

24. Common Council Minutes, 1723–1745, City of Albany, Microfilm A 3284–87 (Aug. 1, 1704); "Journal of Warren Johnson," 260, 265; NYCM, June 19, 1751, 21:424 (two tavernkeepers); DRCHNY, 6:362 (Clement); SWJP, 10:241 ("ruined people"). For other evidence on taverns and alcohol see SWJP, 4:55, 633, 11:45–46, 195, 10:17, 57–58, 69, 387, 13:517.

25. Doblin and Starna, *Journals of Christian Daniel Claus and Conrad Weiser*, 38–39. For evidence of Kast's interactions with the Iroquois see "Diary of J. Martin Mack's . . . Journey," 113–14, 152, 178–80 (wander), 211. For Sarah Maginnis (née Kast) see George Clinton Papers, box 15, "Contingencies, July 22, 1746–March 28, 1747"; for her employment as a translator for Susquehanna Indians see Aug. 12, 1746, entry. See also H. Z. Jones, *Palatine Families of New York*, 1:438, Graymont, *Iroquois in the American Revolution*, 13, 144, 158; claim of Sarah McGin, Loyalist Transcripts, 1776–1831, 21:399–406, reel 10 ("understood"), NYPL.

26. M. W. Hamilton, "Diary of Reverend John Ogilvie," 346; DRCHNY, 6:857–58 (batteaux); NYCMSS, 79:50 (2–3) (Oneida-McMichael). For hostile encounters and

crimes see DRCHNY, 5:385–86, 965, 968; SWJP, 3:165, 5:633, 9:392, 10:512, 564, 683–84, 796 (theft); NYCM, Aug. 28, 1752, May 9, 1723, 12:345, 14:151–52; DHNY, 2:863–68.

27. SWJP, 4:316–17, 177; Smith, *Tour of the Hudson*, 122; Jeff N. Clyde to Lyman Draper, Feb. 11, 1878, Brant Papers, 5F74, SHSW. See also SWJP, 1:208, 10:776. On naming see Sivertsen, *Turtles, Wolves, and Bears*, 207–69.

28. Albany Commissioners' Minutes (WLCL), Dec. 31, 1753; Jezierski, "1751 Journal of Abbé François Piquet," 367–68; DRCHNY, 6:738; NYCMSS, May 10, 16, 1717, 60:163–70 (petitions regarding slaves who ran away to Indians at Minisink), Aug. 15, 1757, 83:253; Hart, "Black 'Go-Betweens.'"

29. Writ of *certiorari* and return to writ, *Solomon Parmalee v. Henry Welch, Jr.*, 1820, New York Supreme Court of Judicature, Writs of *certiorari*, error, *habeas corpus*, and *mandamus*, box 6, folder 11, NYSA, ser. J1025. (I thank archivist James Folts of the New York State Archives for bringing this source to my attention.)

30. SWJP, 7:681, 8:235, 9:779, 795, 864, 871, 10:564, 13:277, 1:205; Daniel Claus, quoted in Sivertsen, *Turtles, Wolves, and Bears*, 167; Charles Lee to Sidney Lee, June 18, 1756, in Lee, *Charles Lee Papers*, 1:2–6; Rohde, "Journal of a Trip."

31. For Dachstaeders see Simms, *Frontiersmen of New York*, 1:165 (Anna Dockstaeder was a patentee of the German Flatts in 1725); SWJP, 2:575 (Ury Adam Dogstader was listed in an Indian account book); Kelly, *Baptismal Record of German Flats Reformed Church*, 60, 69, 76, 82, 91 (also in Sivertsen, *Turtles, Wolves, and Bears*, app. E, 259–62). For other intermarriages see SWJP, 8:210 (Stacey), 235, 9:779 (Spelman), 795 (Hans Croyn), 864 (Jemmy Campbell), 871 (Hamilton), 10:564 (white among Senecas); Graymont, *Iroquois in the Revolution*, 225 (white Hans); Kelsay, *Joseph Brant*, 110 (Johnson's métis son marries a white captive).

32. Petition of Hendrick, Abram Peterson, and Others to George Clinton, Feb. 8, 1753, IIDH, reel 15; Beauchamp, *Moravian Journals*, 204. For more evidence of joint worship see also "Diary of Rev. Eli Forbes," 395; Jonathan Edwards, quoted in Sivertsen, *Turtles, Wolves, and Bears*, 147–48; Feister, "Indian-Dutch Relations."

33. SWJP, 1:130 (Schuyler/Schoharie), 3:407 (Oneidas and German Flatts), 9:629, 716 (Schoharie and German Flatts); DRCHNY, 8:551 (Schuyler); Roscoe, *History of Schoharie County*, 1:359–60 (Joseph Brant); Kelly, *Baptismal Record of German Flats Reformed Church*; Royden W. Vosburgh, ed., "Records of the Reformed Protestant Dutch Church of Caughnawaga," "Records of the Reformed Protestant Dutch Church of German Flatts in Fort Herkimer, Town of German Flatts, Herkimer County, N.Y.," and "Records of Trinity Lutheran Church of Stone Arabia in the Town of Palatine in Montgomery County, N.Y.," in *New York Genealogical and Biographical Society*, 1914 and 1917 (reprinted as appendices in Sivertsen, *Turtles, Wolves, and Bears*, 207–62). The Records of Mohawk Indians at Fort Hunter also contains examples of European settlers acting as sponsors for Indian children at baptism; see Rufus Alexander Grider Scrapbooks, 1:60 (Palatine Church record transcription).

34. Guldenzopf, "Colonial Transformation," chaps. 5–6; Shannon, Indians and Colonists at the Crossroads, 25–27, 30, 163–65.

35. Smith, Tour of Four Rivers, 126; Bridenbaugh, "Patrick M'Robert's Tour, 170; Guldenzopf, "Colonial Transformation," chaps. 5–6; Wonderley, "Oneida Community in 1780," 19–41.

36. For settlers' services to the Indians see NYCM, 25:46; NYCMSS, 58:173–75, 62:148; SWJP, 2:566–645, 3:158–82, 7:807–9, 817 (2,400 Indians at German Flatts), 856–64, 894 (£3,400 in expenses), 9:595, 647, 649, 655, 10:472. 12:690. See also the accounts of the Indian Affairs Department, listed in SWJP, 14:266. See the John Catherwood Memorandum Book, Oct. 1745, George Clinton Papers, for the large amount of food disbursed to Indians. For examples of Indians living at Johnson's homes see SWJP, 7:737, 9:462, 655, 778, 874.

37. For women's production of Indian shirts see SWJP, 2:634, 636, 9:650, 13:573, 188 (Indian women also made shirts); Jelles Fonda Account Book, 1762–1776, Jelles Fonda Papers (NYHS) (p. 13 in new book, under "Elizabeth Styntie Hamers Daugher"); NYCM, Mar. 28, 1723, 14:136. For colonists' and soldiers' acquisition of Indian shoes, see SWJP, 2:636, 13:519, 14:123–26 (clothing).

38. SWJP, 11:398 (Maginnis). Also see the evidence cited on German Flatts farmer-traders; unidentified account book, Schenectady NY, 1756–1764, box 16, Campbell Family Papers (contains accounts for German Flatts farmer-traders, including shipments of rum, wampum, vermillion, pigeon shot, and various kinds of cloth); unidentified account book, Schenectady NY, box 18, Colin Campbell, Account of Goods, Schenectady NY, 1765–1766, box 19, [Campbell & Andrews?] Goods and Accounts, n.p., 1761–1765, Campbell Family Papers (contains accounts for black strouds, vermillion, shot, powder, brandy going to minor Indian traders); John Sanders Account Book, 1752. For dozens of references to colonial adoption of "Indian shoes" see Jelles Fonda Memorandum Books for 1769 and 1772, box 4, items 173, 65, Jelles Fonda Common Account Ledger, Oct. 1774, box 5, and Jelles Fonda Account Book, 1762–1776, all Fonda Papers (NYHS); John Butler Account Book; unidentified account books, Schenectady NY, 1756–1764, boxes 6 and 16, Campbell Family Papers; "Indian Book, 1754–1764," and General Store Accounts, 1771–1774, in Fonda Papers, 1750–1791, coll. 157 (NYSHA).

39. P. A. W. Wallace, Conrad Weiser, 338; Beauchamp, Moravian Journals, 113, 120, 122–24, 134–35; John Aemilius Wernig letter, Sept. 14, 1752, ERNY, 5:3287.

40. Hawley, "Account of Services among the Indians," 53; Jelles Fonda to Stefanes Degova, Sept. 13, 1774, Fonda Papers, folder 4 (NYHS). See Benson, Peter Kalm's Travels, 435–37, for the ginseng trade in New France. For other references to ginseng's continued importance as a trade item in the Mohawk Valley see SWJP, 1:311, 346–47, 373, 376, 3:311, 4:325, 375, 642, 648, 578 (Sarah Magin), 5:341, 400, 8:276–77, 11:398, 581, 12:150–51, 168, 13:126; A. Cuyler to Jelles Fonda, Feb. 26, 1766, and Account Book of Jelles Fonda, 1769, box 4, items 143 and 173, both Jelles

Fonda Papers (SC 7026) (NYSL); Smith Ramadge to Jelles Fonda, Dec. 3, 1772, and Samuel Stringer, receipt, June 17, 1768, both Fonda Papers, 1750–1791, coll. 157 (NYSHA); Colonel Glen to Fonda, Oct. 28, 1765, J. Harris to Fonda, June 20, 1766, and Stephanus D'Egros to Jelles Fonda, Sept. 23, 1774, all in John Wyman Collection (colls. 13, 16, 75).

41. Benson, *Peter Kalm's Travels*, 437; "Journal of Warren Johnson," 255. Cf. the methods of payment of Sir William Johnson's tenants, in "Account Book of a General Store, Albany, N.Y., 1771–1774," SC 7005, NYSL; Indian payments in Jelles Fonda's Indian Account Book 1762–1776, Fonda Papers (NYHS); Indian Book, 1754–1761, Fonda Papers, 1750–1791 (coll. 157) (NYSHA); Guldenzopf, "Colonial Transformation," 78–80, 135–36. For Indians' cash payments and receipts see SWJP, 1:831, 2:553, 8:556 (£2,000 disbursement), 9:15–31, 10:87 13:542, 544; NYCM, 25:324 (counterfeit money from New England); John Butler Account Book; Walter Butler Account Book, 1733–1743, NYSL; Schenectady Account Books, 1756–1764, boxes 6 and 16, Campbell Family Papers; Indian Book, 1754–1761, Fonda Papers, 1750–1791 (coll. 157) (NYSHA). On Indian batteauxmen see SWJP, 3:631, 7:32, 9:430, 463, 10:175, 180–85; DRCHNY, 6:857–58.

42. SWJP, 1:14, 213, 323, 2:540, 3:228, 950, 4:21, 11:120, 13:29; "Account of Indian Trinketts bought for M. Syme," Daniel Campbell, Goods, 1759–1765, box 16, Campbell Family Papers; Huey and Pulis, *Molly Brant*, 25–39; Burch, "Sir William Johnson's Cabinet of Curiosities"; Phillips, "Jasper Grant and Edward Walsh."

43. SWJP, 2:646, 497; "Journal of Warren Johnson," 259, 254, 266; Benson, *Peter Kalm's Travels*, 190–91; Beauchamp, *Moravian Journals*, 64–65.

44. John Butler Account Book (June 1766: Arent Bradt bought five pair of "Indian stockings"); unidentified account book, Schenectady NY, 1756–1764, box 6, folder 1, Campbell Family Papers, 1707–1907 (EP 11062) (Indian gartering, shoes, and cup); Rufus Grider Scrapbooks, 2:21, 39, 7:68; Shannon, "Dressing for Success."

45. Benson, *Peter Kalm's Travels*, 197, 227–28, 258–60, 606; Crèvecoeur, *Letters from an American Farmer*, 360, 378; Butler, *Awash in a Sea of Faith*, 232–33. For other references to medicine see Colden Papers, 3:89–90; SWJP, index (vol. 14): 367–68 (medicine), 540–41(sickness); Burch, "Sir William Johnson and Eighteenth-Century Medicine."

46. Johnson to Lord Adam Gordon, Apr. 4, 1769 (SC 7005), folder 9, Sir William Johnson Manuscripts.

6. Imperial Crisis in the Ohio Valley

1. D. Jones, *A Journal of Two Visits Made*, 18 (Monongahela); Donehoo, *History of the Indian Villages*, 170–73, 113–18.

2. Bouquet to Cochrane, July 12, 1761, BP, 5:630; [Parrish], "Extracts from the Journal of John Parrish," 446; Joshua Elder to John Lukens, Apr. 15, 1769, Miscellaneous Manuscripts, 1570–1938, box 8; Capt. Harry Gordon to Gage, June 15, 1766,

Gage Papers, AS 51; [Cresswell], *Journal of Nicholas Cresswell*, 63, 68–69; Ellis, *History of Fayette County*, 671–73, 727. See also Darlington, *Christopher Gist's Journals*, for descriptions of the Ohio Valley.

3. P. A. W. Wallace, *Indian Paths of Pennsylvania*, 27–30, 100, 109–13. For Native war parties see Wainwright, "George Croghan's Journal," esp. 402–4; Perkins, *Border Life*, 76–77. On the Redstone Country as a granary see BP, 5:690, 299, 6:78–79, 131.

4. J. W. Jordan, "James Kenny's 'Journal,'" 419; D. Jones, *Journal of Two Visits Made*, 18; Alderfer, *Ephrata Commune*, 136–39 (Dunker settlements); [Parrish], "Extracts from the Journal of John Parrish," 446; J. W. Jordan, "Journal of James Kenny," 199; SWJP, 1:634, 7:70–71, 264, 298 (Peter's Kahnawake origins).

5. D. Jones, *Journal of Two Visits Made*, 100–101 (rumor). For references to Captain Peter's murder see SWJP, 5:540, 12:296, 308; Reese, *Official Papers of Francis Fauquier*, 3:1435–39. For references to the Thomlinson and Aron murders see BP, 5:74–75, 6:78–79; J. W. Jordan, "Journal of James Kenny," 152, 158; SWJP, 10:452, 543. For horse thefts see BP, 5:477, 482, 495, 522, 543, 590–92; PA, 1st ser., 4:441–42; McConnell, *Country Between*, 101–2, 156, 161, 217.

6. Dexter, *Diary of David McClure*, 45; Wainwright, "George Croghan's Journal," 365 (Iroquois); Fort Pitt Day Book, Mar. 1767–Nov. 1767, Historical Society of Western Pennsylvania; "Account of Indian Shirts Making, 1771" (microfilm 1294 at PSA); J. W. Jordan, "James Kenny's 'Journal,'" 419; J. W. Jordan, "Journal of James Kenny," 40, 47, 153. On Fort Pitt see Stotz, *Outposts of the War for Empire*.

7. SWJP, 5:375, 744, 8:1141, 12:1116. See George Croghan to Gage, May 26, 1766, Gage Papers, AS 51, for his fear of a general war. For the "dilemma of British policy" over settlement see Bailyn, *Voyagers to the West*, 3–56; Holton, *Forced Founders*, esp. chaps. 1 and 6; McConnell, *Country Between*, 233–79; White, *Middle Ground*, 315–65; Cutliffe, "Sideling Hill Affair"; Sosin, *Whitehall and the Wilderness*.

8. Capt. Harry Gordon to Gage, June 4, 1766, Gage Papers, AS 51; Cutliffe, "Sideling Hill Affair"; Anderson, *Crucible of War*, xix.

9. PA, 8th ser., 7:6136, 6178. For the weakness of government in the colonies see Shannon, *Indians and Colonists at the Crossroads*, chaps. 2–3; Greene, "Seven Years' War and the American Revolution," 85–105.

10. Brumwell, *Redcoats*, 119–27, 309; A. P. James, "First English-Speaking Trans-Appalachian Frontier," 61–63; McConnell, *Army and Empire*; Mayer, *Belonging to the Army*, chap. 1.

11. PA, 1st ser., 4:281, 325. For information on Virginia land companies see A. F. C. Wallace, *Thomas Jefferson and the Indians*, chap. 2. Woody Holton's *Forced Founders* persuasively shows that the Proclamation Line of 1763 vexed Virginia planters, but for many other colonists, particularly in Pennsylvania and New York, the Proclamation was not a hindrance. The explosion of settlements and land grants in Pennsylvania and New York before and after the 1768 Treaty of Fort Stanwix is evidence that the British system worked for many British colonists.

12. Aspinwall Papers, 8:174–23 (Easton Treaty); McConnell, *Country Between*, 129–58; White, *Middle Ground*, 248–68. On Native strategy see Ward, *Breaking the Backcountry* (quote at 58); Dowd, *War under Heaven*, 5, 114–73.

13. Richter, *Facing East*, 151; Post, "Two Journals of Western Tours," 274, 278; SWJP, 12:133–35; J. W. Jordan, "James Kenny's 'Journal,'" 433. See Eric Hinderaker's *Elusive Empires* (185) and Richard White's *Middle Ground* for interpretations that emphasize the British Empire as an imperfect "restraining force."

14. J. W. Jordan, "Journal of James Kenny," 175, 18; SWJP, 10:867; PA, 1st ser., 4:326; Croghan to Gage, Aug. 8, 1770, Gage Papers, AS 94; Ward, *Breaking the Backcountry*, 202 (Philadelphia); Dowd, *Spirited Resistance*; Dowd, *War under Heaven* (Pontiac's War).

15. PA, 1st ser., 4:326; Charles Edmonstone to Gage, Oct. 24, 1770, Gage Papers, AS 97. See Dowd, *War under Heaven*, 2, 82, for the importance of sovereignty.

16. J. W. Jordan, "Journal of James Kenny," 174; Major General Frederick Haldimand to Earl of Dartmouth, Nov. 3, 1773, in Davies, *Documents of the American Revolution*, 6:237–38; Doddridge, *Notes on the Settlement*, 81; Bouquet to Monckton, Mar. 20, 1761, BP, 5:253–56 (quote at 354–55); George Croghan, quoted in Buck and Buck, *Planting of Civilization in Western Pennsylvania*, 144. Population estimates are in McConnell, *Country Between*, 260.

17. John Struthers, quoted in J. C. Dann, *Revolution Remembered*, 252. For examples of petitioners "driven off by the Indians," see *Minutes of the Board of Property*, PA, 3rd ser., 1:139, 223, 189, 234–35, 346, 365, 583, 2:273, 298, 300, 344; Records, "Pioneer Experiences." On Euroamerican motives see Perkins, *Border Life*, 54–60.

18. McDonald to Bouquet, Oct. 25, 1761, Bouquet to Livingston, Feb. 6, 1762, both BP, 5:840, 6:43; Livingston to Bouquet, Feb. 14, 1762, in Stevens and Kent, *Papers of Henry Bouquet*, vol. 19, pt. 1, p. 25; Wainwright, "George Croghan's Journal," 420–21.

19. Darlington, *Christopher Gist's Journals*, 47.

20. Marietta and Rowe, *Troubled Experiment*, 35–37.

21. SWJP, 12:137; *Pennsylvania Gazette*, July 10, July 17, Aug. 7, 1766; Gage to Commanding Officer at Fort Niagara, July 7, 1766, Gage Papers, AS 54; White, *Middle Ground*, 345; Vaughan, "Frontier Banditti and the Indians"; Rowe, "Frederick Stump Affair." For interpretations that emphasize a generalized racial ideology in Pennsylvania by 1763 see works by White, Merritt, Merrell, and Silver.

22. Extract of a Letter from Captain Edmonstone, Nov. 11, 1767, and Report of Ensign [Thomas] Batts, Nov. 10, 1767, both Gage Papers, AS 72.

23. PA, 1st ser., 4:260, 273; SWJP, 7:182. For other instances of attempted murder, assault, and verbal abuse, or rumors of such crimes, see Croghan to Gage, Aug. 8, 1770, Gage Papers, AS 94; PA, 1st ser., 4:217, 413; SWJP, 12:115 (cf. DRCHNY, 7:864) (rumor of prominent Iroquois warriors' death), 12:123 (reports of Indians' deaths elsewhere), 4:769 (fragmentary account of two Indians killed at Redstone Creek),

5:260 (fragmentary account of murder), 8:9–10 (soldier assaulted near Fort Pitt), 9:753 (accidental death). For instances of soldiers and colonists abusing Indians at Fort Pitt see Edmonstone to Gage, Mar. 9, 1771, Gage Papers, AS 100; SWJP, 3:459, 699, 724, 7:86, 182, 211–12, 10:135, 11:862. For examples of Indians' offenses against the colonists see SWJP, 7:942–43, 993–94, 1052–54, 1076–77, 8:227.

24. Franklin, quoted in M. W. Hamilton, "Sir William Johnson and Pennsylvania"; DRCHNY, 7:852.

25. Bailyn, *Voyagers to the West*, 3–56; PA, 8th ser., 7:6076; SWJP, 5:201, 12:376–77; Carter, *Correspondence of General Thomas Gage*, 1:278; D. H. Fischer, *Paul Revere's Ride*, 31.

26. SWJP, 12:380; Gage to Bouquet, May 14, 1764, and Bouquet to Gage, May 20, 1764, both BP, 6:279–81, 539, 542–44; Edmonstone to Gage, Feb. 12, 1768, Gage Papers, AS 74. For Roman precedents see Luttwak, *Grand Strategy of the Roman Empire*. Bouquet had created militia companies at Fort Pitt as early as 1761 (see BP, 5:593, 606).

27. Hinderaker, *Elusive Empires*, 170, 185 ("restraining force"); Dowd, *War under Heaven*, 2. See also Stephenson, "With Swords and Plowshares," which is the best study of how veterans' networks shaped early settlement. Stephenson and I reached similar conclusions independently.

Our research corroborates older narratives that recognized the relationships between the British Army and colonization but did not fully examine all of the evidence: see A. P. James, "First English-Speaking Trans-Appalachian Frontier," 61–63; Buck and Buck, *Planting of Civilization in Western Pennsylvania*, 140.

28. Capt. Harry Gordon to Gage, June 15, 1766, Gage Papers, AS 51; Dowd, *War under Heaven*, 5 ("supply lines"); "Clarkson's Diary, August 6, 1766–April 16, 1767," ISHLC, 11:348–51. On the improvement of roads see Buck and Buck, *Planting of Civilization in Western Pennsylvania*, 98. For British garrisons in the Ohio Country see BP, 6:50; Waddell and Bomberger, *French and Indian War in Pennsylvania*, 90–96. For early censuses of Pittsburgh see "Early Record of Pittsburgh"; "Pittsburgh in 1761"; BP, 5:407–21 (for biographical sketches of each resident). For archaeological evidence of a civilian presence at Fort Ligonier see Grimm, *Archaeological Investigation of Fort Ligonier*.

29. [Tilghman], "Thoughts on the Situation"; Fauquier to Bouquet, Jan. 17, 1762, and Bouquet to Fauquier, Feb. 8, 1762, both BP, 6:39, 45. Colonel Bouquet corresponded with individuals who entertained hopes of planting colonies in the Ohio Valley and desired "to form an estate in Pennsylvania." His own plans for colonization were published posthumously in 1765 in William Smith's *An Account of Bouquet's Expedition Against the Ohio Indians in 1764*. See BP, 5:32–33, 214–15, 6:169–70, 787. For licensed settlers' exemption from removal see SWJP, 11:793.

30. Bouquet to Monckton, Mar. 20, 1761, BP, 5:354; DRCHNY, 10:267–69; Petition of Pittsburgh Inhabitants, Dec. 20, 1767, Gage Papers, AS 73. The petition

contained forty-nine signatures, including some representing "several Small Familys." Gage approved the request for a stockade around the village (Gage to Edmonstone, Jan. 16, 1768, AS 73).

31. Articles Necessary for the Western Department, 1760, BP, 5:227–28 (see 352 and 628 for grain shipments from the "Cuntrey people"); Bouquet to McDonald, Apr. 10, 1762, in Stevens and Kent, *Papers of Henry Bouquet*, vol. 19, part 1, p. 69; Charles Edmonstone to Gage, Aug. 15, 1769, Gage Papers, AS 87.

32. Monckton to Bouquet, June 28, 1761, T. Hay to Bouquet, Apr. 9, 1761, and Ourry: Order to Hay, May 25, 1761, all BP, 5:174–75n4 (Christopher Lems), 587, 507–8, 401; BP, 6:531 (Hugh Reed, tavernkeeper); New Purchase Applications, 1769, Records of the Land Office, PSA, microfilm reel 1.9 (Margaret Stewart's application is #325, dated Apr. 3, 1769); A. P. James, "Early Property and Land Title Situation" (Metcalfe). For taverns see also George Washington to John Blair, May 17, 1768, in Abbott and Twohig, *Papers of George Washington*, 8:87–88.

33. Bouquet: Contract for a Tanyard, Nov. 16, 1762, BP, 6:130–31; Bouquet to Monckton, Apr. 22, 1761 (tavernkeepers), Bouquet to Monckton, Dec. 20, 1760 (need for coopers), Monckton to Bouquet, Apr. 5, 1761 (bricklayers and masons), all BP, 5:437, 182–83, 391–93. For batteaux and ship's carpenters see Gage to Murray, Mar. 14, 1766, and Baynton, Wharton, and Morgan to Gage, Mar. 17, 1766, both Gage Papers, AS 49, AS 50; BP, 5:225, 239–40, 242, 267; Keyser, "Memorials of Col. Jehu Eyre." Brumwell, *Redcoats*, shows that many British regulars were artisans before joining the army (see table 8, p. 320).

34. McDonald to Bouquet, Apr. 20, 1763, in Stevens and Kent, *Papers of Henry Bouquet*, vol. 19, part 1, p. 102 (permit to settle) (for a brief biography of McDonald see BP, 5:125n1); BP, 2:30 (Martha May); Dexter, *Diary of David McClure*, 109; Ourry to Amherst, June 22, 1763, BP, 6:247. For other examples of soldiers turned settlers see Brumwell, *Redcoats*, 290–98, 311; BP, 5:91n2, 121n3, 174–75n4, 184n2, 299n3, 316n7, 505n2, 6:75n3; New Purchase Applications, 1769, Records of the Land Office, PSA, applications 34 (Aneas MacKay) and 613 (Henry Shyrock and William Shearer). For women in the armies see Mayer, *Belonging to the Army*, chap. 1. For examples of women in British garrisons see BP, 5:278, 280, 360, 557, 6:363, 364, 366, 520–21, 627. For military settlement of the Champlain Valley see Mackillop, "More Fruitful than the Soil," 186.

35. For examples of colonists who obtained land through military license see New Purchase Applications, 1769, Records of the Land Office, PSA (microfilm reel 1.9), applications of John Campbell (#39), William Crawford (#374), Thomas Hutchins (#945), James Thompson (#1207), Jacob Toup (#3145), William Brooks (#3383), and Robert Laughlin (#3479); William Henry Egle, ed., *Minutes of the Board of Property*, PA, 3rd ser., 1:609 (*William Beaty v. Patrick Campbell*), 672 (*William Schooly v. Robert Adams*), 728 (*John Perry v. Robert Thompson*), 2:444 (*Thomas Crafts v. Henry Spiers*), 465 (*Casper Taub v. George Croghan*).

36. McDonald to Bouquet, Mar. 20, 1761, McDonald to Bouquet, Mar. 29, 1761, Ourry to Bouquet, June 17, 1761, A. McDonald to Bouquet, Apr. 15, 1762, Blane to Bouquet, June 14, 1762, all BP, 5:359, 380, 557, 6:78–79, 94–95; "Gordon's Journal, May 8, 1766–December 6, 1766," ISHLC, 291.

37. Peckham, *George Croghan's Journal*, 16–17, 23. See also SWJP, 5:560–62.

38. Mohawk Peter often acted as a messenger between the Ohio Country and the Illinois Country. See ISHLC, 16:571. For other references to Mohawk Peter see SWJP, index (vol. 14).

39. SWJP, 11:790–94 (quotes at 791).

40. "Matthew Clarkson's Diary, August 6, 1766–April 16, 1767," ISHLC, 11:357 (Aug. 30, 1766, entry); George Croghan Journal, Aug. 1, 1770, WLCL. For Murray's second expedition see Gage to Shelburne, Aug. 24, 1767, ISHLC, 11:395; Murray to Gage, May 16, June 24, 1767, Gage Papers, AS 65–66. For other British actions against illegal settlement in the early 1760s see SWJP, 12:790–94 (esp. 793). For the Fort Pitt commanders' proclamations and detachments from 1765–1767 see BP, 5:437, 844, 6:43, 71–73; PA, 1st ser., 4:251–52; MPCP, 9:353, 403, 531; SWJP, 5:492, 547–49, 12:111–12, 380; ISHLC, 11:325, 357, 582, 595.

41. Charles Edmonstone to Gage, Mar. 9, 1771, Gage Papers, AS 100; Clarkson's Diary, ISHLC, 11:357; J. W. Jordan, "Journal of James Kenny," 166; George Croghan to Gage, Aug. 8, 1770, Gage Papers, AS 94; Ellis, *History of Fayette County*, 724–25; SWJP, 6:19; Perkins, *Border Life*, 38, 104.

42. SWJP, 5:504, 12:112, 374; Gage to Captain St. John, Mar. 24, 1766, and Gage to Maj. Gen. Burton, Apr. 14, 1766, both Gage Papers, AS 50. For the uneven execution of Gage's orders see Col. John Wilkins to Gage, Jan. 8, 1767, Gage Papers, AS 61; Charles Murray to Gage, Apr. 7, 1767, Gage Papers, AS 63.

43. SWJP, 12:374.

44. MPCP, 9:414–70 (quotes at 414, 487–88); Rowe, "Frederick Stump Affair," 259–88.

45. SWJP, 6:101–2 (McKee), 110, 122, 129; MPCP, 9:422 (Penn). On Stump's escape from jail see 9:458, 462–65.

46. MPCP, 9:481–82 (Lieutenant Governor Penn's Proclamation), 483 (Commission to the Reverend Steel and Cumberland County officials). For provincial politics see PA, 8th ser., 7:6080–79.

47. MPCP, 9:506–9.

48. MPCP, 9:508.

49. MPCP, 9:514–36 (minutes of Fort Pitt Conference), 542 (Guyasutha); McConnell, *Country Between*, 244–54; D. V. Jones, *License for Empire*, 91–92; Abernethy, *Western Lands*, 35.

50. [Croghan], "Letters of George Croghan," 430; Marshall, "Sir William Johnson"; Billington, "Treaty of Fort Stanwix"; McConnell, *Country Between*, 248–54. For

the text of the treaty see DRCHNY, vol. 8. For squatters obtaining preemption rights in 1769 see Buck and Buck, *Planting of Civilization in Western Pennsylvania*, 143.

51. For Steel's list of Redstone and Monongahela Valley squatters, see MPCP, 9:508–9. Using the Records of the Land Office, tax lists, and county histories, I identified approximately thirty-four of the squatters. On the colonists' land companies and scouting trips see SWJP, 7:184–85, 1132, 8:834–35; A. F. C. Wallace, *Jefferson and the Indians*, chaps. 1–2; Hinderaker, *Elusive Empires*, 173–74; James, *George Rogers Clark Papers*, 3–9.

52. White, *Middle Ground*, 321; McConnell, *Country Between*, 237–38, 269; Gage to Barrington, Mar. 4, 1772, in Carter, *Correspondence of General Thomas Gage*, 2:600–601; MPCP, 10:71; SWJP, 8:286 (Fort Pitt expenses); "Letters of George Croghan," 433; SWJP, 8:645 (Indians "well pleased"); "Memorial of the Merchants and Inhabitants of the Town of Pittsburg and Settlements Adjacent," Nov. 24, 1772, and Croghan to Gage, Nov. 24, 1772, both Gage Papers, AS 115; Davies, *Documents of the American Revolution*, 5:44, 70, 201–3; PA, 1st ser., 4:457–58.

53. Hinderaker, *Elusive Empires*, 171; SWJP, 8:889–90, 898.

54. DRCHNY, 8:462. For murders in the spring of 1774 see PA, 1st ser., 4:495–500, 511–13, 569; DRCHNY, 8:462–65; James, *George Rogers Clark Papers*; ISHLC, 8:3–9. See also Selby, *Dunmore*, chap. 2; Skaggs, *Sixty Years' War*.

Epilogue

1. SWJP, 3:328, 647, 5:237, 8:935–36, 938; DRCHNY, 6:362, 8:405–6, 478.

2. See Tiro, "'Civil' War?" for a recent reinterpretation of the Iroquois in the Revolution. I argue that the weight of evidence indicates that the Iroquois perceived and experienced a civil war (broadly defined).

3. Pencak and Frantz, *Beyond Philadelphia*; Knouff, "Soldiers and Violence," 177–78; Sipe, *Indian Wars of Pennsylvania*, chaps. 23–28.

4. Jelles Fonda to James Clinton, Mar. 19, 1779, Fonda Papers (NYHS), folder 4. See Calloway, *American Revolution in Indian Country*; Graymont, *Iroquois in the American Revolution*; Mintz, *Seeds of Empire*.

5. SWJP, 10:571, 8:686, 11:34; Pilkington, *Journals of Samuel Kirkland*; Ronda, "Reverend Samuel Kirkland"; Guzzardo, "Superintendent and the Ministers." For violations of Stanwix see SWJP, 8:262, 1008, 1141, 1164, 12:124, 376–77, 417–18, 421, 494, 587, 674–75, 889; Moyer, *Wild Yankees*.

6. H. Z. Jones, *Palatine Families of New York*, 288–90; John Sanders Account Book, 1752; William Johnson to George Clinton, May 7, 1747, DRCHNY, 6:362, 687–88; SWJP, 1:421, 427, 438, 3:424, 4:54–55; Applications for Land Grants, NYSA, 15:111, 126, 127.

7. NYCM, July 2–5, 1754, 23:196–201; DRCHNY, 6:788 (harm); DHNY, 3:711–13; H. Z. Jones, *Palatine Families of New York*, 288–90; Williams, *Klock-Clock Genealogy*, 2–9 (on file at NYSL); John Sanders Account Book, 1752 (gristmill); May 19, 1769

(no. 29), Fonda Papers (NYSHA); John Wyman Collection (gristmill). For other evidence of Palatine-Iroquois contact see William Johnson to George Clinton, May 7, 1747, DRCHNY, 6:362, 687–88; SWJP, 1:421, 427, 438, 3:424, 4:54–55, 7:666 (boards); Applications for Land Grants, NYSA, 15:111, 126, 127. Klock paid 180 Spanish dollars, or £72 NY currency, for the land on July 5, 1754; lawyer Harmen Gansevoort's signature affirmed receipt of the money. See George Klock certificate, July 5, 1754, Gansevoort-Lansing Collection, vol. 1, 1754–1776, box 1, NYPL.

8. Virtually all studies of Sir William Johnson contrast his benevolent policies with Klock's "rascally conduct": see previous works by Stone, Flexner, Hamilton, Kelsay, Joseph Brant, and Nammack. Only Nellis, *Mohawk Dutch*, chap. 7, exonerates Klock and condemns Johnson with selective evidence.

9. NYCM, July 3, 1754, 23:197. For a few examples of Klock's ability to speak Mohawk and interpret see SWJP, 4:140, 8:1008, 13:274–75; NYCM, Mar. 21, 1763, 25:477–78.

10. George Clinton to Henry Pelham, Dec. 8, 1746, George Clinton Papers; SWJP, 3:367 (bad look); McIlwain, *Abridgment . . . by Peter Wraxall*, 185; DRCHNY, 6:879–80.

11. SWJP, 10:227, 233, 3:339, 4:55, 58, 13:274–75. For Klock's purchase of Livingston patent claims see SWJP, 3:339–40, 356, 364, 648, 4:80. For Johnson's efforts to exclude Klock and block his patenting see SWJP, 3:296, 358–39, 374, 558, 584, 595–96, 615.

12. SWJP, 10:541 (children; my emphasis), 995, 998 (rent); Council Minute, Dec. 21, 1773, Common Council Minutes, City of Albany, vol. 9, 1773–1783, roll 5; SWJP, 3:649 (twenty years), 4:54 (other Germans). For the Canajoharie tenants see Deposition of John Diffendorf, Solomon Miers, Jacob Keller, and Henry Miers, Jan. 14, 1762, Duane Papers, Legal-Misc. Box, 1666–1770. See also Kempe Papers, Misc. Microfilms, reel 49 (*The King v. George Klock*); Alexander Papers, box 48 (Court Papers); SWJP, index (vol. 14). See also SWJP, 4:657, 3:562, 584, 639, 648–49, 726, 737, 880, 945, 4:115–17, 10:216–17, 337, 367, 487, 12:345–36.

13. SWJP, 3:328 (Rogue); Flexner, *Lord of the Mohawks*, 227; Sir William Johnson to Augustine Prevost, Jan. 16, 1771, Augustine Prevost Papers (boorish). For evidence of family squabbles see SWJP, 4:194, 10:621–22 (Jacob Klock's affidavit). For Klock's legal affairs see SWJP, 8:545–49; Deed of George Klock, Sept. 28, 1771, Miscellaneous Manuscripts, 1635–1899 (AT 7003), coll. 12781; Court of Common Pleas Minutes, vol. 1, 1772–1785, transcr. Arthur Beaman, MCDHA (1773–74 entries contain references to debts owed to or by Klock). For Johnson's concern about Klock's landlordship see SWJP, 3:667.

14. SWJP, 3:328, 4:79 ("flathead"), 316–17, 177, 5:400 (Klock and Oneidas), 10:757, 799, 13:274 (Klock's party), 800 (women), 900, 4:165 (Hanyery threats). For archaeological evidence see Snow, *Mohawk Valley Archaeology*, 1:493–95 (Ganada #1); Harrington, *Two Mohawk Strongholds*, 23–26, 34–35. I am deeply grateful to historian

Anthony Wonderley for sharing his thoughts and an unpublished manuscript, "The Oriskany Battle of Oneida Hanyery and Mohawk Joseph Brant" (2003), which highlights the Oneidas' connection to George Klock. See Rooney, *Dockstader Family*, 1:1–32. For other references to Oneida cultural change see Wonderley, "1777," 45–46 (37ff. explains Oneida land claims to the western valley); Tiro, "People of the Standing Stone," chap. 1.

15. SWJP, 10:220, 227 (unbrotherlike behavior). See also DRCHNY, 8:478; SWJP, 3:647, 12:167–68. On Klock's refusals to sign a release see SWJP, 4:575, 5:492, 616; see 4:53–54 for the 1763 meeting's proceedings. Eve Pickerd, a tavernkeeper, and her grandson Cobus Maybe were two particularly troublesome settlers who lived at Canajoharie Flatts; Cobus also tried to inebriate Indians to get them to sign deeds to his land but was eventually ousted by colonial authorities (see SWJP, 4:513–14, 567, 577, 615, 5:469, 556, 493, 492–93, 11:926–27, 950–51). Cobus had some ties to Klock and may have been acting on his behalf in his attempts to defraud the Mohawks. See also Hart, "Black 'Go-Betweens,'" 106–8.

16. DRCHNY, 7:659 (proof); SWJP, 3:367 (settle). For Johnson's gift see SWJP, 3:296–97, 312, 10:248–49; DRCHNY, 6:741–45, 7:839–42, 942–43 (Mohawk gift). See SWJP, 1:421, 428–29, 3:424, 616–17, 5:237, for the conflicting claims of Johnson and Klock. See also William Johnson to George Clinton, Jan. 6, 1750, George Clinton Papers.

17. SWJP, 3:584 (no Pattent), 12:301 (Cobalt), 3:616 (condition). For Johnson's caveats and others' exclusions of Klock see SWJP, 3:419, 558, 573, 584, 595–96, 615–16, 633. For Johnson's offers of land to Banyar and Colden see SWJP, 3:583–84, 367, 373–74, 654–56.

18. SWJP, 10:574 (Difficulties), 717 (Pattent), 12:702 (barratry), 3:649, 672–64, 943; NYCM, 25:434–77; SWJP, 10:587, 717, 756, 927. For records relating to *The King v. George Klock* see Alexander Papers, box 48; Duane Papers; Kempe Papers. For the 1768 charges filed against Klock see SWJP, 6:224, 284, 743–44, 616 ("Common Disturber"), 635, 12:496–97, 698, 702; NYCM, July 29, 1767, 26:101–2; Court of Sessions Minutes, 1763–1782, Albany Hall of Records, Jan. 22, 1768, microfilm reel 74-4-17 (NYSA). Power of Attorney, George Klock and Harmen Gansevoort, June 4, 1768, Gansevoort-Lansing Collection, NYPL, reveals that Klock hired the able attorney and Canajoharie patent shareholder Harmen Gansevoort as his attorney.

19. SWJP, 8:686 (trifle), 7:201–2 (surrounded), 6:769–70 (sole use).

20. SWJP, 12:365, 539–40 (confrontation with Henry Moore). For references to Klock's political connections see SWJP, 3:288, 328, 420, 424, 374, 4:117 (Creatures), 196 (Powerfull Sett), 10:724; DRCHNY, 8:305. See SWJP, 8:1201, for Guy Johnson's perception of ineffective laws regarding Indian disputes.

21. SWJP, 8:1192 (Show), 935, 1060, 1160; NYCM, Sept. 1, 1774, Dec. 7, 1774, 26:408, 414–15; DRCHNY, 8:416; George Klock to the Governor, July 8, 1774, Brant Papers, ser. F, 2:58, Draper Manuscripts, SHSW. For Klock's earlier sponsorship of Mohawk

voyages to England see Hamell, "Mohawks Abroad"; Vaughan, *Transatlantic Encounters*. I am grateful to George Hammell for sending me a copy of his article.

22. DRCHNY, 8:474–80 (Johnson's death); SWJP, 8:1193, NYCM, Sept. 29, 1774, Dec. 7, 1774, 26:410, 26:414–15; "Speech of the Chiefs of the Canajoharie Village delivered to Col. Hendrick Fry Esq. And other Inhabitants of Conajohare y.e 6th Day Septbr 1774," "The answer of Col. Hendrick Fry," and George Klock to the Governor, Nov. 4, 1774, all Brant Papers, ser. F, 2:58–61, SHSW. See Tryon County Committee of Safety Minutes, Aug. 1774–Nov. 1775, NYSHA, 21–22, for the meeting at Frederick Bellinger's home. See also Levinson, "Explanation for the Oneida-Colonist Alliance"; Countryman, *People in Revolution*.

23. Cadwallader Colden to Guy Johnson, Aug. 22, 1774, ser. 1, folder 9, Johnson Collection; DRCHNY, 8:670–71 (Brant's speech to Lord Germain); Wonderley, "Good Peter's Narrative."

24. German Flatts Treaty, 1775, in Penrose, *Indian Affairs Papers*, 28; "Copy of Answer to the Indians Speech, May 23, 1775," and "A Speech from the People of the German Flatts to the Oneidas and Tuscaroras, June 28, 1775," both in Tryon County Miscellaneous Manuscripts, May 1774–June 1775 folder.

25. DRCHNY, 8:474–80. For New York loyalists' perspectives see Gibb, "Colonel Guy Johnson"; Ranlet, *New York Loyalists*; M. Sullivan, "Schoharie Loyalists"; Swiggett, *War out of Niagara*.

26. Joseph Brant, quoted in Kelsay, *Joseph Brant*, 336; "Journal of Joseph Bloomfield, 1776," 278.

27. On Iroquois factionalism see Parmenter, "At the Woods' Edge"; Graymont, *Iroquois in the American Revolution*, chaps. 5–6.

28. Blacksnake, quoted in Graymont, *Iroquois in the American Revolution*, 135; Foote, *Liberty March*.

29. Jacob Zimmerman, quoted in J. C. Dann, *Revolution Remembered*, 287; John Butler, quoted in Mintz, *Seeds of Empire*, 47; Seaver, *Narrative of the Life of Mrs. Mary Jemison*, 62–63; Kelsay, *Joseph Brant*, 190–92; Graymont, *Iroquois in the American Revolution*, 116, 131, 183.

30. Lt. William Barton, quoted in Graymont, *Iroquois in the American Revolution*, 213; Col. Peter Bellinger to Henry Glen, 1778, coll. 11147, NYSL; Graymont, *Iroquois in the American Revolution*, chap. 7; Kelsay, *Joseph Brant*, 214–34; Stefon, "Wyoming Valley"; Knouff, "Soldiers and Violence"; Hinman, *Onaquaga*.

31. Peter Gansevoort to Catherine Gansevoort, Aug. 6, 1779, Peter Gansevoort Military Papers, vol. 5, 1779–1780, Gansevoort-Lansing Collection, NYPL; Francis Barber letter, July 5, 1779, NYHS; "Thomas Grant's Journal of General Sullivan's Expedition from Wyoming to Genessee," July 13–Sept. 25, 1779, NYHS; Graymont, *Iroquois in the American Revolution*, 180–82, 221; Kelsay, *Joseph Brant*, 228, 254–71; Calloway, *Revolution in Indian Country*, 51–53, 108–57; Mintz, *Seeds of Empire*, 106; J. R. Fischer, *Well-Executed Failure*.

32. Sayenqueraghta, quoted in Calloway, *American Revolution in Indian Country*, 132–33; Guy Johnson, Journal of 1781, Johnson Collection, box 1, folder 30, quoted in Graymont, *Iroquois in the American Revolution*, 238; Watt, with Morrison, *Burning of the Valleys*; Kelsay, *Joseph Brant*, chap. 14. On Kanonwalohale's destruction see Wonderley, "Oneida Community in 1780," 19–20. For the Battle of Klock's Field see Watt, with Morrison, *Burning of the Valleys*.

33. A. F. C. Wallace, *Death and Rebirth of the Seneca*, chap. 7; Sewall Hopkins et al., Petition to New York State Legislature, 1800, Native American History Collection; Calloway, *American Revolution in Indian Country*, chap. 10; Lehman, "End of the Iroquois Mystique"; White, *Middle Ground*, chaps. 9–10.

34. Petition of Mohawk Indians to the New York State Legislature, Jan. 12, 1788, Miscellaneous Manuscripts, Indians, folder 3; Penrose, *Indian Affairs Papers*, 100 (threats), 121–33 (plundering); Graymont, *Iroquois in the American Revolution*, 146–48; Faux, "Iroquoian Occupation of the Mohawk Valley"; Huey and Pulis, *Molly Brant*, 46–48.

35. White, *Middle Ground*, 389–96; Hurt, *Ohio Frontier*, 91–92; P. A. W. Wallace, *Thirty Thousand Miles with John Heckewelder*, chap. 15; J. C. Dann, *Revolution Remembered*, 256–57. The story of Schoharie loyalists was communicated to me by a guide in 1999.

36. De Beauvoir, "Visit to Schenectady, 1780," 294; Edward Walsh, quoted in Kelsay, *Joseph Brant*, 19; Thomas Proctor Journal, 1791; A. F. C. Wallace, *Death and Rebirth of the Senecas*.

37. Petition of George Klock to Governor of New York, Apr. 26, 1785, Indorsed Land Papers, NYSA, 37:148; Oneida Sachems to William Colebreath, Aug. 6, 1792, Huntington Manuscripts, 13426; SWJP, 8:1192 ("old Antagonist"). For Klock's post-Revolution land negotiations in Canajoharie see Van Vechten Family Papers, 1678–1880, boxes 1–2; Applications for Land Grants, NYSA, 37:148, 42:117, 45:125; Indenture between Jacob Reed and Conrad Klock, Johan Jost Klock, and Johannes Klock, [Aug. 4, 1794(?)], Schuyler Papers, box 15, reel 7, NYPL; Fort Klock Papers. For other land papers related to Klock's lands north of Canajoharie see Applications for Land Grants, NYSA, May 13, 1784 (16:7), July 3, 1786 (42:117), Dec. 22, 1787 (42:125). For the Oneidas' land negotiations in the 1780s and 1790s see Wonderley, "Good Peter's Narrative"; Tiro, "People of the Standing Stone"; Schuyler Papers, box 15, reel 7A, NYPL; A. Taylor, *Divided Ground*.

38. Speech of Congress to the Six Nations, 1775, Schuyler Papers, Indian Papers, box 13, NYPL.

Bibliography

Manuscript Collections and Unpublished Sources

Albany County Hall of Records, Albany, New York
    Common Council Minutes, City of Albany, 1723–1745, 1773–1783
Albany Institute of History and Art (AIHA)
    Account Books, Eighteenth Century
Albany Revolution War Papers, 1775–1779
    Johannes Rutgers Bleecker Papers, 1738–1753
    Jelles Fonda Papers
    Milton Hamilton Papers, 1911–1987
    Minutes of the Commissioners for Indian Affairs, 1746–1780
    Augustine Prevost Papers
Archives Nationales du Quebec, Montreal
    Archives Judiciaires, Pièces Detachées
Beinecke Library Manuscript and Rare Book Room, Yale University, New Haven, Connecticut.
    Guy Johnson Collection
Hamilton College Library Archives, Clinton, New York
    Samuel Kirkland Papers
Henry E. Huntington Library, San Marino, California
    Huntington Manuscripts (3049, 8172, 13426, 20280, 22693)
Historical Society of Pennsylvania, Philadelphia (HSP)
    Berks and Montgomery Counties, Misc. Manuscripts, 1693–1869

Penn Manuscripts, Official Correspondence
Thomas Penn Papers
Richard Peters Letterbooks, 1737–1750
Richard Peters Papers, 1699–1845
Conrad Weiser Papers
Montgomery County Department of History and Archives, Fonda, New York (MCDHA)
Genealogical Collection
Transcripts of Records of Lutheran Trinity Church (Stone Arabia NY) and St. Paul's Evangelical Lutheran Church (Schoharie NY)
Tryon County Court of Common Pleas Minutes Transcripts
Tryon Court of Sessions Minutes Transcripts
National Archives of Canada, Ottawa (NAC)
Archives Nationales (Paris), Fonds des Colonies, microfilm
Claus Family Papers, 1727–1886
Minutes of the Albany Commissioners for Indian Affairs, microfilm
Haldimand Papers, Series B
New-York Historical Society (NYHS)
Albany County Manuscripts, Canajohary Box
James Alexander Papers
Goldsbrow Banyar Papers
George Clinton Correspondence, 1762–1812
Duane Papers
Jelles Fonda Papers
Thomas Gage Papers
Daniel Horsmanden Papers, 1714–1747
John Tabor Kempe Papers
Archibald Kennedy Papers, 1715–1758
John Henry Lydius Papers
Miscellaneous Manuscripts, Indians
Miscellaneous Manuscripts, Kayaderosseras
Records of Mohawk Indians at Fort Hunter, New York
Sanders Family Papers
Leonard Spaulding. Diary, 1758
Tryon County Court of Common Pleas Records, 1772–1784
Tryon County Miscellaneous Manuscripts, 1774–1794
Evert Wendell, Account Books, 1695–1726, 1708–1758
New York Public Library, New York City (NYPL)
Gansevoort-Lansing Collection
Loyalist Transcripts
Philip Schuyler Papers, 1684–1851

New York State Archives, Albany (NYSA)
> Indian Treaties and Deeds, 1766–1811 (A0448)
> Letters Patent, 1664–1990 (12943)
> New York Colonial Manuscripts, 1638–1800 (A1894)
> New York Council Minutes, 1668–1783 (A1895)
> Records of Deeds, 1640–1884 (A0453)

New York State Historical Association, Cooperstown (NYSHA)
> Jelles Fonda Papers, 1750–1791
> Henry Glen Papers
> Charles Stewart Papers
> John Wyman Collection, Tryon County Court Papers

New York State Library, Albany (NYSL)
> Abbott Collection (BA9691)
> Hermanus Bleecker Papers, 1715–1872
> Rutger Bleecker Papers, 1741–1862 (GO 11846)
> Joseph Brant Letters
> Campbell Family Papers, 1707–1907 (EP 11062)
> Jelles Fonda Papers, 1697–1828 (SC7026)
> Samuel Ludlow Frey Papers, 1706–1912 (SC9829)
> Jacob Glen Papers, 1828–1917 (SC18229)
> Thomas Grant Journal, 1779 (16660)
> Rufus Alexander Grider Scrapbooks
> William T. Hanson, Colonial Manuscript Collection, 1709–1833 (AU7002)
> Sir William Johnson Manuscripts, 1746–1779 (SC7005)
> Sherman O. Klock Collection (SC11170)
> Jonathan Lawrence Diary, 1777 (13419)
> Miscellaneous Manuscripts, 1635–1899 (AT 7003)
> John Ogilvie Diary, 1750–1759 (12878)
> Thomas Proctor Journal, 1791 (1791)
> St. Peter's Episcopal Church Records, 1708–1915 (SC19680)
> Sullivan Campaign Collection, 1779 (HS 12326)
> Transcripts of American Loyalist Claims, microfilm
> Van Vechten Family Papers, 1678–1880 (SC15213)
> Abraham Verplanck Papers, 1758–1784 (SC17169)

Pennsylvania State Archives, Harrisburg (PSA)
> Cumberland County Tax Lists
> Fort Pitt Museum Collection, MG-193, microfilm
> Joseph Shippen, Orderly Book, 1758, microfilm

State Historical Society of Wisconsin, Madison (SHSW)
> Lyman Copeland Draper Manuscript Collection, microfilm
> > Brant Papers, Series F, microfilm

William L. Clements Library, University of Michigan, Ann Arbor (WLCL)
    Jeffery Amherst Papers, 1758–1764
    Canada Manuscripts, 1682–1727
    George Clinton Papers, 1697–1759
    George Croghan Journal
    Jonathan French Journal, 1757
    Thomas Gage Papers, 1754–1783, American Series
    Jehu Hay Diary, 1763–1765
    Miscellaneous Manuscripts, 1570–1938
    Native American History Collection
        Minutes of the Albany Commissioners for Indian Affairs, 1753–1755
    Schoff Revolutionary War Collection
    Shelburne Papers, 1663–1797
    Warren Papers, 1744–1751

Published Sources

Abbot, W. W., and Dorothy Twohig, eds. *The Papers of George Washington, Colonial Series.* 10 vols. Charlottesville: University Press of Virginia, 1983–94.

Abernethy, Thomas P. *Western Lands and the American Revolution.* New York: Russell & Russell, 1959.

"An Account of the Famine among the Indians of the North and West Branch of the Susquehanna, in the Summer of 1748." PMHB 16 (1892): 430–32.

Adair, E. R. "Montreal under the French Regime." *Canadian Historical Association Report* (1942): 20–41.

Adams, Nick. "Iroquois Settlement at Fort Frontenac in the Seventeenth and Early Eighteenth Centuries." *Ontario Archaeology* 46, no. 4 (1986): 5–20.

Adelman, Jeremy, and Stephen Aron. "From Borderlands to Borders: Empires, Nation-States, and the Peoples in Between in North American History." *American Historical Review* 104 (June 1999): 814–41.

Adler, Jeanne Winston, ed. *Chainbreaker's War: A Seneca Chief Remembers the American Revolution.* Hensonville NY: Black Dome Press, 2002.

Alderfer, E. G. *The Ephrata Commune: An Early American Counterculture.* Pittsburgh: University of Pittsburgh Press, 1985.

Alfred, Gerald. *Heeding the Voices of Our Ancestors: Kahnawake Mohawk Politics and the Rise of Native Nationalism.* Toronto: Oxford University Press, 1995.

Alvord, Clarence Walworth, and Clarence Edwin Carter, eds. *Collections of the Illinois State Historical Library.* Vol. 11, *The New Regime, 1765–1767.* Springfield: Illinois State Historical Library, 1921.

Anderson, Fred. *Crucible of War: The Seven Years' War and the Fate of Empire in British North America, 1754–1766.* New York: Alfred A. Knopf, 2000.

Aquila, Richard. *The Iroquois Restoration: Iroquois Diplomacy on the Colonial Frontier, 1701–1754*. Lincoln: University of Nebraska Press, 1983.

Armitage, Susan. "Everyday Encounters: Indians and the White Woman in the Palouse." *Pacific Northwest Forum* 7 (Summer–Fall 1982): 27–30.

Armour, David Arthur. *The Merchants of Albany, New York, 1686–1760*. New York: Garland, 1986.

Aron, Stephen. *How the West Was Lost: The Transformation of Kentucky from Daniel Boone to Henry Clay*. Baltimore: Johns Hopkins University Press, 1996.

———. "Pigs and Hunters: 'Rights in the Woods' on the Trans-Appalachian Frontier." In Cayton and Teute, *Contact Points*, 175–204.

Aspinwall Papers. *Massachusetts Historical Society Collections*, 4th ser., vol. 9.

Aubry, Claude. *The Magic Fiddler and Other Legends of French Canada*. Trans. Alice E. Kane. Toronto: Peter Martin, 1968.

Axtell, James. *After Columbus: Essays in the Ethnohistory of Colonial North America*. Oxford: Oxford University Press, 1988.

———. *The European and the Indian: Essays in the Ethnohistory of Colonial North America*. Oxford: Oxford University Press, 1981.

———. *The Invasion Within: The Contest of Cultures in Colonial North America*. Oxford: Oxford University Press, 1985.

———. *Natives and Newcomers: The Cultural Origins of North America*. Oxford: Oxford University Press, 2000.

Bailyn, Bernard. *Voyagers to the West: A Passage in the Peopling of America on the Eve of the Revolution*. New York: Vintage Books, 1986.

Bailyn, Bernard, and Philip D. Morgan, eds. *Strangers within the Realm: Cultural Margins of the First British Empire*. Chapel Hill: University of North Carolina Press, 1991.

Baker, C. Alice. *True Stories of New England Captives Carried to Canada during the Old French and Indian Wars*. Greenfield MA: E. A. Hall, 1897.

Balvay, Arnaud. "Les rélations entre soldats français et Amérindiens: La question de la traite (1683–1763)." *Recherches amérindiennes au Quebec* 35, no. 2 (2005): 17–27.

Barr, Daniel P., ed. *The Boundaries between Us: Natives and Newcomers along the Frontiers of the Old Northwest Territory, 1750–1850*. Kent OH: Kent State University Press, 2006.

Barsotti, John J., ed. *Scoouwa: James Smith's Indian Captivity Narrative*. Columbus: Ohio Historical Society, 1996.

Bartram, John. *Observations on the Inhabitants, Climate, Soil, Rivers, Productions, Animals, and Other Matters Worthy of Notice Made by Mr. John Bartram in His Travels from Pensilvania to Onondaga, Oswego, and the Lake Ontario, in Canada*. London: Whiston and White, 1751.

Bartram, John, Lewis Evans, and Conrad Weiser. *A Journey from Pennsylvania to Onondaga in 1743*. With an Introduction by Whitfield J. Bell Jr. Barre MA: Imprint Society, 1973.

Bates, Samuel P., and J. Fraise Richard. *History of Franklin County, Pennsylvania*. Chicago: Warner, Beers & Co., 1887.

Beauchamp, William M. "Aboriginal Place Names of New York." *New York State Museum Bulletin* 108 (May 1907): 6–333.

———, ed. *Moravian Journals Relating to Central New York, 1745–66*. Syracuse: Dehler Press, 1916.

Beaulieu, Alain, and Roland Viau. *La Grande Paix: Chronique d'une saga diplomatique*. Montreal: Éditions Libre Expression, 2001.

Béchard, Henri. *The Original Caughnawaga Indians*. Montreal: International Publishers, 1976.

———. "Gandeacteau." DCB, 1:321–22.

———. "Togouiroui." DCB, 1:650–51.

———. "Tonsahoten." DCB, 1:651.

Becker, Marshall J. "Hannah Freeman: An Eighteenth-Century Lenape Living and Working among Colonial Farmers." *PMHB* 114 (April 1990): 249–70.

Benson, Adolph B., ed. *Peter Kalm's Travels in North America: The English Version of 1770*. New York: Dover Publications, 1987.

Benton, Nathaniel S. *History of Herkimer County, Including the Upper Mohawk Valley, From the Earliest Period to the Present Time*. Albany: J. Munsell, 1856.

Berkeley, Edmund, and Dorothy Smith Berkeley, eds. *The Correspondence of John Bartram, 1734–1777*. Gainesville: University Press of Florida, 1992.

Berthoff, Rowland, and John M. Murrin. "Feudalism, Communalism, and the Yeoman Freeholder: The American Revolution Considered as Social Accident." In *Essays on the American Revolution*, ed. Stephen G. Kurtz and James H. Hutson, 256–88. New York: W. W. Norton, 1973.

Billington, Ray A. "The Treaty of Fort Stanwix of 1768." *New York History* 24 (Spring 1944): 182–94.

Blanchard, David. "Patterns of Tradition and Change: The Re-Creation of Iroquois Culture at Kahnawake." PhD diss., University of Chicago, 1982.

———. "The Seven Nations of Canada: An Alliance and a Treaty." *American Indian Culture and Research Journal* 7 (1983): 3–23.

Blessing, Tim H. "The Upper Juniata Valley." In Pencak and Frantz, *Beyond Philadelphia*, 153–70.

Bodle, Wayne. "The Fabricated Region: On the Insufficiency of 'Colonies' for Understanding American Colonial History." *Early American Studies* (2003): 1–27.

———. "The 'Myth of the Middle Colonies' Reconsidered: The Process of Regionalization in Early America." *PMHB* 113 (October 1989): 527–48.

———. "Themes and Directions in Middle Colonies Historiography, 1980–1994." *WMQ* 51 (July 1994): 355–88.

Bond, Beverley W., ed. "The Captivity of Charles Stuart, 1755–57." *Mississippi Valley Historical Review* 13 (June 1926): 58–81.

Bond, Richmond P. *Queen Anne's American Kings*. Oxford: Clarendon Press, 1952.

Bonomi, Patricia U. *A Factious People: Politics and Society in Colonial New York*. New York: Columbia University Press, 1971.

Boyd, Julian P., ed. *Indian Treaties Printed by Benjamin Franklin, 1736–1762*. Intro. Carl Van Doren. Philadelphia: Historical Society of Pennsylvania, 1938.

Boyd, Thomas. *Simon Girty: The White Savage*. New York: Minton, Balch & Company, 1939.

Bragdon, Kathleen J. *The Native People of Southern New England, 1500–1650*. Norman: University of Oklahoma Press, 1996.

Brandão, José António. *"Your Fyre Shall Burn No More": Iroquois Policy toward New France and Its Native Allies to 1701*. Lincoln: University of Nebraska Press, 1997.

Brandão, José António, and William Starna. "'Some Things May Slip Out of Your Memory and Be Forgott': The 1701 Deed and Map of Iroquois Hunting Territory Revised." *New York History* 86 (Fall 2005): 417–34.

———. "The Treaties of 1701: A Triumph of Iroquois Diplomacy." *Ethnohistory* 43 (Spring 1996): 209–44.

Brasser, T. J. "Mahican." In Trigger, *Northeast*, 198–212.

Breen, T. H. "Creative Adaptations: Peoples and Cultures." In *Colonial British America: Essays in the New History of the Early Modern Era*, ed. Jack Greene and J. R. Pole, 195–232. Baltimore: Johns Hopkins University Press, 1984.

Breton, Arthur J. *A Guide to the Manuscript Collections of the New-York Historical Society*. 2 vols. Westport CT: Greenwood Press, 1972.

Brewster, William. *The Pennsylvania and New York Frontier: History of from 1720 to the Close of the Revolution*. Philadelphia: George S. McManus Company, 1954.

Bridenbaugh, Carl, ed. "Patrick M'Robert's Tour through Part of the North Provinces of America." PMHB 59 (April 1935): 134–80.

Brooks, James. *Captives and Cousins: Slavery, Kinship, and Community in the Southwest Borderlands*. Chapel Hill: University of North Carolina Press, 2002.

Brown, George, et al., eds. *Dictionary of Canadian Biography*. 14 vols. to date. Toronto: University of Toronto Press, 1966–98.

Brown, John M. *Brief Sketch of the First Settlement of the County of Schoharie by the Germans*. 1823. Reprint, Cornwallville NY: Hope Farm Press, 1981.

Brown, Richard Maxwell. "Back Country Rebellions and the Homestead Ethic in America, 1740–1799." In *Tradition, Conflict, and Modernization: Perspectives on the American Revolution*, ed. Richard Maxwell Brown and Don E. Fehrenbacher, 73–99. New York: Academic Press, 1977.

Brumwell, Stephen. *Redcoats: The British Soldier and War in the Americas, 1755–1763*. Cambridge: Cambridge University Press, 2002.

———. *White Devil: A True Story of Savagery and Vengeance in Colonial America*. Cambridge MA: DaCapo Press, 2004.

Buck, Solon J., and Elizabeth Hawthorn Buck. *The Planting of Civilization in Western Pennsylvania*. Pittsburgh: University of Pittsburgh Press, 1939.

Burch, Wanda. "Sir William Johnson and Eighteenth-Century Medicine in the New York Colony." In *Medicine and Health: 1990 Proceedings of the Dublin Seminar for New England Folklife*, ed. Peter Benes, 55–65. Boston: Boston University, 1990.

———. "Sir William Johnson's Cabinet of Curiosities." *New York History* 71 (1990): 261–82.

Burke, Thomas E. *Mohawk Frontier: The Dutch Community of Schenectady, New York, 1661–1710*. Ithaca: Cornell University Press, 1991.

Burnaby, Andrew. *Travels through the Middle Settlements in North-America in the Years 1759 and 1760. With Observations on the State of the Colonies*. London: T. Payne, 1775.

Butler, John. *Awash in a Sea of Faith: Christianizing the American People*. Cambridge: Harvard University Press, 1990.

Butterfield, Consul Willshire. *History of the Girtys*. Cincinnati: Robert Clark & Co., 1890.

Calloway, Colin G. *The American Revolution in Indian Country: Crisis and Diversity in Native American Communities*. Cambridge: Cambridge University Press, 1995.

———. *Dawnland Encounters: Indians and Europeans in Northern New England*. Hanover: University Press of New England, 1991.

———. *First Peoples: A Documentary Survey of American Indian History*. New York: Bedford/St. Martin's, 1999.

———. *New Worlds for All: Indians, Europeans, and the Remaking of Early America*. Baltimore: Johns Hopkins University Press, 1997.

———. *The Scratch of a Pen: 1763 and the Transformation of North America*. Oxford: Oxford University Press, 2006.

———. *The Western Abenakis of Vermont, 1600–1800: War, Migration, and the Survival of a Native People*. Norman: University of Oklahoma Press, 1990.

Camenzind, Krista. "Violence, Race, and the Paxton Boys." In Pencak and Richter, *Friends and Enemies in Penn's Woods*, 201–20.

Campbell, William W. *Annals of Tryon County; or, The Border Wars of New-York, During the Revolution*. New York: J & J Harper, 1831.

Campeau, Lucien. "Luc-François Nau." DCB, 3:480–81.

Campisi, Jack. "Oneida." In Trigger, *Northeast*, 481–90.

Campisi, Jack, and Laurence M. Hauptman, eds. *The Oneida Indian Experience: Two Perspectives*. Syracuse: Syracuse University Press, 1988.

Cardy, Michael. "A French Officer among the Iroquois in the Early 18th Century." *North Dakota Quarterly* 55 (Summer 1987): 144–56.

Carter, Clarence Edward, ed. *The Correspondence of General Thomas Gage with the Secretaries of State, 1763–1775*. 2 vols. New Haven: Yale University Press, 1931–33.

Casgrain, H. S., ed. *Collection des Manuscrits du Marechal de Lévis*. Vol. 11, *Guerre du*

Canada: Relations et Journaux de Différentes Expéditions Faites Durant Les Années 1755–56–57–58–59–60. Quebec: L.-J. Demers & Frère, 1895.

Cassell, Abraham H., ed. "Notes on the Iroquois and Delaware Indians." Trans. Helen Bell. PMHB 1 (1877): 163–67, 319–23, 2 (1878): 407–10.

Cavaioli, Frank J. "A Profile of the Paxton Boys: Murderers of the Conestoga Indians." *Journal of the Lancaster County Historical Society* 87, no. 3 (1983): 74–96.

Cayton, Andrew R. L., and Fredrika Teute, eds. *Contact Points: American Frontiers from the Mohawk Valley to the Mississippi, 1750–1830.* Chapel Hill: University of North Carolina Press, 1998.

Charlevoix, Pierre de. *Journal of a Voyage to North America* (London, 1761). March of America Facsimile Series, no. 36. Ann Arbor: University Microfilms, 1966.

Choquette, Leslie. *Frenchmen into Peasants: Modernity and Tradition in the Peopling of French Canada.* Cambridge: Harvard University Press, 1997.

[Claus, Daniel]. *Daniel Claus' Narrative of His Relations with Sir William Johnson and Experiences in the Lake George Fight.* New York: Society of Colonial Wars, 1904.

Colden, Cadwallader. *The History of the Five Indian Nations Depending on the Province of New-York in America.* Ithaca: Cornell University Press, 1994.

Colden, Cadwallader. Papers. In *Collections of the New-York Historical Society.* Vols. 9–10, 50–58, 67–68. New York: New-York Historical Society, 1876–77, 1918–25, 1934–35.

Coleman, Emma Lewis. *New England Captives Carried to Canada Between 1677 and 1760 during the French and Indian Wars.* 2 vols. Portland ME: Southworth Press, 1925.

Colley, Charles C. "Indians in Colonial Pennsylvania: Historical Interpretations." *Indian Historian* 7 (Winter 1974): 2–5.

Coolidge, Guy Omeron. "The French Occupation of the Champlain Valley from 1609 to 1759." *Vermont Historical Society Proceedings* 6, no. 3 (1938): 143–311.

Cossette, Joseph. "Pierre de Lauzon." DCB, 3:360–61.

[Cresswell, Nicholas]. *The Journal of Nicholas Cresswell, 1774–1777.* New York: Dial Press, 1924.

Crèvecoeur, J. Hector St. John de. *Letters from an American Farmer and Sketches of Eighteenth-Century America.* Ed. Albert E. Stone. New York: Penguin Books, 1981.

———. *Travels in Northern Pennsylvania and the State of New York.* Trans. Clarissa Spencer Bostelmann. Ann Arbor: University of Michigan Press, 1964.

[Croghan, George]. "Letters of George Croghan." PMHB 15, no. 4 (1891): 429–39.

Cronon, William. *Changes in the Land: Indians, Colonists, and the Ecology of New England.* New York: Hill and Wang, 1983.

———. "Revisiting the Vanishing Frontier: The Legacy of Frederick Jackson Turner." *Western Historical Quarterly* 18 (April 1987): 157–76.

Cronon, William, George Miles, and Jay Gitlin, eds. *Under an Open Sky: Rethinking America's Western Past.* New York: W. W. Norton, 1992.

Countryman, Edward. *A People in Revolution: The American Revolution and Political Society in New York, 1760–1790*. New York: W. W. Norton, 1981.

Cutliffe, Stephen J. "Colonial Indian Policy as a Measure of Rising Imperialism: New York and Pennsylvania, 1700–1755." *WPAHM* 64 (July 1981): 237–68.

———. "Sideling Hill Affair: The Cumberland County Riots of 1765." *WPAHM* 59 (January 1976): 39–53.

Dann, Catharine Christie. "Kittanning Destroyed." Unpublished manuscript, 1998. In author's possession.

Dann, John C., ed. *The Revolution Remembered: Eyewitness Accounts of the War for Independence*. Chicago: University of Chicago Press, 1980.

Danvers, Gail D. "Gendered Encounters: Warriors, Women, and William Johnson." *Journal of American Studies* 35 (2001): 187–202.

Darlington, William M., ed. *Christopher Gist's Journals*. New York: Argonaut Press, 1966.

Davies, K. G., ed. *Documents of the American Revolution 1770–1783*. 19 vols. Dublin: Irish University Press, 1972–81.

Dawson, Samuel Edward. *The Saint Lawrence Basin and Its Borderlands: Being the Story of their Discovery, Exploration, and Occupation*. London: Lawrence and Bullen, 1905.

de Beauvoir, Francois-Jean, Marquis de Chastellux. "Visit to Schenectady, 1780." In Snow, Gehring, and Starna, *In Mohawk Country*, 292–94.

Dechêne, Louise. *Habitants and Merchants in Seventeenth-Century Montreal*. Trans. Liana Vardi. Montreal: McGill-Queen's University Press, 1992.

Delâge, Denys. "Les Iroquois chrétiens des réductions, 1667–1760." *Recherches amérindiennes au Québec* 21, nos. 1–2 (1991): 59–70.

———. "Les Iroquois chrétiens des réductions, 1667–1770: Rapports avec la Ligue Iroquoise, les Britanniques, et les autres nations autochtones." *Recherches amérindiennes au Quebec* 21, no. 2 (1991): 39–50.

Delâge, Denys, and Étienne Gilbert. "Les Amérindiens face à la justice coloniale française dans le gouvernement de Québec, 1663–1759: I-Les crimes capitaux et leur châtiments." *Recherches amérindiennes au Quebec* 33, no. 3 (2003): 79–90.

———. "Les Amérindiens face à la justice coloniale française dans le gouvernement de Québec, 1663–1759: II-Eau de vie, traite des fourrures, endettement, affaires civiles." *Recherches amérindiennes au Quebec* 33, no. 1 (2004): 31–41.

Delâge, Denys, and Jean-Pierre Sawaya. *Les traités des Sept-Feux aves les britanniques: Droits et pièges d'un heritage colonial au Québec*. Sillery PQ: Septentrion, 2001.

Delisle, Steven. *The Equipment of New France Militia, 1740–1760*. Bel Air MD: Kebeca Liber Ata, 1998.

Demos, John. *The Unredeemed Captive: A Family Story from Early America*. New York: A. A. Knopf, 1994.

Dennis, Matthew. *Cultivating a Landscape of Peace: Iroquois-European Encounters in Seventeenth-Century America*. Ithaca: Cornell University Press, 1993.

Desbarats, Catherine. "The Cost of Early Canada's Native Alliances: Reality and Scarcity's Rhetoric." *WMQ* 52 (October 1995): 609–30.

Devine, E. J. *Historic Caughnawaga*. Montreal: Messenger Press, 1922.

Dexter, Franklin B., ed. *Diary of David McClure, Doctor of Divinity, 1748–1820*. New York: Knickerbocker Press, 1899. Reprint, Waterville OH: Rettig's Frontier Ohio, 1996.

"Diary of J. Martin Mack's, David Zeisberger's and Gottfried Rundt's Journey to Onondaga in 1752." In *Moravian Journals Relating to Central New York, 1745–66*, ed. William M. Beauchamp, 112–20. Syracuse: Dehler Press, 1916.

"Diary of Rev. Eli Forbes" *Massachusetts Historical Society Proceedings*, 2nd ser., vol. 7 (1892): 384–99.

Dickason, Olive Patricia. *Canada's First Nations: A History of Founding Peoples from Earliest Times*. Norman: University of Oklahoma Press, 1992.

———. "From 'One Nation' in the Northeast to 'New Nation' in the Northwest: A Look at the Emergence of the Métis." In *The New Peoples: Being and Becoming Métis in North America*, ed. Jacqueline Peterson and Jennifer S. H. Brown, 19–35. Lincoln: University of Nebraska Press, 1985.

Dickinson, John A., and Jan Grabowski. "Les populations amérindiennes de la vallée laurentienne, 1608–1765." *Annales de démographie historique* (1993): 51–65.

DiVirgilio, Justin. "Rum Punch and Cultural Revolution: The Impact of the Seven Years' War in Albany." *New York History* 86 (Fall 2005): 435–50.

Doblin, Helga, and William A. Starna, eds. *The Journals of Christian Daniel Claus and Conrad Weiser: A Journey to Onondaga, 1750*. Philadelphia: American Philosophical Society, 1994.

Doddridge, Joseph. *Notes on the Settlement and Indian Wars*. Pittsburgh: John S. Ritenour and William T. Lindsey, 1912.

Donehoo, George P. *A History of the Indian Villages and Place Names in Pennsylvania*. 1928. Reprint, Baltimore: Gateway Press, 1995.

Douville, Raymond. "Jacques Hertel de la Fresnière." *DCB*, 1:386–87.

——— "Jean-Baptiste Hertel de Rouville." *DCB*, 2:284–86.

———. "Joseph-François Hertel de la Fresnière." *DCB*, 2:282–84.

Douville, Raymond, and Jacques Casanova. *Daily Life in Early Canada*. Trans. Carola Congreve. New York: Macmillan, 1967.

Dowd, Gregory Evans. "The Panic of 1751: The Significance of Rumors on the South Carolina-Cherokee Frontier." *WMQ* 53 (July 1996): 527–60.

———. *A Spirited Resistance: The North American Indian Struggle for Unity, 1745–1815*. Baltimore: Johns Hopkins University Press, 1992.

———. *War under Heaven: Pontiac, the Indian Nations and the British Empire*. Baltimore: Johns Hopkins University Press, 2002.

Dubois, Paul-André. *De l'oreille au coeur: Naissance du chant religieux en langues amérindiennes dans les missions de Nouvelle-France, 1600–1650*. Sillery PQ: Septentrion, 1997.

Dumouchel, Jean-François. "Calumet de paix, un objet de contacts: étude et analyse d'une pipe amérindienne." *Recherches amérindiennes au Quebec* 35, no. 2 (2005): 29–37.

Dunbar, John R., ed. *The Paxton Papers.* The Hague: Martinus Nijhoff, 1957.

Dunn, Richard S., and Mary Maples Dunn, eds. *The World of William Penn.* Philadelphia: University of Pennsylvania Press, 1986.

Dutrizac, Charles Desmond. "Local Identity and Authority in a Disputed Hinterland: The Pennsylvania-Maryland Border in the 1730s." *PMHB* 115 (January 1991): 35–62.

"An Early Record of Pittsburgh." *PMHB* 2, no. 3 (1878): 303–5.

Eccles, W. J. *The Canadian Frontier, 1534–1760.* Rev. ed. Albuquerque: University of New Mexico Press, 1969.

———. *Essays on New France.* Toronto: Oxford University Press, 1987.

———. *France in America.* Rev. ed. East Lansing: Michigan State University Press, 1990.

Elliott, Dolores. "Otsiningo, An Example of an Eighteenth Century Settlement Pattern." In *Current Perspectives in Northeastern Anthropology: Essays in Honor of William A. Ritchie,* ed. Robert E. Funk and Charles F. Hayes III. *Researches and Transactions of the New York State Archaeological Association* 17, no. 1 (1977): 93–105.

Ellis, Franklin, ed. *History of Fayette County, Pennsylvania, With Biographical Sketches of Many of its Pioneers and Prominent Men.* Philadelphia: L. H. Everts & Co., 1882.

Ellis, Franklin, and Samuel Evans. *History of Lancaster County, Pennsylvania, with Biographical Sketches of many of its Pioneers and Prominent Men.* Philadelphia: Everts & Peck, 1883.

Engelbrecht, William. *Iroquoia: The Development of a Native World.* Syracuse: Syracuse University Press, 2003.

Faragher, John Mack. "Americans, Mexicans, and Métis: A Community Approach to the Comparative Study of North American Frontiers." In *Under an Open Sky: Rethinking America's Western Past,* ed. William Cronon, George Miles, and Jay Gitlin, 90–109. New York: W. W. Norton, 1992.

———. *Daniel Boone: The Life and Legend of an American Pioneer.* New York: Henry Holt, 1992.

Faux, David K. "Iroquoian Occupation of the Mohawk Valley during and after the Revolution." *Man in the Northeast* 34 (Fall 1987): 27–39.

Feeley, Stephen D. "Tuscarora Trails: Indian Migrations, War, and Constructions of Colonial Frontiers." PhD diss., College of William and Mary, 2007.

Feister, Lois M. "Indian-Dutch Relations in the Upper Hudson Valley: A Study of Baptism Records in the Dutch Reformed Church, Albany, N.Y." *Man in the Northeast* 24 (Fall 1982): 89–113.

Feister, Lois M., and Bonnie Pulis. "Molly Brant: Her Domestic and Political Roles in Eighteenth-Century New York." In Grumet, *Northeastern Indian Lives,* 295–320.

Fenton, William N. "The Concept of Locality and the Program of Iroquois Research." In "Symposium on Local Diversity in Iroquois Culture," ed. William N. Fenton, 3–12. *Smithsonian Institution Bureau of American Ethnology Bulletin*, no. 149. Washington DC: Government Printing Office, 1951.

———. *The Great Law and the Longhouse: A Political History of the Iroquois Confederacy.* Norman: University of Oklahoma Press, 1998.

———. "Joseph-François Lafitau." DCB, 3:334–38.

———, ed. "Symposium on Local Diversity in Iroquois Culture." *Smithsonian Institution Bureau of American Ethnology Bulletin*, no. 149. Washington DC: Government Printing Office, 1951.

Fenton, William N., and Elisabeth Tooker. "Mohawk." In Trigger, Northeast, 466–80.

Ferguson, John P. "Reported Missing: One Iroquois Village." *Schoharie County Historical Review* 46 (Fall–Winter 1982): 28–30.

———. "The Schoharie Iroquois?" *Schoharie County Historical Review* 48 (Fall–Winter 1984): 14–18.

Fernow, Berthold, comp. *New York (Colony) Council: Calendar of Council Minutes, 1668–1783.* Harrison NY: Harbor Hill Books, 1987.

Fischer, David Hackett. *Albion's Seed: Four British Folkways in America.* New York: Oxford University Press, 1989.

———. *Paul Revere's Ride.* Oxford: Oxford University Press, 1994.

Fischer, Joseph R. *A Well Executed Failure: The Sullivan Campaign against the Iroquois, July-September 1779.* Columbia: University of South Carolina Press, 1997.

Flexner, James Thomas. *Lord of the Mohawks: A Biography of Sir William Johnson.* Rev. ed. Boston: Little, Brown and Company, 1979.

Fogleman, Aaron Spencer. *Hopeful Journeys: German Immigration, Settlement, and Political Culture in Colonial America, 1717–1775.* Philadelphia: University of Pennsylvania Press, 1996.

Foote, Allan D. *Liberty March: The Battle of Oriskany.* Utica NY: North Country Books, 1998.

Forbes, L'abbe G. "Les Iroquois de Caughnawaga." *Bulletin des recherches historiques* 6, no. 4 (1900): 116–17.

Force, Peter, ed. *American Archives.* 9 vols. Washington DC, 1837–53.

Fort Klock Papers, 1762–1845. St. Johnsville NY: Enterprise and News, 1937.

Fox, Edith M. *Land Speculation in the Mohawk Country.* Ithaca: Cornell University Press, 1949.

Fralish, John Cecil, Jr. *Index of Names in the Tax Lists of Cumberland County, Pennsylvania, For Certain Years, 1758–1767.* Carlisle PA: Cumberland County Historical Society, 1977.

Franquet, Louis. *Voyages et Mémoires sur le Canada.* Montreal: Éditions Elysée, 1974.

Franz, George W. *Paxton: A Study of Community Structure and Mobility in the Colonial Pennsylvania Backcountry.* New York: Garland, 1989.

Frazier, Patrick. *The Mohicans of Stockbridge.* Lincoln: University of Nebraska Press, 1992.

Frégault, Guy. *Canada: The War of the Conquest.* Trans. Margaret M. Cameron. Toronto: Oxford University Press, 1969.

Frisch, Jack. "John Tarbell." DCB, 3:615.

Frothingham, Washington. *History of Fulton County.* Syracuse: D. Mason & Co., 1892.

Gallup, Andrew, ed. *Memoir of a French and Indian War Soldier: "Jolicoeur" Charles Bonin.* Westminster MD: Heritage Books, 2005.

Gelinas, Cyrille. *The Role of Fort Chambly in the Development of New France, 1665–1760.* Ottawa: Parks Canada, 1983.

Gibb, Harley L. "Colonel Guy Johnson, Superintendent General of Indian Affairs, 1774–82." *Papers of the Michigan Academy of Sciences, Arts and Letters* 27 (1941): 595–613.

[Gibson, Hugh]. "An Account of the Captivity of Hugh Gibson among the Delaware Indians of the Big Beaver and the Muskingum, from the Latter Part of July 1756, to the Beginning of April, 1759." *Collections of the Massachusetts Historical Society,* 3rd ser., vol. 6 (1837): 141–53.

Gitlin, Jay. "On the Boundaries of Empire: Connecting the West to Its Imperial Past." In Cronon, Miles, and Gitlin, *Under an Open Sky,* 71–89.

Gough, Robert J. "The Myth of the 'Middle Colonies': An Analysis of Regionalization in Early America." PMHB 107 (July 1983): 393–419.

Grabowski, Jan. "Les Amérindiennes domiciliés et la Contrabande des Fourrures en Nouvelle-France." *Recherches amérindiennes au Quebec* 24, no. 3 (1994): 45–52.

———. "The Common Ground: Settled Natives and French in Montréal, 1667–1760." PhD diss., University of Montreal, 1993.

Grant, Anne. *Memoirs of an American Lady with Sketches of Manners and Scenes in America as They Existed Previous to the Revolution.* 2 vols. Boston: W. Wells, 1809.

Grant, Sir Francis. "Journal from New York to Canada, 1767." *New York History* 13 (Spring–Summer 1932): 181–96, 305–22.

Graymont, Barbara. "Atiatoharongwen." DCB, 5:39–41.

———. *The Iroquois in the American Revolution.* Syracuse: Syracuse University Press, 1972.

Green, Gretchen L. "A New People in an Age of War: The Kahnawake Iroquois, 1667–1760." PhD diss., College of William and Mary, 1991.

Greenberg, Douglas. "The Middle Colonies in Recent American Historiography." WMQ 36 (July 1979): 396–427.

Greene, Jack. "The Seven Years' War and the American Revolution: The Causal

Relationship Reconsidered." In *The British Atlantic Empire before the American Revolution*, ed. Peter Marshall and Glyn Williams, 85–105. London: Frank Cass, 1980.

Greene, Jack, and J. R. Pole, eds. *Colonial British America: Essays in the New History of the Early Modern Era*. Baltimore: Johns Hopkins University Press, 1984.

Greer, Allan. *Mohawk Saint: Catherine Tekakwitha and the Jesuits*. Oxford: Oxford University Press, 2005.

———. *The People of New France*. Toronto: Toronto University Press, 1997.

Griffin, Patrick. "The People with No Name: Ulster's Migrants and Identity Formation in Eighteenth-Century Pennsylvania." *WMQ* 58 (July 2001): 587–614.

Grimm, Jacob L. *Archaeological Investigation of Fort Ligonier, 1960–1965*. Pittsburgh: Annals of the Carnegie Museum, 1970.

Groulx, Lionel. *Roland-Michel Barrin de La Galissonière, 1693–1756*. Toronto: University of Toronto Press, 1970.

[Grube, Bernard A.] "A Missionary's Tour to Shamokin and the West Branch of the Susquehanna, 1753." *PMHB* 39 (1915): 440–44.

Grumet, Robert S., ed. *Northeastern Indian Lives, 1632–1816*. Amherst: University of Massachusetts Press, 1996.

Guldenzopf, David. "The Colonial Transformation of Mohawk Iroquois Society." PhD diss., SUNY Albany, 1987.

———. "Frontier Demography and Settlement Patterns of the Mohawk Iroquois." *Man in the Northeast* 27 (Spring 1984): 79–94.

Guy, Donna J., and Thomas E. Sheridan, eds. *Contested Ground: Comparative Frontiers on the Northern and Southern Edges of the Spanish Empire*. Tucson: University of Arizona Press, 1998.

Guzzardo, John Christopher. "Sir William Johnson's Official Family: Patron and Clients in an Anglo-American Empire, 1742–1777." PhD diss., Syracuse University, 1975.

———. "The Superintendent and the Ministers: The Battle for Oneida Allegiances, 1761–65." *New York History* 57 (Summer 1976): 255–83.

Haan, Richard. "The Problem of Iroquois Neutrality: Suggestions for Revision." *Ethnohistory* 27 (Fall 1980): 317–20.

Hagan, Edward A. "Adam Vrooman." *Schoharie County Historical Review* 62 (Spring–Summer 1998): 33–34.

Hagedorn, Nancy L. "Brokers of Understanding: Interpreters as Agents of Cultural Exchange in Colonial New York." *New York History* 76 (Fall 1995): 379–408.

———. "'Faithful, Knowing, and Prudent': Andrew Montour as Interpreter and Cultural Broker, 1740–1722." In Szasz, *Between Indian and White Worlds*, 44–60.

———. "'A Friend to Go Between Them': Interpreters among the Iroquois, 1664–1775." PhD diss., College of William and Mary, 1995.

Hallowell, A. Irving. "The Impact of the American Indian on American Culture."
    American Anthropologist 59 (April 1957): 201–17.

Halsey, Francis Whiting. *The Old New York Frontier: Its Wars with Indians and Tories, Its
    Missionary Schools, Pioneers, and Land Titles.* New York: Charles Scribner's Sons,
    1932.

Hamell, George R. "Mohawks Abroad: The 1764 Amsterdam Etching of Sychnecta."
    In *Indians and Europe: An Interdisciplinary Collection of Essays,* ed. Christian F. Feest,
    175–94. Lincoln: University of Nebraska Press, 1999.

Hamilton, Edward P., ed. *Adventure in the Wilderness: The American Journals of Louis An-
    toine de Bougainville, 1756–1760.* Norman: University of Oklahoma Press, 1964.

———. "John Henry Lydius, Fur Trader at Fort Edward." *Fort Ticonderoga Museum
    Bulletin* 12 (December 1964): 270–80.

———. "Unrest at Caughnawaga; or, Lady Fur Traders of Sault St. Louis." *Fort Ticon-
    deroga Museum Bulletin* 11 (December 1963) 155–60.

Hamilton, Milton W. "An American Knight in Britain; Sir John Johnson's Tour,
    1765–1767." *New York History* 42 (Spring 1961): 119–44.

———. "The Diary of the Reverend John Ogilvie, 1750–1759." *Bulletin of the Fort
    Ticonderoga Museum* 10 (February 1961): 331–85.

———. *Sir William Johnson: Colonial American, 1715–1763.* Port Washington NY: Ken-
    nikat Press, 1976.

———. "Sir William Johnson: Interpreter of the Iroquois." *Ethnohistory* 10 (1963):
    270–86.

———. "Sir William Johnson and Pennsylvania." *Pennsylvania History* 19 (Janu-
    ary 1952): 52–74.

Hanna, Charles A. *The Wilderness Trail; or, The Ventures and Adventures of the Pennsylva-
    nia Traders on the Allegheny Path.* 2 vols. New York: B. P. Putnam's Sons, 1911.

Harbaugh, H. *The Life of Rev. Michael Schlatter.* Philadelphia: Lindsay and Blakiston,
    1857.

Hardin, George A., and Frank H. Willard. *History of Herkimer County, New York.* 2
    vols. Syracuse: D. Mason & Co., 1893.

Harpster, John W., ed. *Crossroads: Descriptions of Western Pennsylvania, 1720–1829.*
    Pittsburgh: University of Pittsburgh Press, 1986.

Harrington, M. R. *Two Mohawk Strongholds: An Account of the Archaeological Explorations
    in the Ganada Site, Montgomery County, Mohawk Valley, 1905.* Peabody Museum of
    Archaeology and Ethnology, Harvard University, Cambridge MA.

Harris, R. Cole. *Historical Atlas of Canada.* Vol. 1, *From the Beginning to 1800.* Toronto:
    University of Toronto Press, 1987.

Hart, William B. "Black 'Go-Betweens' and the Mutability of 'Race,' Status, and
    Identity on New York's Pre-Revolutionary Frontier." In Cayton and Teute, *Con-
    tact Points,* 88–113.

———. "For the Good of Our Souls: Mohawk Authority, Accommodation, and

Resistance to Protestant Evangelism, 1700–1780." PhD diss., Brown University, 1998.

Hastings, Hugh, ed. *Ecclesiastical Records of the State of New York*. 7 vols. Albany: J. B. Lyon, Co., 1902.

Hatley, Tom. *The Dividing Paths: Cherokees and South Carolinians through the Revolutionary Era*. New York: Oxford University Press, 1995.

Hauptman, Laurence M. "Refugee Havens: The Iroquois Villages of the Eighteenth Century." In *American Indian Environments: Ecological Issues in Native American History*, ed. Christopher Vecsey and Robert W. Venables, 128–39. Syracuse: Syracuse University Press, 1980.

Havard, Gilles. *The Great Peace of Montreal of 1701: French-Native Diplomacy in the Seventeenth Century*. Trans. Phyllis Aronoff and Howard Scott. Montreal: McGill-Queen's University Press, 2001.

———. *Montreal, 1701: Planting the Tree of Peace*. Trans. Phyllis Aronoff and Howard Scott. Montreal: McCord Museum of Canadian History, 2001.

———. "Postes français et villages indiens: Un aspect de l'organisation de l'espace colonial français dans le Pays d'En Haut, (1660–1715)." *Recherches amérindiennes au Quebec* 30 (2000): 11–22.

Havard, Gilles, and Cécile Vidal. *Histoire de l'Amérique Française*. Paris: Flammarion, 2003.

Hawley, Gideon. "Account of Services among the Indians." HMSC 4 (1795): 53.

———. "A Letter from Rev. Gideon Hawley of Marshpee Containing An Account of His Services Among the Indians of Massachusetts and New-York, And a Narrative of His Journey to Onohoghgwage." *Massachusetts Historical Society Collections* 4 (1795): 50–67.

Hazard, Samuel, ed. *Hazard's Register of Pennsylvania*. 16 vols. Philadelphia: W. F. Geddes, 1828–35.

———. *Minutes of the Provincial Council of Pennsylvania*. 16 vols. Harrisburg: Theophilus Fenn & Co., 1838–1853. Reprint, vols. 1–3, Philadelphia: Jo. Severns and Co., 1852.

Heal, Felicity. *Hospitality in Early Modern England*. Oxford: Oxford University Press, 1990.

Henry, Alexander. *Travels and Adventures in Canada and the Indian Territories between the Years 1760 and 1774*. Ed. James Bain. Boston: Little, Brown & Co., 1901.

Herkimer County at 200. Herkimer NY: Herkimer County Historical Society, 1992.

[Hesselius, Gustavus]. "'With God's Blessings on Both Land and Sea': Gustavus Hesselius Describes the New World to the Old in a Letter from Philadelphia in 1714." Trans. Carin K. Arnborg. *American Art Journal* 21 (1989): 4–17.

Higgins, Ruth L. *Expansion in New York*. Columbus: Ohio State University, 1931.

Hinderaker, Eric. *Elusive Empires: Constructing Colonialism in the Ohio Valley, 1673–1800*. Cambridge: Cambridge University Press, 1997.

———. "The 'Four Indian Kings' and the Imaginative Construction of the First British Empire." *WMQ* 53 (July 1996): 487–526.

Hinderaker, Eric, and Peter Mancall. *At the Edge of Empire: The Backcountry in British North America.* Baltimore: Johns Hopkins University Press, 2003.

Hinman, Marjory Barnum. *Onaquaga: Hub of the Border Wars of the American Revolution in New York State.* N.p.: Valley Offset, 1975.

Hirsch, Adam J. "The Collision of Military Cultures in Seventeenth-Century New England." *JAH* 74 (March 1988): 1187–212.

Hirsch, Alison Duncan. "'The Celebrated Mme. Montour': Interpretess across Early American Frontiers." *Explorations in Early American Culture* 4 (2000): 81–112.

———. "Indian, Métis, and Euro-American Women on Multiple Frontiers." In Pencak and Richter, *Friends and Enemies in Penn's Woods,* 63–84.

History of Bedford, Somerset, and Fulton Counties, Pennsylvania. Chicago: Waterman, Watkins & Co., 1884.

Hoffman, Phillip W. "Simon Girty: His War on the Frontier." In *The Human Tradition in the American Revolution,* ed. Nancy L. Rhoden and Ian K. Steele, 221–40. Wilmington DE: Scholarly Resources, 2000.

Hoffman, Ronald, Mechal Sobel, and Fredrika Teute, eds. *Through a Glass Darkly: Reflections on Personal Identity in Early America.* Chapel Hill: University of North Carolina Press, 1997.

Hofstra, Warren R. "'The Extension of His Majesties Dominions': The Virginia Backcountry and the Reconfiguration of Imperial Frontiers." *JAH* 84 (March 1998): 1281–312.

———. "Land, Ethnicity, and Community at the Opequon Settlement, Virginia, 1730–1800." *VMHB* 98 (July 1990): 423–48.

Hofstra, Warren R., and Robert D. Mitchell. "Town and Country in Backcountry Virginia: Winchester and the Shenandoah Valley, 1730–1800." *Journal of Southern History* 59 (November 1993): 619–46.

Holton, Woody. *Forced Founders: Indians, Debtors, Slaves, and the Making of the American Revolution in Virginia.* Chapel Hill: University of North Carolina Press, 1999.

Hough, Franklin B. *A History of St. Lawrence and Franklin Counties, New York from the Earliest Period to the Present Time.* Albany: Little & Co., 1853.

Hsiung, David. "Death on the Juniata: Delawares, Iroquois, and Pennsylvanians in a Colonial Whodunit." *Pennsylvania History* 65 (Autumn 1998): 445–77.

Huey, Lois M., and Bonnie Pulis. *Molly Brant: A Legacy of Her Own.* Youngstown NY: Old Fort Niagara Association, 1997.

Hunter, Charles E. "The Delaware Nativist Revival of the Mid-Eighteenth Century." *Ethnohistory* 18 (Winter 1971): 39–49.

Hunter, William A. "Moses (Tunda) Tatamy, Delaware Indian Diplomat." In Grumet, *Northeastern Indian Lives,* 258–72.

———. "Victory at Kittanning." *Pennsylvania History* 23 (July 1956): 376–407.

Hurt, R. Douglas. *The Ohio Frontier: Crucible of the Old Northwest, 1720–1830*. Bloomington: Indiana University Press, 1996.

Igartua, Jose. "Pierre Trottier-Desauniers." DCB, 3:631–32.

Illick, Joseph E. *Colonial Pennsylvania: A History*. New York: Charles Scribner's Sons, 1976.

Jacquin, Philippe. *Les Indiens blancs: Français et Indiens en Amérique du Nord (XVIe–XVIIIe Siècle)*. Paris: Payot, 1987.

Jaenen, C. J. "Bruyas, Jacques." DCB, 2:106–8.

James, Alfred P., ed. "The Early Property and Land Title Situation in Western Pennsylvania." WPAHM 16 (August 1933): 197–204.

———. "The First English-Speaking Trans-Appalachian Frontier." *Mississippi Valley Historical Review* 17 (June 1930): 55–71.

James, James Alton, ed. *George Rogers Clark Papers, 1771–1781*. In *Collections of the Illinois Historical Society*, vol. 8. Springfield: Illinois State Historical Library, 1912.

Jennings, Francis. *The Ambiguous Iroquois Empire: The Covenant Chain Confederation of Indian Tribes with English Colonies from Its Beginnings to the Lancaster Treaty of 1744*. New York: W. W. Norton, 1984.

———. "Brother Miquon: Good Lord!" In Dunn and Dunn, *World of William Penn*, 195–214.

———. "The Delaware Interregnum." PMHB 89 (April 1965): 174–98.

———. *Empire of Fortune: Crowns, Colonies and Tribes in the Seven Years' War in America*. New York: W. W. Norton, 1988.

———. "Incident at Tulpehocken." *Pennsylvania History* 35 (1968): 335–55.

———. "The Indian Trade of the Susquehanna Valley." *Proceedings of the American Philosophical Society* 110 (1966): 406–24.

———. *The Invasion of America: Indians, Colonialism, and the Cant of Conquest*. New York: W. W. Norton, 1975.

———. "Miquon's Passing: Indian-European Relations in Colonial Pennsylvania, 1674–1755." PhD diss., University of Pennsylvania, 1965.

———. "'Pennsylvania Indians' and the Iroquois." In Richter and Merrell, *Beyond the Covenant Chain*, 75–91.

———. "The Scandalous Indian Policy of William Penn's Sons: Deeds and Documents of the Walking Purchase." *Pennsylvania History* 37 (1970): 19–39.

Jennings, Francis, et al., eds. *The History and Culture of Iroquois Diplomacy: An Interdisciplinary Guide to the Treaties of the Six Nations and Their League*. Syracuse: Syracuse University Press, 1985.

———, eds. *Iroquois Indians: A Documentary History of the Diplomacy of the Six Nations and Their League*. 50 microfilm reels. Woodbridge CT: Research Publications, 1984.

Jetten, Marc. *Enclaves amérindiennes: Les "réductions" du Canada, 1637–1701*. Sillery PQ: Septentrion, 1994.

Jezierski, John V., ed. and trans. "A 1751 Journal of Abbé François Piquet." *New-York Historical Society Quarterly* 54 (October 1970): 361–81.

"John Francis Bannon and the Historiography of the Spanish Borderlands: Retrospect and Prospect." *Journal of the Southwest* 29 (Winter 1987): 331–63.

Johnston, Louise. "Onontio, le grand arbre et la chaîne d'alliance : Le discours du marquis de Beauharnois aux Kanehsata'kehró:non, août 1741." *Recherches amérindiennes au Quebec* 29, no. 1 (1999): 11–21.

Jones, David. *A Journal of Two Visits Made to Some Nations of Indians on the West Side of the River Ohio in the Years 1772 and 1773.* Burlington: Isaac Collins, 1774.

Jones, Dorothy V. *License for Empire: Colonialism by Treaty in Early America.* Chicago: University of Chicago Press, 1982.

Jones, Henry Z. *The Palatine Families of New York: A Study of the German Immigrants Who Arrived in Colonial New York in 1710.* 2 vols. Universal City CA: By author, 1985.

Jones, Maldwyn. "Scotch-Irish in British America." In Bailyn and Morgan, *Strangers within the Realm,* 284–313.

Jones, U[riah] J[ames]. *History of the Early Settlement of the Juniata Valley.* Philadelphia: H. B. Ashmead, 1856. Reprint, Harrisburg: Telegraph Press, 1940.

Jordan, John W., ed. "Bishop J. C. F. Cammerhof's Narrative of a Journey to Shamokin, Penna., in the Winter of 1748." *PMHB* 29 (1905): 160–79.

———. *A History of the Juniata Valley and Its Peoples.* 3 vols. New York: Historical Publishing Co., 1913.

———. "James Kenny's 'Journal to Ye Westward,' 1758–1759." *PMHB* 37 (1913): 395–449.

———. "Journal of James Kenny, 1761–1763." *PMHB* 37 (1913): 1–47.

———. "Spangenberg's Notes of Travel to Onondaga in 1745." *PMHB* 2 (1878): 424–32, 3 (1879): 56–64.

Jordan, Kurt Anders. "The Archaeology of the Iroquois Restoration: Settlement, Housing, and Economy at a Dispersed Seneca Community, ca. AD 1715–1754." PhD diss., Columbia University, 2002.

Jordan, Terry, and Matti Kaups. *The American Backwoods Frontier: An Ethnic and Ecological Interpretation.* Baltimore: Johns Hopkins University Press, 1989.

"Journal de la Campagne de M. de Bellestre." In *Collection des Manuscrits du Marechal de Lévis,* ed. H. S. Casgrain, vol. 11, *Guerre du Canada: Relations et Journaux de Différentes Expéditions Faites Durant Les Années 1755–56–57–58–59–60,* 127–42. Quebec: L.-J. Demers & Frère, 1895.

"Journal of Joseph Bloomfield, 1776." In Snow, Gehring, and Starna, *In Mohawk Country,* 274–91.

"Journal of Warren Johnson, 1760–1761." In Snow, Gehring, and Starna, *In Mohawk Country,* 250–73.

Juricek, John T. "American Usage of the Word 'Frontier' from Colonial Times to

Frederick Jackson Turner." *American Philosophical Society Proceedings* 110, no. 1 (1966): 10–34.

Kammen, Michael. *Colonial New York: A History.* 1975. Reprint, Oxford: Oxford University Press, 1996.

Katz, Stanley Nider. *Newcastle's New York: Anglo-American Politics, 1732–1753.* Cambridge: Belknap Press of Harvard University Press, 1968.

Kelly, Arthur C. M. *Baptismal Record of German Flats Reformed Church (Fort Herkimer Reformed Church), 1763–1795, 1811–1848, 1896–1899.* Rhinebeck NY: By author, 1983.

————. *Baptism Record of St. Paul's Evangelical Lutheran Church (Schoharie, N.Y., 1728–1799).* Rhinebeck NY: By author, 1977.

————. *Baptism Record of the Schoharie Reformed Church.* Rhinebeck NY: By author, 1977.

————. *Marriage Record of the Early Schoharie New York Churches: St. Paul's Lutheran Church, 1743–1899, and Reformed Church, 1723–1892.* Rhinebeck NY: By author, 1977.

Kelsay, Isabel Thompson. *Joseph Brant 1743–1807: Man of Two Worlds.* Syracuse: Syracuse University Press, 1986.

Kent, Barry C. *Susquehanna's Indians.* Anthropological Series, no. 6. Harrisburg: Pennsylvania Historical and Museum Commission, 1984.

Kent, Barry C., Janet Rice, and Kakuko Ota. "A Map of 18th Century Indian Towns in Pennsylvania." *Pennsylvania Archaeologist* 51 (December 1981): 1–18.

Kent, Donald H. *The French Invasion of Western Pennsylvania.* Harrisburg: Pennsylvania Historical and Museum Commission, 1954.

Keyser, Peter D., ed. "Memorials of Col. Jehu Eyre." PMHB 3, no. 3 (1879): 296–307.

Kierner, Cynthia A. *Traders and Gentlefolk: The Livingstons of New York, 1675–1790.* Ithaca: Cornell University Press, 1992.

Kim, Sung Bok. *Landlord and Tenant in Colonial New York: Manorial Society, 1664–1775.* Chapel Hill: University of North Carolina Press, 1978.

Klein, Milton M. *The Politics of Diversity: Essays in the History of Colonial New York.* Port Washington NY: Kennikat Press, 1974.

Klepp, Susan E., and Billy G. Smith, eds. *The Infortunate: The Voyages and Adventures of William Moraley, an Indentured Servant.* University Park: Pennsylvania State University Press, 1992.

Knittle, Walter A. *Early Eighteenth-Century Palatine Emigration.* Philadelphia: University of Pennsylvania Press, 1937.

Knowles, Nathaniel. "The Torture of Captives by the Indians of Eastern North America." *American Philosophical Society Proceedings* 82, no. 2 (1940): 151–225.

Knouff, Gregory T. "Soldiers and Violence on the Pennsylvania Frontier." In Pencak and Frantz, *Beyond Philadelphia,* 171–93.

Konrad, Victor. "An Iroquois Frontier: The North Shore of Lake Ontario during the Late Seventeenth Century." *Journal of Historical Geography* 7 (1981): 129–44.

———."The Iroquois Return to Their Homeland: Military Retreat or Cultural Adjustment." In *A Cultural Geography of North American Indians*, ed. Thomas E. Ross and Tyrel G. Moore, 191–211. Boulder: Westview Press, 1987.

Kopperman, Paul E. *Braddock at the Monongahela*. Pittsburgh: University of Pittsburgh Press, 1977.

Labaree, Leonard W., et al., eds. *The Papers of Benjamin Franklin*. 32 vols. to date. New Haven: Yale University Press, 1959–2006.

Lachance, Andre. *La vie urbaine en Nouvelle-France*. Montreal: Boreal, 1987.

Lafitau, Joseph Francois. *Customs of the American Indians Compared with the Customs of Primitive Times*. 2 vols. Ed. William N. Fenton and Elizabeth L. Moore. Toronto: Champlain Society, 1977.

Lahontan, Louis Armand de Lom d'Arce, Baron de. *New Voyages to North-America*. 2 vols. Ed. Reuben Gold Thwaites. Chicago: A. C. McClurg, 1905.

Lamar, Howard, and Leonard Thompson. *The Frontier in History: North America and South America Compared*. New Haven: Yale University Press, 1981.

Lanctot, Gustave. *A History of Canada*. Vol. 3, *From the Treaty of Utrecht to the Treaty of Paris, 1713–1763*. Trans. Margaret M. Cameron. Cambridge: Harvard University Press, 1965.

Landsman, Ned C. "Roots, Routes, and Rootedness: Diversity, Migration, and Toleration in Mid-atlantic Pluralism," *Early American Studies* 2 (2004): 267–309.

Landy, David. "Tuscarora among the Iroquois." In Trigger, *Northeast*, 520.

Latrobe, John H. B., ed. "Military and Political Affairs in the Middle Colonies in 1755." PMHB 3 (1879): 22.

Lavallée, Louis. *La Prairie en Nouvelle-France, 1647–1760: Étude d'histoire sociale*. Montreal: McGill-Queen's University Press, 1992.

Le Blanc, Jean-Marie. "Jean-Baptiste Tournois." DCB, 3:627–28.

Leder, Lawrence H., ed. *The Livingston Indian Records, 1666–1723*. Gettysburg: Pennsylvania Historical Association, 1956.

[Lee, Charles]. *The Charles Lee Papers*. Collections of the New-York Historical Society, 1871.

Lehman, J. David. "The End of the Iroquois Mystique: The Oneida Land Cession Treaties of the 1780s." WMQ 47 (October 1990): 523–47.

Lemon, James T. *The Best Poor Man's Country: A Geographical Study of Early Southeastern Pennsylvania*. Baltimore: Johns Hopkins University Press, 1972.

Lemon, James T., and Gary B. Nash. "The Distribution of Wealth in Eighteenth Century America: A Century of Change in Chester County, Pennsylvania, 1693–1802." *Journal of Social History* 2 (Fall 1968): 1–24.

Lenig, Donald J. "Archaeology, Education, and the Indian Castle Church." *New York State Archaeological Association Bulletin* 69 (1977): 42–51.

Lepore, Jill. *The Name of War: King Phillip's War and the Origins of American Identity*. New York: Alfred A. Knopf, 1998.

"Lettre de M. de Vaudreuil au conseil de Marine (7 novembre 1720)." *Bulletin des Recherches Historiques* 30, no. 3 (1924): 91–92.

"Lettres de Mère Marie-Andrée Duplessis de Sainte Hélène." *Nova Francia* 3 (October 1927): 39–47.

Levernier, James A. "Indian Lore from Lancaster County." *Keystone Folklore* 22, no. 3 (1978): 17–24.

Levinson, David. "An Explanation for the Oneida-Colonist Alliance in the American Revolution." *Ethnohistory* 23 (Summer 1976): 265–89.

Leyburn, James G. *The Scotch-Irish: A Social History*. Chapel Hill: University of North Carolina Press, 1962.

Long, John. *Voyages and Travels of an Indian Interpreter and Trader*. London, 1791. In *Early Western Travels, 1748–1846*, ed. Reuben Gold Thwaites, 2:1–239. Cleveland OH: Arthur H. Clark, 1904.

Lord, Philip, Jr. "Taverns, Forts, and Castles: Rediscovering King Hendrick's Village." *Northeast Anthropology* (Fall 1996): 69–94.

Loudon, Archibald, ed. *Loudon's Indian Narratives*. Carlisle, 1911. Reprint, Lewisburg PA: Wennawoods Publishing, 1996.

Lunn, Jean. "The Illegal Fur Trade Out of New France." *Report of the Canadian Historical Association* 18, no. 1 (1939): 61–76.

Lustig, Mary Lou. *Privilege and Prerogative: New York's Provincial Elite, 1710–1776*. London: Associated University Press, 1995.

———. *Robert Hunter, 1666–1734: New York's Augustan Statesman*. Syracuse: Syracuse University Press, 1983.

Luttwak, Edward. *The Grand Strategy of the Roman Empire: From the First Century AD to the Third*. Baltimore: Johns Hopkins University Press, 1979.

Lydekker, John Wolfe. *The Faithful Mohawks*. New York: Macmillan, 1938.

Lynch, James. "The Iroquois Confederacy, and the Adoption and Administration of Non-Iroquoian Individuals and Groups Prior to 1756." *Man in the Northeast* 30 (Fall 1985): 83–99.

MacGregor, Douglas. "Braddock's Field: 'How Brilliant the Morning, How Melancholy the Evening.'" *Western Pennsylvania History* 88, no. 4 (2005): 22–29.

Mackillop, Andrew. *"More Fruitful than the Soil": Army, Empire, and the Scottish Highlands, 1715–1815*. Scotland: Tuckwell Press, 2000.

MacLeod, D. Peter. *The Canadian Iroquois and the Seven Years' War*. Canadian War Museum Historical Publication, no. 29. Toronto: Dundurn Press, 1996.

———. "Philippe-Thomas Chabert de Joncaire." DCB, 3:101–2.

Mancall, Peter C. *Valley of Opportunity: Economic Culture along the Upper Susquehanna, 1700–1800*. Ithaca: Cornell University Press, 1991.

Mandell, Daniel R. *Behind the Frontier: Indians in Eighteenth-Century Eastern Massachusetts*. Lincoln: University of Nebraska Press, 1996.

Marietta, Jack D., and G. S. Rowe. *Troubled Experiment: Crime and Justice in Pennsylvania, 1682–1800*. Philadelphia: University of Pennsylvania Press, 2007.

Marshall, Peter. "Sir William Johnson and the Treaty of Fort Stanwix, 1768." *Journal of American Studies* 1 (October 1967): 149–79.

[Marshe, Witham]. "Witham Marshe's Journal of the Treaty Held with the Six Nations By the Commissioners of Maryland, and Other Provinces, at Lancaster, Pennsylvania, June 1744." *Collections of the Massachusetts Historical Society*, 1st ser., vol. 7 (1800): 171–201.

Matson, Cathy. *Merchants and Empire: Trading in Colonial New York*. Baltimore: Johns Hopkins University Press, 1998.

Mayer, Holly A. *Belonging to the Army: Camp Followers and Community during the American Revolution*. Columbia: University of South Carolina Press, 1996.

McAnear, Beverly, ed. "Personal Accounts of the Albany Congress of 1754." *Mississippi Valley Historical Review* 39 (March 1953): 727–46.

McCauley, I. H. *Historical Sketch of Franklin County, Pennsylvania*. Harrisburg: Patriot Publishing Company, 1878.

McConnell, Michael N. *Army and Empire: British Soldiers on the American Frontier, 1758–1775*. Lincoln: University of Nebraska Press, 2004.

———. *A Country Between: The Upper Ohio Valley and Its Peoples, 1724–1774*. Lincoln: University of Nebraska Press, 1992.

———. "Peoples 'In Between': The Iroquois and the Ohio Indians, 1720–1768." In Richter and Merrell, *Beyond the Covenant Chain*, 93–114.

McCullough, John. *A Narrative of the Captivity of John M'Cullough, Esq. In The Garland Library of Narratives of North American Indian Captivities*, ed. Wilcomb E. Washburn, 57:86–113. New York: Garland Publishing, 1977.

McGregor, Robert Kuhn. "Cultural Adaptation in Colonial New York: The Palatine Germans of the Mohawk Valley." *New York History* 69 (Winter 1988): 5–34.

———. "Settlement Variation and Cultural Adaptation in the Immigration History of Colonial New York." *New York History* 73 (Spring 1992): 192–212.

McIlwain, Charles H., ed. *An Abridgment of Indian Affairs Contained in Four Folio Volumes, Transacted in the Colony of New York from the Year 1678 to the Year 1751 by Peter Wraxall*. Cambridge: Harvard University Press, 1915.

Meinig, D. W. *Atlantic America, 1492–1800*. Vol. 1 of *The Shaping of America: A Geographical Perspective on 500 Years of History*. New Haven: Yale University Press, 1986.

———. "The Colonial Period, 1609–1775." In *Geography of New York State*, ed. John H. Thompson, 121–39. Syracuse: Syracuse University Press, 1966.

Mereness, Newton D. *Travels in the American Colonies*. New York: 1916.

Merrell, James H. "'The Cast of His Countenance': Reading Andrew Montour." In *Through a Glass Darkly: Reflections on Personal Identity in Early America*, ed. Ronald

Hoffman, Mechal Sobel, and Fredrika J. Teute, 13–39. Chapel Hill: University of North Carolina Press, 1997.

———. "'The Customes of Our Countrey': Indians and Colonists in Early America." In Bailyn and Morgan, *Strangers within the Realm*, 117–56.

———. *The Indians' New World: Catawbas and Their European Neighbors from European Contact through the Era of Removal.* New York: W. W. Norton, 1989.

———. *Into the American Woods: Negotiators on the Pennsylvania Frontier.* New York: W. W. Norton, 1999.

———. Review of *The American Revolution in Indian Country*, by Colin G. Calloway. *WMQ* 53 (July 1996): 637–39.

———. "Shamokin, 'The Very Seat of the Prince of Darkness.'" In Cayton and Teute, *Contact Points*, 16–59.

———. "Shikellamy: 'A Person of Consequence.'" In Grumet, *Northeastern Indian Lives*, 227–57.

———. "Some Thoughts on Colonial Historians and American Indians." *WMQ* 46 (January 1989): 94–119.

———. "'Their Very Bones Shall Fight': The Catawba-Iroquois Wars." In Richter and Merrell, *Beyond the Covenant Chain*, 115–33.

Merritt, Jane. *At the Crossroads: Indians and Empires on a Mid-Atlantic Frontier, 1700–1763.* Chapel Hill: University of North Carolina Press, 2003.

Merwick, Donna. *Possessing Albany, 1630–1710: The Dutch and English Experiences.* New York: Cambridge University Press, 1988.

Miller, E. Willard, ed. *A Geography of Pennsylvania.* University Park: Pennsylvania State University Press, 1995.

Mintz, Max M. *Seeds of Empire: The American Revolutionary Conquest of the Iroquois.* New York: New York University Press, 1999.

Miquelon, Dale. *New France, 1701–1744: "A Supplement to Europe."* Toronto: McClelland and Stewart, 1987.

"A Missionary's Tour to Shamokin and the West Branch of the Susquehanna, 1753." *PMHB* 39 (1915): 440–44.

Mittelberger, Gottlieb. *Journey to Pennsylvania.* Ed. and trans. Oscar Handlin and John Clive. Cambridge: Belknap Press of Harvard University Press, 1960.

Moody, Kevin, and Charles L. Fisher. "Archaeological Evidence of the Colonial Occupation at Schoharie Crossing State Historic Site, Montgomery County, New York." *Bulletin: Journal of the New York State Archaeological Association* 99 (1989): 1–13.

Moogk, Peter. "John Hendricks Lydius." *DCB*, 4:488–90.

———. "Manon's Fellow Exiles: Emigration from France to North America before 1763." In *Europeans on the Move: Studies on European Migration, 1500–1800*, ed. Nicholas Canny, 236–60. Oxford: Clarendon Press, 1994.

———. *La Nouvelle France: The Making of French Canada: A Cultural History.* East Lansing: Michigan State University Press, 2000.

Monet, J. "Garreau, Léonard." DCB, 1:325.

Moyer, Paul. *Wild Yankees: The Struggle for Independence along Pennsylvania's Revolutionary Frontier.* University Park: Pennsylvania State University Press, 2007.

Muhlenberg, Henry Melchior. *The Journals of Henry Melchior Muhlenberg.* 3 vols. Trans. Theodore G. Tappert and John W. Doberstein. Philadelphia: Muhlenberg Press, 1942.

Mullin, Michael J. "Sir William Johnson, Indian Relations, and British Policy, 1744 to 1774." PhD diss., University of California, Santa Barbara, 1989.

Munger, Donna Bingham. *Pennsylvania Land Records: A History and Guide for Research.* Wilmington DE: Scholarly Resources, 1991.

Myers, James P., Jr. "Pennsylvania's Awakening: The Kittanning Raid of 1756." *Pennsylvania History* 66 (Summer 1999): 399–420.

Nammack, Georgiana C. *Fraud, Politics, and the Dispossession of the Indians: The Iroquois Land Frontier in the Colonial Period.* Norman: Oklahoma University Press, 1969.

"The Narrative of Marie Le Roy and Barbara Leininger, For Three Years Captives Among the Indians." Trans. Edmund Schweinitz. PMHB 29, no. 4 (1905): 407–20.

Nellis, Milo. *The Mohawk Dutch and the Palatines.* St. Johnsville NY, 1951.

Nicolai, Martin L. "A Different Kind of Courage: The French Military and the Canadian Irregular Soldier during the Seven Years' War." *Canadian Historical Review* 70 (March 1989): 53–75.

Nobles, Gregory T. "Breaking into the Backcountry." WMQ 46 (1989): 641–70.

Norris, Isaac. "Journal of Isaac Norris, During a Trip to Albany in 1745, and an Account of a Treaty Held There in October of that Year." PMHB 27, no. 1 (1903): 20–28.

Norton, Thomas Elliot. *The Fur Trade in Colonial New York, 1686–1776.* Madison: University of Wisconsin Press, 1974.

O'Brien, Jean M. *Dispossession by Degrees: Indian Land and Identity in Natick, Massachusetts, 1650–1790.* Cambridge: Cambridge University Press, 1997.

"Observations of Wentworth Greenhalgh in a Journey from Albany to the Indians Westward." In Snow, Gehring, and Starna, *In Mohawk Country*, 188–92.

O'Callaghan, E. B., ed. *Calendar of Historical Manuscripts in the Office of the Secretary of State, Albany, New York.* 2 vols. Albany: Weed, Parsons, & Co., 1865–66.

———. *Calendar of N.Y. Colonial Manuscripts: Indorsed Land Papers in the Office of the Secretary of State of New York, 1643–1803.* Harrison NY: Harbor Hill Books, 1987.

———. *Documentary History of the State of New-York.* 4 vols. Albany: Weed, Parsons & Co., 1849–51.

O'Callaghan, E. B., and Berthold Fernow, eds. *Documents Relative to the Colonial History of the State of New York.* 14 vols. Albany: Weed, Parsons and Co., 1855.

O'Toole, Fintan. *White Savage: William Johnson and the Invention of America.* New York: Farrar, Strauss, and Giroux, 2005.

Otterness, Philip. *Becoming German: The 1709 Palatine Migration to New York*. Ithaca: Cornell University Press, 2004.

———. "The New York Naval Stores Project and the Transformation of the Poor Palatines, 1710–1712." *New York History* 75 (Spring 1994): 133–56.

———. "The Unattained Canaan: The 1709 Palatine Migration and the Formation of German Society in Colonial America." PhD diss., University of Iowa, 1996.

Ousterhout, Anne M. *A State Divided: Opposition in Pennsylvania to the American Revolution*. New York: Greenwood Press, 1987.

Parker, Arthur. *The Constitution of the Five Nations or the Iroquois Book of the Great Law*. Albany: New York State Museum Bulletin, No. 184, 1916.

Parkman, Francis. *Montcalm and Wolfe: The French and Indian War*. New York: Barnes and Noble Books, 2005.

Parmenter, Jon. "After the Mourning Wars: The Iroquois as Allies in Colonial North American Campaigns, 1676–1760." WMQ 64 (January 2007): 39–82.

———. "L'Arbre de Paix: Eighteenth-Century Franco-Iroquois Relations." *French Colonial History* 4 (2003): 63–80.

———. "At the Wood's Edge: Iroquois Foreign Relations, 1727–1768." PhD diss., University of Michigan, 1999.

[Parrish, John]. "Extracts from the Journal of John Parrish." PMHB 16 (1892): 443–48.

Peckham, Howard H., ed. *George Croghan's Journal of His Trip to Detroit in 1767*. Ann Arbor: University of Michigan Press, 1939.

Pencak, William, and Daniel K. Richter, eds. *Friends and Enemies in Penn's Woods: Indians, Colonists, and the Racial Construction of Pennsylvania*. University Park: Pennsylvania State University Press, 2004.

Pencak, William, and John B. Frantz, eds. *Beyond Philadelphia: The American Revolution in the Pennsylvania Hinterland*. University Park: Pennsylvania State University Press, 1998.

Pennsylvania Archives, 9 series, 138 vols. Philadelphia and Harrisburg, 1852–1949.

Penrose, Marilyn, ed. *Indian Affairs Papers: American Revolution*. Franklin Park NJ: Liberty Bell Associates, 1981.

Perkins, Elizabeth A. *Border Life: Experience and Memory in the Revolutionary Ohio Valley*. Chapel Hill: University of North Carolina Press, 1998.

Pettit, Norman. *The Life of David Brainerd*. Vol. 7 of *The Works of Jonathan Edwards*, ed. John E. Smith. New Haven: Yale University Press, 1985.

Phillips, Ruth B. "Jasper Grant and Edward Walsh: The Gentleman-Soldier as Early Collector of Great Lakes Indian Art." *Journal of Canadian Studies* 21 (Winter 1986–87): 56–71.

Piker, Joshua. *Okfuskee: A Creek Indian Town in Colonial America*. Cambridge: Harvard University Press, 2004.

Pilkington, Walter, ed. *The Journals of Samuel Kirkland: 18th-Century Missionary to the*

Iroquois, Government Agent, Father of Hamilton College. Clinton NY: Hamilton College, 1980.

"Pittsburgh in 1761." PMHB 6, no. 3 (1882): 344–47.

Podruchny, Carolyn. *Making the Voyageur World: Travelers and Traders in the North American Fur Trade.* Lincoln: University of Nebraska Press, 2006.

———. "Werewolves and Windigos: Narratives of Cannibal Monsters in French-Canadian Voyageur Oral Tradition." Ethnohistory 51 (Fall 2004): 677–700.

Porter, Frank W., III. "From Backcountry to County: The Delayed Settlement of Western Maryland." *Maryland Historical Magazine* 70 (Winter 1975): 329–49.

Post, Charles Frederick. "Two Journals of Western Tours." In Thwaites, *Early Western Journals,* 1:177–291.

Pouchot, Pierre. *Memoirs on the Late War in North America between France and England.* Trans. Michael Cardy. Ed. and ann. Brian Leigh Dunnigan. Youngstown NY: Old Fort Niagara Association, 1994.

Poyo, Gerald E., and Gilberto M. Hinojosa. "Spanish Texas and Borderlands Historiography in Transition: Implications for U.S. History." JAH 75 (September 1988): 393–416.

Preston, David L. "George Klock, the Canajoharie Mohawks, and the Good Ship *Sir William Johnson.*" *New York History* 86 (Fall 2005): 473–99.

———. "'Make Indians of Our White Men': British Soldiers and Indian Warriors from Braddock's to Forbes's Campaigns, 1755–1758." *Pennsylvania History* 74 (Summer 2007): 280–306.

———. "Squatters, Indians, Proprietary Government, and Land in the Susquehanna Valley." In Pencak and Richter, *Friends and Enemies in Penn's Woods,* 180–200.

———. "The Texture of Contact: Indians and Settlers in the Pennsylvania Backcountry, 1718–1755." Master's thesis, College of William and Mary, 1997.

Ranlet, Philip. *The New York Loyalists.* Knoxville: University of Tennessee Press, 1986.

Records, Spencer. "Pioneer Experiences in Pennsylvania, Kentucky, Ohio and Indiana, 1766–1836." *Indiana Magazine of History* 15 (September 1919): 201–32.

Reese, George, ed. *The Official Papers of Francis Fauquier, Lieutenant Governor of Virginia, 1758–1768.* Charlottesville: University Press of Virginia, 1983.

Reichel, William C., ed. *Memorials of the Moravian Church.* Philadelphia: J. B. Lippincott & Co., 1870.

Reid, Gerald F. *Kahnawa:ke: Factionalism, Traditionalism, and Nationalism in a Mohawk Community.* Lincoln: University of Nebraska Press, 2004.

Reid, John Phillip. *A Better Kind of Hatchet: Law, Trade, and Diplomacy in the Cherokee Nation during the Early Years of European Contact.* University Park: Pennsylvania State University Press, 1976.

Rice, James D. "Old Appalachia's Path to Interdependency: Economic Development and the Creation of Community in Western Maryland, 1730–1850." *Appalachian Journal* 22, no. 4 (1995): 348–74.

Richter, Daniel K. "Cultural Brokers and Intercultural Politics: New York-Iroquois Relations." *JAH* 75 (June 1988): 40–67.

———. *Facing East from Indian Country: A Native History of Early America.* Cambridge: Harvard University Press, 2001.

———. "A Framework for Pennsylvania Indian History." *Pennsylvania History* 57 (July 1990): 236–61.

———. *Ordeal of the Longhouse: The Peoples of the Iroquois League in the Era of European Colonization.* Chapel Hill: University of North Carolina Press, 1992.

———. "'Some of the Them Would Always Have a Minister with Them': Mohawk Protestantism, 1683–1719." *American Indian Quarterly* 16 (Fall 1992): 471–84.

———. "Whose Indian History?" *WMQ* 50 (April 1993): 379–93.

Richter, Daniel K., and James H. Merrell, eds. *Beyond the Covenant Chain: The Iroquois and Their Neighbors in Indian North America, 1600–1800.* Syracuse: Syracuse University Press, 1987.

Robert, Jean-Claude. *Atlas historique de Montréal.* Montreal: Éditions Libre Expression, 1994.

Roberts, William L. "The Origins and Transfer of German-American Concepts of Property and Inheritance." *Perspectives in American History,* new ser., vol. 3 (1986): 115–72.

———. "Samuel Storke: An Eighteenth-Century London Merchant Trading to the American Colonies." *Business History Review* 39 (Summer 1965): 147–70.

Roeber, A. G. "'The Origin of Whatever Is Not English among Us': The Dutch-Speaking and the German-Speaking Peoples of Colonial British America." In Bailyn and Morgan, *Strangers within the Realm,* 220–83.

———. "The Origins and Transfer of German-American Concepts of Property and Inheritance." *Perspectives in American History,* new ser., vol. 3 (1986): 115–72.

———. *Palatines, Liberty, and Property: German Lutherans in Colonial America.* Baltimore: Johns Hopkins University Press, 1993.

Rohde, Friedrich. "Journal of a Trip from New Jersey to Oneida Lake." In Snow, Gehring, and Starna, *In Mohawk Country,* 380–81.

Ronda, James P. "Reverend Samuel Kirkland and the Oneida Indians." In Campisi and Hauptman, *Oneida Indian Experience,* 31–42.

———. "The Sillery Experiment: A Jesuit-Indian Village in New France, 1637–1663." *American Indian Culture and Research Journal* 3 (1979): 1–18.

Rooney, Doris Dockstader. *The Dockstader Family: Descendants of Georg Dachstätter.* 4 vols. Dodge City KS: High Plains Publishers, 1983.

Roscoe, William E. *History of Schoharie County, New York With Illustrations and Biographical Sketches of Some of Its Prominent Men and Pioneers.* 2 vols. Syracuse: D. Mason & Co., 1882.

Rothschild, Nan A. *Colonial Encounters in a Native American Landscape: The Spanish and Dutch in North America.* Washington DC: Smithsonian Institution Press, 2003.

Rowe, G. S. "The Frederick Stump Affair, 1768, and Its Challenge to Legal Historians of Early Pennsylvania." *Pennsylvania History* 49 (October 1982): 259–88.

Rushforth, Brett. "'A Little Flesh We Offer You': The Origins of Indian Slavery in New France." *WMQ* 60 (October 2003): 777–808.

Russell, Peter E. "Redcoats in the Wilderness: British Officers and Irregular Warfare in Europe and America, 1740–1760." *WMQ* 35 (October 1978): 629–52.

"Saint-François Xavier de Caughnawaga." *Bulletin des recherches historiques* 5, no. 5 (1899): 131–35.

Salisbury, Neal. Introduction to *The Sovereignty and Goodness of God, Together with the Faithfulness of His Promises Displayed, Being a Narrative of the Captivity and Restoration of Mrs. Mary Rowlandson and Related Documents,* 1–55. Boston: Bedford Books, 1997.

Sargent, Winthrop. *The History of an Expedition Against Fort Du Quesne in 1755.* Philadelphia, 1856. Reprint, Lewisburg PA: Wennawoods Publishing, 1997.

Sawaya, Jean-Pierre. *Alliance et dépendance: Comment la couronne britannique a obtenu la collaboration des Indiens de la vallée du Saint-Laurent entre 1760 et 1774.* Sillery PQ: Septentrion, 2002.

———. *La Fédération des Sept Feus de la vallée du Saint-Laurent, XVIIe–XIXe Siècle.* Sillery PQ: Septentrion, 1998.

Schaumann, Morri Lou Scribner. *Transcriptions of Original Tax Records at Cumberland County Court House, Carlisle PA.* N.p., n.d. Copy in Pennsylvania State Archives Reading Room.

Schock, Edwin Thomas, Jr. "The 'Cloven Foot' Rediscovered: The Historiography of the Conestoga Massacre through Three Centuries of Scholarship." *Journal of the Lancaster County Historical Society* 96 (1994): 99–112.

Schwartz, Sally. *"A Mixed Multitude": The Struggle for Ethnic Toleration in Colonial Pennsylvania.* New York: New York University Press, 1987.

Seaver, James E. *A Narrative of the Life of Mrs. Mary Jemison.* Syracuse: Syracuse University Press, 1990.

Selby, John E. *Dunmore.* Williamsburg: Virginia Independence Bicentennial Commission, 1977.

Shannon, Timothy J. "Dressing for Success on the Mohawk Frontier: Hendrick, William Johnson, and the Indian Fashion." *WMQ* 53 (January 1996): 13–42.

———. *Indians and Colonists at the Crossroads of Empire: The Albany Congress of 1754.* Ithaca: Cornell University Press, 2000.

Sherill, Charles N. *French Memories of Eighteenth Century America.* New York: 1915.

[Shippen, Joseph]. "The Military Letters of Captain Joseph Shippen of the Provincial Service, 1756–1758." *PMHB* 36 (1912): 367–78, 385–464.

Shirk, Willis L., Jr. "Wright's Ferry: A Glimpse into the Susquehanna Backcountry." PMHB 120 (January–April 1996): 61–87.

Shoemaker, Nancy. "How the Indians Got to Be Red." *American Historical Review*
102 (June 1997): 625–44.

———. *A Strange Likeness: Becoming Red and White in Eighteenth-Century North America*. Oxford: Oxford University Press, 2004.

Silver, Peter. *Our Savage Neighbors: How Indian Wars Shaped Early America*. New York:
W. W. Norton, 2007.

Simkins, Paul D. "Growth and Characteristics of Pennsylvania's Population." In *A
Geography of Pennsylvania*, ed. E. Willard Miller, 87–112. University Park: Pennsylvania State University Press, 1995.

Simler, Lucy. "Tenancy in Colonial Pennsylvania: The Case of Chester County."
WMQ 43 (October 1986): 542–69.

Simms, Jeptha R. *The Frontiersmen of New York*. 2 vols. Albany: G. C. Riggs,
1882–83.

———. *History of Schoharie County, and Border Wars of New York*. Albany: Munsell &
Tanner, 1841.

Sipe, C. Hale. *The Indian Chiefs of Pennsylvania*. Butler PA, 1927. Reprint, Lewisburg
PA: Wennawoods Publishing, 1997.

———. *Indian Wars of Pennsylvania*. Harrisburg, 1931. Reprint, Lewisburg PA: Wennawoods Publishing, 1998.

Sivertsen, Barbara J. *Turtles, Wolves, and Bears: A Mohawk Family History*. Bowie MD:
Heritage Books, 1996.

Skaggs, David Curtis, ed. *The Sixty Years' War for the Great Lakes, 1754–1814*. East Lansing: Michigan State University Press, 2001.

Slaughter, Thomas P. *The Whiskey Rebellion: Frontier Epilogue to the American Revolution*. Oxford: Oxford University Press, 1986.

Smith, John E., ed. *The Works of Jonathan Edwards*. Vol. 7, *The Life of David Brainerd*. Ed.
Norman Pettit. New Haven: Yale University Press, 1985.

Smith, Richard. *A Tour of the Hudson, the Mohawk, the Susquehanna, and the Delaware in
1769*. Ed. Francis W. Halsey. Fleischmanns NY: Purple Mountain Press, 1989.

Smith, William, Jr. *The History of the Province of New York*. 2 vols. Ed. Michael Kammen. Cambridge: Belknap Press of Harvard University Press, 1972.

Smolenski, John. "The Death of Sawantaeny and the Problem of Justice on the Frontier." In Pencak and Richter, *Friends and Enemies in Penn's Woods*, 104–28.

Snow, Dean R. *The Iroquois*. Oxford: Blackwell, 1994.

———. *Mohawk Valley Archaeology*. 2 vols. Occasional Papers in Anthropology, no.
23. University Park: Pennsylvania State University/Matson Museum of Anthropology, 1995.

———. "Searching for Hendrick: Correction of a Historic Conflation." *New York
History* 88 (Summer 2007): 229–54.

———. "Theyanoguin." In Grumet, *Northeastern Indian Lives*, 208–26.

Snow, Dean R., Charles T. Gehring, and William A. Starna, eds. *In Mohawk Country: Early Narratives about a Native People*. Syracuse: Syracuse University Press, 1996.

Snyderman, George S. "Concepts of Land Ownership among the Iroquois and Their Neighbors." *Smithsonian Institution Bureau of American Ethnology Bulletin*, no. 149. Ed. William N. Fenton. Washington DC: Government Printing Office, 1951.

Society for the Propagation of the Gospel in Foreign Parts: The Letter Books, Series B, 1701–1786. Historical Introduction by Belle Pridmore. Microfilm. London: Micro Methods, 1964.

Sosin, Jack M. *Whitehall and the Wilderness: The Middle West in British Colonial Policy, 1760–1775*. Lincoln: University of Nebraska Press, 1961.

Spencer, Charles Worthen. "The Land System of Colonial New York." *New York State Historical Association Proceedings* 16 (1917): 150–64.

Stanley, George F. G. "The Indians and the Brandy Trade during the Ancien Regime." *Revue d'histoire de l'Amérique française* 6, no. 4 (1953): 489–505.

Starna, William A. "The Diplomatic Career of Canasatego." In Pencak and Richter, *Friends and Enemies in Penn's Woods*, 144–63.

———. "Mohawk Iroquois Populations: A Revision." *Ethnohistory* 27 (Fall 1980): 371–81.

Steele, Ian K. *Betrayals: Fort William Henry and the "Massacre."* New York: Oxford University Press, 1990.

———. *Warpaths: Invasions of North America*. New York: Oxford University Press, 1994.

Stefon, Frederick J. "The Wyoming Valley." In Pencak and Frantz, *Beyond Philadelphia*, 133–52.

Stephenson, Robert Scott. "With Swords and Plowshares: British and American Soldiers in the Trans-Allegheny West, 1754–1774." PhD diss., University of Virginia, 1998.

Stevens, Sylvester K., and Donald H. Kent, eds. *The Papers of Henry Bouquet*. Series 21648. Harrisburg: Pennsylvania Historical Commission, 1942.

Stevens, Sylvester K., Donald H. Kent, and Louis M. Waddell, eds. *The Papers of Henry Bouquet*. 6 vols. Harrisburg: Pennsylvania Historical and Museum Commission, 1951–94.

Stevens, Sylvester K., Donald H. Kent, and Emma Edith Woods, eds. *Travels in New France by J.C.B.* Harrisburg: Pennsylvania Historical Commission, 1941.

Stone, William L. *The Life and Times of Sir William Johnson, Bart*. 2 vols. Albany: J. Munsell, 1865.

———. *The Life of Joseph Brant—Thayendanegea*. New York: G. Dearborn and Co., 1938.

Stotz, Charles Morse. *Outposts of the War for Empire: The French and English in Western*

Pennsylvania: Their Armies, Their Forts, Their People, 1749–1764. Pittsburgh: University of Pittsburgh Press/Historical Society of Western Pennsylvania, 1985.

Sturtevant, William C., ed. *Handbook of North American Indians.* Vol. 15, *Northeast,* ed. Bruce G. Trigger. Washington DC: Smithsonian Institution Press, 1978.

Sullivan, James, et al., eds. *The Papers of Sir William Johnson.* 14 vols. Albany: State University of New York, 1921–63.

Sullivan, Mark. "Schoharie Loyalists, 1775–1784." *Schoharie County Historical Review* 48 (Spring–Summer 1984): 13–16.

Swiggett, Howard. *War out of Niagara: Walter Butler and the Tory Rangers.* New York: Columbia University Press, 1933.

Szasz, Margaret Connell, ed. *Between Indian and White Worlds: The Cultural Broker.* Norman: University of Oklahoma Press, 1994.

Taylor, Alan. "The Bad Birds." *New Republic,* August 9, 1999, 45–49.

———. *The Divided Ground: Indians, Settlers, and the Northern Borderland of the American Revolution.* New York: Alfred Knopf, 2006.

———. *William Cooper's Town: Power and Persuasion on the Frontier of the Early American Republic.* New York: Alfred A. Knopf, 1995.

Taylor, Gavin. "Ruled with a Pen: Land, Language, and the Invention of Maine." PhD diss., College of William and Mary, 2000.

Terry, Wyllys. "Negotiating the Frontier: Land Patenting in Colonial New York." PhD diss., Boston University, 1997.

Thompson, John H., ed. *Geography of New York State.* Syracuse: Syracuse University Press, 1966.

Thomson, Charles. *An Enquiry into the Causes of the Alienation of the Delaware and Shawanese Indians from the British Interest, and into the Measures taken for recovering their Friendship.* London: J. Wilkie, 1759.

Thwaites, Reuben Gold, ed. *Early Western Journals, 1748–1765.* Cleveland: Arthur H. Clark, 1904. Reprint, Lewisburg PA: Wennawoods Publishing, 1998.

———. *The Jesuit Relations and Allied Documents: Travels and Explorations of the Jesuit Missionaries in New France, 1610–1691.* 73 vols. New York: Pageant Book Co., 1959.

[Tilghman, James]. "Letter from Thomas Penn to James Tilghman, November 7, 1766." WPAHM 57 (April 1974): 239–48.

———. "Thoughts on the Situation of the Inhabitants on the Frontier." PMHB 10 (1886): 316–19.

Tiro, Karim. "A 'Civil War'? Rethinking Iroquois Participation in the American Revolution." *Pennsylvania History,* special issue, *Explorations in Early American Culture,* 4 (2000): 148–65.

———. "The People of the Standing Stone: The Oneida Nation from Revolution through Removal, 1765–1840." PhD diss., University of Pennsylvania, 1999.

Tousignant, Pierre, and Madeleine Dionne-Tousignant. "Picoté de Belestre, François Marie." DCB, 4:633–36.

Trelease, Allen W. *Indian Affairs in Colonial New York: The Seventeenth Century*. Intro. William A. Starna. 2nd.ed. Lincoln: University of Nebraska Press, 1997.

Trigger, Bruce G. *Natives and Newcomers: Canada's "Heroic Age" Reconsidered*. Montreal: McGill-Queen's University Press, 1985.

———, ed. *Northeast*. Vol. 15 of *Handbook of North American Indians*, ed. William C. Sturtevant. Washington DC: Smithsonian Institution Press, 1978.

Turner, Frederick Jackson. *The Frontier in American History*. New York: Henry Holt, 1953. Reprint, New York: Dover Publications, 1996.

Usner, Daniel H., Jr. *Indians, Settlers, and Slaves in a Frontier Exchange Economy: The Lower Mississippi Valley before 1783*. Chapel Hill: University of North Carolina Press, 1992.

Vaughan, Alden T. "Frontier Banditti and the Indians: The Paxton Boys' Legacy, 1763–1775." *Pennsylvania History* 51 (January 1984): 1–29.

———, ed. *The Roots of American Racism: Essays on the Colonial Experience*. New York: Oxford University Press, 1995.

———. *Transatlantic Encounters: American Indians in Britain, 1500–1776*. Cambridge: Cambridge University Press, 2006.

Vaughan, Alden T., and Daniel K. Richter. "Crossing the Cultural Divide: Indians and New Englanders, 1605–1763." In *The Roots of American Racism: Essays on the Colonial Experience*, ed. Alden T. Vaughan, 213–52. New York: Oxford University Press, 2006.

Veech, James. *The Monongahela of Old; or, Historical Sketches of South-Western Pennsylvania to the Year 1800*. Pittsburgh, 1910.

Vogel, Virgil J. *American Indian Medicine*. Norman: University of Oklahoma Press, 1970.

Volweiler, A. T., ed. "William Trent's Journal at Fort Pitt, 1763." *Mississippi Valley Historical Review* 11 (December 1924): 390–413.

Vrooman, John J. *Forts and Firesides of the Mohawk Country*. Johnstown: Baronet Litho Co., 1951.

Waddell, Louis M. "Justice, Retribution, and the Case of John Toby." In Pencak and Richter, *Friends and Enemies in Penn's Woods*, 129–43.

Waddell, Louis M., and Bruce D. Bomberger. *The French and Indian War in Pennsylvania, 1753–1763: Fortification and the Struggle during the War for Empire*. Harrisburg: Pennsylvania Historical and Museum Commission, 1996.

Wainwright, Nicholas B., ed. *George Croghan, Wilderness Diplomat*. Chapel Hill: University of North Carolina Press, 1959.

———. "George Croghan's Journal, 1759–1763." PMHB 71 (October 1947): 305–444.

Wallace, Anthony F. C. *The Death and Rebirth of the Seneca*. New York: Vintage Books, 1969.

———. *King of the Delawares: Teedyuscung, 1700–1763*. Philadelphia: University of Pennsylvania Press, 1949.

———. "The Origins of Iroquois Neutrality: The Grand Settlement of 1701." *Pennsylvania History* 24 (1957): 223–35.

———. "Political Organization and Land Tenure among the Northeastern Indians, 1600–1830." *Southwestern Journal of Anthropology* 13 (1957): 301–21.

———. *Thomas Jefferson and the Indians: The Tragic Fate of the First Americans*. Cambridge: Belknap Press of Harvard University Press, 1999.

———. "Woman, Land, and Society: Three Aspects of Aboriginal Delaware Life." *Pennsylvania Archaeologist* 17 (1947): 1–35.

Wallace, Paul A. W. *Conrad Weiser: Friend of Colonist and Mohawk*. Philadelphia: University of Pennsylvania Press, 1945.

———. *Indian Paths of Pennsylvania*. Harrisburg: Pennsylvania Historical and Museum Commission, 1965.

———. *Indians in Pennsylvania*. 2nd. ed., rev. Harrisburg: Pennsylvania Historical and Museum Commission, 1993.

———, ed. *Thirty Thousand Miles with John Heckewelder*. Pittsburgh: University of Pittsburgh Press, 1958.

———. *The White Roots of Peace*. Philadelphia: University of Pennsylvania Press, 1946.

Ward, Matthew C. "An Army of Servants: The Pennsylvania Regiment during the Seven Years' War." PMHB 119 (January–April 1995): 75–93.

———. *Breaking the Backcountry: The Seven Years' War in Virginia and Pennsylvania, 1754–1765*. Pittsburgh: University of Pittsburgh Press, 2003.

———. "Fighting the 'Old Women': Indian Strategy on the Virginia and Pennsylvania Frontier, 1754–1758." VMHB 103 (July 1995): 297–320.

———. "*La Guerre Sauvage*: The Seven Years' War on the Virginia and Pennsylvania Frontier." PhD diss., College of William and Mary, 1992.

———. "The Indians Our Real Friends": The British Army and the Ohio Indians, 1758–1772." In Barr, *Boundaries between Us*, 66–86.

Watson, John F. *Annals of Philadelphia, and Pennsylvania in the Olden Time*. Rev. ed. 3 vols. Philadelphia: Edwin S. Stuart, 1884.

Watt, Gavin K., with James F. Morrison. *The Burning of the Valleys: Daring Raids from Canada against the New York Frontier in the Fall of 1780*. Toronto: Dundurn Press, 1997.

Way, Peter. "The Cutting Edge of Culture: British Soldiers Encounter Native Americans in the French and Indian War." In *Empire and Others: British Encounters with Indigenous Peoples, 1600–1850*, ed. Martin Daunton and Rick Halpern, 123–48. Philadelphia: University of Pennsylvania Press, 1999.

Weber, David J. *The Spanish Frontier in North America*. New Haven: Yale University Press, 1992.

Weiser, Frederick S., ed. *Johan Friederich Weisers Buch Containing The Autobiography of*

John Conrad Weiser (1690–1760). Hanover PA: John Conrad Weiser Family Association, 1976.

Weslager, C. A. "The Nanticoke Indians in Early Pennsylvania History." PMHB 67 (October 1943): 345–55.

White, Richard. The Middle Ground: Indians, Empires, and Republics in the Great Lakes Region, 1650–1815. Cambridge: Cambridge University Press, 1991.

Williams, Helen Laura Clock. Klock-Clock Genealogy. Cleveland: typescript, n.d. On file at the New York State Library.

Wonderley, Anthony. "Good Peter's Narrative of Several Transactions Respecting Indian Lands: An Oneida View of Dispossession, 1785–1788." New York History (Summer 2003): 237–73.

———. "An Oneida Community in 1780: Study of an Inventory of Iroquois Property Losses During the Revolutionary War." Northeast Anthropology 56 (Fall 1998): 19–41.

———. "1777: The Revolutionary War Comes to Oneida Country." Mohawk Valley History 1 (2004): 15–48.

Wood, Jerome H. Conestoga Crossroads: Lancaster, Pennsylvania, 1730–1790. Harrisburg: Pennsylvania Historical and Museum Commission, 1979.

[Zeisberger, David, and John Martin Mack]. "An Account of the Famine among the Indians of the North and West Branch of the Susquehanna, in the Summer of 1748." PMHB 16 (1892): 430–32.

Zoltvany, Yves F. "Louis-Thomas Chabert de Joncaire." DCB, 2:125–27.

———. Philippe de Rigaud de Vaudreuil: Governor of New France, 1703–1725. Toronto: McClelland and Stewart, 1974.

Zuckerman, Michael, ed. Friends and Neighbors: Group Life in America's First Plural Society. Philadelphia: Temple University Press, 1982.

In The Iroquoians and Their World

Nation Iroquoise
A Seventeenth-Century Ethnography of the Iroquois
By José António Brandão

Your Fyre Shall Burn No More
Iroquois Policy toward New France and Its Native Allies to 1701
By José António Brandão

Gideon's People, Volumes 1 and 2
Being a Chronicle of an American Indian Community in
Colonial Connecticut and the Moravian Missionaries Who Served There
Translated and edited by
Corinna Dally-Starna and William A. Starna

Iroquois Journey
An Anthropologist Remembers
By William N. Fenton
Edited and introduced by Jack Campisi and William A. Starna

William Fenton
Selected Writings
By William N. Fenton
Edited and introduced by William A. Starna and Jack Campisi

Oneida Lives
Long-Lost Voices of the Wisconsin Oneidas
Edited by Herbert S. Lewis
With the assistance of L. Gordon McLester III

The Texture of Contact
European and Indian Settler Communities on the Frontiers of Iroquoia,
1667–1783
By David L. Preston

Kahnawà:ke
Factionalism, Traditionalism, and Nationalism
in a Mohawk Community
By Gerald R. Reid

A Description of New Netherland
By Adriaen van der Donck
Edited by Charles T. Gehring and William A. Starna

To order or obtain more information on these or other University
of Nebraska Press titles, visit www.nebraskapress.unl.edu.

Printed in the USA
CPSIA information can be obtained
at www.ICGtesting.com
LVHW041253071223
765824LV00001B/26